The Obscene Diaries of a Michigan Fan

by Craig Ross

First Page Publications
Livonia, Michigan

First Page Publications

12103 Merriman • Livonia • MI • 48150
1-800-343-3034 • Fax 734-525-4420
www.firstpagepublications.com

Craig Ross, 1948–
Library of Congress Control Number:
2005927261
The Obscene Diaries of a Michigan Fan
/Ross, Craig
ISBN # 1-928623-50-6

Summary:
Humorous commentary, analysis and statistical observations about college and professional sports, with emphasis on University of Michigan teams.

To Sue

Preface

Who am I to write a book about sports? Author James Kunen, answering a similar question in a radical polemic of the sixties said, (something like), "Let's not worry about it. I'm just writing it. You're just reading it." This probably works in most worlds, whether literary or historical or aesthetic. But sport occupies a place in the American consciousness where credentials seem a mandate. Books about sports are written by athletes or ex-athletes or those with an established media identity. It is a closed set. You want to write a novel? Be my guest. You might even be welcomed and encouraged by established writers. Indeed, anyone who has poked around a bookstore in the past few years knows that writers, even famous writers, love to get their fingers in the pie or (better yet) a piece of the action. Yesterday, for example, while wandering around Border's in Ann Arbor, I ran across a new title by Mike Lupica:

> "*Sniff My Socks* is a taut, raunchy and metaphorical thriller set against the timely backdrop of the whaling industry. Thar . . . she . . . blows . . ."—Herman Melville

> "*Sniff My Socks* . . . is . . . the . . . second . . . coming . . . of . . . the green . . . light . . . at . . . the end . . . of . . . the dock. It just . . . sucks . . . the marrow out . . . of . . . reality . . ." —F. Scott Fitzgerald

> "*Sniff My Socks* . . . just . . . smells . . . so . . . familiar." —Dr. Scholl

Honest. You can look it up. So, if you want to write about Mussolini coming back to earth as a transsexual space alien, you will be welcomed by both the masses and, who knows, maybe even Umberto Eco. On the other hand, if you think you have some insight on the offside trapping guard from the 1961 Cleveland Browns (Gene Hickerson or John Wooten, it escapes me at the

1

moment) and why he was ineffective against Packer middle linebacker Ray Nitschke, think again. The topic, hot and controversial as it may be, needs press credentials. In homage to Dr. Larry Fine and cohorts Dr. Howard and Dr. Howard, it is press and press. And pull, of course.

You want to criticize Kant or Hume? You really be good, especially in the university presses. You think Regis Philbin has a sound metaphysical argument for the existence of God? Well, editors might not like it but publishers will be enthusiastic. Bingo! The title—*Notre Dame, God, Dopey Leprechauns, and Saint Regis*—is too sexy to ignore and, hey, this is serious stuff. None of that banal sports drek. Still, it contains a certain promise. Notre Dame wins! Ray Nitschke was wrong! The best of all possible outcomes in the non-secular world. Okay, I said, I get it now. *The shortest distance between two points is a straight line.* So what if I write a treatise explaining the exegesis of Jose Azcue, Joe Charboneau, and Jerry Dybzinski and how they formed a sort of trinity cum *Zeitgeist* of the Cleveland Indians that became a metaphorical proof against the existence of God? (Essentially, the Indians always suck. There must be no God.) Nope. Sorry. Snake eyes. Not in your job description. Hmm. *Except in a place where someone is always throwing you a curve.* And, anyway, I was told, the manuscript makes no sense. Nitschke and God are dead? Only the Browns (and Indians and Cavaliers and Barons) were dead. Then and now.

The landscape of this was impossible for me (as an outsider) to comprehend. I assumed that since complete, pathetic morons had made it big in this profession, I had some reasonable chance to inch my toe through the door. Hey, I wasn't born yesterday. I understand Venn diagrams and subsets. So as an example of your own personal standing, I propose a test that will prove your own credentials as a disturbed human. Here it is. Name the sports icon noteworthy for his ability to be wrong somewhere in the vicinity of a hundred percent of the time, but one who remains a revered prognosticator by his cohorts and the networks. (Clue: I guess he was right about Ron Powlus and his three Heisman Awards. And the call about Penn State dominating the Big Ten in football turned out to be dead on the money.) You right. Beano. Face it. There is something wrong with you if you had the answer. And, no doubt, it goes down on your permanent cosmic record. I'll award you extra credit either way.

One of my favorite Beano calls came after Notre Dame's unseemly and hypocritical firing of head football coach Bob Davie. Two hours after it was plastered all over the internet that John Gruden had turned down the ND job and that the Fighting Irish would hire Georgia Tech coach George O'Leary, Beano was reporting his "inside scoop" that Gruden would be the next Notre Dame coach. Of course, O'Leary didn't last long either—two days if I recall. Beano then tried to weasel out of his Gruden projection by claiming there were "typographical errors" in the O'Leary résumé. "Hell, I thought the guy was a Ph.D. in nuclear physics," Beano lamented. This proved to be a notable revision on Beano's part when Notre Dame turned in another direction, to the light-hearted Tyrone Willingham. (A reporter from the East Coast said Willingham makes Leonid Brezhnev seem like Mary Poppins.) Notre Dame, really piling on its coaches, gave the dignified, intelligent, and ethical Willingham three years before breaking their word to him. Tyrone's personality may be better suited for sergeant-at-arms of the Stasi, but no one but the Golden Dome would deny his character and competence. (Beano's status is beyond mystifying, where, as far as I can tell, the networks actually pay this guy to make predictions that never come to fruition. A groundhog would be a better hire.)

Rodents aside, the network hiring practices defy reason. Now, I admit that Brent Musburger is as famous as Einstein, but he was hired, last time I checked, to call football games. And, as chance would have it, Brent is as clueless about the sport as was Albert concerning his own unified field theory. Or, more to the point, Brent is as clueless about football as Einstein. I hope, in saying this, Brent will make some connections and in a future book these words will find their way to the fly jacket: "Ross . . . equates . . . Musburger . . . to . . . Einstein."

All this said, I have to admit that Brent has impeccable credentials for his rumored forthcoming book or speaking tour on "How to Tell if Momentum Has Changed." In the January 1, 2000 Michigan-Alabama Citrus Bowl, "momentum changed" so many times in the second half (according to Brent) that the concept became as obvious and meaningless as the cliché it is. A Northwestern graduate, Brent thinks "coincidence" is the same word as "irony." And, I swear, he once intoned that a player "is six feet, three inches tall but his body formation makes him taller than that." I assumed this meant either (a) the guy had long arms, or (b) a short head. But one never knows. Explanations for Brentisms can be sent to P.O. Box WhoKnows.

It ain't just me. Even Howard Cosell felt it necessary to be defensive about the fact that he was a lawyer and mere hanger-on in the professional jock culture. In retrospect, Howard should have saved the angst for his demonstrated lack of knowledge about sports (perhaps excluding boxing) and the fact that he consistently misused the language. Cosell's successful book, *I Never Played The Game*, would have been better titled, *I Never Correctly Used An Adverb*, or some other appropriate irony. This said, I admit my own weakness for Cosell. He was and made *Monday Night Football*. It will never be the same. Worse, I am beginning to warm to Musburger. Have mercy on me as long as you are at it. Yeah, yeah, yeah, Brent. He does have "deceptive" speed. He is a lot slower than he looks.

So who am I? Just another lawyer. In Ann Arbor, a place some call "fifteen square miles surrounded by reality," every third person is a lawyer and many aren't very enthusiastic about this admission against interest. To be honest, the majority of local counsel seems to have nominal psychic ties to the profession, though, praise be to Enron, many now exalt their status in the hierarchy above used car salesmen *and* accountants. For my part, I was sanguine about being a lawyer—then and now—and went to law school in Boston, as opposed to an alternate opportunity in California, because I believed my car wouldn't make it from exit eight on the Ohio Turnpike to Beverly Hills. I thought there was a chance the beater would last to Boston, a chance that came to pass. (And then there was that four hundred dollar balance in my checking account, about one-twentieth of Maurice Clarett's walk-around money at OSU. Chris Webber? I don't wanna talk about that. Why do you keep asking me that?)

Pretty thin, you say? Got any other qualifications? Lemme think. Well, I have been a Michigan fan since my father took me to my first game in 1957. Anything else to say? Not much. And I don't have any special connection to the university, except for my status as a graduate and the fact that Lloyd Carr routinely ignores my emails (as he should). What about athletic ability? Pretty much a hack. At fifty-seven I continue to play some organized tennis and unorganized basketball. Not all that well. You saw some bricks thrown up at Burns Park last month? Might have been mine. I golf now and again. Yep. Those fat shots and dribblers could be mine, too. I hit your car on Ann Arbor–Saline Road with an impossible hook? Must have been my pal Lee Bollinger. We look a lot alike. I used to play volleyball. The double hits? Could be. I have played a lot of baseball and softball. A mediocre shortstop with limited power and one who couldn't hit the curve. And football. But not since ninth grade, when Cyclops Klaus kicked me in the head as I whiffed at his feet on a power sweep. Think of me as yourself, a person who reads the sports pages first, is pretty average at some sports, and who is tired of the lame stuff published in the local and national rags. But take your pick. Even the great writers (Mitch Albom, Tony Kornheiser, Michael Wilbon) won't tell you much. Mostly, they talk about people. Or tell jokes. Or just fill up the page with laments about how close they were to a Pulitzer. Or won one, for all I know. Think of this as an extended diatribe. What you might say to yourself. And, perhaps, what a sportswriter cannot say and maintain standing with coaches and his or her colleagues. Or, perhaps, the human race. This might not apply, however, if "Beano" came to your mind as a first choice. Extra credit, indeed.

This is a real view from the outside. My first goal is to make rumor, innuendo, and pure speculation a staple and, as fate would have it, I have few enough assets to make myself judgment-proof (no problem here) and immune from libel actions. And my second goal is to not pay too much attention to anyone who is supposed to know. Boxer Sonny Liston once said, "A sportswriter looks up at the sky and asks, is the sun shining?" Most of what is passed off for sports reporting is nothing more than this. Rain today, but only maybe. Locally, there may be a firm grasp of the obvious. But probably not. Anything else? Well, I

4

have a friend (quoting the Talking Heads) who says he was "born in a house with the television always on." And, to this day, he lives in a three-room apartment with four TVs. He estimates they are turned on, more or less, eighteen hours a day. I appreciate the life-long impact of these sorts of things. I was born in a house with the radio always on (this creates a sort of privacy, according to Marshall McLuhan), where all family intercourse was punctuated with left-wing political discourse and heated argument. Was Rosa Luxemburg truly a revisionist? Did Karl Liebknecht (Rosa's lover) cede power to Hitler with a "guaranteed to lose" political strategy? Was Stalin a running dog exile from the czar's secret police (the Okhrana)? Is pacifism preferable to activism? Was the Kennedy coup d'état the work of Richard Nixon? (The answers were [in order]: Probably not. Probably not. Absolutely yes. Probably yes. I would bet my life on it.) Other questions were, of course, why the hell didn't you make your bed this morning, and didn't I tell you to sweep the freakin' garage out?

These are the starting spots. That and the fact this is not an attempt at any sort of objective commentary. At times, I might try to be "objective." At other times I might be objective in fact—though this may be an accident. I admit, at the least, I am a complete Michigan homer. But not Homer. I have two eyes and two ears, too, for chrissakes. And I hate Duke basketball. Well, Coach K actually, whom I perceive as a complete low life, a sniveling, slimy, and pathetic snake in the mud. But don't give up on me yet, Duke fans, since I recognize my own consciousness on point to be somewhere between irrational and pathetic. And, as long as I am admitting biases, I don't care much for Tom Izzo either. Is Izzo a good coach? No. He is a great coach who runs a great program. But that don't mean I gotta like him or his stooge ref, to be named later. Or his pathetic endorsement of Drew Sharp as a journalist with "integrity." Or his sneaky and passive-aggressive whining, carefully crafted from the Coach K alma mater, Whiner and Crybaby U. (Hey, wait a minute, I graduated from that school. Somebody hand me a mirror.) And before I start, I admit my tendency to the irrational and make room for dissenting opinion. Even *rational* dissenting opinion, though I would prefer ranting as a salve to my own sense of reality. I admit this much up front. Beyond this, I will concede most biases that are apparent on these pages. It ain't fair? Big deal. Go write your own book and you can be as fair as you want. Then I'll send you twenty bucks and I can get in your face.

Oh yeah, one other thing. I want to dedicate this to my father's mother, who was desperate to reach the twenty-first century but didn't come close. She was born in Russia before 1900 and, somehow, loved baseball (especially the Indians) and took it seriously, as an art form. Bertha Ross was not a physically attractive woman. She was stumpy and possessed a head shaped like a shoebox. Her ears looked pinned to her skull like the W on those ratty Wisconsin football helmets—just waiting for the right wind to change angle or, in a treacherous air, to flap away. She had lips like giant earthworms swollen from the spring storms. But, a genetic improbability, she precursed reasonably attractive grandchildren—though, if one looks closely, there is the dominant shoebox head as a family characteristic. Reunions of cousins resemble the Containers "R" Us wing of the International Shoe Makers. But Bertha was as beautiful a person as humans produce. An ultra left-winger in a family of socialists and communists, she represented the conservative faction of her generation. And, always, she was the representative of optimism in the gloom. In her mid-eighties, losing her memory, she told me that "forgetting is a good thing, because I know which books I love but I just can't remember the stories. So I put my favorites on one shelf and can read them again and they are brand new." This was, as always, spoken in English with the heavy inflection of old, czarist Russia. Grandma, raised in a shtetl where Jews were forbidden education, found reading to be the ultimate freedom, yet struggled with her own language—a mix of Yiddish, Hebrew, Russian, and English—for her entire life.

After my grandfather died, Bertha lived in Lorain, Ohio, with her sister Anna. Anna, a supposed beauty in her youth, represented the far-left element of her generation, a true commie. Anna and Bertha argued politics. They argued about who was the more wretched bridge or canasta player. They argued whether Larry Doby was better than Duke Snider. They argued about the space in their refrigerator. And they argued, most of all, about who was older. In these arguments, the worst that could be said was, "Go to sleep," as in, "Go to sleep, Bertha; Garcia has a better curve ball than Lemon."

In my freshman year at Michigan, suffering from homesickness, my mother bought me a subscription to my hometown paper, the *Lorain Journal*. Opening the paper one gray day in November, I saw Bertha's old Pontiac angled through the window of a downtown carpet store. Terrified, I read the story impatiently to find Bertha and Anna were fine. However, each had listed her age to the reporter as seventy-five. Could this be? Could they be twins? Neither would ever tell me, and the historical record proved no restraint on the argument. Now, in their celebrity, they argued about who should bear the blame for the accident. I suspect my grandmother's revisionism was profound as she became the heroine, steering the woeful Pontiac into a carpet store as a way of escaping the carping Anna's vitriol about Duke Snider, betrayed revolutions, and poor murdered Trotsky.

So kids, pay attention. Those with the patience of Job will learn in this book (a) how to unravel the unified field theory, (b) the secrets to understanding Marshall McLuhan, (c) what the word "slobberknocker" really means, and (d) how to beat the point spread. In this, I hope that I cover the field.

* * * *

On a mid-April weekend when I began to write this book (2000), I sat through parts of the Michigan water polo, softball, and baseball games. Water polo is a physically demanding sport, but I leave it aside for the moment. Revise that. I leave it aside forever because I don't think I had the slightest clue as to what was going on. (No one can sell this game, not even a Michigan player who was quoted in the *Michigan Daily* as saying, "It's a brutal sport. It is young women in shape in bathing suits. And who knows when those suits are going to come off.") The juxtaposition of the softball and baseball games of the weekend was marked, a demarcation that defined the best and worst of amateur athletics for me. The Michigan baseball team, in the wake of a surprising three-game winning streak against a superior Ohio State team, was hammered on Sunday. The team seemed listless and fundamentally unsound. The base running was woeful and some of this was coach-inspired, runners being sent in hopeless situations and being held when the extra base was obviously there. The defense, particularly in the infield, was shaky. But the play was better than in the Big Ten opening series a few weeks prior, where the Michigan team set a never-to-be-surpassed world record by committing more errors (eighteen) than hits (seventeen) in the four games played over the weekend. The crowd was apathetic. Even the sizeable Ohio State contingent, stunned by the prior losses, seemed unconcerned about Sunday's result. I love baseball, but the games were serious and morbid and a drag.

On the adjoining field, the Michigan softball team, twelfth in the country, was pounding a good Penn State squad. Unlike the sullen and quiet dugouts in the men's field, the Michigan women "chirp-chanted" during their own at bats, the usual happening in the women's game. When the lithe and athletic Pam Kosanke led off in the first inning it was, "P-A-M-M-Y, Pammy, Pammy, make it fly." And then, "R-O-P-E, rope it. R-O-P-E, rope it." And she did, sending the first pitch into the tall pines that separate the baseball and softball diamonds. The Michigan team has an endless supply of sing-song chirps. And they are relentless, ahead or behind. Between innings, the Michigan players danced, together and apart. Rap music blasted. And then polkas. The kids had fun. The team had fun. And this went on, if to a mildly lesser extent, on the Penn State side of the field.

I sat with another local attorney, Kurt Berggren. Kurt, now in his sixties, played varsity basketball at Virginia Military Institute. (He claims he is known as "Old Number 35" in VMI circles and he makes his wife call him this.) His backcourt partner at VMI was Bobby Ross, once coach of the Lions (more successful with the Chargers) and the winner of a freakish national championship when he coached at Georgia Tech. Kurt has met Fidel Castro. Honest. (I sent him with baseballs to be autographed but Fidel was suspicious of the possibility of exploding ones, and rightfully so. Kurt gave the balls away to kids on the street in Havana.) He once rode from Ann Arbor to Nicaragua in a dump truck. Honest. He got shot at by the contras and has a steel plate in his head. I know these things to be facts. Kurt claims he once played against Jerry West and "held him to forty-six points," but he admits this was "before the three-point line and it could have been worse." This may or may not be fact. Indeed, Kurt admits, "It might have been forty-seven points and I think West only played in the first half."

I coerced Kurt into attending softball games three years ago (after my wife, Sue, coerced me), and this is now his spring preference (as it is mine) to the men's game. The men, relatively woeful as they were at that moment, are absurdly good athletes. The women are (at present) markedly better players and athletes than the men, verging on world-class. They have the bonus of personalities and I find their passing from the program a personal loss, though I have never spoken to one of them. As Kosanke's shot settled into the pines in left field, Kurt turned to me and said, "Michigan should start recruiting baseball players who can dance." Perfect. And exactly what I was thinking. (In 2004, the softball/baseball energies began to merge. The softball team, an extremely close group according to coach Carol Hutchins, was serious and intense. The baseball team, now lead by the young and energetic Rich Maloney, loosened up. At the 2004 softball regionals in Ann Arbor, Maloney and his team showed up to cheer for the softball Wolverines in their showdown against powerful Oregon State. Maloney's group didn't just cheer. They chanted, ragged, and cajoled the crowd and the Wolverines to the regional title.)

* * * *

This book was written originally as a diary and, at times, I quote from those notes. I have retained the luxury of the title after reputable publishers turned me down. That left me with the others. Oh, yeah. One more thing. Most of what is written in this book is true, where "true" means "my opinion" as based upon the rumors and stories I have heard around town. I will try to clue you in when I am serious and when not, but most everything I have heard has come from reasonable sources, where "reasonable" means either "me" or "educated persons not institutionalized or in drug rehab at the moment the information was imparted." Though, I admit, one UM coach (twenty-five years ago) was drunk as a skunk when he gave up the story. Sometimes, most of the time in fact, I actually saw the events in question. But I admit to creating occasional composites of events—though these instances are obvious and the truths elsewhere. Essentially, some or most of this book is trustworthy.

One *The Mind Connects*

The day after the Michigan-PSU softball weekend mentioned in the preface, I was on an air flight to the west coast. I was surprised to find myself seated next to Jerry West. Now, aside from Howard Cosell (in an elevator in Vegas) and Eddie Sutton (in an elevator in Lexington), I can't say that I have ever bumped into anyone famous, save for Ann Arbor celebrities or Jeff Feiger lurking around the Washtenaw County Courthouse. So I was surprised. My normal inclination would have been to leave West in peace, but just the day before, Kurt ("Old Number 35") had been bragging about his defensive prowess against West in a game between VMI and West Virginia. One day prior. It seemed too coincidental (not ironic, Brent) to ignore, so I asked West if he remembered playing against a guy named Kurt Berggren.

"Not offhand," West answered. "Who did he play for?"

"VMI. He played with Bobby Ross."

"I remember playing against VMI. Not to be mean, but they weren't much competition." West smiled politely. "I vaguely remember Bobby Ross. He couldn't really play, but he tried hard as hell."

"What kind of teams did VMI have? Did they run?" I asked.

West laughed. "To be honest, they were mostly clutch and grab. But they were pretty slow and not very big either. But they played hard. They were tough and didn't give up."

"Kurt says that he held you to forty-six or forty-seven points." I added, "But, to be fair, he mentioned that it was prior to the three-point line. Plus, he thought you might have only played about eighteen minutes in the game and were playing on a sprained ankle."

"That was kind of him." West paused and thought. "You know, I don't recall much about the games against VMI. And I don't remember Kurt. But I can say that if he held me to forty-six or forty-seven points—even if I only played half the game on a *broken* ankle—then he must have been one hell of a defensive player."

My encounter with West was one of those things that happens more often than would seem to be dictated by chance. Indeed, I have a basket of such stories/incidents. We all do. My most confounding sports-related coincidence took place as I wandered into Crisler Arena in July of 2001. Michigan was conducting its annual basketball camp and I walked into the arena to check out the action. The Michigan basketball staff had changed and I was curious as to how the new administration was handling the operation. As I walked through the Crisler tunnel, I bumped into Tommy Amaker, the new Michigan basketball coach. I tried to move around Amaker but, instead, he held out his hand and introduced himself. Surprising enough. After all, Amaker had no reason to introduce himself to some random street person. We chatted for a few minutes and I was stunned by how intelligent, personable, and thoughtful Amaker was. In a fugue of bad manners I mentioned that I despised Duke basketball, most specifically, Coach Mike Krzyzewski.

As opposed to the coldness I deserved for my comments, Amaker (a Duke grad) was interested as to why I harbored these ill feelings toward his old coach, the poster person for the "good side" of college basketball. I said it was the juxtaposition of the image and the reality that bothered me. Anyone who has paid attention to the college game—and especially anyone who has sat near Coach K during a game—knows he is among the most foul-mouthed referee-baiters in the history of college basketball. Much worse, to be honest, than the reportedly deranged and generally reviled Coach Robert Knight, Coach K's old mentor at Army. I mentioned this to Amaker. He said, "He thinks that's part of his job."

"I can see that," I responded. Amaker smiled at my attempt at deflection. "And I respect the fact that coaches need to feel some sense of control over their working environments. But Bob Knight is vilified for his treatment of officials and he tends to be much less consistent in his terrorization of the refs." Indeed, Knight is now comatose about half the time when he watches his team play. I suspect medication.

I continued. "Knight is considered a boorish thug. Coach K is considered an angel. But watch K during a game, cursing and swearing at the officials over anything that resembles a close call. The truth is that he is worse, game in and game out, than Knight ever was. He just doesn't throw chairs."

"Do you think it works?" Amaker asked.

"No question," I said. "Look at Shane Battier. The color guys at games marvel over the number of charges he takes but the truth is the guy, for all of his ability, is just a plain old shameless flopper. Battier is what, six-nine, about 230 pounds, and he gets tossed around the court like a rag doll by 160-pound point guards. The guy can be completely out of position or sitting in the first row of the stands wolfing down a chili dog—he will still get the damn call."

"So Mike is effective during games?"

"Yep. But it reminds me of Dean Smith's cigarette behind the back routine. Do you remember that?"

"Of course. Did that bother you?"

"Well, it bothered me because Smith was a legitimate bleeding heart left-winger and a terrific coach. Maybe one of the best. But he was a cigarette addict. Everyone knew it, so it made sense for him to be up front about it, as opposed to trying to hide the things behind his back."

"I see your point. What about the four-corner offense? You think that was good for the game?" Amaker asked.

"That's a sore spot. I have to admit that Dean almost single-handedly ruined the game with that crap. On the other hand, the four corners and the control freak coaches put the shot clock in the game—a good thing, I think. And more than this, Dean took Mahktar N'diaye off our hands. I think all Michigan fans owe Carolina a debt of gratitude for that one."

"That seems pretty attenuated and lame," Amaker noted.

I had to admit that it was. But none of the foregoing is the point. It is preamble. After my conversation with Amaker, he said there was someone in Crisler who I might be interested in meeting and he introduced me to Juwan Howard, who was watching a scrimmage of young kids while seated in the Crisler bowl. Howard, then playing for Dallas in the NBA, left school to play in the pros at the end of his junior season. However, Juwan came back to school and, six years after the start of his first year at UM, received his degree. Howard feels a continuing connection to the program now that Amaker is the head coach and Brian Ellerbe has been banished to parts unknown. He had agreed to speak to kids at the Michigan camp that afternoon and, as I was introduced, he was waiting for his ride to Metro Airport. He and I chatted basketball for a few minutes and he stated that Dallas (his team) would be very tough to beat in the coming season. (This turned out to be a better prediction than any that Beano ever made. It also turned out that Juwan was banished to parts unknown—Denver—by mid-season.) I then mentioned to Juwan that he was the author of my all time favorite sports quotation. Indeed, it was a comment so clever that I used it in a paper I wrote on alimony theory, a paper that can be found on my web site at www.marginsoft.net. Howard, perplexed, asked about the quote.

"Well, it was when you were playing in a holiday tournament in Hawaii with the Fab Five. I think, at the time, Mitch Albom was writing his book about you guys and he asked whether you had been down to the beaches . . . what you thought of the beaches or something like that."

"What did I say?" Howard asked.

"You don't remember?"

"No idea."

"Albom quoted you as saying that you had no interest in the beaches. He

11

asked why and your response was, 'too much sand and shit.' As a person who hates the beach, I found the response to be right on the mark and perversely brilliant."

Howard laughed and said he still did not recall saying that but he thanked me for my recollection. Or the exaltation of his remark.

In any event, you might be wondering about the circle of the supposed connection. Be patient. That's how the mind works, after all. I talked with Howard in the late afternoon. As I walked into my house after the trip from Crisler, the phone was ringing. I picked it up on the last ring before it hit the answering machine. It was an F-14 fighter pilot stationed in Japan. An educated and intelligent man, he had been surfing the internet when he came across my theories about alimony and the connected software that I publish. He wanted to purchase the software and talk about "what was fair" in his pending divorce case. Unlike many prospective payers that I speak with, the pilot was extremely concerned that his wife would not have sufficient resources to get by after the divorce. To this end, he had read my papers about alimony theory.

"I am pretty amazed by that," I said, "since my guess is those writings have been read by, uh, maybe upwards of five people."

"They were very useful," he replied, "and very funny."

"I tried to make them interesting, since the topic is not exactly inspiring. But, even so, one attorney told me nobody actually breathing could get through this stuff."

"He was wrong. And the Juwan Howard quote is one of the best lines ever."

"It's funny you should mention that," I said, "since it is a favorite of mine, too. Even funnier since—and I know you are not going to believe this—I met Juwan Howard for the first time about ten minutes ago and talked with him about that exact quotation."

"You are kidding me."

"I am definitely not."

So let's examine this. First, Amaker, unlike any other head coach in the history of the galaxy, extended himself to talk to an average fan who had made no attempt to talk to him. Second, after the fan pointlessly insulted his alma mater and mentor, the coach remained urbane and thoughtful (and a fair cross-examiner) and then introduced the fan to one of the ten best players to ever suit up for Michigan. Third, by happenstance, the conversation turned to a quote by that player. Fourth, within the next half hour, a guy from halfway around the world called the fan and, with no prompting, mentioned the same quote. Fifth, despite the fact that the writing and the quote had been "out there" for more than five years, no one had ever mentioned it to the writer before. No one has mentioned it in the three since years since the incident and I suspect no one will mention it in the future. I admit this is not exactly cataclysmic stuff. The side of a hill did not even *sorta* swing open. Still, I have a difficult time putting it down to mere chance. From an analytical point of view, however, the story is both the problem and the solution, since we make these sorts of jumps every day, particularly in the world of sports analysis.

Bill James, the baseball statistician, has pretty much invented logical thought as it is applied to baseball. Prior to James's analyses, the theory of the game was dominated by old-time baseball pedagogues spewing homilies about the sport that were little more than holistic. These truths were sacrosanct and undeniable—until James showed up—despite the fact they were nothing other than things just said. Examples are:

Pitching is 75 percent of baseball.

It is a mistake for a runner on second to try for third when a ground ball is hit to the shortstop.

Part of what James did was to examine these homilies to discern the elements of truth therein, or the lack thereof. The classic example is the notion that "pitching is 75 percent of baseball," meaning, presumably, that a team's pitching staff is three times more important than its hitting and defense combined. Or, perhaps, that a team with good pitching and poor hitting will be markedly better than a team with these qualities in the precise inverse. James's work proves the obvious truth (in the rearview mirror), that offense (hitting and base running and scoring runs) and defense (pitching and fielding and preventing runs) are equivalents; that a team will win a predictable number of games (over a large number of trials, such as a major league baseball season) as based upon the number of runs scored versus the number of runs allowed.

I share James's fascination with the way the mind establishes order, but he is less yielding to the temptation to connect those elements that, perhaps, should not be connected. There is, in his work, no right brain allowed. There are two aspects to this. The first, where I disagree with James, is his notion that things don't really run in streaks any more than ordinary chance would dictate. James believes that the mind tends to connect events in ways that make them appear to be continuous, as opposed to the actual fact of independent trials. And, in this, streaks are nothing other than the usual application of chance.

I don't buy it, at least, not all of it. I think luck runs in streaks. And I think that once I experience something that I never have before, I am more likely to experience it again in the following week—and then never again. "Too much sand and shit" focuses a reasonably current example. But it is more than this, since these connections happen every week. As a measure of illustration I include portions of transcripts from two different cases I heard (as a neutral) within a week of the time of this writing. Both litigations are divorce cases and concern the division of property. In the first case, the parties owned more than five million dollars in real estate in Ann Arbor with very limited debt on these properties. However, the parties owed eighty-five thousand dollars in credit card debt for consumer items and, at this juncture of the hearing, I sought to resolve this relatively small item with a few questions for the husband.

(All questioning by the referee.)

Q: What about this credit card debt?
A: What about it?
Q: Don't we need to dispose of the liability or, at the least, assign it?
A: Why?
Q: Well, it has to be paid off or liquidated in some fashion, right?
A: No.
Q: Okay. Humor me. How was the debt accumulated?
A: Easy. I applied for a card. Not all that much to it. Then we ran it up to the max.
Q: Then what happened?
A: Got another card. We ran it up to the max again.
Q: So it was a pyramid scheme? You paid on the first card from distributions from the second card?
A: No. I applied for another card.
Q: And ran it up to the limit again?
A: Yep.
Q: Did you use any of this third card to pay off the other two?
A: No.
Q: So what did you do?
A: I just kept getting more cards and kept on running them up. Nobody seemed to be paying any attention.
Q: And you never made any payments?
A: Not that I can recall.
Q: Maybe I am wrong, but my assumption has always been that lending institutions prefer you pay these obligations. At some point they are going to pursue their remedies.
A: You are really beginning to irritate me.
Q: Okay, but paying the debt seems rational. First, it seems like the right thing to do. Second, the creditors are going to come after you and the debt is accruing interest at double digit rates. Right?
A: What kind of a fucking idiot are you? No one pays their credit card debt. No one. At least, I don't know anybody who does. How did you get this damned job, anyway?

Word for word. The real world is often like this and it may be why many of us are driven to the world of sports and sports-talk. I think Woody Allen said he preferred to deal with reality "only as a tourist," something that feels right to me after the foregoing kind of interaction. Still, the credit card guy was unusual and I couldn't imagine I would ever come across another person like him. And I haven't, except for the next day in a similar hearing. A portion of the transcript is (again) faithfully reproduced, except that the names and addresses are altered. The transcript commences with Mr. Smith, one of the parties, and the first witness in the session.

(All questioning by Attorney Jones.)

Q: Mr. Smith, for the record, would you state your full name and address?

A: Karl L. Smith. Capital k, small a and r and an l, capital l, and then Smith starting with a capital s and then mith. I reside at 245 Maxwell Street in Livonia, spelled capital m, small a and x and then small well. I do stay in Ann Arbor occasionally . . .

Q: Where in Ann Arbor?

A: I think . . . well, at home with my wife.

Q: In Ann Arbor?

A: Well, I thought we were going into property. I object to that question.

Mr. Ross: Please just answer the question.

A: We're wasting so much time on foolishness. It's a house in Ann Arbor. I'd like to get to the meat of this. We are wasting so much time on foolishness.

Mr. Ross: Actually, we just started the hearing a minute ago.

Q: Please just answer my questions. Now, you are an attorney?

A: Yes.

Q: How long have you been an attorney?

A: I have no idea.

Q: Can you tell me approximately?

A: Well, I am seventy-two and I passed the bar at age twenty-five.

Mr. Ross: So that would be forty-seven years.

A: No, that's not right.

Q: Well, how long has it been?

A: I don't know. Maybe forty-seven years.

Q: What kind of law practice do you have?

A: Well, good. Or sometimes bad.

Q: All right.

A: Mostly bad, according to my wife.

Q: Let me rephrase my question. Would you describe your specialty? Do you have a general or a specialty practice?

A: I don't know.

Q: Do you derive income from any other occupation except law?

A: Really, I don't know.

Q: You don't know?

A: What do you mean? It's all interrelated with law—I own properties, but is that a part of law? I don't know. It depends upon how you look at it. I have legal problems with the properties.

Q: Mr. Smith, in the pleadings to this case, didn't you describe yourself as a real estate investor?

A: Yes, I guess so. It could be. I don't remember. If it says that I did so, then I guess I did so.

Q: All right, are you a real estate investor? Let's get that cleared up.

A: Well, what do you mean by "a real estate investor?" I don't know what you are talking about and when—do I do it individually? The answer is no; I haven't invested myself, that I remember, in real estate for years. I have been in companies that invest.

Q: Do you own an interest in these companies?

A: I own an interest but I am not an individual investor.

Q: I didn't ask whether you invest individually.

A: You asked me if I invested in real estate, to be exact, and I don't know.

Q: And your answer is you don't know?

A: Depends on what you mean.

Q: Do you understand that you are under oath?

A: No, I don't understand that.

Q: Can you tell me why you don't understand that?

A: Because it's a foolish question. Of course I know I am under oath. You think I can be an attorney for forty-seven years and not know that?

I intervened at the foregoing point, not that my intervention did all that much. Mr. Smith wasn't about to help me or the court, and, after eight hours, we had a transcript that looked not much different from the above portion.

Q: What does any of this have to do with Michigan sports?

A: Well, good question. But it depends upon what you mean.

From my consciousness, I viewed Mr. Smith as a force of nature, something vexatious yet mystical in its ability to endure, sorta like Beano, Wayne Newton, or Wisconsin football. But that's off the thread. The point here is that I am unlikely to see anyone like these two characters again. Indeed, I have not. But I saw these two "clones" back to back.

Postulate One of this book is "things run in streaks." The axiom is, "When you just evidenced something really weird, look out, you're going to see it again—soon." Bill James can be damned on this point. But the tendency to connect is, in fact, a minor point in the structure of James's argument. Here, James's point is crucial to the understanding of the way sports "theory" is perceived. He explains his point by noting that he had a friend who died by being sucked from his car by a tornado. This friend had, apparently, lived his life in a sort of random fashion, skipping from job to job and town to town and woman to woman. Because of this, James said that the deceased's friends tended to connect the way he lived and the way he died. The randomness of his life and the randomness of his death allowed others to mitigate the pain of such an awful event and give it a certain rational and non-random character. As James pointed out, he died, in some sense, in the way he lived. This is the "natural" way the mind works.

James goes on to argue, however, that this is just the mind's tendency to connect. To make sense. To deny the arbitrary and random nature of existence. The problem with this "natural" tendency is a focus of James's early writings about baseball. As an example, James points out that management of the Cleveland Indians (pre-1995) consistently misunderstood "that a bearskin stuffed with hamburger is not a bear." The aphorism was made in the context of the "logical" thinking that occurs in sports, with particular application to the 1978 Indians. In 1978, the Indians finished 69–90 despite having an average team ERA and batting average. Tribe management (the woeful and inept Gabe Paul) looked at his team and decided the Tribe needed power and speed, quantities missing in 1978. Coming to this seemingly sensible conclusion, the Indians acquired power and speed for 1979 in the form of Toby Harrah and Bobby Bonds. Both players had power. Both could steal bases. This was a rational way to shore up the obvious weaknesses in the team.

Needless to say, the acquisitions did not work; the Indians did not improve. The problem was that the Indians had attempted to remedy their situation by a logical process imposed via (in Jamesian terms) an "irrelevant" fashion. Bonds was thirty-three years old at the time of his acquisition. Harrah was thirty, perhaps the best player in the league in 1975. But it was 1979. And by 1979, Harrah's speed and power were in decline. And there was little tread left on Bonds. In 1978 (and in most any other year post-1959), the Indians needed to begin to build a new foundation for a decayed franchise. (If your teeth are rotting, putting caps on won't help. Start with a root canal.) Instead, the Indians chose to build around players that were beginning to fade in ability. This had been a typical Tribe conception and theory. Gee, Joe Adcock is available. Wasn't he a good player once? He was. And so, the Indians snatched him up and blocked the young Walter Bond at first base, ultimately souring on the younger player and dealing him off. Same story for (among others) Tommy

John, Tommy Agee, Luis Tiant, Norm Cash, Sonny Siebert, Roger Maris, and numerous others. The ultimate blunder, of course, was the Rocky Colavito for Harvey Kuenn trade. The Tribe traded Colavito to Detroit when he was in his prime for a lesser player who was past his prime. But never fear, they reacquired the Rock five years later when he was also in his descendency. It is almost a surprise that the Indians did not attempt to trade Joe Carter for Babe Ruth. After all, wasn't the Babe a good player once? (The more or less moral equivalent of Indians management was Calvin Griffith at Minnesota, who prided himself as being a great businessman as compared to, say, George Steinbrenner. James points out that if Calvin was such a great businessman, how come he lost games and money while Steinbrenner was moving in the opposite direction? James labeled Griffith as the "north end of a south-bound Brontosaurus," and suggested that Griffith's notion of being a successful businessman was akin to "running out of gas in the middle of the desert and then congratulating yourself because you're driving a high-mileage car." Yeah, my advice is to buy James's books. They are brilliant.)

Almost all the commentary about sports (including much of my own, no doubt) contains some element of this frail connectivity. These logical conundrums tend to confound sports fans more than most. There was, for example, a general feeling among Michigan fans, going into the 2000 football season, that Anthony Thomas was "just another back" because of Michigan's woeful running game in 1999. In retrospect, this may be hard to believe, since the Michigan running game was dominant in 2000 and the A-Train finished his career as the all-time leading rusher in the history of the program. But at the time, Michigan internet sites and radio call-in shows were rife with criticism that Thomas was slow, and there was a general clamor for Justin Fargas (later transferred to USC after two years of awful injuries) to be inserted as the starting running back. The reasoning was (a) the running game sucked last year, (b) Thomas was the primary ball carrier, (c) Thomas looks slow, and (d) Fargas is fast, and generally regarded as the top high school running back recruit. There was, indeed, very little opposition to the foregoing syllogism. But if one looks back at the film of the 1999 season (Help me. I did. Over and over.) what one can see is that AT was routinely dodging linebackers at the line of scrimmage. The creases, generally, were just not there.

Lloyd Carr knew that AT was his best back, not just from a ball carrying perspective, but in all elements of the game. Thomas is, in fact, the best pass blocking back I have seen since Jim Brown and, where Michigan could only move the ball through the air consistently, taking Thomas out of the lineup would have been suicidal. The solution was not to bench AT or limit his carries, as argued for by the fans. The "logical" response was, "Our running game is not going, let's get someone else in there." Or it was, "Let's abandon the run." I heard/read both of these in spades. There was almost zero dissent

18

from this view, except from Lloyd Carr.

Lloyd Carr knew (but did not say at the time) that the 1999 offensive line was very beat up, many playing with nagging injuries that made drive/run blocking tough. These injuries made it necessary for Michigan to show a running attack, as much on reputation as anything. Ultimately, Carr played to his strengths in that season: Tom Brady, solid pass blocking, and his talented wide receivers, David Terrell, Marcus Knight, and Marquise Walker. Carr's response was the relevant solution to a major problem. He neither abandoned the running game, nor abandoned his best player. He balanced the offense in a way that discouraged defenses from sitting on the pass. Unlike Indians management, Carr found the relevant response to the problems he faced. This is, in part, why Michigan football is what it is. And it is why the Indians were what they were and, alas, what they would become. (In the 1999–2002 period, the Tribe made an attempt to relive its gloried past [last place for thirty consecutive years] by trading away all of its good young prospects—Jeremy Burnitz, Brian Giles, Sean Casey, Jeff Shaw, Jeff Kent, Danny Graves, Julian Tavarez, and Richie Sexson—for guys named Roberto Rincom. It looks like the Tribe only wants position players over thirty-five years old or those with a dubious history of achievement. Is Joe Adcock still around? Died in 1999? Okay, okay, okay, I admit they are stocking up on "young arms." Maybe it will work. Yeah. You right. It won't.)

Well, what about Michigan streaks? Okay, let's pick one that was a source of mystery on the Michigan posting boards: Bo Schembechler's record in close games. In the Schembechler era, the Wolverines won 79 percent of their games. Yet, in games decided by two or fewer points in Bo's tenure, the Wolverines were 7–18–8. Excluding ties, Bo lost ten straight two-point games between 1971 and 1985. I will get into the topic of close games in chapter three, but bear with me in assuming that a team that wins 79 percent of its games should win 50 percent of all close games, at a bare minimum. This means the odds of losing ten such games in a row is about one in 1,024. Assuming the win percentage for a 79 percent team in such (two-point) games is 55 percent, the odds increase to one in 3,405 that Michigan would lose ten in a row. From a two-point perspective, Schembechler accomplished in this fourteen-year period what had previously taken the Wolverines sixty-nine years to do. Between 1879 and 1948, the UM two-point record (not counting ties) was 20–10. In the pre-Schembechler period between 1949 and 1968 (about the weakest years in Michigan history), the two-point record was 8–8, not including ties.

It seems there are a few things one could make of this. One is that Bo was a poor coach since, after all, the "good teams win the close games." Anyone who raises his or her hand on this proposed answer is an idiot. And that includes OSU fans thinking the same of Woody Hayes. Bo might have had a certain stubbornness about the forward pass that was problematic, but it also led to a toughness that implied Michigan would rarely or never (well, once) get blown out in his tenure. The fact is that Bo inherited a not-quite-moribund program and took it back to something in the vicinity of its historical accomplishment. This was not a random occurrence.

A more likely argument is that there was something unique in Bo's coaching style or philosophy that led to disaster in these contests. Michigan grad (and lawyer and political commentator) Paul Campos has suggested such. Maybe. But maybe it was the case that these were better teams than Michigan and Bo's style allowed the Wolverines to hang around in games to a greater extent than talent levels would dictate. I would argue, at the least, that this was true in the 1984 Sugar Bowl 9–7 loss to Auburn (think Bo Jackson, among others), where Michigan's ability to stay with the Tigers seemed almost mystical. The same was true in the Wolverines' 1979 loss to North Carolina (think Lawrence Taylor). Moreover, if there was something in Bo's style that was problematic in two-point games, how come it did not raise its head in three-point games? In the same fourteen-year period, the Wolverines were 11–4 in three- or four-point games, games likely to be no more or less close than the one- and two-point losses. Okay, maybe there is something weird about Bo's record. But maybe it is no more weird than flipping a coin and having heads come up ten times in a row. After all, if one makes enough attempts, this has to happen. The latter, I admit, would be Bill James's point. Nevertheless, I suggest that all fans continue to say the following mantras. And, I believe, you will be better off for it.

Things run in streaks.

Be careful about connecting events that may not be connected.

A final stray thought on these notions. In looking through the Michigan record book, I discovered back-to-back 7–6 wins in 1937 followed by a 13–12 win. One-point games are rare. Winning three straight one-point games is downright weird. And consider this question. How many 7–6 games has Michigan played since 1937? Yep. You got it. In the sixty-seven years since those back-to-back games, the answer is none.

* * * *

April 8, 2002. Reading back on the above, I noticed the phrase "parts unknown," and this brought back powerful memories. When I was growing up (in the fifties), before pro rasslin' became an identifiable part of slick culture, most pro rasslers were just big fat guys with great flexibility and coordination. No steroids. No Gold's Gym. Just big dudes gone to seed. At the time, there were two things you could count on in the Cleveland rasslin' scene. First, if a new or lightly known guy was introduced as a "local talent," you could be certain he was gonna get clobbered. Second, in any sequence of rasslin' matches, there was always some character named the "Masked Marvel" or the "Unknown Terror," a mean-spirited, bad-guy rassler who wore a mask and was rumored to be banned from rasslin' in some other venue (either Canada or South America or more likely Mexico) for poor ethical behavior. Either that or he accidentally (wink) killed someone in the ring and was "rumored to be" banned from the sport. Presumably, in the latter event, the rassler never took off his mask, in the fear that someone might discover his true identity. In my kid vision, the Masked Marvel wore his mask at dinner, in the shower, at the movies. He was forced, perhaps at his own doing, into a life of terrorizing and terror, a tragic not-hero on the lam from the wrestling (or other) police and never at peace with himself. Sort of like the average UM basketball fan during the Brian Ellerbe tenure.

Of course, these matches were always the same. The good guy (he was dirty too, but it was in a just cause), after pummeling the Masked Man into submission, lost interest in winning the match and turned to tearing at his opponent's mask to reveal to the world (well, Cleveland actually) the true identity of this low life. At this juncture the script generally took one of two turns. One possibility was that the Masked Man, being given a respite from the beating, would pull a "foreign object" from his trunks (the damn ref just never sees this), and use the instrument to turn the tide. Or, after the object was pulled, the good guy, being completely cheesed by this lack of fair play, would go on a nut and be disqualified by the cretin referee. Two other things were inevitable. First, Masked Men always wore tights, as opposed to trunks. This was a sign of being a bad dude. Second, these guys were always from "parts unknown." Always.

I took pro rasslin' quite seriously. Until I visited my grandparents in Detroit and discovered that the world champion in Detroit was Dick the Bruiser. Hey, this ain't right. The world champion in Cleveland is the Sheik! I had just left home that morning and I knew this stuff didn't change that fast. I wasn't a very smart kid but I knew—even though Detroit and Cleveland were in separate states—they were still in the same world. Something was fishy. And it seemed even fishier when Fritz Von Erich, a notorious bad guy in Cleveland with his fabled, loathed, and lethal "claw hold," was a good guy in Detroit. How could this be? How could the world have so many champions and, more puzzling, how could there be so much ambiguity about what was good and what was evil? My confusion was manifest.

The blurring of right and wrong, the blurring of black and white in the world, is a hard lesson for latency-aged boys (and college sports fans in general). And a few weeks later, my life changed forever when, in our own private rasslin' room (our sisters' bedroom when they weren't around), I threw a vicious flying drop kick at my brother John. I nailed it and him. Neither Argentina Rocca nor Ilio DePaulo ever did it better, I was sure. But John wasn't fazed at all by the maneuver. On the other hand, I took a beating as my body crashed to the floor. I knew, looking up at John's smiling face and suffering a very bruised back, that there was something not right in the world. It took quite a number of years for me to figure out what it was. Ultimately, I had to look it up.

It is a fact that most of the first-rate sports reporting is now done on the internet. The best writing and analyses are generally written by those who are not professional journalists, who are not being paid, and who are likely to absorb some immediate and visceral reaction to their commentaries. Getting banned is quite easy, and then you only have yourself to yammer at. Given the lesser chance of public vilification, there is a greater willingness for the internet journalist to go out on a limb, to take a chance, and to make some attempt at thought. At least as to Michigan sports, actual thought in the print media has pushed zero, excluding the recent efforts of Jim Carty in the *Ann Arbor News*. Carty, a young guy new to the scene, is trying to change the landscape of local history.

In the spring of 2000, there was more than the ordinary excitement about Michigan's football team and its coming season, since it would be Drew Henson's first genuine opportunity to show his stuff. Moreover, Henson would be backed by a loaded offense in the skill positions and an offensive line as talented as any Michigan line of the past twenty-five years. Making the spring game more interesting was the fact that Michigan had little in the way of proven players on the defense in the front seven. Not only was the offense the strength of the team, it might have had to carry the defense over much or all of the season. This was layered with the enigma of Michigan's woeful running game in 1999. In that season, Michigan averaged a measly 3.2 yards per carry—the worst in who-knows-how-long—and the Wolverines were out-rushed by their opposition for the first time in forever.

The Wolverine prospects in 2000 seemed a gold mine for the average sports journalist, particularly in relation to writing about the Michigan spring football scrimmage—an opportunity to evaluate and predict what the Wolverines might look like in the fall. Instead, Jim Cnockaert, an experienced and popular football writer, informed his readers in the *Ann Arbor News* that (a) football practices are "hard and boring," (b) a scrimmage is more fun than practices, (c) playing in front of people should "build excitement" for the players, (d) "there are more defensive backs than last year," (e) Justin Fargas won't play (his leg had been demolished and this was common knowledge), (f) the position switches were worth checking out, and (g) Drew Henson can play, so pay attention to the back-up quarterbacks. In other words, nothing. Not one single piece of corn in this dung heap. Not even the souped-up and tangerine-flaked version outlined above.

Well, okay, Cnockaert is an extremely nice and sincere man, and his article must have been written before the scrimmage, though after the spring practices as a whole. Moreover, he is a historical (versus analytical) writer, the latter role being left at the time to Rich Thomaselli. I assumed, naively, that Thomaselli would provide some insight into the status of the Michigan team. Well, it got worse. Thomaselli wrote (after the scrimmage) that (a) Henson is the starter (gee, thanks), (b) "he's the man" (honest), (c) Tom Brady has graduated (Thomaselli got paid for this), (d) "Henson can be a great quarterback" but, (e) "he needs to improve," (f) Michigan's defensive uncertainties are less important than Henson and "Michigan will go as far as Henson takes them," and (g) we will know how far Henson can take them "after the fifth game" of the season. Well, let me guess. If Michigan is 5–0, the answer is "pretty far." And if Michigan is 2–3, the answer is "not very far." I surmise that Rich wrote this at breakfast and didn't see five minutes of the scrimmage. Either that or he was so clueless that the scrimmage meant nothing to him.

It would seem a sports columnist should be willing to go out a limb. Have an opinion. The writer should be able to tell us what he thinks is likely in the coming year. Not that (per the above), "if Michigan wins all of its games, it will be doing well." Beano Cook, your basic rock collection, will go out on a limb, even if his track record is . . . well . . . it is Beano. Still, the Thomaselli /Cnockaert standard is ordinary. Knowing little about what they saw, they imparted nothing. Beano, knowing nothing about what he sees, makes it up. Sad to say, in this environment, Beano is a star.

Not long after Thomaselli wrote the foregoing non-article, he secured (I assume) a promotion to a paper with much greater circulation. Since he had covered the Ann Arbor sports scene, the new publication assigned him to write about the Michigan football prospects for the 2000 season. The resulting article was picked up by the reasonably prestigious *Sporting News*, this publication believing, apparently, it was the best they could find on Michigan football for the coming year.

Thomaselli's sum total analysis was "Lloyd Carr is still the coach so that means a lot of running the football and conservative passing." The most enlightening part of this sentence is the observation that Lloyd Carr neither died nor was fired in the off-season. In this, Thomaselli was accurate. The point of the remainder of the sentence, I surmise, is that in 1999, Michigan's theory had been to run the ball as opposed to having a more balanced offense.

The second point, presumably, is that when Michigan does pass, Lloyd tends to favor a "conservative" game, whatever that might be. These contentions do not withstand scrutiny. Indeed, they are just something Thomaselli made up. It was his job to pay attention. And he wasn't.

In 1999, Michigan passed the ball on 44 percent of its plays. Historically, this was a high percentage for a college team, though in more recent seasons, the college game has moved more to the pass. Indeed, in 1999, Michigan passed the ball 22 percent more often than its opposition, a relatively high differential for a successful team, a team that was typically ahead at the end of games. However, the percentage underestimates how many pass plays were called by the Michigan staff, since Brady, Henson, and Jason Kapsner rushed the ball seventy times over the course of the year, and the vast majority of these were sacks or scrambles, not called runs. Adding, say, sixty of these plays to the mix, Michigan called pass plays as often as running plays in 1999. In other words, the Wolverines had a completely balanced attack that year, without looking to the intricacies of down and distance.

But, presumably, the reference to Lloyd Carr and "a lot of running" must have some comparative aspect. Since it wasn't the Michigan opposition in 1999, my instinct was to give Thomaselli the benefit of the doubt and assume the reference is to the prior coaching regime. So I checked Gary Moeller's last year, the 1994 season. Moeller was known as an offensive innovator and, indeed, he ran an unusual no-huddle offense for a year and a half until he felt that defenses had caught on. In 1994, the Michigan QB was Todd Collins, a future NFL player who, to this day, holds the Michigan record for completion percentage (64.3 percent). Indeed, Collins's percentage is one of the highest in the history of college football. And Collins was in his senior season, and was throwing to Amani Toomer, Mercury Hayes, and Jay Riemersma, a trio that rivals any that Michigan has ever produced. So, Michigan had an innovative offensive coach, a terrific quarterback, and great receivers. Yet, in 1994, Michigan threw the ball 37 percent of the time. Counting sacks and scrambles, that places it in the 42 percent range. In other words, in 1994, Michigan threw the ball about 16 percent less often than they did in 1999. Again, the assertion was not proven.

But, thinking again, I thought that Thomaselli might have been making a prediction about 2000. That he really wasn't talking about the past (fat chance). Well, indeed, he stunk here too. While Michigan passed less in 2000 than in 1999 (the running game was lousy in 1999 and terrific in 2000), the Wolverines still had the most effective passing game in the Big Ten that year. The numbers from the UM website are as follows:

Yardage	2772	(third)
Completion percentage	59.2	(second)
Interceptions	5	(first)
Touchdowns	26	(second)
TD/INT Ratio	5.2	(first)
Yds/Pass	8.6	(first)
Yds/Completion	14.7	(first)
Efficiency	155.3	(first)

These numbers are impressive when it is considered that Drew Henson broke his foot in the fall and Michigan used a completely untested quarterback, John Navarre, for the first three and a half games of the 2000 season. This is even more impressive when Henson's numbers are compared to those of Drew Brees at pass-happy Purdue. There is no comparison. Henson blew him away. From a national perspective, the numbers also hold up quite well, with Michigan finishing third in overall passing (efficiency) in the country, behind Boise State and (slightly) Florida State. (The fans and media were legion in their complaints about the 1999 offense. And, indeed, the complaint was that the offense was too "conservative." But no one complained at the end of the 2003 regular season, when the Wolverines threw 46 percent of the time and only slightly more often than their opposition. What "conservative" means is, in fan and commentator lingo, "what doesn't work.")

But Thomaselli said "conservative" passing. I guess I don't know how to evaluate this, but Michigan's "yards per completion" would seem to be one measure of such a notion, and the Wolverines were, by a huge margin, the leaders in the Big Ten in that statistic. I also note that the Wolverines spread the offense around in 2000, with the wide receivers catching 163 balls, the tight ends 53, and the running backs 43.

Thomaselli's commentary underscores a popular fan vision, that the sine qua non of offensive football is fooling the defense, as opposed to a focus on execution: blocking and throwing and catching. The point of his writing is that, perhaps, Michigan should bring back the underused quick kick or triple reverse or the always-surprising Statue of Liberty play. This one worked well for Ronald Reagan in *Bonzo Goes to College*. And what about the drop kick? After all, the last time the Wolverines used this tactic was in 1916 when Cliff Sparks executed it successfully against the Michigan Agricultural College. Since tapes of the 1916 game do not exist, this should be a real surprise to any opponent on the Michigan schedule. No one will expect it and, in this, it should be a tactic embraced by Rich and the media. (Tom Harmon actually had a cameo in the *Bonzo* flick as a color commentator, and while watching the chimp throw a TD pass, he said, "I sure am glad I didn't have to face Bonzo during my playing days at Michigan." I think the line must have precursed the ordinary color commentary of the moment.)

The point here isn't Thomaselli. The point here is that he is reflective of a media that pays no attention—a media that just says stuff without taking the effort to evaluate its instincts.

Thomaselli's article in the *Sporting News* was typical of the somnambulist media. The article's prediction about the UM defense was, "The defense, though also unproven, will return to the aggressive, opportunistic style of three years ago." Right. I have this vision of Lloyd Carr talking to Coach Herman (the UM defensive coordinator) prior to the 1998 season. It goes something like this. Indeed, I overheard and taped this exact conversation, and I pulled out the transcript:

Carr: I know we just won a national championship with an opportunistic, aggressive defense, but what if we change it up this year?

Herman: What do you mean, coach?

Carr: Well, my vision is that we might try to use a non-aggressive scheme this time around.

Herman: Huh?

Carr: Yeah. I thought we might install a defense that has a tendency to not take advantage of opportunities presented to us.

Herman: You mean, this year let's experiment and see if we can win games without actually hitting anyone?

Carr: That would be a start.

Herman: And we could not play very hard and drop some easy interceptions and not recover some fumbles.

Carr: Perfect. Exactly what I had in mind.

What the hell is Thomaselli talking about? How can any person covering sports come up with this drivel? And why would anyone pay him for this? The difference between 1997 and 1998 was Charles Woodson, the best defensive player I have seen on any Michigan team, and Glenn Steele, whose pass rushing ability was not replaced on the 1998 team. These losses, and the fact that early in the season Michigan was hit with a rash of injuries at the linebacking positions (necessitating playing time for first-year players, one walk on, and certain players not competing at full health), were the downfall of the Michigan defense in 1998. Also relevant was Donovan McNabb, the Syracuse quarterback, whose incredible ability made the Wolverines look just plain silly. Occasionally, it is useful to view the world in this light. Syracuse just hammered us that year because they were better and UM had no answer for McNabb. Not because, as it was ludicrously yammered, we threw "conservative" passes.

The difference between the 1997 defense and those that have followed is that there have been personnel changes (and injuries), and did not arise out of the creeping imbecility of the coaching staff or all of the sudden not wanting to be "aggressive and opportunistic." Aside from this, it was hard for me to understand the basis for Thomaselli's impression that the Michigan defense would improve to 1997 levels in year 2000. At the time I wrote:

> The secondary should be good, perhaps very good (and deep), but it is unlikely whether Michigan will have a difference-maker like Charles Woodson. The linebacking corps seems to have some talent and speed, but it is mostly unproven talent. And I doubt if Ian Gold will be adequately replaced. And the defensive line is completely green and an absolute enigma. There is, at the very least, no proven pass rusher in the group. I hope Rich is right. He could be. But it seems to me Michigan will be fortunate to be as good as it was (defensively) in 1999. Forget about 1997. Ain't gonna happen.

I made some bad predictions that year (I will relate some later), including one genuine Beano, but I think this one was as close to the mark as anyone's, particularly in my concerns about a pass rush. Despite Herman's attempts over the course of the season to get at the opposing quarterback by blitzing from every conceivable formation and position, the Wolverines could generate no heat on the QBs in 2000. Michigan, relying on the blitz (and fires from the corners), had twenty-one sacks over the course of the season, near the bottom of the conference. (Ohio State, much less of a blitzing team, had forty-six sacks.) The lack of synergy was devastating and put too much pressure on the defensive backs; against teams with better than adequate quarterbacking, the Wolverine defense collapsed.

Of course, the most reviled sports reporter for Michigan fans is Michigan graduate Drew Sharp of the *Detroit Free Press*. Sharp, unlike most writers covering sports, has opinions. For this, he deserves his due. The problem is, his opinions often seem disingenuous. And he is a one-trick pony, a Big Ten, Michigan and local sports team basher who makes his mark, like a bad guy in pro rasslin', by repeating the same mantra over and over. Most reporters, like Rich Thomaselli or Joe Falls in the *Detroit News*, reached their analytic heights with commentary that projected the future like the Oracle of Delphi. Falls or Thomaselli or the average columnist might write, "If Michigan wins all or most of their games, they will be doing pretty well." Sharp's theme, to the contrary, has been something like, "The Big Ten teams suck again and will lose every bowl game by at least thirty points. There is not a quarterback in the conference who can throw the ball more than twenty yards. The coaches are all dolts. The teams are all slow. The coaches in the South are all smart. The teams in the South are all fast. It is a fact that players from the South are faster. Robert Smith and Desmond Howard and Charles Woodson and Tyrone Wheatley weren't really fast. They just looked fast as compared to cheeseheads and guys from Iowa. The teams in the West are all creative. The teams in Texas are all inventive." Gee, thanks again, Drew. And then, somehow, when the Big Ten goes 5–2 in bowl games (as in 2002), he will write it off as a fluke, then predict the Big Ten will lose every game out of conference in the next three years. Proof, indeed, that Sharp is just ahead of his time.

Drew Sharp is the king of the revisionists, but one has to admire his persistence, monomania, and complete lack of shame. He will go out on a limb. The problem is, it is the same old limb and, of course, sometimes he is right. Predict tails often enough, and now and again (let's see, I would call it 50 percent of the time) it will pan out. Incidentally, Drew Sharp is not an idiot. Not even close. He is just all shtick, the Masked Marvel of the local journalistic scene. (In the 2002 pro football season, Drew managed to predict, as of this writing, about 43 percent of all games against the spread. This is worse than random. A number like 47 percent would be bad, what one would expect from a coin or an inanimate object or a groundhog as applied to the ordinary randomness of events.)

The worst example of Sharp's brand of journalism came in the 2001 Michigan football season when he lambasted Michigan DB Jeremy LeSeur for having "brain lock" in committing a penalty that allowed MSU to win in ersatz OT against the Wolverines. Lloyd Carr was furious with the comment, particularly since LeSeur's brother has a physiological brain disorder, and Carr felt the comments were too personal and hurtful to Jeremy and his family. I think it is probable that Carr, upset over the loss to MSU and feeling the need to protect a kid he cared about, went avant-garde on Sharp, since it seems highly unlikely that Sharp knew about Jeremy's brother. Indeed, there was almost no chance. That said, I think Sharp might arguably have crossed the line when he criticized a college player in this fashion, though I can understand Sharp's posture and, push comes to shove, I (hate to but have to) maintain that he did not go too far. But what Sharp should have understood was that it was completely reasonable for Carr to call him out on the matter, regardless of whether or not Sharp's comments were inbounds.

It is in Sharp's job description to be critical. I concede this. It is definitely in Carr's job description to care about his players. Instead of perceiving these legitimate lines of demarcation, Sharp acted like a complete baby, lashing out at Lloyd and another one of his players (two weeks later), after Michigan's failure in the 2001 OSU game. In the attempt to get even and prove who was really in charge, Sharp wrote:

> In this new era of sensitivity at Michigan, you must tread carefully with criticism. You can't say that John Navarre stained his pants against Ohio State with four interceptions and a lost fumble because there might have been a history of bed wetting in his family.
>
> You can't say the Wolverines collectively choked at home against an unranked nine-point underdog with a novice quarterback and a prehistoric offensive game plan because that's unnecessarily ripping unsuspecting kids.
>
> Yet somewhere in this attempt to spare feelings is the reality that the toughest football teams are most likely the victorious. Thickness of heart and sturdiness of soul are usually the determining factors on the field of battle.
>
> That's where the Buckeyes had the most decisive edge Saturday. And that should disturb the Wolverine coaching staff more than anything else.
>
> Ohio State physically and mentally overmatched the Wolverines, proving that it can not only beat Michigan, but it can also beat them up in the process.
>
> The 26–20 outcome looked deceptively close at final glance but the Buckeyes were far and away the better team. Jim Tressel was far and away the better coach . . .

Now, it was a fact that the Buckeyes outplayed the Wolverines in this victory. I didn't hear a single Wolverine fan say otherwise. But the rest of this was nothing more than a petulant shot at Lloyd Carr for his reasonable attempt to protect his player.

Sharp had no ethical right to criticize John Navarre in this fashion. Navarre played a less than terrific game, that was true. And it was fair for Sharp to point this out. But the claim that Navarre lacked courage or a thick heart or a stout soul was moronic pabulum. Sharp's first paragraph was as shameful as Navarre was courageous in speaking to the media after the game and taking much of the blame—too much, in fact—on his own shoulders. Navarre just had a poor first half, a fact that was compounded by excellent OSU defensive play. Let's face it, we got whacked in this game and the Buckeyes deserved their victory. But in the second half, Michigan was not that far from pulling the game out, and some of this was due to Navarre's play, his determination and refusal to give up. And the same can be said for the entire Michigan team, particularly the defense for limiting the in-the-shell Buckeyes to one first down in the second half.

Instead of the pointless trashing of college kids trying to do their best, I suggest that Sharp and his colleagues actually attempt some kind of analysis or explanation for their readers. They might be taken more seriously if they did. Instead, since they understand little of what is in front of them, they sink to the level of cliché generalizations about the "field of battle."

A notable failure by the media happened after the incredible and classic loss to Northwestern (54–51) in 2000. Despite the fact that the game should have been a second guesser's paradise, there was not a single coherent word printed in the local papers about what happened to the Michigan defense in the game. The coaches, naturally, never speculated to the media about the genesis of their defensive failures (except for laments of "bad tackling"), and the media, on its own, made little or no attempt. At the close of the 2000 season I was still ruminating over the game, and I shot a question out to my then-favorite internet site, the Wolverine Den, about possible structural flaws in the Michigan defensive game plan. I was particularly interested in Northwestern's success against Michigan as compared to the Wildcats' collapse against Nebraska in their bowl game. I received two responses more interesting than the commentary I saw anywhere else. The first, from "jon," stressed a simple but plausible theory as follows:

> What we did on defense against NU was treat them like an option team. Basically, that means having players assigned to stop the quarterback and pitchman on both sides of the offense. Having to respect the offense like this severely constrains the defense's flexibility in stopping both the passing game and the normal running game.
>
> Nebraska, from what I could tell, did something different. They recognize that NU is different from most option teams in one crucial respect: They can only run the option in one direction. The Northwestern offense has its halfback set off

to one side of the quarterback, rather than directly behind him, and, if it runs option, can only run it to the side the halfback is deployed.

You could see the difference on TV. When NU shifted its halfback from one side to the other, our defense basically didn't react. When they shifted the halfback against Nebraska, the Husker defense moved along with it. I'm not sure precisely what adjustment Nebraska made. But the basic idea was that they freed up more defenders to play regular, aggressive defense by doing this.

Some caveats: I didn't read any newspaper coverage of the game, so I haven't seen any confirmation from the coaches about this. Also, I'm not saying that this accounted for the entire difference between Nebraska's defensive performance and ours—merely that it was a very important factor.

Another poster, calling himself "hurryup," wrote as follows:

What I remember about the UM-NW game is this. All week Lloyd talked about how NW had a run-first offense out of the spread and how we had to stop the run. So what we did was play nickel and dime defenses all day, forcing our small, young DLs to make all the plays on the runners, with usually only one LB in position to help. Of course, with their WRs dragging our DBs all over the field, once a RB gets past line and shakes that one LB, he has all kinds of room to run.

I cannot verify that either of these analyses is correct, though I think they both have merit (more on that later). But right or wrong, these writers took a chance and attempted to explain what happened in one of the most incredible games (maybe *the* most incredible game) of my lifetime. The foregoing posts were thoughtful and thought-provoking, unlike anything in the mainstream media.

Reasonably, the Michigan coaching staff was mum about the Northwestern game, save for boilerplate generalizations, since commentary by the coaching staff would have served no useful purpose. But what about the average sportswriter in the Michigan or Illinois papers? Doesn't it seem that someone would attempt to analyze why a defense that had shut out two consecutive opponents would give up fifty-four points in a game where the Northwestern offense was given zero help by its defense? Instead, I saw not a single written word of explanation or any attempt to analyze or understand.

Of course, it is not only Michigan sportswriters who give the public next to nothing. At least some local reporters (Sharp and the too-good-so-he-won't-be-around-long Jim Carty) will criticize the Wolverines, even if these criticisms are, well, often Beanoisms. MSU reporting is equally bad (probably worse), though it has its own, distinct brand of homerism. *Oakland Press* stalwart and dope Rich Caputo, prior to the UM-MSU game in 1997, said something like, "MSU corner Sorie Kanu is every bit as good as Charles Woodson. He just doesn't get the same level of publicity." Nice analysis. Woodson (as of 2003) remains one of the premier corners in the NFL. Kanu? Sorie. Two years ago, a reporter in Lansing (the wretched Jack Eibling) made up a quote from a Michigan player in order to put some heat under the Spartans and their already-hot followers. Since MSU and its fans in the post-Duffy era (excluding Muddy Waters's brief tenure) have lived on the bubble of their emotions, it seemed purely coals to Newcastle to make this sort of stuff up. But this also seems indigenous to MSU; it is just never hot enough in East Lansing. If you root for the Spartans, you can never have a large enough sleeve upon which to wear your heart. Indeed, to the brie-eating UM faithful (me, for example), there is a lesson in this.

In July of 2000, Jemele Hill, an MSU grad who covers the Spartans for the *Detroit Free Press*, wrote about the NCAA's decision to allow Zach Randolph to be eligible in the 2000–2001 basketball season. Hill tackled a tough topic—full marks on this—but her writing proved to be nothing other than a PR stunt for MSU. The NCAA had declared terrific MSU freshman "big man" Zach Randolph eligible, despite the fact that he skied out at an 810 SAT score, a level that implied freshman ineligibility, given his grade point average of 2.7. The SAT score was twenty points shy of the minimum level required. This was an odd and awkward ruling by the NCCA since, by my understanding, it had not been waived for others, perhaps ever, though I can't say I have studied the matter. I wrote the NCAA about this and queried, specifically, about a kid at Indiana, call him GL. This kid, also a fine prospect, scored an 820 on the SAT and had a *higher* GPA than Randolph. This kid, unlike Randolph, had no criminal convictions. Nor had he ever been implicated, unlike Randolph, in the sale of automatic weapons. Yet the NCAA denied GL's request.

The Randolph decision seemed particularly bizarre given the kid's prior troubles. There would seem no compelling equity for the agency to go out of its way to look inconsistent and silly on behalf of a kid with a history of criminal problems, even if he was truly a good kid. I also began to wonder about Randolph's 2.7 GPA. It had been reported previously that at the close of Randolph's junior year, he had a 2.2 GPA. This implies (assuming an even level of credits over four years) a 4.27 GPA in his senior year. I suppose this is possible. But does it seem likely that a kid who has the ability to do A+ work in his senior year of high school could only score 810 on the SAT? This is a woeful score or, at least, a surprising score for someone ostensibly capable of A+ course work. Well, who knows? And perhaps the previous reporting was erroneous. I have no way to verify it. But it is certain that Randolph's GPA made big gains in his senior year. This was verified by Randolph's high school coach, Moe Smedley.

Ms. Hill noted the NCAA decision with approval, despite the fact that the agency had been silent about the reasons for the decision. Given this, Hill speculated that the correct decision was made, since (a) Randolph worked hard to raise his GPA to a 2.7 (see above), (b) he didn't declare for the NBA draft, (c) Tom Izzo had a reputation equal to or bordering on that of Coach K, (d) MSU deserved consideration, since it was the defending NCAA champion and MSU rarely loses players early to the NBA, and (e) it might make up for "all of the foolishness Jason Richardson was put through in his freshman season." As to (e), Hill states the NCAA was "ready to take away (Richardson's) first season over a class he had taken as a ninth-grader." I am not compelled by these arguments. No one should be. First of all, the arguments could be made for just about any kid who has not qualified. Certainly the arguments apply to GL. I assume GL could claim he worked hard at his studies. And, while GL was a top high school prospect, he also didn't declare for the NBA draft. The prominence and competence of Tom Izzo cannot be questioned. But he is not as prominent as Bob Knight (the Indiana coach at that time), certainly among the most successful coaches in college history. Knight is a loose cannon and a person I don't care for, but no one can dispute the fact that the Indiana program has been as clean as any program in the country. More so than Duke or Michigan or North Carolina or Kentucky or even MSU. Indeed, among the top twenty-five programs, I doubt if there has been a more ethical one than Indiana, at least when one looks at the level playing field considerations mandated by the NCAA. Indiana also almost never loses players to the NBA. I recall only three (Jay Edwards, Isaiah Thomas, and recently Jarrod Jeffries) over the past thirty years, even though Indiana has been a national power for most of that period and MSU has been up and down over the decades in question.

It was certainly the case that MSU was the defending national champion. But this would seem a reason to grant the program less slack, as opposed to more. It would seem, if anything, that the NCAA would grant more leeway to a historically clean program (say Northwestern or Vanderbilt) that is courageous enough to bang against a brutal schedule year after year, as opposed to the big guys on the block. Even when compared to has-been and for-a-short-period-sorta-was basketball big guys like UM.

However, even if this was right, even if it is the case that MSU deserved a different set of rules for its recent (and periodic) prominence, would that not also apply to Indiana? Certainly, the two years prior to the Randolph decision evinced better basketball in East Lansing than Bloomington. But there can be no debate that Indiana has been a more successful program over the years than MSU. Indeed, it isn't even close. When one thinks of the top five programs in the country one thinks of Indiana, not MSU, though there may come a time when that will change. (As it turns out, it isn't likely to change too soon, since Indiana wandered into the 2002 national championship game. I also checked out the AP top twenty-five since its creation in 1948. Disregarding the recent forfeit of 117 games [give or take five] by UM, the Wolverines are listed at number eleven on the composite poll, as measured by weeks in the top ten. Indiana is number six. MSU is number twenty-three. And, to be honest, Michigan is hardly part of the nation's basketball elite.)

The most bizarre aspect of the Jemele Hill argument is the notion that the NCAA almost did not allow Jason Richardson to compete during his freshman year. I would title this argument, "If My Aunt Had Wheels She Would Be a Trolley Car." I have no idea whether the Richardson decision by the NCAA was correct or not, though, from what I know now, I would say the organization made the right call in allowing Richardson to play. But it seems a completely inane notion that "the NCAA ruled in our favor recently, so they should rule in our favor again." Jason Richardson did not miss one minute of his freshman season due to eligibility concerns and, hence, MSU deserved no "payback" from the agency, even if such "paybacks" were within any sort of ethical boundary. Of course, Hill's crowing about players staying at MSU was also short-lived; Richardson, Randolph, and Marcus Taylor all jumped to the NBA within the period of a year. In the spring of 2003, big man Ezrem Lorbeck also defected.

Hill also complained that the "folks in Indiana . . . are whining more than usual because of what happened to Randolph." Now, I admit, there are significant numbers of Indiana fans with a continuing reverence for the probably-not-very-balanced Bob Knight that is hard to explain or understand. However, as an experienced recipient of Indiana whining and MSU whining, I can state, with absolute certainty, that the latter is always more profound.

Compare, for example, the Indiana and MSU internet posting boards. The Indiana boards, at least, show some level of introspection. The MSU boards evince little more than mindless ventilation, bitching about Michigan, and various theories as to how the world, led by the arrogant University-of-Michigan-controlled press, conspires against MSU. Any show of self-examination is unusual, though there are more than a few excellent Spartan posters. But, even if the whining characterization is accurate—and, indeed, I can't argue that UM fans whine less—do not the Indiana fans have a point? GL had a higher GPA than Zach Randolph. He had a higher SAT score. He has no criminal history. And the NCAA denied his appeal. If the tables were turned, would not MSU fans (or Michigan fans or any other fans) be howling? I would suggest so, and would further suggest the complaint would be completely justified, at least absent some coherent explanation from the NCAA. The agency's failure to explain or rationalize its decision as applied to one specific student-athlete is completely understandable. But these explanations can be made in the abstract, something the agency refused to do in relation to my inquiries or in any other published venue.

Hill did approach one argument of possible consequence. She stated (I can't verify her statement as fact) that 49 percent of "all eligibility" appeals from NCAA decisions resulted in the original agency result being nullified or modified. The problem with this, of course, is that the statistic is not connected to the Randolph eligibility concerns. Rather, the percentage relates to the entire spectrum of eligibility and other issues. Presumably, Jason Richardson's case would be included in these numbers (no resemblance to the Randolph/GL decisions), as might, say, Duane Goldbourne's legitimate sixth year of eligibility at MSU due to his history of injuries. The use of the statistic is like saying that 49 percent of all criminal convictions are set aside by appeals courts so Charles Manson should be released.

After my letters went unheeded, I emailed the NCAA about the Randolph/GL distinction and I received an email in response which stated that they would get back to me. And they did, several days later, with the communication that they are proscribed from discussing circumstances as to individual student athletes by federal regulation. No surprise, though I can't figure out why they would have to "get back with me" to relate the rule. And the rule might make sense, unless you are Indiana trying to figure out why decisions were made. In any event, I emailed the NCAA another note asking the question as a complete hypothetical. My questions were (among others) (1) how many other student athletes have had the GPA/test score criteria waived, and (b) what factors would go into granting such a waiver? I recieved no response.

My parting shot on this is that Ms. Hill also argues that Zach Randolph deserved more consideration than GL, since Randolph took the SAT test more times than GL. Well, what can I say? Assume it is a pole vault competition. Competitor A clears 6 feet. And then Competitor A misses at 6.5 feet. Three times. Competitor B clears 5.9 feet, but then misses at 6.5 feet ten times. The winner? In Jemele's world, it is Competitor B, since he failed more times at the higher height.

In one respect, Ms. Hill touched upon a reality of the watchdog functions of the NCAA. It is a historical fact that the NCAA is much more likely to scrutinize, and punish hard, the minor league college program as opposed to its more successful brethren. (This changed in the spring of 2003 when Michigan got hammered. It was well deserved. More later.) Don Yeager, a Florida reporter, wrote a book (published in 1991) called *Undue Process: The NCAA's Injustice For All,* where he outlined the NCAA's disparate treatment of Marist with regard to Rik Smits, as compared to much more significant problems at UCLA under John Wooden. Yeager's writing extended support for the Hill piece, albeit in a perverse way. Yeager might say, "of course Ms. Hill is right," since the NCAA is arbitrary and capricious in its treatment of student-athletes and institutions and is a front-runner in protecting the successful program.

So was the NCAA right or wrong in the Randolph case? I would guess they were wrong, in the absence of some public and written policy that explains the level of the agency's discretion in the waiver of the rules. But even this would seem tough, pushing the agency into very difficult decisions as to why one kid should be ineligible (GL) while another in the same or worse situation (Randolph) is not. I am not certain the NCAA's reliance on SAT or ACT scores makes any sense, particularly where it is likely that there is some significant element of cultural bias in these exams. On the other hand, without these exams, a laudable purpose of the NCAA (the carrot to get kids to study) may be stripped away, since any reliance on high school grades for superstar athletes is, at best, a complete and naive act of faith.

In the big picture, I would concur with the idea that any academic rules about pre-college performance and college admission and eligibility for competition purposes represent a dubious policy. If MSU or UM prefers to grant scholarship money to an illiterate ballerina or cretin bassoon player or even a minor league criminal football player, then it seems it should be that institution's choice. The institution lives with its reputation and the sense of pride and connection shared by its alumni. If MSU believed it could make a good citizen out of Randolph, who are we—at UM or other institutions—to throw stones? Wouldn't it have been legitimate for MSU to argue, "We saw real glimmers of intelligence and humanity in Zach and thought that the exposure to Tom Izzo—soon to be knighted by the queen and granted sainthood by the pope (by the way)—and the exposure to our academic and basketball programs would be good for both Zach and MSU." And shouldn't this have been MSU's choice? Wasn't this MSU's judgment to make, regardless of how jaded or cynical outsiders might have been of the choice? But this assumes a set of rules that does not exist.

An example at Michigan was Gil Chapman, the "Jersey Jet," recruited by Schembechler prior to the advent of Prop 48. Bo had to fight with the university to allow Chapman's entrance, since his high school academic record was reported to be marginal, to say it graciously. But Chapman became a good student at UM, got his degree, and later went on to receive his MBA from Rutgers, a very good business school. Artificial rules about entrance criteria might have made these achievements unlikely. MSU, to be certain, owns similar stories.

Hill's argument, as it stands, is pathetic. However, the argument, "Hey, it's our business who we choose to accept and why" is hard to deny. I certainly won't deny it. Discounting the system, Randolph's status at MSU should have been up to MSU.

In the context of the status quo, it is difficult to figure out what in the world the NCAA was doing in the Randolph case. Of course, the big picture issue is that if Michigan admits an idiot bassoon player, then MSU will feel compelled to do the same thing. And once MSU admitted Zach Randolph, UM had to take a chance on a problem child like Jason Brooks. Blather. The big picture is that the "level playing field" is a complete crock of something. Why should we care if the playing field is level? We just need to concern ourselves with what we are and what we prefer to be in the future. Let others make their own choices.

In retrospect, the Randolph decision by the NCAA was a complete rent-a-player. I thought Randolph was an incredible talent as he entered MSU in 2000, and predicted that he could be the best big man in the conference. Randolph was a monster on the boards and, more unlikely, saw the court very well and had an uncanny ability to pass out of the post. My prediction was, "If Randolph plays (and even if he doesn't), MSU will win the Big Ten again. It might make a run at another national championship." This proved accurate but Randolph's presence may have had only a nominal impact on MSU's success in 2000–2001. The kid reported to MSU out of shape and, with other talented inside players (notably the very tough Andre Hutson), Izzo limited Randolph's minutes to about nineteen per game. His thirty-minute-per-game stats would have been points 16.9, rebounds 10.3, assists 1.3, steals 1.0, blocks 1.1. Not bad at all, especially for a first-year player, though Zach had some issues on defense. But Zach's ability was not lost on NBA scouts, since he declared for the draft and was taken as a lottery pick. Moreover, I heard a rumor from many (including MSU students) that Zach did not attend a single class in his last two and a half months at MSU. I cannot state this as a matter of fact, but, assuming it was true (or even if not), it is hard to figure out what the NCAA accomplished in its eligibility ruling on Randolph. To make sure Zach got a quality education? To make sure he attended some classes? Any classes? To make sure he got to hang around East Lansing and attain, by osmosis, the advantages of a college atmosphere? I don't blame MSU for this. Or even Randolph. He will be richer than I can ever imagine. And MSU did nothing wrong. But it seems if the NCAA is serious in its quest to have competitions between legitimate student-athletes, their ruling made no sense.

In the wake of the Randolph decision and other affairs, I would argue for eliminating the ACT/SAT requirements. And I would argue for eliminating grade requirements; they are likely phony for some percentage of big-time athletes anyway. Let the individual institution make its own rules, consistent with the institution's vision of its purposes. This would, of course, drive schools like Michigan, Notre Dame, and Northwestern nuts, never knowing exactly where to draw the line. But shouldn't this be the way it is? Shouldn't Michigan and Notre Dame actually have to define where their priorities lie, as opposed to someone else, like the NCAA, doing it for them?

* * * *

Unlike local sports reporting, the internet has created writers who are both more and less restricted than ordinary journalists. More, in that any idiotic comments are going to be hammered by those paying attention. Less, in that language (so-called vulgarity) is not restricted and there are no space or editorial limitations. In this environment, one sees a broader spectrum of writing than can be found in ordinary print media. Jason Foster, aka Sparty Speaks, is a very talented writer who focuses on MSU and Big Ten sports issues. His comments on Spartan star tight end Eric Knott's legal troubles while in high school were more thoughtful and incisive than any of those printed in the Detroit papers. On the other hand, there is the ubiquitous "jim9," a supposed Notre Dame or OSU fan who penned comments such as this:

> ohio state will be giving all players a chance to play on sat. getting ready for next year. they know michigan will run the score up but at least cooper will have an excuse, several players will be able to show their skills.someone told me that many players will not even have their names o on their jersey"s. Also they will be wearing different helmets. More later when I get new information from a friend who lives in ashtabula ohio that is near Geneva on the lake stay tuned.

This is exactly as written. And exactly so, I expect. But the most appealing part of the internet is its capriciousness and flexibility, the fact that posters will stray from sports to politics to movies in a way that is outside of the static, warm-bath newspaper medium.

My favorite poster on the old Wolverine Den was Paul Campos, a Michigan alum and lawyer living in Colorado. Campos is a law professor and a spectacular journalist; his writing moves from sports to politics to history to statistics with an unusual grace and fluidity. A recent contribution is reproduced: a response to a conservative's complaint about paying taxes. The complaint focused on the "nauseatingly large portion of my income stolen . . . for inefficient, costly, unnecessary, and even harmful programs" funded by the government. Campos's response was as follows:

> More than 80% of all federal tax revenues go to pay for just four things: servicing the national debt, defense, social security and Medicare.

Paying the first item isn't really optional.

Although one can always argue about how much money ought to go to national defense, I doubt there are too many pacifists in this thread. And defense spending was far higher under Ronald Reagan, who is the patron saint of the anti-tax sentiment, despite the fact that his budgets produced the gigantic debt whose servicing now eats up one quarter of all federal revenues.

Social security and Medicare, these are enormously popular social welfare programs that no politician dares touch in any serious way. You may dislike that use of federal money, but the political process that makes those programs untouchable is called "democracy." The notion that property should be immune from democratic redistribution is curious. Property rights are no more "natural" than the infield fly rule is "natural"; the whole concept of property only exists within the context of a web of social relations. In other words, you have property rights because the legal/political system says you do. The idea of "property" outside of whatever legal-political regime defines the characteristics of that concept is meaningless.

If you don't like our taxation system, your argument is mostly with your fellow citizens—not with the government. In this case, at least, the government is pretty much doing what the vast majority of people want it to do: pay the debt, fund the military, and provide a relatively modest portion of the retirement income of older Americans, as well as paying most of their medical expenses . . .

The notion that somehow it is the government's fault that we voted for a bunch of expensive programs we weren't willing to pay for is one of the more annoying aspects of contemporary political rhetoric.

I can't say there is something this thoughtful (whether you agree or not) found on the Michigan boards every day, but the interactive nature of the web will (has, actually) make ordinary sports reporting dead in the water—at least in terms of the relative quality of information. I'd like to reproduce one other non-sports example that I have been carrying around in my briefcase.

40

Unfortunately, I have long since lost the identity of the author, whose thoughts on Clinton's liaisons with Monica Lewinsky and "Zippergate" follow:

Opinion #1: It's about lies, not sex.

Some individuals say it's not the sex, it's the lying that's the real problem. But it's not a general kind of lying that's the problem, it's specifically the president's unwillingness to share details of his sex life with every human being in the world. By that standard only Geraldo Rivera and Dennis Rodman would qualify to be president. If lying is damnable, let's say we decide to impeach every politician who lies to the American people. They'd be dropping like flies. I forget how the chain of command works but I think that after the president and vice president you have the Speaker of the House and then members of the cabinet and on from there. It would take about two months before a near-sighted postal clerk has the nuclear launch codes.

When the politicians who vote on impeachment tell us they will be non-political, asking us to believe they will ignore the fact that Al Gore would become president, do you think they are telling the truth? And if they aren't, should we impeach them too?

Opinion #2: How can Clinton govern now?

I have this image in my head of Yasser Arafat visiting the White House. Clinton offers him a presidential cigar and Arafat says,"If you don't mind, could I have one that is still in the original wrapper?" This ugly incident turns into a towel fight and triggers World War III. That's the best scenario I could come up with in which the president's ability to govern is affected by Zippergate.

I guess there's one other possibility. Suppose Congress passes some legislation and it comes to Clinton's desk for signature, but Hillary has broken both of his arms. That might slow him down. But he could still grip a pen in his teeth and sign the bill into law. And if Hillary punched out his teeth too, all you really need is a bottle of dripping ink and a cute intern to improvise a solution . . .

Opinion #3: Any CEO would be fired.

The pundits keep saying that any CEO who has an affair with an employee would be fired. But on my planet, Earth, CEOs routinely boff the staff, literally and figuratively, and I know of no example where any CEO ever got fired for anything except falling stock prices . . .

Opinion #4: You can't do that in the military.

Pundits point out that the president would be kicked out of the military for his behavior, if in fact he were in the military. We can extend this brilliant analysis to see how he would be treated by organizations to which he does not belong. For example, I also believe he would be kicked out of the Girl Scouts for his behavior. That sort of activity is very disruptive to the meetings. And I don't think you can participate in the Big Sister program with that on your record either. I also believe he would be fired as editor of *Cigar Aficionado* magazine if he worked there, which he doesn't.

Opinion # 5: It's sexual harassment.

Some say that because Monica was a White House employee and Clinton had the power to influence her career, it is sexual harassment by definition. I suppose it is possible that Monica thought she would get a cabinet job after her internship was over, or possibly become ambassador to Great Britain. And I suppose it's possible that Monica was afraid of being demoted from her lucrative intern job. So I guess that's the best point I've heard so far.

* * * *

After I wrote the foregoing section, I was accused of shooting fish in a barrel and, more to the point, being unfair to local sportswriters. Friends chastised me, saying that local writing really isn't all that bad. Okay, I thought, maybe they are right. But at the exact moment my guilt came to the surface, a local, unnamed sportswriter wrote an article explaining why Lloyd Carr's record against ranked teams was 23–11 and against teams in the top ten, 11–1. This was, indeed, a fair topic for analysis. How was it possible that Carr's record against the best competition could be so good? I wanted to know. First, the writer suggested, "Michigan's talent has something to do with these numbers." Second, he postulated, "Coaching is critical too." Third, he argued, "Of the head coach's many responsibilities, the most important is to make certain his team is mentally prepared to play each week." Finally, the writer contended that the trinity of talent, motivation, and coaching was a surprise to Carr, and that, "it took Carr two solid seasons to fully understand this." I thought, what the hell, I could ask Lloyd about this. The transcript follows:

Ross:	Lloyd, I know you were a head coach at the high school level, and an assistant coach at Michigan for fifteen years, including terms as defensive coordinator and position coaching. Despite this history, there must have been something that surprised you when you became head coach.
Carr:	Is that a question?
Ross:	I guess so.
Carr:	Well, what surprised me was that you needed good football players.
Ross:	You are kidding.
Carr:	No. When I was defensive coordinator, I thought that you could win games with any old guys off the street. But it didn't take me long to be disabused of that notion. It takes football players to win football games. Generally, it is better if they have played the game prior to playing at Michigan.
Ross:	How about against good teams?
Carr:	Against good teams, your players have to be even better. If you want to win against really good teams, you have to have really good football players. As I told a local writer (name deleted), it took me a solid two years to understand that.
Ross:	How about coaching?
Carr:	Once we started to get the really good players, I thought it was possible we could just line them up single file, throw out a ball, and then let them go at it. It turns out, however, there are certain procedural requisites you have to follow.
Ross:	Like what?

43

Carr:	A key one is that you have to put seven guys on the line of scrimmage on offense. Otherwise, those little fat guys in the striped shirts keep marching the ball in the wrong direction. On defense, though, we still kept lining them up single file. No problem there. As I told a reporter over at the *Free Press* it took me two solid years to figure out that coaching is an important part of the game.
Ross:	What about motivation?
Carr:	No big deal there. We just let the players read the columns in the *Ann Arbor News* and the *Free Press*. As I told those guys, it took me two solid years . . .

So, given this, I guess that the local reporting hasn't been so bad; it did take Lloyd two (solid) years to understand that he wasn't going to win games without good players. You read it here second.

* * * *

I was heartened to discover that I was not the only one being driven insane by the lunatic ravings of Jemele Hill. In February of 2002, this parody (posted by "Jemele Hill") showed up on the Wolverine Den:

> University of Michigan Head Football Coach Lloyd Carr announced several catastrophicable shakeups in his coaching staff on Thursday.
>
> Michigan, still reeling from its last-second loss to Michigan State in November, loses the services of Defensive Backfield Coach Jim Morrisson, as well as Head Offense Coach Lance Parrish. Morrisson is leaving for health reasons. Sources speculate that he has grown tired of catching colds and the flu from being around so many young players. Parrish is leaving after a late-night sumo wrestling battle with Coach Carr on Wednesday night.
>
> Carr announced that Morrisson would be replaced by noted Las Vegas oddsmaker Danny Sheridan. Officials at Michigan, still embroiled in controversy after the resignation of Assistant Basketball Coach and noted numbers runner Ed Martin, refused to comment on Sheridan's gambling background. No replacement for Parrish has been announced. However, I got several email messages stating that Offensive

Receivers Coach Gary Moeller is a leading candidate to replace Parrish. Moeller was Michigan's head coach until he was arrested after a late-night shootout with the FBI at a metropolitan Detroit restaurant.

It is expected that an announcement regarding Parrish's replacement will be made after the rest of Michigan's staff, as well as all of its fans, returns from the Ku Klux Klan national convention in Skokie, Illinois.

Michigan lost to Michigan State in November after a controversial finish that led to a large increase in racism among its fans.

This would be funnier if it wasn't so close to the bone of Hill's actual work.

Three *A Lot of Running and Conservative Passing*

The average person, when he walks into his doctor's office, does not assume he knows as much or more than the physician. Even if the patient reads about medical issues in the *NY Times*, has an uncle who is a physician, and once won an insurance dispute with Blue Cross, he is unlikely to make the leap that he knows better than the doc. Aside from this, those of us who are not professionals in an arena, whether it be auto mechanics or architecture, are unlikely to assume that we know more or could do it better than the professional we have consulted or observed. Yet, somehow, the casual football fan (or sports fan) often thinks that he (rarely she) "knows better" than the coach. That schmuck. Putz. Fool. Moron. Idiot. Corso. Beano! I won't say Michigan fans are worse in this regard than other fans. But they are definitely not better.

Kent Weichmann, a brilliant Ann Arbor attorney, finds this to be a variation on what he calls "Casey Stengel syndrome." Kent, as a child, could never understand why the managerial decisions Casey made during a game tended to work, while those of, say, Bob Elliot of the Kansas City A's or Charlie Grimm of the Cubs never worked. Until he went back to the team rosters as an adult and realized that, for example, in 1960 the Yankees had three catchers—Yogi Berra, Elston Howard, and John Blanchard—who were all certifiable stars or Hall of Fame caliber players. Each of these players hit more than twenty home runs (in 1961 when twenty was a real number) and one of these guys was always on the bench (no DH at the time), meaning that Stengel never had any concern about a fresh player to pinch hit or catch. So, in 1960, the catching position looked like this:

Yankees	A's	Cubs
Elston Howard	Pete Daley	Elvin Tappe
Yogi Berra	Danny Kravitz	Moe Thacker
John Blanchard	Harry Chiti	Sammy Taylor

To be sure, it is amazing that the Yankees could put together a team with three catchers of such quality. But it defies belief that the Cubs could arrange to have Elvin Tappe, Sammy Taylor, and Moe Thacker on their roster at the same time. It seems to me it would be difficult to arrange to have three such you-fill-in-the-blank players on the same roster over the course of an extended period, let alone at a single moment. Until one looks at the poor A's. The best of this lot was Harry Chiti, who averaged .236 over a ten-year career and overachieved by pounding out an average of four home runs and eighteen RBIs per year. To be fair, Chiti is a prominent baseball footnote, since he was once traded for himself, the only player to hold that distinction. How did this happen? He was traded to the New York Mets by the Cleveland Indians (who else?) for a "player to be named later." And who was this not-named player? Harry Chiti. Honest. The Tribe couldn't even wrangle Arnold Portacarrerro or Hobie Landrith in return.

Now, lest one think I have unfairly stacked the deck, the Yankees in 1960 had five good starters—headed by Whitey Ford, Bob Turley, and Ralph Terry—and a team ERA of 3.52. And a bullpen with the great Louis Arroyo, as well as Ryne Duren, and a terrific young pitcher, Bill Stafford. The A's? Well, their best starter was probably Bud Daley, who finished with a 16–16 record and a 4.56 ERA. The best reliever was Marty Kutyna, who parlayed a 3.92 ERA into four saves. He was backed by guys who would have trouble at AAA. The Cubs did have two decent starters in Don Cardwell and Dick Ellsworth, but both had ERAs well above the Yankee team. And after these two, it was not pretty. Don Elston managed to scrape out eleven saves on a decent ERA, but he was backed by guys like Joe Schaffernoth and Dick Burwell. The less said the better.

So if Casey left Ford in the game, it was likely to work. If he brought in Arroyo, it might work too. And if he brought in Blanchard to pinch hit for a hung-over Mickey Mantle, there was a chance that might work. But if Grimm left Barney Schultz in, or pulled him for Schaffernoth, the result was likely to be the same. Cubs lose. Cubs lose. Cubs lose. Cubs lose. Such is the genesis of genius and something less than genius. Did I mention, "Cubs lose?"

So, go to sleep; what's the point? Are coaches fungible, mere victims of the vagaries of talent? I think not—consider the phrase "John Cooper." Should they be, as often seems their reaction to criticism, completely above the slings and arrows of those who care? Nope. These guys make a fortune, and second-guessing is inbounds. But in making evaluations of coaches—even John Cooper (a completely competent coach, though one who catered to the NFL aspirations of his players over the construction of his team)—it seems to me the analyses are generally as flabby as the events sought to be criticized. Typical in the Michigan football world is the Thomaselli "prediction," or criticism, coming into the 2000 season, that Michigan would evince "a lot of running and conservative passing." The phrase "conservative passing" is a curious one to me in its implied criticism of the Michigan offense, and interesting in the fact that this is the most typical criticism of Lloyd Carr made by Michigan fans and the press. It has become cliché that Michigan "will not throw over the middle," or throws only "safe passes," or just won't take any reasonable chances. Or, most common, it is just "too predictable."

The Thomaselli phrase also piqued my interest by reminding me of a piece that Paul Zimmerman wrote for *Sports Illustrated* a number of years ago, where he noted that fumbles lost in the NFL correlated, slightly, with wins, while interceptions correlated, overwhelmingly, with losses. At the time, I put this down to junk science, despite the fact that Zimmerman is one of the few reporters out there who seems to really know the game. Indeed, Zimmerman's out-of-print treatise, *An Intellectual's Guide to Pro Football*, is the best thing ever written for the serious fan.

Despite my respect for Zimmerman, it seemed to me that the conditions of winning and losing caused the statistic, and not the other way around. In other words, if you are getting beat up at the line of scrimmage, you tend to be passing more, and the defense is far more likely to be sitting on the pass. Ergo, more interceptions. And teams that are winning easily are more likely to be running the clock. Ergo, more fumbles. Regardless, I thought it might be interesting to evaluate a database of Michigan games and explore the correlations between winning and losing.

My database consists of 113 games from 1993 through mid-2000 and includes all bowl games from 1970. The games chosen are inclusive and random, save for the bowl games, included to increase the number of losses in the database, since our "Bo bowl record" predominates (by a large margin) in the loss column. Of those 113 games, Michigan won 77 and lost 36. This is a winning percentage of 68.14, somewhat lower than the 75 percent historical level, due to the inclusion of the bowl games. In this database, the correlation between turnovers and winning or losing is profound:

Michigan Record in Database	77–36	68.14	percent
Michigan Record When Fewer Turnovers	52– 8	87.7	percent
Michigan Record When Even Turnovers	13–10	56.5	percent
Michigan Record When More Turnovers	12–18	41.8	percent

When UM was the recipient of more turnovers than its opponent, they won 88 percent of the games. When it lost the turnover stat, it won 41 percent. Considering the database has a certain number of excessive losses in relation to Michigan's actual winning percentage, the numbers make perfect sense and are about what I would have guessed. And my surmise is that there is no surprise in these numbers for anyone. Breaking the numbers down Zimmerman-style still perplexes me, regardless of my initial feelings about mixing the cause and effect of interceptions. The numbers look like this:

Michigan Record When Fewer Fumbles	32–15	68.1 percent
Michigan Record When Equal Fumbles	20–11	64.5 percent
Michigan Record When More Fumbles	25–10	71.4 percent
Michigan Record When Fewer INTs	51– 6	89.5 percent
Michigan Record When Equal INTs	16– 8	66.7 percent
Michigan Record When More INTs	10–22	31.3 percent

(Note that all references to "fumbles" are to "fumbles lost.") It still seems to me that the interception percentages are explainable, at least in significant part, as a matter of effect and not cause. The fumble percentage is harder to explain. How can it be, in the big picture, that fumbling has no statistical correlation with winning or losing games? I posted the foregoing on the Wolverine Den under the title "Are All Turnovers Created Equal?" I concluded the post with the following note:

> My suspicion is there is some (possibly significant) mixing of
> cause and effect, but (in any event) it seems odd to me that
> fumbles (in a macro view) seem to have a limited impact upon
> outcomes. Any thoughts on this?

There weren't many thoughts. There was some mild irritation that I was attempting an argument for never passing the ball. There was one comment about "passing when behind," implying a greater rate of interceptions. And there was one post suggesting that I not send Lloyd Carr these numbers, since "he might try to fumble the ball more often."

The above numbers still bugged me. So what if we just looked at the games where the yardage gained was close? Wouldn't this tend to separate out those instances when a team was just passing when they were behind and try-ing to catch up? Moreover, it would tend to minimize the "being beaten up at the line of scrimmage" argument. And, in any event, it seemed a review of games where yardage was close might be interesting.

Well, I was surprised again. I decided to divide the database into three seg-ments. These were (a) those where Michigan gained at least seventy-five more yards from scrimmage than its opponent, (b) those where Michigan gained at least seventy-five fewer yards than its opponent, and (c) all other close games. I chose seventy-five yards, since this represents one field-long drive. The num-bers are below:

Record When UM Gains More Yards	47– 4	92.2 percent
Record When UM Gains Fewer Yards	4–12	25.0 percent
Record In Close Games	26–20	56.5 percent

Looking to the forty-six close games, the turnover record is exactly what one would suspect:

Record When Michigan Has Fewer Turnovers	20– 2	90.9	percent
Record When Michigan Has More Turnovers	3–13	18.75	percent
Record When Turnovers Are Even	3– 5	37.5	percent

But, looking specifically to fumbles and interceptions, the numbers again tend to show a more profound correlation with interceptions:

Record When Michigan Has Fewer Fumbles	13– 7	65	percent
Record When Michigan Has More Fumbles	6– 7	46.15	percent
Record When Even Fumbles	7– 6	53.85	percent
Record When Michigan Throws Fewer INTs	16– 0	100	percent
Record When Michigan Throws More INTs	2–15	11.8	percent
Record When Even Interceptions	8– 5	61.5	percent

Thus, while fumbles in close games have some correlation with winning and losing, interceptions have an extremely high coincidence. Some of this, there is no question, is merely reflective of the fact of losing and is not the cause of losing. Still, it is hard for me not to conclude that interceptions, other things being equal, represent more profound events than fumbles.

However, I tried it out one other way. What if, for example, we look only to games where there was a two-fumble or two-interception advantage? Wouldn't this, in part, create a comparison between fumbles and interceptions that tends to minimize the end of the game interception that may skew the data? Looking at it from Michigan or its opponent's point of view (in all 113 games in the database):

Record (either team) When two Fewer Fumbles	16–14	53.3 percent
Record (either team) When two Fewer INTs	35– 4	89.7 percent

Two or more lost fumbles has no correlation with winning or losing. Two or more interceptions is almost a lock to coincide with a win. #$%$ %#^*#. Okay, okay, I take it all back. Let's try it out one more time, but this time, just in the close (seventy-five yards from scrimmage) games. I would predict/assume that in these games, where yardage from scrimmage was within one drive, a two-interception or two-fumble advantage would show a very favorable (and very similar) win percentage.

Record (either team) When Two Fewer Fumbles	5–9	35.7 percent
Record (either team) When Two Fewer INTs	18–0	100 percent

Basically, we get the same result. The problem is that the two-fewer-fumbles games also have interceptions in the mix, sometimes working in the same direction. So, what if we hold fumbles and interceptions as constants? Looking at all games, either team, and only in those games where the interceptions thrown by each team were equal, the record of the team fumbling less often was 10–7, or a winning percentage of 58.8 percent. Looking at those games where fumbles were equal, the record of the team throwing fewer interceptions was 23–2, or 92 percent. Viewing it only from a Michigan perspective, the numbers are thus:

Michigan Record When Even Fumbles and More INTs	1–8	11.1 percent
Michigan Record When Even Fumbles and Fewer INTs	15–1	93.75 percent
Michigan Record When Even INTs and More Fumbles	4–3	57.1 percent
Michigan Record When Even INTs and Fewer Fumbles	8–3	72.7 percent

For the moment, I am left with the conclusion that an interception is a more consequential occurrence than a lost fumble. Hey, I didn't believe it either.

The foregoing seems a pretty sound argument for conservative passing, assuming this means not throwing interceptions. Interceptions, more than any statistic other than points scored (one hundred percent in any individual game), correlate with winning and losing. Well, what about "a lot of running?" A recent internet posting by Paul Campos again aroused my curiosity on this topic. In speaking of the relative impact of running/passing, he wrote:

> There is a much better correlation between yards rushing and yards rushing allowed and winning/losing than there is between yards passing and yards passing allowed and winning/losing. I haven't quantified it, but it's certainly true that a team that gains three hundred yards rushing and one hundred yards passing in a particular game is going to have a much higher winning percentage in such games than a team that passes for three hundred and rushes for one hundred.

Looking at the same base of games used above, Michigan was 66–10 (86.8 percent versus the win rate of 68.1 percent in the sample) when it outrushed its opposition, and 10–27 (27 percent) when they did not. On the other hand, the sample does not show much difference in outcomes based upon the differential in passing yardages. When Michigan had more passing yards, it was 41–19, a percentage equivalent to the win rate in the sample. When it was outpassed in yards, its record was 35–18, not a significant difference. Looking specifically to the issue posed by Campos, there were forty games in the database where (a) yards gained by each team were within sixty of each other, and (b) the team running for more yards passed for fewer yards. In those games, without distinguishing the level of the yardage differential, the team that rushed for more yards won thirty-two of the contests, a rate of 80 percent. So we now know that (a) interceptions are likely to be more consequential events than fumbles, (b) the level of consequence between a fumble and an interception may be profound, (c) winning the running game is strongly correlated to winning games, and (d) winning the passing game is not strongly correlated to winning games. I would add (e) Lloyd Carr knows that (a) through (d) are true. As did Bear Bryant, Woody Hayes, Joe Paterno, and Bo Schembechler. There are, I suspect, some connections. But the connection that seems most plain is that all of these guys built their teams around "a lot of running and conservative passing." And they all won a lot of games. A whole lot. You might not like it. I might not like it. But games are won and lost, in general, by the effectiveness of the running games and the ability of one team to force the interception.

I can't say I know with any certainty why this is, but it seems to me that games, especially at the college level, are won by the ability of the front seven of each team to control the line of scrimmage. In chess, if you control the middle of the board, you are likely to win. The same is true in racket sports. And my guess is, football is no different. The team that is best able to control the action—to play the game at its tempo by neutralizing the opposition—is the team that is likely to win. The irony is that the most anonymous players, the players that the fans and writers pay the least attention to, may be the most important.

I could not find a game in my database, incidentally, that exactly fit the Campos hypothetical. The closest was the 2000 UCLA game where Michigan outrushed the Bruins 263 to 126, lost the passing game 111 to 268, and yet lost the game 23–20. What was in the mix, however, was a Michigan interception and one fumble lost, as compared to three UCLA fumbles lost and no interceptions. For dogmatic types (maybe me), the interception was just too much. The truth is, the contest was a star-crossed affair for the Wolverines. After beating up on a very weak Bowling Green team and a not-very-good Rice team, the Henson-injured Wolverines traveled to the coast to play the Bruins, a team with athletes of equal quality to UM. And, unlike the prior opponents (no passing game by Rice, no running game by BGSU), UCLA had balance in its offense. Michigan stopped the UCLA running game; the Bruins gained twenty-eight yards in the first half and not much thereafter. And, despite the fact that UCLA seemed to have receivers open, the Bruin QB, Ryan McCann, had difficulty making a play. His throws wobbled and were often inaccurate but, when it counted, he had enough to get it done. John Navarre, conversely, had a tough-to-awful game. He missed open receivers at times; at other times, he could not find the open man, though, on TV, it was hard to tell if any existed. Michigan was able to run the ball some against a UCLA defense that seemed to be playing honest (seven in the box), but the passing game continually sputtered and failed. Indeed, from my biased eyes, Michigan seemed to outplay UCLA, but a spate of bizarre plays, Michigan screw-ups, poor quarterback play, and awful officiating dictated the outcome. Let me count the ways.

(1) On UM's third series, after a first down near midfield, a drive stalls when Navarre stumbles on a handoff and then misses open receivers on consecutive plays.

(2) James Whitley drops an easy interception on the UCLA twelve yard line with an open field in front of him.

(3) After Anthony Thomas breaks a third and one at the Michigan thirty-two for a sixty-eight-yard touchdown, Hayden Epstein misses the extra point.

(4) On Michigan's fifth series, after a poor screen pass, Navarre mishandles the snap. Then, after a nice slant pass for a first down, Justin Fargas loses a yard when he misses a hole, and Navarre makes another poor throw, stalling the drive.

(5) UCLA finally gets a drive going late in the first quarter, a drive that is kept alive when the UCLA tailback, DeShaun Foster, fumbles a ball seven yards upfield into traffic and recovers the ball himself.

(6) Late in the first half, with Michigan holding a 13–3 lead, Epstein is roughed while punting by two UCLA defenders. No call.

(7) In UCLA's first possession of the second half, the Bruin drive is kept alive by a "roughing the passer" call. A good call, but a pointless play by the Wolverines. Then, in a key play, McCann throws a wobbly, end-over-end ball well short of his receiver. Jeremy LeSeur, the young Michigan corner, is in position to make the interception, but he misjudges the floater, runs back toward the line of scrimmage, overruns the ball, and allows it to plop into the receiver's hands for a big gain. UCLA scores on the next play. Now it is 13–10.

(8) On Michigan's next series, they move to their own forty. On third and five, Navarre again overthrows a receiver. UCLA gets the ball back at its own twenty and loses a fumble on

54

the first play of its drive. The officials miss the fumble.

(9) After Michigan goes ahead 20–10 on a drive punctuated by a thirty-seven-yard waggle to David Terrell, Julius Curry intercepts at midfield, but the officials again miss the call. This one is key and obvious. This is followed by another poor call (an uncalled offensive pass interference), and then a tipped pass that goes for a UCLA completion. Then, a pass hits the UCLA tight end in the helmet, bounces about five feet in the air, and then falls back in his hands. On the next play, McCann makes an excellent throw into the corner of the end zone for a touchdown. UM leads 20–17.

(10) Navarre continues to struggle, but a long draw play moves the Wolverines to the UCLA thirty-two early in the fourth quarter. The drive stalls and Epstein misses a forty-six-yard field goal by a foot.

(11) A UCLA drive is thwarted when they fumble, but Navarre still can't make a play, and UCLA breaks a long run to put the Bruins ahead 23–20 with 6:30 left to play. The Bruins help out with their own missed extra point.

(12) Michigan drives the field with long runs by Fargas and A-Train but Epstein misses a chip shot from twenty-three yards. On the replay, if Epstein missed, it was by an inch. Worse, according to Jim Brandstatter and Frank Beckman calling the game on the UM radio network, UCLA has twelve men on the field during the attempt. (From my tape it is impossible to tell.)

(13) As time is running down, Michigan holds the Bruins and Ronald Bellamy returns a punt thirty-five yards to the UCLA thirty-six. A double reverse moves the ball to the UCLA twenty-six. But Hayden Epstein never gets his opportunity for redemption when, on first down, Navarre misses BJ Askew, open at the UCLA ten. On second down, Navarre misreads the UCLA safety, who picks off a pass over the middle to end the Wolverines' hopes. It is, from either side of the field, a terrific and maddening game.

The UCLA game illustrates a reality we often minimize as fans: luck, or the mere randomness of events. The vagaries of chance are pivotal in games of any sort and, in any sequence of short trials, chance can be the most important variable. And, of course, the closer the game, the more likely the element of chance will predominate. The cliché the media and the fans buy into is that "good teams know how to win the close games." Nothing could be further from the truth. Michigan football, over its history, qualifies as a good team. Indeed, the Wolverines have won more games than any I-A team (Yale was passed during the 2001 season) and are now (at the close of the 2004 season) two games ahead of Notre Dame in all-time winning percentage.

I don't want to diminish anything ND has done, but if one looks at the teams it has beaten, there are more than 115 wins (I would call it 118–6) against complete meatball competition, such as Engelwood High School, the South Bend Athletic Club, Harvard Prep School (not Harvard), four wins against St. Viator, three against Rush Medical, five wins over Haskell (Eddie Haskell?), seven over Chicago Physicians and Surgeons, four (each) over Ohio Northern and Ohio Medical (ouch), five over American Medical (eech), eight each over Drake and Depauw (ducks and feet), ten wins over Wabash (ouch again, on da head), three against (Ben) Franklin, three against (Carole?) Lombard, one each against Rose-Hulman Tech, Bennet Medical, Goshen, Indianapolis Light Artillery (they ducked Indianapolis Heavy Artillery), Christian Brothers, the famed DeLaSalle Institute, and others too embarrassing to name. Michigan has won against many of these non-teams also, but a lot fewer (call it forty or fifty) than ND. As a matter of legitimate comparison, UM's Big Ten record evinces 73 percent wins. Notre Dame's winning rate is 66 percent against the Big Ten, despite playing forty-seven games against generally humble Northwestern and only four against the admittedly formidable OSU—where ND has split 2–2 with the Buckeyes. Michigan, it is true, has also faced the Cats sixty-three times. But they have played OSU one hundred times. And here's a clue. The Buckeyes can really play, particularly over the past fifty-five years. When one looks at the level of competition, Notre Dame ain't close. Okay, I will call them close. But second.

Thus, over the course of college football, Michigan has been not just a good team, but (being generous to ND) among the two best teams. If the cliché is true, then Michigan's record in close games should be something in the vicinity of its historical winning percentage. That is, if "good teams win close games," it would seem likely that great teams also win such affairs.

In fact, Michigan's record in close games is much less than spectacular and about what one would surmise from any of the top twenty-five or so programs in the country. In games decided by nine points or fewer since 1900, the Wolverines are 174–122–35 for a quite respectable 57.8 percent winning percentage, but well below the program's historical win rate. In games decided by six points or fewer, the record declines to 110–83–35 and the percentage falls to 55.9 percent. In games decided by a field goal or less, the Wolverines are 59–53–35, a winning percentage of 52 percent. In one-point games, the record is 21–19, a percentage of 51.3 percent. In a statistical curiosity, Michigan is even in tie games. Two things are evident. First, the Wolverines are much more likely to win if the game is a blowout. Good teams, indeed, win these affairs. Second, the closer the game is, the less likely it is that a good team (in this case Michigan) will prevail.

There are two reasons for this. First, in a close game, it is more likely than not that the teams are evenly matched. Hard to believe that we forget this, but the score tends to indicate the relative abilities of the teams, even if we rationalize it to be "at least on that day." Second, in a close game, the randomness of events is more likely to be a determinant of the outcome. A stray bounce is meaningless in a 58–0 game. In a 32–31 game, any bounce can be consequential. The meaningful cliché should be that good teams are likely to win slightly more than half of their close games. And I would add the corollary that good teams almost always beat bad teams. There. I have really gone out on a limb. I expect royalties from Brent Musburger when he uses this one.

Some may complain that the foregoing is old data. What do the numbers look like since the commencement of the Schembechler era in 1969? Since that time, in fact, the Michigan winning percentage is 78.7 percent (296–77–8). In games decided by nine points or fewer, the Wolverines are 69–54–8, or 56.2 percent. In six-points-or-fewer games, the record is 54.17 percent. In games decided by three or fewer, the Wolverines are 21-31-8, or 41.7 percent. Ouch. I suppose there are three possibilities. One is that Michigan coaching has been lousy in close games. A second is that Michigan coaching has been spectacular in keeping the Wolverines in games where they were outmanned. A third is that it is pure random chance, a function of Bo's run of ten straight losses in one- or two-point games. In making one's choice consider, at least, that the post-1969 Wolverines have been 62–36, a pretty imposing 63.3 percent, in games decided by three to nine points. My choice? Mostly pure random chance. This doesn't mean that losing close games doesn't drive me nuts or that I, like most fans, don't rummage around for the salve of explanation.

Paul Campos pointed out in mid-September of 2000 that over the 1997 through early-2000 seasons, Lloyd Carr's teams had been involved in nineteen nailbiters (according to his holistic, game-by-game analysis), with Michigan winning sixteen of those games. Over the same period of time, Carr was 36–6 overall. Thus, Carr's overall percentage was .857 while his record in games where the outcome was in doubt to the end was an impossible .842. Campos contended, "the chance that a team would have this good of a record in close games merely because of luck is no more than 5 percent. In other words, it seems very likely to me that Carr's record in close games is statistically significant—that it indicates something positive about the abilities of his teams, just as Bo's notably poor record in close games during the first half of his career indicated something negative about him and his teams." Paul went on to guess that the reason for this might be the "psychological effect Carr's coaching has on his players." He argued that "Michigan's record in such games indicates that the players must have enormous confidence in their ability to pull these games out. Part of that, of course, is a product of the players themselves, but part of that must be a reflection of the attitude that Carr and his staff instill in those players."

Campos admitted the record was likely to be unsustainable and that the "tendency of Carr's teams to play such a large number of games is a weakness, just as their ability to win them is a strength." I admire Campos's ability to distill a certain essence of history as well as his ability to create aphorisms descriptive of that history. But isn't the foregoing subject to James's criticism of connecting events that might not be connected? Say this mantra: *Luck runs in streaks.* On the other hand, as Campos predicted, the 2000 Wolverines continued to play in nailbiters, sneaking by Illinois, Ohio State, Wisconsin, Auburn, and (arguably) MSU, and losing to Purdue and Northwestern. Campos's point that Carr's teams have played a hard-to-fathom number of close games is a fact. But whether this is a weakness (playing to the level of the competition) or a strength (a weaker team playing to the level of the competition) or the function of all teams moving to the same level via the eighty-five-scholarship limitation, is impossible to prove.

In 2001, the Wolverines lost two out of three close games; if one includes OSU, UM lost three out of four. In 2002, the Wolverines won a one-point, luck-filled affair (bad officiating to our benefit) against Washington, then lost a two-pointer to Notre Dame when, among other conditions, the Domers got a freebie TD from the Big Ten officials when they forgot the rule of actually carrying the ball over the goal line. The Wolverines went on to win a nailbiter over Wisconsin, an overtime game against Penn State, and an arguable toss-up game against Purdue. They then lost a definite white knuckler against OSU, in the wake of two woeful pass-interference calls by the dreadful LaPetina officiating crew, pushing the 2001–2 record in these games to a more ordinary 5–5. In 2003, the Wolverines were incredibly lucky in a three-point win over Minnesota—a game they had no business winning—and incredibly unlucky in three- and four-point losses to Iowa and Oregon, doomed by poor punting games in both contests. In 2004 it began to swing the other way, the Wolverines winning all four games that came down to the wire. Since the Campos note, Carr's close game record looks more ordinary: 10–7 in such games. The vigorish is grinding the number down.

Many left-handed and right-brained types may complain, "Hey, what does this have to do with the elegance and smashmouthness and slobberknockerness of the games?" They have a point. The game is blocking and tackling and throwing and catching. It is not a game of moving pieces around on a game board. To these fans, and I guess that includes me, the ambiguity of the equation is what makes a beer taste good, what makes it worthwhile being alive. Is there anything better than a cool and sunny October day and the anticipation of Michigan versus MSU and all of the history and hubris implied in the contest? Doesn't the glow of a hard win or the bitterness of a tough loss give meaning to our lives, particularly when we all know, we all really know, that the outcome of the game does not really amount to a hill of beans? The score is

27–26. MSU leads. No time is left on the clock, but Michigan has just scored and is attempting a two-point play. Elvis Grbac drops back and looks to his left. Desmond Howard runs a quick slant from the wide left to the middle of the field. He beats the defender, cornerback Eddie Brown, sitting in man coverage. As Desmond clears the defensive back, he is grabbed and then tripped in desperation. Eddie Brown falls to the ground, now out of play. Elvis zeroes in and throws the ball on a line. A strike. More than 106,000 fans follow the spiral of the ball. The spin is tight and pristine; it hangs in the air, uncertain, unimportant. And so important that all 106,000 are completely uninvolved with the ennui or tragedy of their day-to-day lives. The only thing that matters is the path of the ball and the impossibly small and skinny wide receiver struggling to keep his balance. Completely stuck in time the crowd is going crazy yet, in my mind, there is complete silence. Not a sound. Stumbling forward now, almost falling but not quite, the ball strikes Desmond in the chest. He catches the ball, losing his balance at last, and as he lands on his back the object squibs away, the random bounces a parody of the game. He caught the ball! It is incomplete. He was held and interfered! No penalty is called. And none of it really matters save for the indelibility of the moment and the despair of the Michigan partisans. And the joy, relief, and celebration in East Lansing. And the certain notion that on another day these emotions will change. And, when that day comes, will come the truth and delusion that there is justice in the world because Desmond really . . . just . . . well . . . I hate the despair and embrace it. And I know that the joy is an artifice. A trick. But I am a junkie. I can't get by without it. Nor can others. And because of this many of us come back to the moment that is rife with the joy and the pain. If we had just . . . Why didn't we try . . . Why are we so predictable . . . It is just all of that running . . . That and the conservative passing.

* * * *

After I wrote about turnovers, I stumbled across a terrific book (but only for the analytically inclined) called *The Hidden Game* by Bob Carroll, Pete Palmer, and John Thorn. Palmer and Thorn have baseball roots and they go to great lengths to explain why baseball and football stats are not comparable, and how football stats, particularly individual stats, are misleading or wrong in ignoring the time and space contexts indigenous to football. I am certain they are right in their general principles. I am also inclined to the work, since they note, as a preamble, that Benny Friedman made Michigan one of the few campuses in America where "pass" wasn't a four-letter word. Plus, in their appendices, the authors note that the number one player not enshrined in the Pro Football Hall of Fame (but should be) is Al Wistert, one of a trio of great brothers (all played tackle and wore the now-retired number eleven) who played prior to 1950 for the Wolverines. On the other side of the coin, they perceive Paul Hornung as a "shaky" HOF choice. More and more plusses, though I would call Hornung a "pathetic" choice. (Just joking, Irish faithful. I am pretty much clueless on the issue.)

The authors of *The Hidden Game* conclude that, in the big picture (over the course of a number of games), penalties tend to be reasonably neutral in determining who wins games and why. While admitting that a call or non-call can be decisive in any individual game, *The Hidden Game* finds no correlation between penalties and winning or losing. This, indeed, corresponds to the information in my database, though not with my instincts. I would like to say that penalties and non-penalties are decisive or critical in nearly every close contest. That, indeed, in all close games, the decision to call or not to call a penalty may determine the outcome of that game. It's just that we can't tell, after the fact, what the alternative outcome would have been (think Desmond in 1991).

And, in the long run and big picture, these sequences of decisions are inevitably random and push to the middle. Aside from this, *The Hidden Game* is right. There is no correlation between penalties and wins/losses in individual games. At least I don't see it.

Palmer and Hunt then examine turnovers, and conclude they are "overrated as a source of victory or defeat," but that there is "a measurable effect"—a fumble costing fifty yards of field position and an interception costing forty-five. *The Hidden Game* concludes, "In general, a positive ratio of two turnovers will make almost a touchdown's difference. However, because of different offensive philosophies, turnovers do not affect all teams equally. Conservative offenses are hurt more by turnovers than high-risk offenses. And, obviously, teams with weak defenses are hurt more." If this sounds like genuine gibberish to you, then you just joined my team. If not, well, you can root for whoever the hell you want to. The problem here is the admission that a turnover is worth, by and large, about 3.5 points, and the connected conclusion that the event is "overrated." In 2001 in the NFL, 55 percent of all games were close (within eight points, or one touchdown and a two-point conversion), and nearly 22 percent were decided by a field goal or less. Indeed, the most common point differential was three, a number that defined the difference in 18 percent of all games. In that there is a turnover differential in more than 85 percent of all games played, I would argue that turnovers play an important role in more than 40 percent of NFL contests. At least assuming the predicate of *The Hidden Game* argument. But let's check it out. What was the correlation in 2001 in the NFL between turnovers and winning (for the first sixteen weeks of the season)?

Record When More Turnovers	49–139	26.1 percent
Record When More Fumbles Lost	55– 95	36.7 percent
Record When More INTs	45–129	25.9 percent

It seems to me that the *Hidden Game* authors have some explaining to do. If turnovers are overrated, how come the team turning the ball over more often loses three-fourths of the time? I can think of explanations, but the authors don't confront it. And, if a fumble is actually worse (by five yards of field position), how come interceptions are 40 percent more correlated with losing than are lost fumbles? I am not saying there are not answers, even great answers. But *The Hidden Game,* a terrific work, hides them.

Two other related matters. First, if conservative teams are hurt more by turnovers than high-risk offenses, why is there a greater correlation with interceptions and losing than with fumbles and losing? Hey, I don't know either. Second, what about Tennessee versus Michigan in the Citrus Bowl at the end of the 2001 season, if you're so smart? Didn't they run for fewer yards than Michigan? Well, it is true they did; Michigan gained six more yards on the ground in a veritable 103–97 stomping. But I don't think I have ever claimed this kind of a rushing differential has any significant meaning at all. More important in that contest was the Tennessee 406 to 240 passing yards differential. And a lot more important were the three turnovers to one and one interception to none. Oh, yeah. One other thing. The biggest problem here is that Tennessee just happened to be a lot better than Michigan was, all over the field. If I haven't mentioned it before, I think I should now. Axiom. It is almost always the case that when one football team is markedly better than the other, the markedly better team will win. I think we can look this up.

As a final note, my current editor, Ms. Smarty Pants, suggested I throw some new stats into the mix, since that database of 113 games is just not enough to make the point. And, as certain friends of mine believe, the game was actually born last year, and the changes since 2002 are likely to show that fumbles are, indeed, as consequential as interceptions. The final tallies for the 2002 through 2004 Michigan seasons are below:

Record Of Team Throwing Fewer INTs	18–4	81.8 percent
Record Of Team Losing Fewer Fumbles	13–9	59.1 percent

Eliminating intercorrelation, it is:

Record Of Team Throwing Fewer INTs	10–2	83.3 percent
Record Of Team Losing Fewer Fumbles	5–8	38.5 percent

So it goes.

Four *Bill Buntin, Ed Martin, Lee Bollinger, Nike, and Bulgarian Shoes*

To make any sense of the Ed Martin saga, it must be placed in the context of the fan perception of Michigan athletics and the history of the Wolverine basketball program. It was a Michigan homily for many years that Michigan wanted to win, but "wanted to do it the right way." This meant that Michigan alums and fans preferred that the program pay attention to NCAA rules and run a clean and honorable athletic program. Michigan fans wanted student-athletes and programs to be proud of as much as they wanted to win. (Well, okay, some of us did.) Because of this, Michigan fans became known as arrogant, particularly to schools that were getting their knuckles whacked by the NCAA. I don't think this is what the word "arrogant" actually means, but then, I guess it is no worse than Musburger's confusion over the words "irony" and "coincidence" or "fortune."

Much as Michigan fans might prefer it otherwise, we will never know, with certainty, what the historical realities are vis-à-vis the Michigan Athletic Department's commitment to the spirit of fair play, since even the most respected programs have come into question. It comes down to this: you can't trust any school to level with you about its private history. Not Duke. Not Cornell. Not OSU. Not Michigan.

John Wooden, still mythologized as the pinnacle of basketball genius and ethics, ran a particularly nasty and unethical program at UCLA, according to Don Yaeger in his book, *Undue Process: The NCAA's Injustice For All.* Yaeger claims that Sam Gilbert was the multimillionaire sugar daddy at UCLA, and he was, as the *Los Angeles Times* described him, "a one-man clearinghouse [who enabled] players and their families to receive goods and services usually at a big discount and sometimes at no cost." Gilbert arranged abortions for the girlfriends of basketball players, scalped tickets for individual players (including Kareem), and signed them to professional contracts while they were still playing for Wooden. And this is likely the tip of the iceberg. Keith Erickson, a star on the 1965 Bruin NCAA championship team (they beat the Buntin-and-

Cazzie-led Michigan team in the finals), admitted that Sam "knows what the rules are and thinks they are rubbish. So he does what he believes is right." It was, in fact, a little worse than Sam's ethical stance against NCAA rules, since his source of income was money laundering from the sale of narcotics. I suspect that what Sam thought was right was a pretty private notion. After Gilbert was indicted on federal racketeering charges, Wooden's comment was that he was "surprised" and described Gilbert as "a friend to me and the university."

At UCLA, boosters other than Sam Gilbert would pay individual players, for example, for each rebound a player gathered. Former Bruin player Jack Hirsch said, "It was a helluva feeling to pick up [$100] for a night's work." And Gilbert was key in keeping stars in school through big payments and benefits. Lucius Allen, the great playmaking guard, said that "UCLA wouldn't have won any championships without athletes . . . and without Sam Gilbert they wouldn't have had any athletes." Yet, to this day, Wooden is revered. And, to this day, former Bruin players rationalize the handouts and rule violations at UCLA with the bromide that "it was going on at all universities." Star UCLA player David Greenwood, in making this statement, might have been right. Who knows? But, until 1963 at least, Michigan wasn't getting any bang for the buck, assuming monkey business was going on.

Of course, one school with a similar consciousness to Michigan is Notre Dame. Indeed, more than any other school, Notre Dame seems protective of its image as an institution that plays fair and follows the rules. I think—unlike UCLA and like Michigan—Notre Dame has had good intentions. At least it did until Lou Holtz showed up. Gerry Faust, one of the most successful coaches in Ohio high school history, was hired to lead the Notre Dame football team for the 1981 season. Faust was and is a wonderful person, in many ways the poster boy for what Notre Dame professes a coach should be. But he was unprepared for the rigors of coaching at the college level. Over a five-year period, his teams were 17–23, and the Irish faithful were furious. In the Don Yaeger and Douglas Looney book *Under the Tarnished Dome,* the authors relate Bo Schembechler's private comments after beating a Notre Dame team: that the Irish were completely lacking in football fundamentals. This reality was not lost on the Irish fans or administration.

After Faust's contract expired (full marks to ND on this one), the Notre Dame administration made a determined choice that wins were more important than the image of the institution. Lou Holtz, known as a brilliant coach, was also known as a coach who left trouble in his wake. At Arkansas, Holtz pandered to kids who had significant criminal issues. Ultimately, Holtz's greed in pursuing commercial endeavors that were at odds with the wishes of the university. That, and his aggressive public support for Jesse Helms, led to his termination. Holtz landed at Minnesota, where he became a part of a pay-for-play system that included cash handouts to prospective recruits, some directly—allegedly—from Holtz. Certain scholarship players were funneled significant amounts of cash. When the NCAA circled in, Holtz called players and asked them to lie, and to communicate with one another to make certain there were no inconsistencies in their stories.

Three days prior to leaving for Notre Dame, Holtz had promised the Minnesota administration and players that he was the Minnesota coach for life. In a press conference where reporters asked about the leaks that Holtz was heading for greener pastures, Holtz denied that he was going anywhere, and he became quite edgy when pressed about rumors to the contrary. These denials and the coach's checkered history seemed to have no impact on the Notre Dame administration. The Golden Dome gobbled Holtz up amidst great fanfare and enthusiasm.

Holtz did turn the Notre Dame football program around. The man can coach, and there was never any doubt about his ability to return ND to its glory. But it wasn't without a cost. Many players reported that Holtz endangered their long-term well-being by aggressively "encouraging" them to play while hurt. If the player would not succumb to the encouragement, he was shunned by the coach. Holtz yelled at and embarrassed assistant coaches in front of players, and routinely humiliated players by grabbing their facemasks or cursing at them. But the worst was the introduction of steroids in South Bend. Yaeger and Looney concluded, "First Lou Holtz arrived at Notre Dame. Then a lot of steroids did." Indeed, according to their interviews with players, Notre Dame was rife with steroids during the Holtz regime, a fact well-known and, according to some players, encouraged by the coach.

If Notre Dame and John Wooden have skeletons in their closets, then David Greenwood might be right in his assessment that all colleges do. Michigan fans would be naive to believe that similar events could not have happened in Ann Arbor. Up until 1963, however, Michigan must have been pretty unsuccessful in any funny business in the basketball program, since it hardly ever won any games. From 1950 through 1962, the Wolverines amassed zero tournament bids (either NIT or NCAA), one finish above fifth in the conference, eight finishes between eighth and tenth in the conference, and an overall Big Ten record of 51–119 (30 percent). In a word: Northwestern.

It all changed in 1962 when, by mere chance, an assistant coach, Jim Skala, participated in a recreation league in the Detroit area with a big kid named Bill Buntin. Buntin was a fair high school player in Detroit in his junior season, but he broke his leg prior to his senior year and disappeared from everyone's radar screens. Michigan had not recruited Buntin. Nor had anyone else. Skala reported back to head coach Dave Strack that he had a real prospect for the team and, eventually, Buntin was offered a scholarship. Within a year of the Buntin find, Michigan recruited Cazzie Russell from Chicago and picked up solid players such as Oliver Darden, George Pomey, Larry Tregoning and John

Thompson. These were all tough and athletic guys, and the 1963–66 Michigan teams were the precursors of Isiah Thomas's Pistons and formed what became known as "bloody-nose lane." And, for the first time ever, Michigan was a national basketball power.

Unfortunately, though the Michigan teams could shoot, rebound, and play defense, they were never quick enough to compete with UCLA's best, such as Gail Goodrich, Walt Hazzard, and Keith Erickson. Michigan was, in these four years, a top three to five team in the country. But they were not UCLA or (surprise) Texas Western (now UTEP) or Kentucky.

Cazzie Russell, to be sure, was the prominent name from the era. Certainly, he was Michigan's star player and is generally credited with elevating Michigan from the doldrums. But it was Buntin who turned the program around. Buntin was a dominating college player, and he destroyed, for example, future Hall of Famer Paul Silas in a game against Creighton. Silas, known as one of the toughest and best defenders in the history of the NBA, was powerless against Buntin, with the Michigan forward putting in twenty-five points and pulling down twenty-two rebounds while being checked by Paul. Silas's totals were half of those numbers. Buntin was drafted by the Pistons in the first round, and the Detroit team tried to make the six-foot, seven-inch Buntin a center. The experiment flopped. And when Buntin and Coach Dave DeBuscherre could not see eye-to-eye, Buntin began to eat. And eat. Until he ate himself out of the league and a profession. In 1968, in his mid-twenties, Buntin died of a heart attack in a pick-up game in the Detroit area.

Post-Buntin-and-Cazzie, Michigan returned to its historical basketball ways, winning twenty Big Ten games (while losing thirty-four) over the next four years. Then, in 1971, John Orr turned the program around for good. "For good" meaning UM was a "generally top twenty program" until Ed Martin showed up. Through (more or less) 1973, it seemed the Michigan program was about as clean as a major program could be. This may be, I admit, faint praise. I have talked to players and those around the program through this period of time and no one suggests any improprieties were taking place. Indeed, in my freshman year (1966–67), I lived across the hall from a potential NBA player, Dave McClellan. He was the high school player of the year in Ohio and, at an agile and strong six foot, five inches, he could play the physical game and shoot the ball with accuracy to twenty feet. Freshmen were not eligible in McClellan's first year, but early in his sophomore season he was a starter and wowed Kentucky coach Adolph Rupp with a twenty-plus-point performance against the Wildcats. After the game, Rupp called McClellan "as good as any young player I have seen in some time."

Unfortunately, McClellan's career did not last long; a severe knee injury made it impossible for him to ever reach his potential. But, at the time, if there was any player for whom Michigan would have provided extra benefits, it would have been Dave. Dave and I were not close friends, but I saw him on a daily basis and we did hang together on occasion. He dressed little better than I did, and I was woefully clad. He lived in the dorm as a sophomore, did not drive a car, and occasionally borrowed a quarter from the ten dollars a month my family sent me. There was no way McClellan was on anyone's dole. He was just another guy in the dorm with no money.

George Pomey, who played with Cazzie and who was later an assistant coach for the Wolverines, denies there was anything untoward in the period of his tenure, a period that stretched through the mid-seventies. Pomey states, "It wasn't a part of my consciousness as a player or as a coach that we would ever do anything in violation of the rules. It was a given that we would play fair, even if that meant we would lose a recruit or a kid in the program." Those around the Michigan program at that time concur with Pomey, but did tell me a few stories about recruiting ethics. One story goes that many of the top basketball stars of the sixties and seventies were never on scholarship in their respective programs, but instead were on the payrolls of corporations or businesses with rooting interests in the local schools. One mega-star (HOF in the NBA) is said to have received a one-hundred-thousand-dollar-per-year retainer from an LA film studio as an extra—they never used him—while he was in college. Michigan lost a recruiting war with OSU on another future NBA player (one that John Orr was certain he would get) when the player turned down a scholarship and was placed on the payroll of a large Ohio insurance firm as an agent. I doubt that he spent a lot of time writing policies. A third player, whose sister was a student at UM, was thought to be a lock for the Wolverines, since his sister was very happy in Ann Arbor, and the player communicated to the coaches that he was bound for Michigan. Until the coaching staff got a call from the kid, who told John Orr he was headed to UCLA (during the Sam Gilbert era) because "they gave me an offer I couldn't refuse, but I am not really comfortable talking about it."

I have no clue, incidentally, whether any of the foregoing, if true, posed any violation of NCAA rules. It might have been the case, at the time, that as long as you did not receive a scholarship, these sorts of deals were completely legitimate. The rules were pretty loose, there is no question. Bud Withers of the *Seattle Times* has noted, as a minor example, that teams used to "hide out" recruits right before signing day in order to keep the players away from the enticements of other schools. According to Withers, "Knowing the heat on a prospect was going to be intense down the stretch before signing, a coach would simply find a motel nearby and hole up the recruit there for a couple of days."

Coaches, then and now of course, will push to the limits of what is allowed. Many years ago, MSU won a recruiting war with Michigan for a major league (future NBA) talent. A part of the MSU offer was a job for the kid's dad (just out of prison) "where he wouldn't have to work too hard," and football press box access for the recruit's family, including some young kids. Despite the recruit's success, MSU later regretted the decision, especially when the kids wreaked havoc in the press box and caused the school some embarrassment. This was not, however, any sort of a violation by MSU, though by my understanding, they never made the press box offer again.

A routine inducement for a major star, of course, is the hiring of his father or high school coach for an assistant's job. This happened with Danny Manning at Kansas (Ed Manning became an assistant and disappeared when Danny did), and may have been relevant in Michigan's hiring of Perry Watson (Jalen Rose's coach), though Perry had been an incredibly successful high school coach and his ties to the Public School League would have made him a valuable commodity for any team. Indeed, Perry's record at the University of Detroit has proven that he knows what he is doing. Still, my guess is that Perry's relationship to Jalen Rose was a qualification near the top of his résumé.

A more subtle way of pushing the rules involves the scheduling of the pre-season exhibition games against teams such as the "EA All-Stars" or the "Double Pump All-Stars." The point of these games is pure revenue enhancement for college teams by allowing them to charge their season ticket holders for these exhibitions. Otherwise, why not just add two legitimate games to the schedule? Or why not just play exhibitions against local teams? At the present time, for example, Steve Fisher (San Diego State) is upset over the use of these games, since a coach he is recruiting against has extended a godfather offer to a touring team for a series of pre-season games. What's the big deal? Well, the story is that this coach/program is paying the touring team over market value for exhibition games played prior to the season. And the contract with the team is for a few years. So? The punch line is that the coach of the touring team is also coach of an AAU team. On this AAU team is the kid that Fisher wants and, apparently, won't get. Fisher believes that the AAU coach will steer his kid to the program where he has been "bribed." There are two things to note about this. First, this isn't a violation of NCAA rules—at least at the moment. Second, a number of these "exhibition" coaches also coach AAU teams and, apparently, this is a fairly common gambit—one that many reputable schools have felt they had to play.

In the main, Michigan has tried to play foreign national teams or Athletes In Action, but they have scheduled a couple of the for-profit touring teams, though I have no clue if recruiting was involved in any of these games. I am pretty certain that Michigan received no recruiting edge in scheduling the Sam Ragnone All-Stars, a touring team sponsored by a lawyer from Flint. Ragnone's team often had ex-pros (John Long and Earl Cureton come to mind), and was intended to promote Ragnone's law practice. Or so it seems. A very good Michigan team once lost to a Ragnone team when a skinny, thirty-five-year-old guard named Spider something-or-other scored his age against the Wolverines with an array of off-balance and acrobatic shots. (After the game, Spider was asked about his accomplishment and whether he felt a sense of pride by putting up so many points against a good team at Crisler. His response was something like, "I don't know, man. I am just a little upset right now because I missed my bowling league tonight.")

Of course, it is not just players and coaches who have their hands out. Anyone with an angle or connection to a highly recruited kid may take a shot at earning a few bucks. A number of years ago, Michigan assistant coach Jim Boyce went to the home of Sam Bowie (who was later drafted in front of Michael Jordan after a fine career at Kentucky) in the attempt to persuade the kid to come to Michigan. When Boyce arrived at the home, there was a man waiting outside the residence. Boyce tried to go around the guy but was stopped. The man said, "You have to pay me two hundred and fifty dollars to go into the house."

"What do you mean?" Boyce asked.

"Ain't that tough to figure out."

"What if I don't?" Boyce responded.

"Then you don't get in."

"Who are you?" Boyce demanded.

"That's none of your business. And next time you come, it will be five hundred dollars, and then seven-fifty, and then a thousand and so on."

Boyce left the home and went to call John Orr. Orr told his assistant to "get the hell out of there." Boyce did. And so ended the recruitment of Bowie. To this day (or so the story goes), neither Boyce nor Orr has a clue as to who the guy was. But they knew they didn't want any part of the game. Of course, the Bowie story is small potatoes. It is normal for the high profile high school hoops big-timer to have a posse to satisfy. And if your name is Yao Ming, the posse is pretty large. As I heard someone say, "China." You right. A substantial bribe is involved.

Certainly, after 1963, it is a fact that Michigan was rarely able to secure a big-time recruit until Bill Frieder came on the scene. John Orr's best teams were composed of football castoffs (Steve Grote, Rick White), midget point guards who almost nobody wanted (Joe Johnson), midget small forwards who weren't the subject of national recruiting battles (Wayman Britt) or any recruiting battles at all (Johnny Robinson), midget power forwards (Henry Wilmore at six foot, three inches), and occasional Ohioans reportedly not recruited by OSU (Phil Hubbard) due to the then street-rumored OSU policy of limited recruiting of black players. Now and then Michigan might have grabbed up a local star such as Campy Russell or the less-than-advertised Ken Brady, but most of these, during Orr's tenure, went elsewhere. Very big-time high school stars such as Ralph Simpson, Lindsay Hairston, and Terry Furlow went to MSU. Spencer Haywood, though playing pick-up games in Ann Arbor against

Bill Buntin, went to the University of Detroit. PSL stars Eric Money and Coniel Norman attended school outside of Michigan. Aside from Campy Russell, perhaps Rudy T, and Rickey Green (a JC transfer), Michigan was not on the winning ledger of very many major recruiting wars.

Not that they didn't try. In the late seventies, Michigan was in the hunt for a national recruit of prominence, a recruit who was well-known by fans since his sophomore year in high school—in a day when fans didn't know this stuff—and a recruit considered to be the best player nationally in the senior class. This was the sort of talent, like a Jabbar or a Magic Johnson, who could turn an also-ran into a power. Or so it was thought at the time. On his recruiting trip to Ann Arbor, according to a Michigan coach not in the basketball program, the kid asked for fifty-thousand dollars in cash, as a starting spot for Michigan to be in the game. Without this, the kid stated, he was willing to hang out in Ann Arbor for the weekend, but had no real interest in talking to anybody about the school as a final destination. Michigan refused the offer and discontinued its recruitment of this star, who later ended up in a top academic program in the east that has a reputation as being one of the more honest schools in the country.

The dividing line is Frieder, of course. Until Frieder, I am fairly (change that to "borderline") confident that Michigan ran an honest program. Or, perhaps more accurately, according to people who were around the program and should know, there seemed to be nothing or very little untoward going on. Once Frieder became the head coach, Michigan started to win its share of the recruiting wars, and there was always some vague anxiety among Michigan fans that maybe things were not all they should have been. There is some irony in that consciousness since, at the time, the most publicized recruits secured by Frieder—Tim McCormick, Richard Rellford, Antoine Joubert, and Paul Jokisch—turned out to be significant and good players, but not program makers. Generally, they were less than advertised. In those instances where Michigan finished second in close recruitments—Earvin Johnson, Clark Kellogg, Derrick Coleman, and Derek Harper, for example—the players always seemed to be every bit as good or better than their high school clippings. Frieder's success was predicated on players like Glenn Rice (only Iowa State and John Orr seemed really interested) and Roy Tarpley (only Michigan seemed to know he was a senior in high school after he had transferred from a school in Alabama) and others who came to the university with more limited fanfare. On the other hand, Frieder was successful in bringing in Terry Mills and Rumeal Robinson (both Prop 48s), and Gary Grant, highly regarded national recruits.

I think the suspicion concerning Frieder arises from areas of concern that are mostly lamentable and superficial considerations. First is the fact that Frieder presented himself as a wheeler-dealer personality. Frieder is, in fact, a brilliant man, and he possesses a strong analytical mind and an extraordinary memory for numbers. He never shied away from letting it be known that he had been banned from casinos in Las Vegas due to his ability as a counter, and this was a fact sometimes reported in the media. (Frieder's buddies say it is absolutely true and I suspect it is.) Whether this is true or not, it is certainly the case that, after his coaching stint at Arizona State, Frieder became a highly successful investment broker. Indeed, the *Wall Street Journal* wrote about Bill as one of the more prominent people in the profession. So Frieder is and was sharp, and was inclined to play the angles. The extension of this is that he didn't know when to stop.

A second, related predicate for the worry or belief that Frieder was unethical was grounded in his personality and appearance. Frieder liked to tell others that he only needed a couple of hours of sleep every night. I took this as typical Frieder shtick that was given credence by the fact that the coach always looked like he hadn't slept. Frieder, with his uncombed hair and disheveled appearance, just didn't care about what he looked like and rationalized it with the no-sleep story. I was disabused of this notion when, over the course of a year, I received two phone calls from Frieder between one and three in the morning. I later met people who were the routine targets of these calls. The guy did not sleep. Once, Frieder's good friend Clem Gill was late to a wedding when he found Frieder blocking his driveway, asleep at the wheel of his car. The coach had been up for days and ultimately collapsed in the Gill driveway. It took some effort to move him.

Many people have connected Frieder's oddball brilliance—his analytical ability, his claimed success at the gaming tables, the fact that he was a night owl and looked like a complete slob—with a lack of ethics. With the above conditions as underpinnings, the well-publicized rift between Schembechler and Frieder was an impetus toward believing the worst about Bill. While Don Canham always liked Frieder, Bo made it plain he thought the guy was a flake and, in his dress and demeanor, not a "Michigan man." (Clue: This is ironic, since Bill has an undergraduate degree and an MBA from Michigan. Bo's degree is from Miami of Ohio, the best academic public institution in Ohio, but not, apparently, *the* Ohio State University.) Since the general consciousness about Bo is that he is a part of the (possibly deranged) Bob Knight "straight arrow" axis, then Frieder must be something else; in other words, not honest. Overlaying this, I fear, is the fact that Frieder is Jewish. While I don't believe it is a conscious part of many people's thoughts, when you add up the other conditions, I believe there may be some element of "It would be just like . . ."

Finally, I believe that Roy Tarpley's alcohol and drug problems while in the NBA implied, to many, that Frieder ran a loose ship. The assumption was that Tarpley must have had these problems while at Michigan and Frieder—it would be just like him—turned a blind eye in the spirit of winning games.

I know for a fact that Frieder and Tarpley had some rockiness while Roy was at Michigan. The nature of these problems has not been made public, but it was certain they often did not see eye to eye. (Frieder once said, referring to Tarpley, "I know when there is more [trash] talking on the court than basketball, there ain't no question about who started it.") What is known, at a minimum, is that Tarpley did not have the criminal issues posed by Scott Skiles or Mateen Cleaves, yet the MSU coaches who did seemingly little with these problems, Jud Heathcote and Tom Izzo, are local icons. I do not intend any criticism of Heathcote or Izzo, or even any criticism in how they handled their troubled players. These matters, in my mind, were up to Jud and Tom. I only make the comparison to point out that there has been a separate set of rules for Frieder, rules brought out by Frieder's idiosyncratic personality and the fact of Michigan's insistence that it was above the maelstrom.

What has also not been made public, and what few know, is that Frieder ran his own spy network while he was the coach of the Wolverines. Frieder would convince a player's friends (and most notably, his girlfriend) to keep tabs on him and report back on any problematic behavior. He convinced girlfriends, in particular, that it was in a player's best interests for him to know what was going on. Indeed, if a player was organizing or attending a party, Frieder might well be the first guest to arrive. Frieder would talk to the professors of any player he had academic concerns about and ask the prof to contact him if the player was missing classes or even if the kid was habitually late. Frieder was completely obsessed with knowing what his kids were doing and obsessed with the notion that their behaviors might, somehow, reflect badly upon him.

I have talked to Frieder on a few occasions. More significantly, I have talked to those who knew Frieder quite well, and were around the program on a day-to-day basis when Frieder was the coach. Everyone I spoke to agrees that Frieder would take full advantage of the rules. And the vast majority agree he was paranoid about not crossing the line. It is true that others are not so sure, and this includes certain friends.

Don Canham, like Frieder, tended to be a lightning rod when it came to the impressions of others. People either admired or despised Canham. But even those who had issues with the former AD (often because of his failure or perceived failure to support women's athletics) admit that "what you saw is what you got"; that Canham told you what he thought without any sugarcoating or ruses, regardless of whether his opinions cast a negative light on the university. In Canham's book, *From the Inside,* he made it clear that he had a high regard for Frieder and, had he remained AD at Michigan, he was "quite certain he would still be Michigan's basketball coach." Canham, for certain, saw nothing untoward in Frieder's regime as coach. But when Frieder took the Arizona State job, I believe there was a collective sigh of relief from many Michigan fans, since there was a general, public distrust of Frieder. And when the Steve-Fisher-led Wolverines won their first NCAA championship with Frieder's team, the relief turned to exaltation.

Local attorney Jon Rowe, also a notable novelist, argues, "If Frieder was so clean, how come I saw certain players of his driving pretty fancy vehicles?" I can't say I can answer this one. Maybe because Jon has a point. Or maybe because the rules were looser at the time. As it turns out, they still might be pretty loose. In April of 2003, Josh Porter, a staff writer for the *New Orleans Times-Picayune,* wrote about Chris Duhon's (Duke) fancy wheels, despite the player's lack of income. According to Porter, Duhon's deal with Duke included a job for his mother, supplied by a Duke booster. Or, spinning it Duke's way, she just happened to find a job in Durham with a Duke booster. This job, never posted, allowed her to buy the car for her son. The article suggests Duhon's case isn't singular, pointing out, in addition, that Carlos Boozer's father was provided a job in Durham by a close friend of Mike Krzyzewski. Duke's position is that the job had nothing to do with Duke, that it was an arrangement between the elder Boozer and the booster, and was within NCAA rules. Out of this I have two thoughts. First, Jon Rowe may well be right and the entire system is and was a game, one likely played by UM and everyone else. Second, even if Duke is clean vis-à-vis NCAA rules in relation to Boozer and Duhon, how much different is (a) friends of the Duke family providing jobs for parents from (b) friends of the Michigan family handing out cash to players? Hell if I know the difference.

Steve Fisher was the antithesis of the noisy and eccentric Frieder, save for their mutual love of basketball. Fisher is quiet, introspective, and extremely considerate of the feelings of others. I have bumped into Fisher at seven in the morning after a bad loss on the prior evening, and he was always willing to acknowledge my comments in good humor. Fisher believed that if he treated his players as mature adults, they would respond in kind. He found Frieder's spy practice to be demeaning, and felt that it was the individual's responsibility to behave appropriately, without any Draconian tactics from the basketball office. Where many had mixed or bad feelings about Bill Frieder, no one had anything bad to say about Steve Fisher. He was kind and polite to all. He was and is a singularly thoughtful and sincere man.

With Steve Fisher came a renewed sense that Michigan would continue the tradition of taking the high road. No one could be more thoughtful or kind than Steve Fisher, and with this came the fan group-think that Michigan would escape the ethical quagmire into which college basketball seemed to be sinking. My spin is that, ultimately, Fisher's trusting nature and his belief in the basic good and honesty and integrity of others cost him the job that he loved. The cost to the Michigan Athletic Department and Michigan has been profound, and will take decades to overcome. I believe that Steve Fisher became the victim of his own trusting or naive nature, for with Fisher came Ed Martin. Frieder, suspicious and analytic, would have been unlikely to (and didn't) allow a character like Martin much of a toehold inside the program. Or, for those more skeptical, Frieder was smart enough not to get caught. Fisher, trusting and open, was more likely to fall victim to the less-than-honorable intentions of others. Until the Ed Martin indictments, the university's formal posture was that there were minor violations in Martin's presence as a possible/probable (pick one) booster of the program. The Detroit papers, to the contrary, claimed it was possible (if they were UM writers) or a lock (if they were MSU writers) that Martin either loaned or gave Michigan players tens of thousands of dollars. Maybe a lot more. It turned out that the MSU folks were a lot closer to the facts, though even they underestimated the possible quantity of the Martin booty.

My diary entries about the handling of the Ed Martin affair are reproduced below. Also included, since it was going on at the same time, is the university's baffling "Nike-Gate" experience. Let me preface the foregoing with the comments that (a) I can't imagine the Martin affair being dealt with more ineptly, but (b) we will never know what the university's (President Lee Bollinger) theory was in the matter. As to (b), I admit that it is possible that Bollinger had a strategy/set of tactics that made sense. As of this moment, however, the latter is hard to perceive.

April 18, 2000. The Minnesota basketball program has been ruptured by academic fraud. Academic fraud, it seems to me, is among the worst of all violations, since it takes place with the sanction of the athletic department and the university. This said, Minnesota has handled its problem with a greater dexterity than Michigan has in the Ed Martin fiasco. As opposed to letting the wrongs of the past fester, Minnesota has admitted its culpability, and has imposed sanctions that look severe, most notably the termination of its coach (the successful and popular Clem Haskins) and the reduction of scholarships. My guess is the self-imposed penalties will keep the NCAA away from Minnesota and the program will right itself. The university might even get credited for honorable behavior, though the penalties are deceptively light. While the reduction of scholarships poses a major issue for a football program, it may actually benefit a basketball program by the guarantee of playing time. The fact is that thirteen players (the number of scholarships allowed) will not see significant time on any major college program. And neither will players number ten through twelve. Eight or nine players will carry the minutes on most teams, and the scholarship reduction allows the coach to prove to the recruit that minutes are available. Indeed, the Minnesota athletic director was upfront in admitting this potential. A one- or two-year scholarship limitation puts a limited crimp in a program. If the NCAA was sharp, it would reduce the number of scholarships penalized, but spread the term over a longer period of time. This limits the PT argument, yet makes a program plan carefully and pay for mistakes, unless the school is willing to run kids off. The latter is allowed by the NCAA, much to the shame of the member schools.

Michigan didn't learn from Minnesota's dexterity. UM completely mishandled the Ed Martin connection to its program, despite the fact that Lee Bollinger, a brilliant academician and first amendment expert, was either calling the shots or should have been calling the shots. Bollinger fired the Michigan basketball coach, Steve Fisher, with the majority of Michigan fans criticizing the move (at least until well after the fact), since the nexus between the firing and the Martin affair was smoky and poorly explained. Indeed, there were *rallies for* Steve Fisher, something that I think may look silly in the light of the present probabilities. Worse, Michigan hired a law firm to sweep the matter under the rug (in effect, if not in intent) with the imposition of self-imposed (and extremely) nominal penalties. This might have been appropriate if the internal investigation had turned up what it did after talking to all the relevant parties. But, the fact is, Ed Martin wouldn't talk to Michigan. And Chris Webber wouldn't talk to Michigan. And (perhaps) others of interest in the Martin investigation would not talk to Michigan. The administration of the university was being shut out.

At this juncture, the Michigan position should have been (a) we don't know if there has been any wrongdoing, and (b) if there was wrongdoing, it was done by players without the university's knowledge or sanction, and by an individual with very tenuous connections to our program, but (c) since Coach Fisher has not been able to convince Mr. Martin or his players to talk to us, we have to release Coach Fisher (much as this pains us) from his position, and (d) we have to assume the worst about our program. Michigan should have concluded, "We will assume, despite the lack of any compelling evidence," that Ed Martin gave money to basketball players, and this was a probable NCAA violation due to Martin's probable status as a booster. Michigan could have then said, "This assumption is made because we value our integrity as a university and our history of playing by the rules. We prefer to punish our program because it may be guilty of infractions. Not because we know it is. But we feel that we cannot merely brush it aside and retain our intention to be an institution with values." I assume a lawyer as sharp as Bollinger would have been more elegant in his *mea culpa* ("my bad," in basketball parlance).

In other words, Michigan should have admitted, since relevant persons would not talk or cooperate with the investigation, that "Michigan might be culpable," and "even if we are not," there was an appearance of impropriety that could only be cured by self-imposed penalties. These penalties should have been even more severe than those levied by Minnesota. I suggest that (a) firing the entire coaching staff with specific reference to Ed Martin, (b) reducing two scholarships over three years, and (c) a year tournament ban would have fit the crime or the theoretical crime. And, in fact, this would have helped the program in the short and long run. Michigan could have said (to outsiders and itself—and honestly so) that it was punishing itself without concrete knowledge of its own guilt. This would have allowed recruiting to continue without negative commentary or hints from other programs that Michigan was in trouble, and allowed the (greater) guarantee of playing time. Indeed, if the university had chosen a nine-scholarship penalty over three years, the upside would have still outweighed the "twisting in the wind" path chosen by Bollinger. The program would have suffered, as it deserved to, but that would have been small compared to the hit taken. If the university was truly innocent, we could still feel good about ourselves as Michigan fans and alums. And, if Michigan was guilty, the price had been paid, or mostly paid. There would have been limited incentive for others to keep it alive. Consider the following quote from President Bollinger:

> In this country, as a whole, basketball, from junior high up, is a system that has lost its moorings. Leadership at a national level is very much needed to address troubling issues. Meanwhile, at Michigan, we are unwavering in our belief that we must adhere to the highest standards in sports, as in any other area.

Given this, it would seem Bollinger and I are on the same page. But he had the opportunity to provide leadership. Instead, we got the opposite, a sort of sniveling and whining strategy of avoidance. I don't get it.

I found Michigan's handling of the affair, then and now, to be a baffling attempt to weasel out of an embarrassing trap. And this attempt has left a residue that has been impossible to shake. My fear is that it may get worse. While the federal prosecutor is denying any gambling is involved, the rumor is hot in Ann Arbor that a player shaved points in an NCAA tournament game. I have watched this game and, I think, the rumor is unfounded. The player in question was just beaten by a superior basketball player (an NBA player).

I don't know Bollinger. But I have friends who know him well and respect him. This said, I cannot believe that many attorneys would have handled it the way he did. The theory of the case has been self-destructive, a plan guaranteed not to work, even if the university/Fisher/the players are completely innocent of the charges leveled in the newspapers.

April 20, 2000. An aside on Lee Bollinger. The day Bollinger fired athletic director Tom Goss, he called a press conference. At the conference, he was asked (and rightfully so) the reasons for Goss's termination. Bollinger's answer was that the matter was "too complicated" to discuss at the press conference (or, presumably, in any other public forum). Well, last time I checked, this is not a town of imbeciles. I graduated from Michigan with a reasonable GPA and managed to get through law school. I ain't no genius, but I am reasonably intelligent. Pretty much the average person in Ann Arbor. And my guess is, I would not have been too mystified by answers like, "He ran the athletic department into the ground financially," or "He has refused to keep me apprised of critical issues in the athletic department," or (even) "The guy is a complete knucklehead, and we should have hired a pet rock before we hired him." I am pretty certain I would have had some *clue* as to what Bollinger was talking about. And my guess is that even the media would have gotten it. Or at least come close.

This is not to assert that Bollinger had to tell the public what was going on with Goss. I don't feel I have any right to know. But then, why call a press conference? Why not just publish a press report that Goss is gone and the reasons are to remain private in the best interests of Tom Goss and his family? Or just say he is gone. Or just say he and Bollinger could never see eye to eye, and it was better for one of them to go, and "between me and him, I chose him." Or just say Goss was a closet Sparty. It seems a very bizarre move to call a press conference and then insult the attendees and general public with the explanation that only Lee Bollinger is smart enough to understand the reasons behind the Goss dismissal. Maybe Bollinger didn't anticipate the question. Well, okay, I admit it. Unless Lee had been hanging out with Dennis Hopper and inhaling laughing gas for three weeks prior to the press conference, this is just not possible.

Meanwhile, the university has just announced it has hired a consulting firm to find a replacement for Goss. The firm is to be paid something in the range of seventy-five thousand to one hundred thousand dollars. I am stunned by this. In my career as a lawyer (admittedly, I have always worked for the government), I have never earned as much as seventy-five K in a year. In fact, I have not even been close. And, in my average work year, I generally get a few things done.

Certainly, even those who think I'm a slug will admit that I accomplish more in a year than a single hiring choice. It is more than a curiosity that it should take this level of expenditure to find a suitable candidate to run the athletic department. There must have been someone at one of the largest and more well-regarded universities in the country who could have handled the task without the expenditure of these monies. And last time I checked, Michigan was rumored to have one of the three or four best business schools in the nation. It seems to me that the chore of finding an employee could have been assigned to the faculty at the B school.

Given Bollinger's track record with Goss (assuming the firing made any sense), I can understand why he would want to turf the responsibility. As the levels of his seeming miscalculations vis-à-vis athletic issues mount (think "Halo," as long as we are at it), it makes sense for him to have somebody else to blame in the future. But I am at a loss to understand why the university felt incompetent to handle the responsibility. Hell, I'll find someone who can do the job for free. Indeed, I offered. No response. No surprise.

May 11, 2000. The month commenced with more Ed Martin. Hell, the next four *years* will probably start with Ed Martin. (Note: I thought I was exaggerating at the time I wrote this.) The *Ann Arbor News* reported today that Michigan has rehired the law firm of Bond, Schoeneck, and King to assist in the deposition of Mister Ed. The rumor is that this is a terrific law firm. They got MSU off with a knuckle slap a few years back and, somehow, Michigan must believe the firm did brilliant work in limiting the damage in the Martin case. After all, almost nothing about the affair has cropped up in the papers in the recent past. Well, maybe so. But I think falling on our collective swords would have been more honorable and useful and allowed us to think better of ourselves. And let's not think about the $140,000 paid to the firm, with more to come. (Note: In August of 2004 the *Ann Arbor News* reported the outsourced attorney fees to be $350,000.) I know. I know. Somebody once said something like, there is more honor in being a polar bear than a human. (PJ O'Rourke?) But, naive or otherwise, I like being associated with an institution that at least tries to take the high road.

Michigan rationalizes more money down this rat hole with the notion that it is useful to have some "institutional memory" about events. Well, it is true the Martin affair happened last century, but it seems like there should be plenty of attorneys employed by the university who were around then. Not to mention Bollinger and other lawyers at the law school. I can find a few guys in town who know what they are doing, and will depose Ed Martin for the sport of it.

As long as I am on this (again), two things are worthy of note. First, the recent *Ann Arbor News* article hints at the first public denial that "no point shaving" was going on with Michigan players. It is just a hint, a limited implication. Though it might just be his attempt to look insightful and have a plausible denial when the hint turns out to be unfounded. Second, the deal with the federal prosecuting attorney, at least as reported, references Ed Martin's obligation to talk to be limited to Michigan and about Michigan players. That is, in exchange for leniency from the feds, Martin only has to spill the beans on Michigan and not any other school. There is no question that Martin has had relationships (of whatever quality) with players who attended Missouri, UNLV, and Iowa. He may have had relationships with players who ended up at Syracuse, MSU, Purdue, Detroit-Mercy, and numerous others, but this is less clear.

One would think that Michigan might like to lift the muck from the bottom on this. It has to be tempting. But I don't think they will. And, even if they try to, my guess is that Martin won't talk, and he will be protected by the federal prosecutor. Odd, if fact. But maybe this is how it should be. Michigan, by its transgressions (construed or otherwise), should not be given the role of prosecuting or digging up dirt on other schools. And the fact Martin did his evil work elsewhere is no defense for what has happened here.

In any event, if the worst is true about Martin's handouts to Michigan players, Michigan fans will howl like wolves (understandably, if wrongly) when Martin clams up (or isn't questioned) about his relationships with players at other schools. And, if my speculation is correct, an incredible oddity exists in the nature of Martin's deal with the feds, particularly where nothing Martin has done vis-à-vis Michigan or its players is a crime. The feds disavow any point shaving. Martin is involved with many players, the probable majority not attending Michigan. And the deal is? Why not mandate, as a condition of the plea bargain, that Martin must talk to other schools? And how come no one in the papers is talking about this? Well, let's just see what happens first.

May 20, 2000. It didn't take long for the Michigan strategy on Ed Martin to take another turn for the worse. Now Ed says he isn't going to plead, and he isn't talking to UM, because he can beat the rap if he goes to trial. I have a (lawyer) friend who has done some criminal practice in federal court. He claims that Ed Martin is a small fry, and the "big dudes" don't want Ed talking to anyone, else he might swim with the fishes. I have heard variations on this theme in numerous conversations among lawyers over the course of the day. It makes no sense to me, unless Ed thinks he can beat the rap and has no need to plead. And, in any event, Ed would only be talking to Michigan lawyers about Michigan players. I can't think of a single reason for him to speak to Michigan about some theoretical superior in the numbers racket food chain.

Meanwhile, the federal prosecutors are having a snit and are threatening to widen the net on their investigations. The whole thing is weird, since it appears Martin was getting a good deal (limited jail time, he keeps his house) on offenses that are portrayed in the papers as slam dunks for conviction.

The Martin strategy is odd, but perhaps less odd than Bollinger's decision to toss a twelve-million-dollar Nike contract into the circular file. I can't say this makes sense or doesn't make sense, but let's start with the basics. I admit to being a radical pessimist. I also admit to being a vegetarian. And, I admit, I don't wear plastic shoes. I can't say my vegetarianism is either forged on health concerns or my belief that animals are no less important than humans, though it is muddled somewhere in these notions. (My cat? Beano Cook? An easy call. Plus, Beano might qualify as a legitimate vegetable.) In response to the "Why?" of my vegetarianism, I generally say something like, "I just don't eat meat," because this is about as honest as I can get without being too contradictory or too idiotic. So, my question concerning the Nike deal is not whether the choice was right or not. It is, rather, "Didn't we just fire an athletic director because the athletic department is losing a lot less money than two million dollars per year?" Oops. I forgot, Goss was fired for reasons that were too complicated for me to comprehend. And I also wonder if Lee (say) owns any properties that were manufactured in third-world countries. And it wouldn't stun me if, as speculated in the *Michigan Daily*, Lee and 99.9 percent of the Michigan student body have shoes in their closets made by Nike or some other manufacturer as venal as Nike or worse. And let's not think about the slaughterhouse.

Well, I am not being critical here, and I won't criticize non-vegetarians or those who are vegetarians on ethical grounds. And, I admit, I can't say radical pessimism is a particularly useful way to view the world. It does allow for a certain level of sloth, one of my favorites among the seven deadly sins. I will allow speculation about my ordering of favorites. You can send your answers to Lee Bollinger. He won't respond. But in thinking about this, I am reminded of PJ O'Rourke's notion that the iron curtain did not fall because of political ideology or repression, but because, after a significant bout with television and media from the west, no one wanted to wear Bulgarian shoes.

June 5, 2000. More rumors. Word has it that the person most pissed about the Nike giveaway is UM equipment manager Jon Falk. Counting walk-ons, Michigan has 105 football players to outfit. It turns out that each player is supplied with (at least) eight pairs of shoes for the season. Apparently, Falk needs somewhere in the vicinity of one thousand pairs. With no equipment deal on the radar (at least as far as anyone knows or is talking about), Falk is in an impossible situation in finding shoes for the team. And, where in the world is Falk going to find plain, generic shoes, aside from a possible raid on the Penn State equipment room? And shoes would not seem the only problem. The Nike logo is on all of the Michigan uniforms and Michigan needs to either (a) purchase new uniforms without logos, or (b) cover up the existing logos. Proposition (a) seems a pretty expensive one and I suspect, even if they buy the uniforms from Wal-Mart, there is a reasonable chance the uniforms may have connections to some third-world sweat shop. As to (b), the only thing I can think of is to cut a deal with the duck tape company and shill for the all-purpose nature of the product. This would work better, I admit, if Michigan's nickname were the "Ducks," or the "Tapirs," or even the "Fighting Silver Blemishes." But that isn't the case. And, Bollinger's taste (the Halo) aside, I can't imagine he would let the football team look this shabby. How Michigan solves this might be one of the more interesting developments of the summer.

The other rumor of the day comes from an attorney (via one level of hearsay) representing a Michigan basketball player alleged to be involved with Ed Martin. That attorney answered one of my prior questions—why the federal prosecutor would demand Martin talk to Michigan, but not to any other school where he was involved with players—with the comment that two FBI agents involved in the probe are avid ND fans (perhaps graduates) who have a rabid antipathy for Michigan sports, and they intend to keep the heat on to embarrass the university as much as is possible. I just don't believe this one. Not for a second. First of all, Notre Dame fans have too much to worry about to play these sorts of games. They've got their own problems. Second, it seems the federal prosecutor would have plenty to lose with this kind of silliness. The cost/benefit is just too high. Third, I think (though I could be wrong) that the key prosecutor investigating the case is a Michigan grad. And, I would guess, the prosecutor is the one calling the shots, not the FBI.

June 16, 2000. More Nike. Michigan and Nike are doing a lot of spinning on the tale. First, it appears the money on the table was between twenty-two and twenty-six million dollars, about twice the amount of the initial report. Michigan says that Nike killed the deal because of Nike's decision to "strike out" at universities "committed to finding appropriate ways to safeguard and respect human rights." Nike admits that Michigan's political issues were "a part of it," but avers that several other "last minute demands" by Michigan were "bigger problems" for the company. These demands would have given Michigan "most favored university" status, forcing Nike to match Michigan's compensation to that received by any (bigger) deal with any other university, as well as giving Michigan COLA adjustments, and denying Nike the right of first refusal to match offers made by other companies.

Michigan counsel Marvin Krislov admits these proposed changes, but contends they were a part of ordinary negotiations. Maybe so, but it sure looks like Michigan was overbearing in the negotiations. The first refusal condition was pointless and insulting. When someone is handing you this level of cash, you don't deny him or her the right to match competing deals, particularly where you are asking for "most favored university" status. And the other conditions look petty and chiseling when measured against the quantity of money on the table. But who knows. These conditions might just be Nike's way of denying its true motivations. Indeed, Nike canceled its contract with Brown (so it seems) out of concern with Brown's joining the Workers' Rights Consortium. And Nike has pulled the plug on contributions to Oregon (Phil Knight's alma mater) due to Oregon's WRC connection. Oregon is reconsidering its decision, but I doubt if Bollinger is willing to look so shameless.

Meanwhile, Nike insists that being a member of the WRC "does not impact whether we will do business with you." Hmmm. Someone is not being completely honest. In this instance, my guess is that it is Michigan, but call it at 50.1/49.9, Mr. Ed. But even if Nike is telling tales, this doesn't minimize Michigan's seeming ineptness in the negotiation.

Well, once again, this gets worse, except for Jon Falk. It turns out Michigan is going to *buy* Nike equipment for the coming year. And the cost will be (for football alone, I think) $760,000. So, let me get this straight. Instead of getting

Nike equipment at no charge and receiving compensation—in the millions—in exchange for wearing Nike gear (and the implicit advertising), Michigan has chosen to pay for the equipment, receive zero additional compensation, and still provide Nike with the advertising benefits. And the sense of this is? And this meets Michigan's human rights concerns how? It seems to me the revised deal continues to put Michigan in bed with Nike, continues to provide Nike with the same advantages that Michigan has pissed away. Indeed, all that has gone on is that Michigan has increased Nike's coffers to the tune of many millions of dollars. I assume Phil Knight is laughing his ass off. Now, perhaps this will only be a one-year deal, and next year Michigan will replace some of the Nike loss with an agreement with Reebok. I don't know, but my guess is Reebok (or Adidas or any other of Nike's primary competitors) doesn't manufacture shoes in Switzerland or Hoboken. And my guess is their wages are not all that much different than those paid by Nike. But, then again, I admit I don't know.

June 20, 2000. I neglected to mention that in the new Nike deal, Michigan will receive (something in the range of) 7 percent royalties on Michigan Nike gear. How this corresponds to deals passed on by UM isn't clear. But if Nike sells ten million dollars worth of Michigan Nike stuff, the royalty is only seven hundred thousand dollars. But I remain very confused. Even if the purchase and wearing of Nike uniforms does not make Michigan a business partner of Nike, doesn't allowing Nike to manufacture Michigan items (and Michigan taking a slice) place us in such status? And, if this logic holds, doesn't this imply that Nike was telling the truth? They seem more than willing to do business with Michigan, and this would seem to indicate (as Nike has stated) that politics wasn't at the core of their issues with Michigan. That it was, simply, Michigan's style of negotiating and Michigan's inclination to push too far. An MSU fan might characterize this as greed. Or arrogance. Those nasty guys. (Note: Michigan ultimately kissed and made up with Nike.)

September 7, 2000. Well, it has been a few days since I have heard anything about Ed Martin. The most recent story on the street is that subpoenas have been/will be issued for Steve Fisher, Perry Watson, Brian Dutcher, and perhaps other assistant coaches from the Michigan program. I have a hard time making much sense of this. The federal prosecutor only has the jurisdiction to investigate crimes, and it is difficult to understand how Michigan coaches would know anything about Ed Martin's gambling rings in any auto factory.

Two possibilities come to mind. First, if the Michigan coaches have information about large sums of money passing from Martin to players, this may bear upon an income tax evasion charge via a net worth prosecution. I have been involved in one such prosecution (against a noted mobster, real noted, and it received a lot less publicity than the Mr. Eddie gambling ring) but in that case, all witnesses were so tight-lipped (with good reason) that the government had little choice but to examine the expenditures of the defendant. In this case, there seems no shortage of evidence (if the papers are right, a leap of faith) directly implicating Ed Martin with illegal gambling activities, including the testimonies of those directly involved. Given this, it is hard to discern why any net worth prosecution would be necessary. And, in any event, it seems unlikely the Michigan coaches would be much help. Somehow, I just can't envision Steve Fisher testifying, "Oh, yeah, I knew Ed Martin was funneling significant amounts of cash to my players. That's why I kept Martin around the program and did not intercede in the transactions. Yeah, I knew a lot of funny stuff was happening with Martin, but what the hell, I needed players."

So what can it be? My guess is that the prosecutor is concerned about point shaving or game fixing. This happened at the (very) respectable Northwestern, and has a significant history in the college sport. Assuming the prosecutor is acting in good faith—and I assume this—it is hard for me to envision any other rational possibility.

December 3, 2000. Two weeks ago, Geoff Larcom published a new Ed Martin column in the *Ann Arbor News* proving, of course, that we will continue to go home again, and by the time this thing is over, we will have created the first ever self-imposed decade-long probation. There must be a few people out there that haven't been called by the grand jury yet. Leopold and Loeb, perhaps. What about Spiro Agnew? He has some experience with transactions made via brown paper sacks in the dead of night. After all, this is a prosecution of the world's number one criminal, (alleged) numbers runner Ed Martin. I know, for example, that Jud Heathcote hasn't been called, and I am certain he would like to help out. And it got me to thinking, as I heard someone point out somewhere, how come there are no pictures of Ed Martin? There are pictures of lowlife fascist dictators. There are pictures of minor league mobsters. There are pictures of spies. There are pictures of criminals in Murmansk. There are pictures of terrorists and alleged terrorists and guys-that-might-be-terrorists-if-you-gave-them-half-a-chance. There are pictures of Carlos the Jackal and real jackals and retching jackals posing as space aliens or the Loch Ness Monster in grocery store tabloids. There are even pictures of John Gotti for chrissakes.

But nary a picture of Ed Martin. This is particularly weird given the official scrambling to disavow any knowledge of the guy, and the fact that the *Detroit Free Press* pisses all over itself attempting to make the Martin story a bigger issue than the JFK assassination or the Bush "election," just to name two of the more recent coups. (By the way, Lee Harvey Oswald didn't do any shooting. This much is a lock. After that, it gets pretty cloudy.) As to the former, it is, "Ed Martin? I thought he was Michael Talley's father." And, "Was he the guy who used to wear the Malcolm X baseball cap?" And, "Is he a white guy?" I swear to something, I have heard all of the above from people either in or having significant connections to the athletic department. Or maybe from Mitch Albom. Perhaps this should be no surprise since, through all of this hoo-haw, (a) it is probable that very few people in Ann Arbor really knew who the hell the guy was, and (b) there has never been a picture of Martin in the papers, despite all of the publicity surrounding him and his federal prosecution for numbers running and other sins. I guess the *Free Press* just doesn't get over to the federal court very often, since it must be at least a one-hundred-yard walk from the exit ramp of the *Free Press* and the consortium just doesn't really care very much about publishing a picture of the guy. No big deal, right?

Larcom's article is the one I have been waiting to see, an attempt to figure out what the hell is going on in the grand jury subpoenas of every former Michigan assistant basketball coach going back to the days of the peach basket. Now, before I get going, I want to make a confession. I don't like Larcom in the abstract (I don't know him; he might be Gandhi), because he has published a piece of crap sports page (excepting Jim Carty and long ago, Jeff Mortimer) for years, and is non-responsive to legitimate inquiries about his publication. Bollinger doesn't respond to my notes either, but my guess is he has a lot more on his mind, and I can't hold it against him, particularly where I have suggested my libel will go on without any response from him if he so pleases. Plus, as a college president excised from sports, I think Bollinger might even be one of my heroes. At the very least, I think he should have earned every alum's respect for his stance on affirmative action, his support of the arts, and his willingness to go nose to nose with the not-such-a-great-guy-in-my-humble-opinion John Engler.

Michigan athletic director Bill Martin, incidentally, has always responded to my notes, a fact that I find pretty stunning. But Larcom? A guy who knows zero about sports, and wrote one of the most boring and uninformed columns in the history of bird cage flooring, can't even get it together to respond to a long and thoughtful (okay, you can disagree) letter. I think he might have responded with, "I don't like you and I wish you would leave me alone. Love, Geoff." Or, "Drop dead, you complete idiot. Love, Geoff." Or even the déclassé, "Thank you for the inspiring words suggesting I tear out my own liver and feed it to the squirrels and worms in my garden. Sincerely, Mr. Larcom." And that would have been enough in my mind. No disrepect to Bollinger (Mr. Halo) in this, by the way.

Anyway, Larcom does ask an absolutely legitimate question, one that I have not heard others asking. It is, why are the Michigan coaches being called before the grand jury? The transcript, from the day I walked into his office (before his thugs at the *Ann Arbor News* tossed me out) is below:

Larcom:	It was startling to see Steve Fisher and two of his former UM assistants, Perry Watson and Brian Dutcher, going into a building that deals with some of society's most menacing criminals.
Ross:	Yo, Geoff. Don't get too worked up over this. This is *federal* court and it's mostly run of the mill gangsters. That and judges and attorneys, and I think it's a little exaggerated to call them "menacing."

A bad start. But then Larcom suggests the reason for the testimony, according to a law prof at the University of Detroit, "is to fill in the details of the targeted person," and to get "an idea where the Martin money went." Well, maybe. But I doubt it. Why the hell would the federal prosecutor care where the money went? Did they call in Ed's local grocer and barber? His paperboy? His masseuse? Or even his bookie? This ain't a net worth prosecution for tax evasion (I surmise this would be a slam dunk without the Michigan ex-coaches, unless Ed claims he *lost* money running his gambling operations), and the fact of "where the money went" would seem pretty irrelevant to Ed's clandestine activities.

But even assuming the prosecutors are attempting to show Martin had more money than can be accounted for in his legitimate business (being retired), what would they expect to get out of (say) Perry Watson? I can imagine this testimony, Perry admitting that (a) he took money from Ed, and (b) he knew that Ed was giving out all kinds of cash to his players, but he just thought, "it would be stupid for me not to get my hands into the till," and "I didn't think it was all that important anyway." Coach Watson elaborates, "Eddie can give money to whoever he wants. It ain't against the law, is it?" Except for the word "Eddie" (Perry always calls Martin "Eddie"), and the fact it isn't "against the law" (probably not), the prosecutors had to know exactly what they would get from the ex-Michigan coaches. Bupkis. (Though one never really ly knows. In the Warren report, there is a copy of Jack Ruby's mother's dental chart. Warren critic Mark Lane suggests that such evidence would not have been relevant, even if it were claimed, "Ruby gummed Oswald to death.")

My guess, contrary to the "filling in the picture" view, is that the primary reason the federal prosecutor was interested in the assistants' testimonies related to the possibility of point shaving or just plain fixing games. How big of a stretch is this? Martin is allegedly involved in gambling. Martin is allegedly involved in giving money, perhaps significant amounts of money, to Michigan players. Doesn't the prosecutor have the obligation to put A and B together? Or at least to look into it? It is true that the papers have denied (via the prosecutors) there was any funny business going on in the Michigan games. (UM

85

was so wretched in some of these games I would be happy to know the players were dumping/shaving. It would help me put some sense to my world, if no one else's.) The "filling in the picture" scenario might be right, but it seems a lame explanation. In any event, after a dubious start, Larcom then gets full marks for the following observations:

> Will the NCAA slam UM? For Michigan, the most difficult aspect of all of this is the court of public opinion. As long as this drags out, opposing coaches can use the NCAA specter as leverage against UM in recruiting and fans will wonder about the program . . . But UM officials will tell you that nearly any NCAA penalty would be better than this waiting game.

Arghhhhhhhh. I want to tear my own liver out. Of course the foregoing is true. Indeed, this is a synthesis of a communication I sent to Larcom (that he did not acknowledge) about a month before his writing. But big deal. Anyone with the sense of a planarian or a rutabaga can figure out that it would be better to just get the specter removed and the penalties defined. Even a hack quasi-socialist lawyer can discern this one. But Geoff's article concludes with the above thought, without any examination of a solution.

Larcom's problem is that he assumes the NCAA is investigating Michigan and, of course, it is not. At this juncture, it remains within the discretion of the university to make a decision. Get it, Geoff? It is all in our own ballpark. We have met the enemy and it is us. And etcetera. And, while the time has passed for Michigan to spin the negative of Ed Martin into a positive, it seems we could still fall on our own sword in a way that would provide a practical solution, if not create the sort of public relations coup that was available in the past.

The answer at this point is called, "How we blew our summer vacation." Michigan calls a press conference and says, "We made a mistake a few years ago. At the time when it was clear that we could not secure cooperation from those within or connected to our program, it would have been most appropriate to punish ourselves for the appearance of impropriety. In the interim it has become possible or probable that a possible booster of our program gave money to some of our players in violation of NCAA rules. It is possible the amounts of money were substantial, in the tens of thousands of dollars. Perhaps more. This possibility has caused us to fire a popular coach and, for the past four years, we have endured a de facto probation while a criminal prosecution of the alleged booster has lingered and the program has been pilloried in the media. Our program cannot continue to twist in the wind while the criminal prosecution stagnates, and we have decided to impose penalties on the program. These penalties are implemented, despite our consciousness that the program has already been gutted by public opinion, and the inability to recruit in a way that we would generally prefer. And they are imposed, despite the fact that the period of limitations may have run out on some or most of the allegations. If and when the criminal prosecution of Mr. Martin has terminated, and we are able to secure more information about occurrences within the basketball program, we will revisit the penalties at that time. But we do not anticipate any further penalties against the program at this moment."

Now the penalties do not have to be all that severe in light of what has taken place at Minnesota and the fact that it is undeniable that Michigan basketball has already taken a de facto hit, regardless of any formal penalties. But the imposition of penalties, two scholarships over three years, probation, and a year ban from tournaments, is likely to put an end to the waiting game lamented by Larcom.

The alternative (and present plan) allows the federal prosecution to keep the Michigan basketball program in a state of permanent probation. And it only gets worse on the (extremely unlikely) possibility of monkey business in the federal prosecutor's office, or just plain bad timing in the sequence of events. Let's say, as appears to be a real possibility at the moment, the Michigan basketball team goes in the tank this year. And let's say Brian Ellerbe gets the ax and Michigan goes on a coaching search in the summer of 2001. Michigan finds exactly who they want, but just as the hiring is about to be made the Martin case is concluded and Martin tells UM that Louis Bullock was paid xyz dollars when Fisher was here and abc dollars thereafter. Martin says yeah, Fisher knew what was going on, and so did Perry Watson, and so did persons A, B, and C in the athletic department. The denials of Fisher, Watson, and A, B, and C will be believed by no one but a minority percentage of Michigan (and U of D) fans. And Steve Fisher's family. What happens then? Does the coach take the job? Or do we go through a coaching search with a sort of caveat emptor warning, discouraging those who Michigan might find to be the best candidates. And, does that throw us into the arms of, say, the (possibly) deranged Bob Knight? He is, after all, the only living candidate with the sort of ethical credentials that make it a certainty Michigan will conform to the even playing field sought to be created by the NCAA rules. And, with no penalties then imposed, doesn't Michigan have to go back to the drawing board, as opposed to saying, "We anticipated this and that's why we imposed the prior penalties, and we have supplemented them with (something relatively trivial) to make certain that this never happens again and Michigan basketball will always comply with the law and spirit of NCAA rules."

February 18, 2001. Today in the *Free Press,* Perry Watson is quoted by Lynn Henning as stating that he has/had known Ed Martin since the eighties, when Martin would buy Perry's high school team post-game meals. At some point, according to Henning/Watson, the coach believed that Martin had "crossed the line" when he began to take players to Pistons games. Because of this, Watson claims he severed his relationship with Martin before the coach was ever hired by Michigan. At Michigan, Watson states he warned Steve Fisher about Martin, but claims that he saw nothing going on that was outside of NCAA rules. Watson admits that Martin and Chris Webber seemed to be friends, but he stresses the lack (from his perception) of any impropriety, or a relationship between Martin and anyone else on the team. Watson claims that Fisher and assistant coaches Jay Smith and Brian Dutcher knew Watson had no relationship with Martin, but Watson implies that he is being hung out to dry as the fall guy by the other coaches. Let me revise this. It is more than an implication, since Watson claims his initials were forged on UM tickets left for Mr. Ed.

So what's this all about? Why, at this moment, does this particular story show up in the *Free Press*? I can only think of one reason, that Coach Watson sees the handwriting on the wall, the probability that Brian Ellerbe will be terminated, and he is attempting to clear his name for a possible showdown on the Michigan job. There is no other (reasonable) possibility since, in relation to one's name and the name of Ed Martin, the only good news is no news. Forget it, Perry. You are a good coach. You may be innocent of all wrongdoing. You may be the patsy, the Lee Harvey Oswald of the Martin affair. But you are not getting the Michigan job in your lifetime. And neither is anyone else associated with Ed Martin. And that includes Jay Smith (Central Michigan), and it definitely includes Brian Dutcher (San Diego), other Fisher assistants over the period in question.

February 12, 2002. The Martin affair has been pretty quiet since the spring of 2001 and the hiring of Tommy Amaker. The only note that appeared in the papers (in months) was the fact that a new prosecutor had been appointed to the office handling the case. This could mean nothing or everything, but it feels like the grand jury will drag on and, in another decade or so, a continuing small cadre of moronic Spartan fans will be clamoring about Michigan's impending "death penalty." And an equal group of idiot Wolverine fans will insist Fisher got a raw deal.

The Michigan AD's office appears to be treating the matter as something between a dead issue and a dead carp. This would seem particularly so where Amaker has made some vague noises about reaching out to former players such as Robert Traylor and Maurice Taylor, individuals who might have been involved with Ed Martin. This condition, and the fact that Michigan is intent on using all of its scholarships (for the first time in many years), indicates that UM is less than worried about any further blowback from the Mr. Eddie gambling prosecution and three-ring circus. Somehow, I ain't so sure.

I assume Bill Martin, the new Michigan AD, knows what he is doing. There is every indication that he does. But I do not believe the Ed Martin saga will die an easy death. On September 10, 2001, Dan Wetzel, who gets my vote for most acerbic if not the best college basketball writer in the country, published an extended article about the tasks facing Tommy Amaker. In the article, Wetzel notes that the Michigan program is one of "incredible power and potential" while being plagued by "obvious shortfalls and contradictions." The latter, of course, comes in the package of Ed Martin. Wetzel notes, six years after the fact and three athletic directors later, the university has not come to grips with what actually happened. He also stresses that the university has not yet admitted the level of culpability of its coaches, though I would argue the termination of Steve Fisher and his staff presents a powerful clue.

Wetzel believes, in opposition to the implicit message of the Michigan AD's office, that the basketball program remains at risk since, once details come out, "it could be one of the most troubling scandals in NCAA history." I disagree with this, since regardless of the activity of Ed Martin and Michigan players, it is unlikely that coaches or university employees were directly culpable in facilitating Ed Martin's "level playing field" violations. Rather, what is more likely is that any NCAA violations that occurred took place in an environment of insufficient vigilance or less than curious attitudes by the coaching staff and athletic administration. Moreover, and this could be critical to the present AD's thinking, the NCAA has a formal proposal on the table that would allow players to borrow up to twenty thousand dollars against future wages. As I understand it, this proposal has a reasonable chance of passage. The proposal, of course, throws the baby of amateurism out with the bath, since any enforcement of the nature and amounts of the loans will verge on the impossible. More to the present point, it is going to be pretty tough for the NCAA to punish a school for violating rules that were later abrogated by the organization. More than pretty tough. More like two chances. Slim and none. But this is a footnote on the issues facing Bill Martin. It is public perception that counts and, in this, the public relations strategies of the university have been a complete failure.

Wetzel says it best with the note that, among Amaker's other problems, the university "has yet to come to terms with its past." In this, it is not any potential NCAA penalties that matter. First, given the fact that Michigan has been on a tether of its own making for more than five years, it seems quite possible the NCAA would not do very much, even if the new loan proposals do not pass. Second, given what has gone on at Minnesota, any potential penalties, in the big picture, are likely to be something UM can live with. Rather, the specter that Michigan faces is itself, the failure to confront what has happened—or what is likely to have happened. The biggest argument in favor of whacking UM, at least at this moment, is the fact that we have kept our head in the sand. Yep. The enemy in this one has been some real bad lawyering in that the lawyer and the client were likely the same person. Or maybe just naive lawyering by a guy (Bollinger) too long in the teeth of the ivory tower. Bollinger should head off in the sunset to some institution (like, say Columbia) that has no athletic issues. He did that? Oddly, this saddens me.

It is, I promise, the calm before the storm. Wetzel has read the tea leaves, and I believe that Michigan's history of probable or perceived or advertised "fair play" posed a stumbling block to confronting events that were outside of the rules defined by the NCAA. Wanting to cling to this, there was a failure to confront the bad news. I still believe there is time for the university to remedy the problem, as opposed to allowing events, and the ultimate court of public opinion, to define the solutions for the university. It won't happen, though. Michigan has chosen its course.

April 1, 2002. I would like to say "I told you so" after the most recent revelations came forth, but I wasn't quite prepared for the number of $616,000, the amount the feds are alleging was laundered by Ed Martin to four players. To be honest, I didn't expect anything close. The sheer quantity of dollars makes a difference in the public perception, and it might make a difference to those in the NCAA as they review Michigan's actions (inaction) in dealing with the issues. Not because a million dollars is any different than 10K in the scheme of the rules, but because the public relations of this level of dollars is hard to escape, and the PR realities are unlikely to be ignored by the NCAA.

Bill Martin and his counsel, Marvin Krislov, have a major problem on their hands. In the words of Hunter Thompson, they are about to get hit with a "thousand-pound shit hammer" unless they are creative in spinning the conditions into a new tale. My suggestion is, as always, that we admit more wrongdoing than we are culpable of, including the Hindenburg disaster, Jerry Lewis movies, Regis Philbin's birth, Mrs. O'Leary's cow, and anything else that doesn't seem all that bad at the moment. I don't think we should take credit for anything Nixon did. We can leave the apologies arising out of the recent publication of his virulently racist and anti-Semitic ravings to his homies at Duke. We can make our apologies for Gerald Ford and Thomas Dewey and the wretched Anne Coulter, our own crosses to bear.

Previously, the interesting question was how Michigan was going to deal with the problem. As I have argued, the decision to wait and see if it was going to go away seemed pretty naive, particularly when Mr. Ed refused to plead, and where there remained alternatives, though as time wore on those alternatives looked more stale and convoluted. Now, the question of penalties is not an interesting issue at all. Michigan is going to have to do something. Either (a) they now assume the allegations to be true and negotiate with the NCAA for the appropriate action, (b) they stay the course on the thread that the FBI has blown it, that the story is not as bad as portrayed in the indictment, or (c) Michigan really stays the course to see if they can throw the swill back at themselves and everybody else who has been imbibing at the same trough. I would say (c) won't happen. This one is pointless. I would say that (b) has some possibilities, but I can't imagine (absent some pretty remarkable information) that this is the course that is going to work out best for the long run interests of the university. That leaves (a). It is, I believe, just a matter of time.

Others can't quite see it and I suppose I can understand this since Bill Martin's comments have been a two-edged sword. On one hand, he states that Michigan needs to act decisively to get the matter behind us. On the other hand, he has stated that he doesn't want to act in a premature fashion, until he has the opportunity to investigate the fiasco as best he can. His comments on point are legitimate but too late, albeit a lateness that must be laid at the feet of others. It seems to me this is what we should have been doing in the past years, as opposed to waiting for the other shoe to drop. If, in fact, Michigan thought there was little untoward going on, how come we fired Steve Fisher? And if we did think that something wasn't right, how come we either didn't just do something sensible and limit the future damage or begin a further investigation at the time of the firing?

At the present moment, the general media brouhaha is that Michigan needs to handle the problem right away. I can understand this. Indeed, five minutes after the indictment came down, I sent a stream of annoying emails to Bill Martin and Marvin Krislov suggesting Michigan end its part of the matter now, whatever it might take. Indeed, some journalists are already criticizing Michigan about "not doing anything" when the most recent allegations only occurred in the past week. I would think, at the least, that whatever Bill Martin does it should take place after April 4, 2002, the day of the basketball bust, and before April 6, the day of the NCAA hockey finals. This is nothing other than elementary manners. Writers suggesting anything to the contrary (e.g., Theresa Brennan's comments in *USA Today*, a generally good writer and a Northwestern grad but a UM fan) are candidates for the Thomaselli Award as the country's biggest dope, almost always awarded to either Jesse Helms or Geoff Larcom. (Larcom gives this award to me, I would hope. Maybe Thomselli gives the Ross award to Larcom. Plaque buildup accrues in this fashion.) My guess is, before the season starts, Michigan will have acted. And my guess is this action will have had the "blessing" of the NCAA. My bet is that UM will be the first school on a nine- or ten-year probation (counting the de facto five or six years that have already taken place). If nothing else, the NCAA should hammer us for being so damn stupid and stubborn.

So what is the interesting stuff? Well, first of all, I would sure as hell like to know what Michigan is doing behind the scenes to figure out what really went on. I know, for an absolute fact, that private entreaties were made to get Steve Fisher to come clean on everything he knew. A prominent attorney in Ann Arbor contacted another attorney who is best friends with Fisher. This attorney was to beg Steve to come out with everything he knew, both for his own good and for the good of those left behind. This entreaty was done with the knowledge and the (possible) tacit approval of Bill Martin, though UM was not directly involved. In this, Bill Martin stood up, and was willing to take what came his way, regardless of what Fisher revealed. I don't know what happened in this reaching out. I do know, a few days after the indictment, Fisher was interviewed on national TV and repeated (three times) that he was proud of his experience at Michigan and that he ran a program that had "integrity." Fisher, taking a page from John Wooden, would not admit that he might have been less than vigilant. He would admit nothing other than he ran a clean program and that he, as coach, demonstrated the highest level of ethics. His exact words were, "I did it the right way (both in coaching and recruiting), and I did it with honesty and integrity. I did it in a fashion that I will continue to be proud of." Most frustrating in the Fisher interview was Steve's failure to speak about the specifics of the allegations. Fisher's comments were completely generalized, a rehearsed denial. That isn't to conclude, at least from Steve's subjective vision, that his comments are not true, though I ain't playing the pass line on this one. Still, it seemed like a fake show. And there is one thing Steve didn't add up correctly. John Wooden is an icon of whom no bad can be spoken. Steve ain't in this particular league.

I also have strong reasons to suspect that the AD's office has made some (direct or indirect) attempt to again talk to the players involved. We will see what comes of this, but at this moment all that we have heard is Chris Webber's sense that the indictment/revelations are annoying to him, and Jalen Rose's message (Jalen is not accused of taking money) that Ed Martin was not a bad man, that he did a lot of good. Webber's annoyance is understandable, since he is accused of taking $280,000 (some, maybe most, while he was in high school). Webber also complained to Mitch Albom that he believed he was exploited while in college because, despite his role in enhanced earnings for the U (finding its way into, among others, the pockets of women athletes or men's minor sport athletes), he was unable to afford a date or a pizza. Somehow, I doubt if Webber has ever had a shortage of candidates on the female companionship front, even if he didn't have a nickel in his pocket. But if I couldn't afford a pizza, I would be pissed about hearing about all the money I had, too. Hell, I couldn't afford a pizza in college, either. But no one ever accused me of salting any dough away.

Well, Webber's thoughts strike a chord with me since the NCAA has legislated a small island of socialism in the capitalist maelstrom. Michigan makes a lot of money on football, and some in basketball, and a little in hockey. The other twenty-two sports are losing propositions, some of them big-time. And so the money from football makes it possible for a water polo player to go to school. And if contributions to the U are enhanced because of a great basketball team, perhaps the campus looks nicer or the computer facilities are better or the U can offer a few worthy students a less expensive ride. So Chris is probably right. It is highly likely that he and the rest of the Fab Five made money for Michigan. But, in the main (excepting, perhaps, Steve Fisher and Perry Watson), no one got rich on C Webb's back. Other just as legitimate but less visible athletes received the opportunity to compete in their sports. And maybe some kids, hopefully some poor kids, were given the opportunity to make their lives better because of "help" arising out of Webber's largesse.

All of this said, I admit that it is very naive to believe that an island of socialism is going to remain pristine and uninfected in an environment that espouses something very much the opposite (think Olympics), an environment with the predicate that it is every person for himself. We gotta face it. Even in an organic paradise, some pesticides are going to wash ashore. In this spin/light, even if Webber did take money, there is no scandal in the Ed Martin affair. It is, rather, nothing other than the exercise of Webber's ordinary if not constitutional rights. Or his own personal revolution, intending to upset the socialist apple cart. Or, more accurately, to live with the socialist ideal while taking advantage of the benefits outside of the island. I can't say I agree with this vision, because I don't, but I can't say it is crazy.

And then think about it from another direction. Let's say a kid from the Detroit suburbs comes to Michigan on a soccer scholarship. His family, among the more wealthy in his community, sends him with a Mercedes, and with as much money as he wants, in the range of fifty thousand dollars per year. They are proud of him. After all, he is a good student and a good son, and he has worked hard at his sport and his academics. And the problem is? None, of course. And there is no violation of NCAA rules. But let's take Athlete B, a kid from a poor part of Detroit with no means of support. His father is out of the picture. His mother scrapes by in a low-paying job. Athlete B comes to UM, and he comes with a fancy car that a longtime neighborhood friend provides. The kid, despite living on the streets, has managed to get through school and is a reasonable student. He has worked diligently on his academics and even more so on his sport, spending hours every day perfecting his craft. The kid stays away from gangs and drugs and trouble with the law. He is, in a real sense, a self-made person.

The neighborhood friend, who helps many in the community, is proud of his protégé. When at UM, the neighborhood friend transfers cash when the player needs or asks for it, sometimes a lot of cash. The friend had done some of the same things while Athlete B was in high school. The differences between Athlete A and Athlete B? I have to admit, I have a hard time seeing the difference, except that it's easier to admire one than the other. In this regard, Jalen's comments mirror those I heard by Detroit residents who knew Ed Martin, including the estimable Jim Spadafore, a Detroit sports reporter. Both seem to regard Martin as a sort of benign guy, a man doing nothing other than what the casino moguls do. The difference is, unlike the casino moguls, that Ed Martin gives back to the community. The lore goes that Ed gives clothes to kids who need them. And, of course, he has (or is alleged to have) given money, apparently big money, to major league athletic talents. For many in Ed's community, he is a local hero, a working class hero, a Robin Hood doing the right thing. In Spadafore's case, he gets full marks for even perceiving this point of view, let alone arguing it, since he has already taken some shit for even expressing such a vision. Okay. I admit it. This is complete spin. But isn't it a spin that in the big picture (excised from Michigan's problems or deserved shame) we should pay some attention to? (As it turns out, the NCAA has turned a blind eye to the "solution" to the Martin affair. Guardianships. You got it. You are a wannabe Mr. Ed? Just secure guardianship of the talent you like, and you can transfer all the dough you want. No problema. And it is happening in your school right now.)

Of course, if the allegations are true, Ed Martin was also laundering money from illegal gambling, and may have expected a major return from the Michigan players. (I would suggest this gives new meaning to the laundry business term "martinizing.") And, of course, the Michigan players and Martin placed their own interests over the long-term interests of the university, their coaches, their teammates, and the players who followed. Whether Martin's activities can be rationalized or not, the players and Martin must have known of the dangers to the UM basketball program. To me, this leads to the most intriguing element of the hoo-haw: why don't the players involved just come out and admit what they did? If it is a slam dunk that the money was taken, if there have been such admissions in front of the grand jury, why not come forward and admit it now, but protect the university with the admission that Fisher neither knew nor should have known about the transfers? The players have little to lose in this. They have done nothing illegal, and their names are already mud in Michigan basketball history. It would provide them with some small element of redemption.

These players might say, if it is true, the transactions were sufficiently clandestine, that it was reasonable for the AD's office not to know, for Fisher and other coaches not to know. Or, at least, they might say they were warned about taking cash from Martin (Perry Watson claims he warned Jalen and Fisher; it is certain Louis Bullock was explicitly warned to stay away from Ed Martin) but they went ahead, against the express warnings of the coaches. Perhaps the reason they haven't done this is that none of it is true. Or perhaps it is the fact that none of them took any money. But then, why not say it? Why not deny?

Of course, the one unknown layering all of the above is the level of proof underscoring the indictment. Either the players came clean in the grand jury, or the evidence lies exclusively in the documentary evidence found in the search of Ed Martin's residence. Since the players ain't talking (except to deny), and the rumor is there were varying levels of cooperation with the feds, my guess is that the predominant element of evidence, certainly as to the amounts of money transferred, lies in the handwriting of Ed Martin. And the reason we should trust Mr. Ed is? Remind me, please. So here is the part to watch. Bill Martin and Marvin Krislov are not exactly Charlton Heston. They actually graduated from school, someplace. (He went to Northwestern? Sorry.) And they don't have Bollinger around to bollix things up. Given this, my guess is that if Michigan doesn't have a plan announced prior to the start of the basketball season, either (a) something really is fishy with the indictment, (b) Bill Martin and Marvin Krislov have concerns that the Mr. Eddie story is less than kosher, or (c) the NCAA has put their fingers on the scale and demanded/mandated Michigan proceed in a certain fashion. Personally, I wouldn't put up with (c), and I would play to the public with a plan for self-immolation, at last.

Oh yeah. One last thing. How come Ed Martin isn't pleading guilty? Why *is* the old coot going to trial? Because he knows the feds have a slam dunk for conviction? Or because the feds actually offered zip in the guilty plea, since they had little interest in Martin, but were more concerned with other elements of the prosecution? The latter seems inconsistent with the public pronouncements from the federal prosecutor's office. But this remains the weirdest part to me, particularly where Martin's crime was practicing gambling without a license, not exactly the biggest crime that has hit southeastern Michigan in the recent past.

April 4, 2002. Webber speaks. Now Chris says, "There is no way in the world that I took $280,000 . . . and in no way do I want to mess up the nature of college basketball, especially my university, the University of Michigan, which is the greatest university in the world . . . I don't want to put a bad mark on my family's name, so as I said before, no, I did not accept the money. And why do you take the word of a criminal, anyway?" The word "before," apparently, references Webber's testimony before the grand jury. So Webber doesn't appear to share Jalen's vision of Ed Martin as Robin Hood. And the foregoing quote sure makes it tough on Krislov and Bill Martin. In conjunction with Steve Fisher's TV interview, it must give them pause. We are innocent?! Well, personally, I would be relieved and ecstatic if this is true. But I won't go dancing naked in the streets. And these statements underscore, I suppose, the strategy of taking a wait-and-see approach. But I think it is the same old trap. Especially where Webber's attorney is saying Webber took something, but it was only a couple of meals (gruel, no doubt) from Mr. Ed and an unstated amount of cash not even close to $280,000.

Well, of course, they should get their stories straight. And this admission by the attorney is bad news, since this is more than the Kansas City law firm uncovered. Gee, the snootful of dough for these characters in KC was really worth it. All UM bought was the longest probation in history. Aside from this, I would suggest that Bill Martin now has a window of opportunity, albeit an awkward one, to come forward with the "appearance of impropriety" spin once again. At the moment, he can legitimately say that Michigan had no clue what the hell went on, but it is time to just get beyond it, so we are punishing ourselves because of the smoke and the fact that we just don't know, and we can't continue on a de facto probation. Unless Bill knows a lot of weird stuff, or other revelations are forthcoming. Or unless the NCAA has put its feet on his fingers. I am guessing the latter.

April 15, 2002. Chris Webber finally joins Jalen's team and admits he took a sequence of twenty dollar bills from Mr. Ed, starting in seventh grade. Sometimes, it seems, Chris says he conned Ed into giving him the dough, much to the consternation of Chris's dad. Other times, it seems like Chris avers he earned the money the old fashioned way, by mowing Ed's lawn. As to UM, Chris appears to admit he took an occasional handout, but (piecing it together) the money he took while in Ann Arbor was (at most) in the 1–3K range, not the amounts listed in the indictment. Chris, like Jalen and Spadafore, is now painting Ed as a sort of neighborhood Mr. Rogers, just a guy helping out kids. A nice man who just happened to not have a license for his chosen occupation.

The more Chris talks, the harder it gets for Bill Martin and Marvin Krislov. It is difficult to argue with the notion that the uncertainty of the facts makes it problematic to levy a punishment. How the hell can UM negotiate with the NCAA prior to any clarity of the facts? On the other hand, doesn't the ambiguity allow UM a window to revise a seemingly "dead" opportunity, to punish before the fact and then revisit? I guess the answer to this depends upon what UM thinks about the Webber stories and the testimonies of the other three players before the grand jury. If their stories mirror Webber's, I guess I can understand the present waiting game. If, on the other hand, these stories are consistent with the indictment, the Webber reality may make little difference.

July 27, 2002. The local papers are now printing speculation that the feds will prosecute Webber for perjury due to his testimony in front of the grand jury. Maybe. But since *I* heard this story more than a month ago, my guess is this is disinformation from the feds and a way to put a clamp on Webber's flapper. And, for those inclined not to trust the face value of the Martin prosecution in the first place, a way to keep the heat on Bill Martin. These kinds of prosecutions are rare, and generally reserved for big-time criminals when the feds are having a difficult time in ordinary prosecutions. It is an unusual back-door for individuals otherwise not involved in criminal behavior and would be a three-ring circus and risky for the prosecutor's office. Why, for example, should any jury (at least innately) believe Ed Martin over Chris Webber? Doesn't Ed Martin have every bit as much motivation (actually, about fifty times greater motivation) to lie as Webber? It might happen. But I bet the don't pass line.

Meanwhile, Mr. Ed is set for a late-night deposition in August. My guess is that the U shows up with its biggest guns (Martin, Krislov, Johnny Cochran, and Raymond Burr), but will have all of their questions monitored and limited by the federal prosecutor and Mr. Ed's attorneys. I surmise the NCAA will send an observer. Too bad this one doesn't make it to cable. (Note: As it turned out, UM never got to talk to Mr. Eddie. They only got to talk to his attorney.)

September 15, 2002. I lose the don't pass bet, as Webber is indicted by the feds for perjury, just as my source predicted months ago. Michigan is still hanging tight, and has committed to a full package of kids for the 2003–4 season. (Note: During the season this decreased to eleven, with one defection and the termination of one of the two Ellerbe holdovers.) So, in this penalty phase, I assume the negotiations center round (a) forfeiture of games (I assume this will happen), (b) pulling down banners (ditto), (c) giving back NCAA revenues (probable), (d) probation (certain), (e) banishment from the NCAA tourney (maybe, for one year), and (f) some TV limitation and limitation of TV revenues (my guess is UM wants to draw the line here). It would not appear that scholarship limitations are on the table.

The Webber prospective is now the most tantalizing element, since he seems to want to go mano-a-mano with Mr. Ed and the federal prosecutor (Rick Convertino) at the risk of some big-time punishment. But let's look back at this. Here's what we have:

1. Incredible leaks by the feds (or someone) to the press and others well in advance of the grand jury process. What exactly was the point of this?
2. Use of a grand jury for a victimless and chickenshit offense like gambling without a license. There was, in fact, no reason to call a grand jury except to end the non-criminal investigation. The cost of this to the public was enormous and the gain, on the criminal side, was zilch. The only reason to convene the grand jury was to investigate a non-crime, the siphoning of funds to third parties.
3. A grand jury process that lasted longer than the Warren Commission and called every irrelevant witness under the sun, for the (seemingly) exclusive purpose of the embarrassment of those individuals. What, for example, could Brian Dutcher have to say about numbers running in a downriver auto plant? He might have a lot to say about

Webber and cashola, but since when is this (a) a crime, or (b) the province of the FBI?

4. Continued leaks by the feds (or someone) during the grand jury process. Ask yourself why the feds (probably the FBI and not the prosecutor, but who knows) felt compelled to do this.

5. A plea offer to Ed Martin that (as leaked by the feds or someone) was later rejected by Martin. Maybe. But my guess is that it was the prosecutor who was playing games. Why would Martin turn down a godfather offer only to accept the same damn deal a lot later? Because the numbers racket left him broke? Because he wanted to spend the rest of his life in jail? My guess is that the feds didn't want the deal because they wanted to subpoena Fisher, Webber, Elmer Fudd, and the Mormon Tabernacle Choir, even though these "witnesses" had nothing to do with the crime in question.

6. Indicting Webber for perjury. Check around. This just doesn't happen all that often. Particularly where the person indicted committed no crime (and is not thought to have committed any crime) other than the fact of his testimony. And where the perjured testimony had zero to do with the crimes being charged. So why are they indicting Webber? Maybe, as the king of arrogance, he just pissed them off. Maybe. But when you think about why they are indicting Webber's aunt (for lying about the existence of a meeting with Mr. Eddie??), doesn't this stink to high heaven? To me, this looks like pure vindictiveness by the feds. But, maybe (a) they want to make an example of Webber, and (b) they've got something in the way of evidence other than Mr. Ed. Certainly, condition (b) is lent credence in that it is the only info they haven't leaked. So, maybe. But it is hard to see the purpose in the example to be set, since lying in front of the grand jury about matters that are non-crimes is not exactly an epidemic, even in the Mr. Eddie gambling shakedown.

Webber may be a truly offensive person, but this prosecution seems like nothing other than machismo that will prove nada. Indeed, aside from punishment for this old coot, the entire prosecution was a waste of money, a prosecution that accomplished zero. Let me give Convertino a clue. People will still gamble on the number. And everything else that moves. I know this is startling info to Rick and the feds, but there it is. I even have it on good sources that there are a few people in town who gamble a dollar or two on the NCAA basketball tournament. And, as an aside, this happens in just about every single office in the USA. And some even play rotisserie baseball. And some of these are, honest, I ain't lying, cops and lawyers and judges and politicians. There are, I guarantee it, even some in the federal prosecutor's office. And most of them are good folks who pose no danger to the public in that dollar they threw down on Wahoo State to run the table. It was a dollar better spent, for certain, than on that next Whopper. Second, the prosecution of Ed Martin cost a lot of money, time, and energy that could have been used on legit prosecutions, as opposed to this trivia. But I guess Convertino doesn't understand the notion of opportunity cost. Not when he can shoot fish in a barrel and especially if the resulting slime is political currency.

But, I admit, I don't really know. After all, I lost my last bet. And I don't suggest for a second that Convertino is a fool or that the leaks painted an accurate picture of what has been going on in the Martin case.

September 20, 2002. Jalen Rose was a guest on the national Dan Patrick radio hookup yesterday, and commented that he had been on the sidelines during the UM-ND football game and wanted to express his appreciation "for all the love I received from the Notre Dame fans." When asked about the Ed Martin affair, Jalen stated, "I never took anything while I was at Michigan," stressing that the small amounts he received accrued prior to attending UM. Apparently the federal prosecutor believed Jalen, since he was not named in the Martin indictment and not charged with perjury, something the prosecutor's office has made clear it was willing to do.

But Jalen is skeptical that Webber took any money, at least while he was at Michigan. Jalen argues that if Chris was taking money, there would have been some manifestation of the transactions, and (a) "if Chris was taking money how come he didn't have a car and we drove around in my beat up old Dodge Omni?" and (b) "if Chris was taking money, how come we didn't have the money to put much in our refrigerator?"

The answer, of course, could be Detroit Country Day and subsequent interest at loan shark rates, and a resultant pissing match between the Webber and Martin families. This would, of course, minimize UM's culpability, and might explain Steve Fisher's seeming unwillingness to admit *anything*. More to come, no doubt.

November 17, 2002. Michigan finally caves in and punishes itself. About freakin' time. We add 117 losses to the ledger, pushing the UM all-time record to the bottom of the Big Ten, or the near-bottom at least. Banners come down. Two years probation. One year ban from tournaments. And $450,000 goes to the NCAA coffers. My guess is the NCAA will add something else. Probably not TV revenues. Maybe a scholarship or two. Possibly one more year on the tournament ban. Bill Martin makes it clear we are humiliated. The scene shifts to Chris Webber as he still fights his indictment, and has now filed a motion to dismiss, citing a lack of specificity in the filing.

It would be nice, of course, if any of these characters (Webber, Taylor, Traylor, Bullock) stood up and took the blame, and took a little bit of the heat off others. For Mo Taylor's part, it is "old news," and he still whines that he was just a small cog in the inhumane treatment of college athletes. From Mo's point of view, he *should* have been paid and, hence, the suffering of those in his wake is just plain irrelevant and tough luck. Not his problem. Just ours. Thanks, Mo. And I assume you are broke lately. Right? That NBA contract just won't stretch very far. (Note: After this was written, Mo decided he would talk about the Ed Martin affair, and his innocence as previously proclaimed to the grand jury, after the NBA season. Yeah. Right. I won't hold my breath. Note: It never happened, to my knowledge.)

February 18, 2003. Ed Martin is dead. No one suggests any foul play. His death may well make it impossible for the feds to pursue their indictment of Chris Webber. In this respect, Martin's death benefits him. For Michigan, however, it closes the coffin on the chance of any partial redemption. Michigan never got to talk to Martin, they were left with the comments of his counsel. And the rumor is that Martin never testified to the grand jury, even if his testimony would (somehow) be admissible in Webber's trial, despite his unavailability for cross examination. So Michigan gets hammered on the supposed words of a dead man, a man never confronted by those with contrary interests. (But, possibly, Bullock, Taylor, and Traylor anted up in front of the grand jury and admitted their sins—though this is testimony that is unlikely to be revealed, and it is less than clear that any of these characters cooperated with UM either.) Ultimately, Martin's death puts a lingering stench on the prosecution and raises, at least, two questions. First, the *Detroit Free Press* reported that "the lawyer for Webber's aunt, Steven Levy, said that the government may have missed an opportunity last year by refusing to go along with a request by defense lawyers to have Martin testify under oath in a deposition." Given Martin's age (sixty-nine) and the real possibility that he might die before the Webber trial (check out the actuarial tables for men of African heritage), it would seem the feds would relish the opportunity to have Martin on record. Second, it would seem the notions of fair play that are an inherent part of the prosecutor's responsibility would mandate an accession to the defense request. This refusal to allow access to Martin, to me if no one else, implies some *ultra vires* motivation of the federal prosecutor in the case. I suggest that the Martin case was never really about gambling in a downriver auto factory. Or, at least, this was a complete sideshow to the main event.

I note that the *Free Press* also reported "the government allowed [Martin] to plead guilty to one count . . . in exchange for cooperation in the investigation against Webber." Maybe this is sloppy writing. But this, if true, endows the Martin prosecution with its most indelible aroma in the pursuit of issues, to wit, non-crimes (NCAA violations) outside of its jurisdiction and the investigation of one person subject to the (probable) Martin handouts when many others were (probably) involved.

The stains on Michigan and Webber are very likely to be deserved. But in looking for villains, there may be other, legitimate candidates in more fiduciary roles. But out of all decay arise good things. In this instance, it is the seeming commitment of Michigan to not let things of this ilk happen again and the ultimate presence of Tommy Amaker, the perfect bromide for the university's ills.

May 30, 2003. Cubs lose. The NCAA hammers UM, and the fact is, we deserve all that was handed out. But let's go through what the NCAA has said about this. First, the NCAA concludes UM administration has acted appropriately and honorably in dealing with the Martin issue. Second, the agency finds there was no evidence that Steve Fisher and/or any assistant coach acted improperly. Essentially, the conclusion is that neither Fisher nor the AD's office knew, nor "should have known," that handouts were being given and, hence, even though the NCAA has jurisdiction to punish these coaches (all are active), no punishments have been levied. Third, in response to the question of why players from other schools (also being given money by Ed Martin) were not the subjects of investigation, the NCAA states that it chose not to pursue this because such players were outside of the limitations period. The questions stop at this point. The follow-ups should have been:

Q: Aren't the Michigan players also outside of the limitations period?

A: Well, yeah. But not Louis Bullock.

Q: But isn't it a fact, by the time Bullock took his loan from Martin, that Michigan had specifically and officially banned Martin and told Bullock (and all others) to stay away from him?

A: Yes.

Q: Isn't it a fact, by the time Bullock took his loan, Michigan had shown Bullock a picture of Martin and said, "stay away from this guy?"

A: Yes.

Q: So at the time of the only violations within the limitations period, Ed Martin wasn't a Michigan booster?

A: Not at that moment.

Q: So hasn't the NCAA either "bootstrapped" the "booster" notion from outside of the limitations period or merely used "limitations" as an excuse to not conduct a full investigation of the Martin affair?

A: Uh . . .

Q: Given that Martin's booster status accrues from prior to the limitations period, doesn't this imply that the NCAA is just jackin' us about its choice not to look at the other schools where Ed Martin was connected?

A: (Nothing coherent.)

Aside from the foregoing little piece of dishonesty by the NCAA, the decision to not punish Fisher (and the rest) is telling. Let's say the NCAA punishes Fisher. In about five minutes, Fisher sues the NCAA, à la former UNLV coach Jerry Tarkanian. Fisher says (a) Ed Martin didn't give the players any money, (b) if Martin did, he wasn't aware of it, and (c) he should not be construed with such awareness. Fisher then parades Webber, Traylor, and Taylor (and Bullock?) to the stand, and they testify they took nothing after they came to UM and what they took in high school was nominal and Steve Fisher didn't know about it. And who testifies for the NCAA? Ed Martin's corpse? The NCAA goes down the drain on this one. Fisher receives an injunction and millions in damages. And then the Michigan-left-holding-the-bag scenario looks pathetically lame, particularly where the bag-holders were five to nine years old when the whole hoo-haw accrued.

The NCAA cannot prove that Steve Fisher did anything untoward. They can't prove any assistant coach did anything to break NCAA rules. They admit the university administration always acted above board. They have no evidence of any lack of institutional control. They suspect the Michigan basketball program was rotten to the core, with Steve Fisher selling his soul to the devil. I suspect this too. And any decent MSU fan knows it. But the truth is, at this point, every element of the Martin affair is a pure dog and monkey show, with the NCAA and the feds being the biggest bozos on the bus. Still, read my lips, we deserved everything that came down and maybe more, if for nothing else, because of our stupidity and refusal to live by our own proclaimed standards.

October 1, 2003. In the NCAA appeal of the infractions committee [won by UM in reducing the two-year post-season ban], the NCAA concluded UM received no competitive advantage in the Martin payments, and that "the student-athletes would have competed [at Michigan] even absent the violation." The NCAA opinion goes on to conclude that the penalties should be reduced due to UM's "unique level of cooperation." Curiously, the appeals panel also concluded the "institution's extraordinary efforts transcended cooperation," and that, absent UM's insistence that Ed Martin's plea agreement include cooperation with the NCAA investigation, "there likely would have been no NCAA enforcement case."

C Webb, you can bet your last cent on it, will never go to trial on anything remotely concerning his testimony in front of the grand jury. Webber doesn't want this. Neither do the feds. In this case, it isn't just a lot of saber rattling and the fact that the emperor has no clothes. No one does. I would have thought it wasn't just Michigan that wanted Ed Martin's ashes swept under the rug, but the NCAA appeals conclusions give me pause. (While the Martin matter was pending, I engaged *Ann Arbor News* reporter Jim Carty in an informal debate about the reliability of the FBI and the federal prosecutor's office. Carty believes these officials are beyond reproach and anything said must be taken as the truth. I am, obviously, quite less trusting. While I had no reason to doubt Convertino or the specific agents involved in the Martin prosecution, there is plenty of historical data that should make one skeptical of any "political" prosecution. On January 29, 2004, an AP article appeared in the *Ann Arbor News* noting a justice department probe of Convertino and the Detroit field office of the FBI, due to the alleged failure of the feds to turn over exculpatory evidence to the defense in the prosecution of another case with political overtones, two individuals charged with and convicted of drug trafficking and financial support of Hezbollah terrorists. In addition, the probe is investigating the allegation [made by a government informant] contending the head of the FBI office [the same office involved in the Martin prosecution, I believe] told the informant "to break the law by stealing mail from people the government identified as terror suspects."

Meanwhile, Convertino has sued the justice department and, as of late March of 2004, the pissing match was ugly. Federal judge Gerald Rosen will likely conduct hearings in the summer of 2004 focusing on why more than one hundred pages of potentially exculpatory documents were not turned over to the defense.

In the late summer of 2004, Convertino got into another political cat fight, this time with the mayor of Las Vegas. The Detroit office claimed that the mayor had ignored FBI warnings about terrorism in that city. Mayor Goodman claimed there were no warnings, and this was some weird political charade being played by Convertino.)

Five *What Color Guys Say and Why We Don't Know Why They Say It*

A "color man" is a so-called expert in the broadcasting booth, whose role is to explain the intricacies of the game to the viewing or listening public. It was, in its inception, a brilliant idea, a way of making the game more accessible to the average fan and more explicable to the novice or casual viewer. The theory was to convey intelligent information about the sport, by an insider, and in the process, allow fans to become more knowledgeable about what they were viewing. In my opinion, the best football color man was Hank Stram, former coach of the Kansas City Chiefs, who won a Super Bowl in the old AFL. Stram, either on radio or television, made it clear it was never beneath him to explain basic elements of the game, such as the notion that running the football was "mostly checkers," the attempt to overload more defenders or blockers to the direction the ball carrier was going.

While driving from Cleveland to Ann Arbor on a Monday night many years ago, I heard Stram explain the point of putting a receiver in motion. He noted that the motion-back allowed the quarterback to read the defense. If, in fact, a defensive back scrambled across the formation to cover the wide receiver or the player in motion, there was a good chance the defense was playing "man," that is, certain defenders would be responsible for covering certain receivers. If, on the other hand, the adjustments in the defense were more subtle, it is likely the defense was in a zone, or some variation of a zone, where the defenders would be responsible for defined areas of the field. Theoretically, since many offenses now use sight adjustments on pass routes, the quarterback and the hot (primary) receiver read the reaction of the defense and respond (hopefully on the same page) to the route the receiver will run. Aside from this, the motion allows the offense to take advantage of a possible overload for running purposes or even to run plays away from the motion if the defense tends to overreact to the action.

Nowadays, some defenses, even at the college level, will show a "man" adjustment in a zone defense. The game has evolved to rock/scissors/paper, bluff and counter-bluff. In the fall of 2003, Michigan QB John Navarre was asked about changing plays at the line of scrimmage. He responded that this was relatively unusual in the Michigan offense, since every play called in the huddle has alternatives and, at the line, it is the QB's job to put the offense in the choice that appears most likely to work against the defense shown at the line of scrimmage. In other words, a play called in the huddle might have three variations and, when Navarre comes to the line, he calls a "color" (or number or other code) to put the offense into the variation that seems best suited for the defense he sees.

Stram conveyed the foregoing information over the course of two or three plays, and it helped my understanding of the game. Aside from this, I can't say that my limited understanding of football has ever been facilitated by the comments of a color man. To the contrary, aside from Stram, they are generally overbearing, less than literate, and complete bores.

I think that the best college football duo of the recent past has been Brad Nessler and Bob Griese (color guy), but even they provide little insight into what is going on during the game. This is pretty stunning, since Griese was known as one of the most cerebral quarterbacks who ever played, both at the college (Purdue) and the pro (Miami) level. And his son's status as a college QB (at Michigan) and NFL (minor) star should give him a unique ability to convey something challenging or interesting about the game. I think Griese is about as good as it gets in the college world, but only because he and Nessler are nearly singular in their ability to not irritate. It is rare for Griese to give the fan very much. Or, at least, you have to pay very close attention.

One of my favorite sequences of the 2000 season took place in the Michigan-Indiana game, a game I attended. With Indiana trailing 10–0, the Hoosiers drove the ball to the Michigan twenty, behind their exciting and unpredictable quarterback, Antwaan Randle-El. On the next two plays, it all unraveled for the Hoosiers, as they lost thirty-five yards and were faced with a third and forty-five. At this point, Nessler made a prescient call—that Indiana might want to try a quick kick out of a short punt (shotgun) formation. This was, indeed, a reasonable tactic, and Indiana coach Cam Cameron elected the option. He forgot, however, to tell Randle-El to kick the ball higher than six inches from the ground. In a punting motion that was reminiscent of a stray swipe at a croquet ball, the Indiana QB knocked the pigskin into the back of his center. The ball bounced backward, and all twenty-two players stared at it, not sure what to do. The ball rested on the turf, forlorn and alone. No one moved. The ball was lonely. The officials stared at one another. No one moved. And then the players milled around. Big crowd today, huh? But no one touched the ball. Anthrax? Doo-doo? Too icky to touch? No one moved. Finally the referee blew the play dead. Everyone assumed it was Michigan's ball, even

Nessler and Griese in the broadcasting booth, with Griese giving praise to Nessler on his prediction.

But it was not Michigan's ball, apparently, because a blocked kick that does not cross the line of scrimmage and is not recovered by the defense does not automatically become the defense's ball. (No, I didn't know this either. No fan knew this, because no one had ever seen such a meshuga play before.) Ordinarily, of course, the ball would belong to the defense, since the offense had run out of downs. But in this case, it was third down. My brother, dubbed by another (possibly deranged) Indiana coach as the Worst-Fan in the United States (more later), was beside himself in the stands. How the @#$#^&% can any team be so lucky? And, I admit, the worst fan's brother thought the zebras had blown it, and (carefully and incorrectly) explained to everyone in the stadium how it should have been called.

As Indiana went into an ordinary punting formation, Griese congratulated the referees on getting it right. Like Griese had any clue whatsoever as to what the hell was going on. And, in any event, the referees did blow it by whistling the play dead as the ball snuggled the turf, naked and unwanted. None of it mattered, of course, since Cameron resorted to an old intramural ruse on fourth and forty-nine, and instructed his punter to have the next punt blocked, almost certainly the first time in history that consecutive plays resulted in consecutive blocked punts. This time Indiana executed correctly, and Michigan obliged by running the ball in for a touchdown on the way to a 58–0 win.

In an afternoon in September of 2002, I heard two pairs of commentators that threatened Nessler and Griese. The first, the ND duo of Tom Hammond and Pat Haden, were objective and even-handed in the call of Notre Dame's 25–23 victory over the Wolverines. I can't say I learned anything from the pair, but they were smooth and inoffensive in calling the upset. So much so that I hardly noticed the game was being called. Later I watched much of the MSU-Cal game, hosted (on ESPN2) by Pam Ward and Chris Spielman. This crew goes to the head of the class. Ward has a terrific voice and demeanor, and she never gets in Spielman's way. Spielman really knows his stuff and, like Hank Stram, is not above pointing out the basics. As an isolated example, Spielman explained the meaning of "one technique," where a defensive tackle or nose guard lines up in the gap between the center and guard in an attempt to split the defense and break down the blocking schemes. This level of commentary is truly rare, and this pair is so far ahead of everyone calling the game right now, including the NFL pairs, that I worry for their existence. And, yes, I am jealous that OSU beat us for Chris's services. He is impressive. Did I mention that Thomas Dewey was a UM grad? What? He didn't win the presidency? We are blessed. The venal and pointless Anne Coulter is still a Michigan law grad? Can we trade her for Harry Chiti? [Note: Spielman was out of the "color" business in 2004.]

The most salient color for me in the 2000 season was conveyed in the Michigan-Ohio State game, containing both the most subtle and least informative commentary of the season. The duo in the booth was Nessler-Griese, and they were backed by Lynn Swann on the field. Over the course of the 2000 season, I developed a sort of paradigm of teams that Michigan played well against and those they failed against. Against balanced teams, particularly teams that had spread the field (Purdue, Northwestern, UCLA) the Michigan defense had been inept. Against more standard pro-style offenses, the Wolverines looked very good, particularly if the opposition's quarterback was less than a star in heaving the ball (MSU, Wisconsin, Penn State, Indiana). The paradigm predicted a pretty close game against the Buckeyes, since OSU looked a lot like MSU, Wisconsin, and Penn State, and not a bit like Purdue or Northwestern. The difference for me was that the game was played on the road (where Michigan had played poorly against all of its opponents), and my instinct that the John Cooper jinx just could not continue.

OSU had won two of its last twelve games against Michigan, and some of those OSU teams were markedly more talented than the Michigan teams they faced. Now, I admit, this is the everyday person's notion of the law of averages. So let's go back to basics. I toss a coin twenty times. It comes up heads twenty times in a row. What is the likelihood of the coin coming up heads on the next toss? Yep. You're right. The answer is "about 50 percent." Or "exactly 50 percent," if you are into such things. But don't tell this to the average Northwestern fan (call him Brent), who will insist that the law of averages means it is much more likely that the twenty-first toss will be tails. This said, I couldn't shake the belief that OSU was going to kick us around. It was about time, wasn't it? This streak of heads had to stop some time, didn't it? So, on the one hand, you had (a) a good OSU defense, but not as good as MSU or Wisconsin, (b) a good OSU running game but not as good as Wisconsin, (c) a quarterback who was mobile and athletic but an erratic thrower, sorta like PSU, and (d) not much in the receiving corps, sorta like all of the above. Logically, if the Michigan offense could click, this was a game Michigan should win. Still, I just could not get beyond the feeling that UM was due for some evil juju. Keeping it simple, my magic eight ball called it a Michigan loss. My diary entry after the OSU game is reproduced. The entry includes the best and worst of the color man universe.

November 20, 2000. Of course I am wrong. Call me Beano. And, maybe, good-bye to John Cooper. I hate to see him go, since, or so I guess, OSU will hire someone who ups the competitive ante. OSU opens the game with an eighty-yard kickoff return, and then, on fourth and inches from the Michigan ten, breaks a play for a TD. OSU misses the extra point, but intercepts Drew Henson on the first Michigan series. The UM defense holds, but OSU converts a short field goal. 9–0 OSU, and the crowd seems moderately excited. And the game has hardly started. The Buckeye defense is playing with extreme abandon, pressuring the line of scrimmage and Henson. On third and ten from their own thirty UM offensive coordinator Stan Parish calls a screen pass to Anthony Thomas, a perfect call against the OSU rush, and the A-Train outruns and outfights the OSU secondary for a seventy-yard touchdown. No. Wait. It was a predictable call. Michigan fans hate predictable calls. And John Madden says (ad nauseam), a screen play on third and long is a "give up" play. I know. I have a solution. Let's not count it.

On OSU's third series, the Michigan defense has the Buckeyes bottled up with a fourth and twelve at the OSU thirty-eight. Michigan rushes the punter and Brandon Williams blocks the kick, the ball bouncing away from the line of scrimmage. This must be the year for weird kicking events, since an OSU player scoops up the ball and runs twenty-five yards downfield for a first down. Like the third down punt in the Indiana game, it is an event I have never witnessed in the thousands of games I have seen, except when we used to do this intentionally when we played in the backyard as kids. And, like the Indiana event, (a) I cursed the football fates and Michigan's awful juju, but (b) the next play reversed the course of the game like a McLuhan tetrad at warp speed. On first down, Bellisari drops back and throws a meatball into the hands of Michigan linebacker Larry Foote. Henson then throws the ball twice to David Terrell. The second is for a TD. It is 14–9 Michigan, and I have never heard it so quiet in Columbus. OSU's fans, rarely the frontrunners like the UM faithful, seem to have given up with a mere five-point deficit.

In the broadcast booth, Brad Nessler and Bob Griese are crowing about the fact that the game is becoming an atypical UM-OSU affair. In other words, some points are actually going to be scored, so they can put down their bottles of Wild Turkey. At this juncture, Griese also mentions that he bumped into several OSU fans on the way to the game who suggested that Griese would root for Michigan. Griese informed these folks that he was a Purdue graduate and fan, despite the place of his son's matriculation. And, he stressed, Purdue and Michigan were yet competing for the conference championship and Rose Bowl berth. Apparently the Ohio State fans weren't one hundred percent convinced of Griese's objectivity. I called Griese, and he was kind enough to provide me with a transcript of the exchange:

OSU Guy: Hey, Mr. Griese, don't you think there may be an ethical violation with the fact that you are calling the game and you are a Michigan fan?

Griese: I graduated from Purdue.

OSU Guy: Didn't your son play for Michigan?

Griese:	Yes. But I am a Purdue fan. Brian doesn't play for Michigan anymore.
OSU Guy:	Perhaps. But don't you have a sort of fiduciary obligation to the audience to be unbiased, and might not some find this to be somewhat bothersome?
Griese:	Well, actually, I am a Purdue graduate and fan.
OSU Guy:	Even if I take that at face value, don't you think there is an appearance of impropriety that should be disclosed?
Griese:	I don't root for Michigan. I always try to be even-handed.
OSU Guy:	And don't you think it might be right for you to make no commentary on anything but the ministerial aspects of the game?
Griese:	Well, Brent Musburger graduated from Northwestern. Todd Christenson from Stanford. Kirk Herbstreit, who does subjective commentary about the Big Ten, graduated from OSU. Lee Corso coached at Indiana. I think Tim Brant might have graduated from third grade, though that's uncertain. All of us in the business have biases, but we attempt to be honest about them and call the game as fairly as possible.
OSU Guy:	Isn't this really an ontological issue that you have not completely dissected in a rational fashion . . .

Exactly. I have had numerous conversations with OSU football fans in Columbus (when they weren't occupied torching cars after a big victory), and they were all very much like this. And, I am sure, that's why Griese brought it up in the clever and sideways way that it came out. I, at least, appreciated it, for these urbane confrontations with OSU football fans are truly stimulating, and the civility of the conversation must have stuck in his mind. As they have mine.

In any event, it seems what Griese and Nessler are rooting for is a shootout, but the next two series both stall, with Michigan punting to the Buckeyes early in the second quarter. The Buckeyes then falter at their own thirty-eight and, on fourth and three, they attempt a fake punt, the punter passing the ball to a receiver in the flat. The play is well-executed and, from the film, I would surmise there was a 99 percent possibility the receiver would make the first down. Except for one thing. He drops the lob pass. But Michigan returns the favor, driving to the OSU twenty and, on fourth and five, they attempt a fake field goal. Hayden Epstein fakes the kick while John Navarre picks up the snap and runs. It is also a reasonably well-executed play, but Navarre gains four-and-a-half yards, not enough for the first down. In the midst of these two series, Brad Nessler comments that Steve Bellisari "is never gonna be one of those guys who completes 75 percent of his passes." Oh really? And exactly what subset of guys are completing passes at the rate of 75 percent, Brad?

Between plays I looked it up, and it turns out it is a null set, since no one has ever finished a career (or season) completing 75 percent of his passes. The closest for a season is Daunte Culpepper at Central Florida in 1998 (now with the Minnesota Vikings) with the startling (to me) percentage of 73.6 percent. The highest percentage for a career is owned by Tim Couch (of Kentucky), who completed passes at the rate of 67.1 percent. There is no subset of 75 percent passers. There is no subset of 70 percent passers. And, in fact, there is no real subset of "one of those guys" who completes 65 percent of his passes. Now, it is fair to write Nessler's comment off as mere puffing, a sort of "touchdown named desire" in the realm of the senses. And, after all, who am I to complain about exaggeration? And maybe Nessler felt some compulsion to compete with the moronic stuff that Brent spews. But since there is only one guy *ever* who has completed 67 percent of his passes, isn't Nessler's comment like saying, "Bye Bye Balboni has never really been one of those guys who's going to hit .432," where a .432 batting average reflects the relative difference between Culpepper's 73.6 percent and 75 percent and Rogers Hornsby's (record) of .424 and .432? Or, in relation to Ty Cobb's .366 lifetime average and Couch's 67.1 percent, substitute .410. Wouldn't whoever came up with this one be pilloried? Okay, I am making too much of this. What Nessler should have really said was, this is a "fake" Michigan-OSU game, a comment that would have been appropriate in the context of the game's history and moment. And exactly in conformity with Griese's comment about his urbane conversations with OSU fans.

Meanwhile, it is punt, punt, and punt in the game, even with a sixty-yard gain (counting a face mask penalty) on a long pass from Drew Henson to freshman Calvin Bell. OSU gets the ball back on its own eighteen with a little more than two minutes left in the half, and on this drive, Bellisari looks like "one of those 75 percent passers," slicing the Michigan defense like some Kustok cheese. But as the field shrinks, Michigan tightens up and OSU kicks another short field goal. 14–12 UM at the half.

The Wolverines start with the ball in the second half, and Michigan grinds a drive to the OSU thirty-five. On fourth and two, Michigan tries another fake field goal (I am absolutely certain that Michigan, at least since 1966, has not tried two fake field goals in a game), and this time it works, BJ Askew gaining a first down. Henson follows this with a strike to the end zone to David Terrell. Michigan leads 21–12 and, on the next series, Bellisari makes an ill-advised throw and the ball is intercepted. Michigan then lucks out when Henson is hit as he is throwing and the ball flutters twenty-five yards downfield to Marquise Walker. The Wolverines can't score, but Hayden Epstein kicks a field goal. And, within a minute, Bellisari makes another bad read, with Julius Curry picking off a pass and racing to the end zone for a touchdown. It is now 31–12 and Ohio State is three and out on their next series. Michigan has the ball on its own twenty. There is 2:33 left in the quarter and the Wolverines manage to eke out a first down. On third and five from the thirty-five (the first play in the fourth quarter) Stan Parish returns to the screen and AT rambles for a sixty-five-yard touchdown. The play, however, is nullified by an illegal block in the back (a good call) and a draw play on third and fifteen is stuffed. Michigan is up by nineteen and it is the fourth quarter, but I am beginning to feel the collar.

Michigan punts and the Buckeyes put together an impressive drive, pushing the ball to the Michigan sixteen. On third and two, Bellisari's pass is blocked by Carl Diggs and the ball floats in the air, hanging above the ten-yard line for a jump ball. OSU wins the jump and gets the first down, but then the OSU quarterback throws consecutive incompletions. On third down, Bellisari throws to the end zone and Todd Howard's coverage is perfect, but pass interference is called. OSU punches it in on the next play and it is 31–19 with 10:20 to go.

The Michigan offense then opens the gates with a three and out, punting to OSU at midfield. It takes five plays for OSU to score, and it is 31–26 with 7:03 left in the game. Michigan goes back to the screen and it works again, Thomas gaining nineteen yards. Two A-Train runs yield a first down at midfield, but then the Michigan drive ends as two long passes to Terrell fall incomplete. Michigan punts to the OSU nine. Bellisari throws two incompletions, and a short pass gains nine yards. It is fourth and one at the OSU eighteen with 3:30 left in the game. OSU has all of its timeouts. It is a difficult decision, but Cooper goes for it. The crowd is in a frenzy until an off-tackle play is stopped for no gain. Michigan takes over and five plays later, the Bucks have used their timeouts and Michigan has a fourth and goal at the one-yard line. A minute and 23 seconds is left on the clock. Now Carr is faced with a difficult choice, since an 8-point lead means OSU will have to (a) traverse the field with no timeouts (call it one in four), (b) score a two-point conversion (one in three), and (c) win in OT (one in two). In other words, if Michigan kicks the field goal, OSU wins about one time in twenty-four. But Carr goes for it, since (a) moving ninety-nine yards with (about) 1:18 and no timeouts left is probably no better than one in ten, and (b) scoring from the one (an absolute win) is about one in two. Probably not much different than a push, but Carr's choice seems more satisfying than backing into the game. And particularly so when the Michigan staff has a play it has not used all year and one it must have believed had a better than fifty-fifty chance to score. Michigan loads the formation to the right side with two blocking backs and a tight end. On the snap, Henson pivots to the overloaded side of the formation and seems to hand the ball off to AT, who dives toward the end zone. But it is a fake, Henson hiding the ball behind his leg, reversing the pivot, and sprinting left to the end zone. It is no contest, Henson goes in standing up. Michigan wins 38–26. On the sidelines, David Terrell and David Brandt hug. Coach Carr and assistant coach Fred Jackson hug. And John Cooper is frustrated and unhappy, stomping and cursing at the air. I have to admit, I feel sorry for Cooper. Legitimately sorry. But not sorry enough to try that last play again. Hang on, Sloopy.

* * * *

After Thanksgiving, I watched the Michigan-OSU tape for the first time. On Michigan's last drive, as it appeared that the Wolverines might again lose a lead in the fourth quarter, Bob Griese suggested that Michigan has had trouble over the season by "sitting on leads." I think, in the main, this was an inaccurate commentary, though it is one that can be argued. Lynn Swann, however, picked up on this thread and noted (slurring his words heavily) that Michigan in the "entire second half did not throw a pass from their side of the field." Well, it was cold and I don't know if Lynn had been passed the Wild Turkey from the broadcasting booth or if he had just discovered some stray anti-freeze on the sidelines, but, *exactly one play* prior to this comment, Michigan had thrown a pass (for a nineteen-yard gain) from its own twenty-one-yard line. Lynn is a legit icon and perhaps should be excused for some short-term memory problems. I have some of my own. But let's look at the half:

> First Series: Michigan had five plays on its side of the
> fifty. They threw on two of these plays, for gains of six and
> twelve yards. As an aside, Michigan threw twice in OSU terri-
> tory, the second for a thirty-three-yard touchdown.

> Second Series: Michigan received the ball at the OSU forty-
> three. There were no plays in Michigan territory. Michigan did
> gain twenty-five yards on a pass play in Buckeye territory on
> the way to a field goal.

Third Series: Michigan intercepted the ball and ran it in for a touchdown. There were no plays from scrimmage.

Fourth Series: Here, Swann was arguably right. Michigan gained a first down on three runs. They ran twice more and then threw a sixty-five-yard touchdown pass. The play was called back, and then a draw lost yards. Swann's accuracy here is strictly technical.

Fifth Series: Three plays, all in Michigan territory. Michigan threw on third down. Incomplete. They also called a pass play on second down, but Henson was pressured and scrambled for no gain. So, two of our three calls were pass plays. I know that is hardly any, so I guess it is fair to characterize it as "none."

Sixth Series: This is where Swann made his comment, one play after a nineteen-yard gain (a pass) from the UM twenty-one to the UM forty. But, heck, it is only one pass, so we might as well call this "none" also.

Okay. I know it was cold on the field. And I know I have had some bad days at work too. But how in the world can the guy be this far off? What the hell was he doing most of the half? Dancing with the cheerleaders? Trading nut pick-up lines with Brutus the Buckeye? Looking for the Michigan mascot? I think the latter is the most likely. Then Lynn Swann could (accurately) report that he had been searching for the Michigan mascot for the entire half, and can now report that Michigan must have been very pessimistic and distressed about the outcome of the game to have not even sent a single mascot to the contest.

The worst color man, in my opinion, is Tim Brant. First, he is an idiot. Second, he is really an idiot. Third, he tends to root for teams (PAC Twelve teams against Midwest teams) within the pretense of objective commentary. If Brant would just root straight up, like Bob Ufer or Johnny Most (the old Celtics broadcaster), it would be no big deal. Or if he would just admit his biases and do his best, I would have no issue. In this vein, Griese's inevitable rooting for Michigan when his kid played never bothered me. He tried to be neutral, but it was no secret, when his son was the QB at Michigan, where his heart was. The same was true in 2000 in the Northwestern-Michigan game. The game was called by Brent Musburger and Gary Danielson. Brent is a Northwestern graduate. Danielson's son was a backup quarterback for the Wildcats. It was certain the duo was rooting for Northwestern, but this was no secret; they would have been less than human if they were not rooting for the Cats.

Moreover, while admitting their biases, the duo bent over backward to be fair to the Wolverines, the same as Griese tended to do in calling games where his son was a participant. In Brant's case, his pretenses are less irritating than his stupidity. (Note: In 2002, I heard [I hope] Brant doing play by play. He wasn't bad. He should stick to this and drop all color commentary.)

In the 2000 UCLA-Michigan affair, Brant was paired with the truly great (but now really losing it) Keith Jackson. Early in the game, Tim whined about an obviously illegal block against UCLA with the complaint that the Bruin offender "tried to pull back," as if *mens rea* (intent) had anything to do with the call. In Brantland, apparently, officials can or should only call violations if they are volitional. In the third quarter, after John Navarre threw an out pass into the hands of a linebacker (dropped), Tim intoned that, "Navarre never looked off the receiver." He then proclaimed the reason the linebacker dropped the ball was that "it surprised him." Hmmm. What is it? If the LB was watching the QB to the level suggested, it would seem unlikely that surprise was the cause of the dropped pass. If it did surprise him, then it would seem that the fact that Navarre was "locked on" was irrelevant.

When Julius Curry intercepted a pass and he was (erroneously) called out of bounds, Brant's explanation/rationalization was that it was "called right away" and, apparently, this mitigated the replay that showed the interception to be easily inbounds. Okay, I get it. If a UCLA player commits an illegal block, it should be questioned because Brant can discern that the guy "didn't mean it." But if a Michigan player intercepts a pass and the replay shows the call to have been blown, it is okay because "it was called right away." What if Curry didn't really mean to intercept the ball? Would that make any difference? What if it was called right, but not "right away?" Should we take it back? What if it took the refs a minute to decide, and the replay showed they were right, should they then be the subjects of criticism?

Then—a complete Brant classic. Navarre missed an open receiver for a TD. On the same play, he had a receiver open (and uncovered) about ten yards down the field. Brant's commentary was, "Navarre very wisely threw it away," proving, apparently, that the QB is "calm under fire." Navarre did seem calm. He didn't take his helmet off and I didn't take his pulse, but he did seem calm. But missing two open receivers, one for a touchdown, hardly seems proof of the wisdom of the pass or evidence of being calm. Later, halfway through the fourth quarter, Brant complained that "penalties are just killing UCLA" after the Bruins received a five-yard procedure call. Keith Jackson pointed out, at this juncture, that it was the first penalty against UCLA in the half. No response from Tim on this one.

Brant and Jackson also called the 2001 Michigan-Washington game. Keith, sadly, has moved from the great to the near-senile, illustrating merely a shell of his former magnificent abilities. And Brant, though not as bad as in his 2000

UCLA effort, was inept beyond comprehension. One of my favorites in this game was Tim's woeful attempt to use a telestrator. After John Navarre was sacked in the first half, Brant tried to show that a blitz from both of the inside linebackers did Navarre in. He circled the LBs and then drew arrows to show where the LBs filled the gaps between the defensive linemen. One problem. Once the film rolled, it was apparent that both of these Washington players were in coverage, neither blitzed. Silence from Keith.

Midway through the third quarter, as the Michigan offensive line seemed to be gaining momentum in controlling the Washington defense, the following colloquy occurred between a fan and Brant. I admit, of course, that only Tim's side of the conversation could be heard, but I have a reliable tape of the exchange:

> Ross: Hey Tim, doesn't it look like the Michigan offensive line is taking over the game? Doesn't Washington need to change it up? As the biggest Washington homer since the White House, what would you advise?

> Brant: Now the safeties have to recognize the formation, make the calls. They have been able to do that because of Michigan's tendencies in certain formations and the Huskies know, they key on the recognition.

I cleaned up the grammar but otherwise, this was exactly as conveyed and now, I know, I really am beginning to understand the game. From here on in, I promise to "key on the recognition."

Aside from being incoherent, Brant's major contribution to football theory is his continual harping about quarterbacks "looking off" or "locking onto" receivers. This, to be fair, is a standard mantra of color guys and a continual bitch by fans. I have always been suspicious of this analysis, and my guess is, in the main, this is just something people say since they appreciate little of what is going on before them. First, in my admittedly limited experience playing defensive back, I can never recall watching a quarterback's eyes while I was in man coverage. I was too busy keeping track of my man and, once he looked back, I then looked for the ball. My best estimate is that no DB chasing Braylon Edwards all over the field has the ability to concentrate on the quarterback's line of vision. And, if there is someone so able, my money is on the probability that he is getting burned. Zone coverage is another matter, but my surmise is that this advantage of the quarterback is still overrated. A quarterback generally has about three seconds to throw the ball and, given this, he does not have the opportunity to swivel his head all over the field. If he has significantly more time than this, he might. But give any quarterback a lot of

116

time to throw, and you are going to be in trouble, regardless of whether he looks off receivers. And it might be the case, after all, that at the moment the QB looks away from the primary (best) receiver, that receiver comes clear. But this is just my instinct. I decided to watch some tape.

I watched a lot of tape. And, at the college level at least, almost no one ever looked off a receiver. And, when they did, it was absolutely no guarantee of success. To the contrary, "looking off a receiver" instances (though pretty rare) tended to be no more successful than those cases where the quarterback completely "locked on" to one receiver. I focused, in particular, on the 1999 Purdue game. Since Drew Brees was the most successful quarterback Michigan played against in that year, it would seem if anyone looked off receivers, it would be Brees. In fact, except when he was being pounded to the turf, Brees almost never looked off a receiver in the Michigan game. The more I have paid attention to this, the more I am convinced it is a complete flat-earth theory. This is not to assert it is not important for a quarterback to see the field. I would suggest this ability is absolutely key. But this seeing engenders a range of skills: (a) knowing whether the defense is in zone or man, (b) feeling the pressure of the rush, (c) understanding where your receivers are in relation to the defense, and (d) (the most important factor) understanding what throws are safe in conditions (a) to (c) and probably a lot of others. But there is no way that defensive backs are reading the quarterback in the fashion suggested by critics on anything but a very now-and-then circumstance. And, by my best guess, a good quarterback does not need to swivel his head to see the field. My surmise is Brees is able to read the defense, know where his receivers are, and has the ability to see a broad range of activity before him without moving his head.

When I mentioned this "lock on" stuff to another fan, he suggested I had stacked the deck by looking at the 1999 Purdue game, a game dominated by Michigan. "Why not look at the 2000 game?" he suggested. "Because that was a complete shoot-out and both quarterbacks had a high level of success." I had to admit this was a reasonable point. I watched the game. In that contest, Drew Henson completed twenty-six of thirty-five passes for 256 yards. How many times did Henson lock on a receiver? Every time. One hundred percent. What about Drew Brees? He was thirty-two of forty-five for 286 yards. Brees did, on four instances, look off a receiver. The first of these, when he had about six seconds to throw, was incomplete. The second, a designed look-off play, was intercepted, the only turnover in the game. The third and fourth throws, when pressured (nominally) in the pocket, were also incomplete. That's it. So when Brees locked on a receiver, he was thirty-two of forty-one or 78 percent. When he "looked off," he was 0 for 4 with one interception. Less than zero percent. This locking on stuff is a very exaggerated notion.

In the 2002 Michigan-Notre Dame game, there was criticism of John Navarre when he forced a ball into coverage on a two-point attempt near the end of the game that would have tied the score. Many fans pointed out that BJ Askew came clear and was open in the end zone on the other side of the field. The fans were right, except that Askew was blocking and only came clear at the moment that Navarre threw the ball. And, if Navarre looked back to his left, it is possible that any opportunity with the primary receivers would have evaporated. Or he might be sacked. The real problem on the play was that the wideouts ran routes that were too shallow, and ran the DBs to the same area of the field, creating a traffic jam.

The locking-on notion has become a fan epidemic. A virus. Two weeks after the 2002 Notre Dame loss, Navarre shredded an Illini defense that was intent upon pressuring the line of scrimmage and taking away the run. This left mostly man coverage over the course of the game, and Navarre took advantage of the Illini gamble, throwing for four TDs with no INTs. Incredibly, many UM fans still whined about the performance, complaining that Navarre was still locking on. Maybe we are just dumber-than-average fans.

Brant (again, he shares the frailty with other color men) also consistently complains about "slow developing" plays. I know, for a fact, coaches stay up nights devising new variations on slow plays so that their offensive lines are pressured and the coaches will look stupid to the average fan. Here's the tape on this one:

> Coach Carr: Hey Coach, do you think we can design some slow
>   developing plays this year to give the fans and Tim
>   Brant something to complain about?
>
> Coach Malone: Can do, Coach. That way, when the offense goes
>   in the tank, I can be the scapegoat.

Yep, just like this. Let me give you a clue. A slow developing play is either a trick play or a reverse, something that is never complained about as slow developing, or it is a play that the defense blew up. There is nothing to discern in the commentary. Next time you hear one of these guys complain about slow development, you should know he is clueless. If he tells you why a play didn't work, you can pay attention. But unless it is Spielman, you might not be hearing anything of value.

A final note on color men. One should not write about the topic, at least in relation to Michigan football, without keying on the recognition that Tom Harmon once played the role of a color man in the famed movie *Bonzo Goes to College*. With Bonzo the chimp leading Unknown U to victory, Harmon intoned, "I sure am glad I didn't have to face Bonzo in my playing days at the University of Michigan." Honest. The lead actor in the movie? Who else? The Gipper. Yep. Ronald Reagan.

My thoughts about *Bonzo* led me to consider who might be the greatest Michigan quarterback of all time. During the Bo years, I think many would have viewed this as strictly local color, though Schembechler did have three fine option QBs in Dennis Franklin, Rick Leach, and Steve Smith. Plus, Bo inherited Don Moorehead, a terrific throwback combination run/pass quarterback who led the Wolverines over Ohio State in 1969. Of course, once Bo recruited Anthony Carter, the days of the option were nearly over, Bo reluctantly resorting to John Wangler and other passing QBs. Post-Bo, the issue becomes quite problematic, since Michigan has seen quarterbacking that is as good (or probably better) than any other major college program. Michigan fans have had the luxury of enjoying the consistently good QB play of Elvis Grbac, Todd Collins, Brian Griese, Jim Harbaugh, Drew Henson, and Tom Brady. And, I promise, there is more to come in the person of Chad Henne. I doubt if any school has ever had a better run of players at the position. Or, at least, such instances are unusual.

Any discussion of Michigan QB play has to start with Benny Friedman (UM, 1924–26), the QB portion of "Benny to Bennie" (Oosterbaan) during the final years of Fielding Yost's coaching tenure. Though I never saw Friedman play (very few living have), I admit a bias toward him, since he was a scrawny kid from Cleveland and was the first great passing quarterback in the history of the game. Friedman played in the NFL at a time when there were few viable franchises, and the competition for a genuinely paying roster spot was more fierce than today. Few realize that Friedman was a star in the NFL and an All-Pro selection for five consecutive years. While comprehensive records were not kept in the NFL in that era, it is known that in 1928 Friedman lead the NFL in rushing touchdowns and touchdown passes, something no other player has accomplished. No player will accomplish this feat in the future. In 1929, Benny threw twenty touchdown passes in the season, a record that stood for many years. As a comparison, Hall of Famer Ernie Nevers threw six TDs that year, a relatively high number at that time. Sammy Baugh, in his first three years in the NFL (1937–1939) threw a total of nineteen touchdown passes, despite playing with a more aerodynamic ball.

Friedman was originally signed by the Cleveland Bulldogs, but moved to the Detroit Wolverines in 1928. He was so dominant in Detroit that the New York Giants made numerous entreaties to the Detroit franchise to procure his services. When the Wolverines refused to part with Benny, the Giants purchased the entire team. New York then released most of the players and signed Benny to a ten-thousand-dollar-per-year contract, the highest amount ever paid a football player. Some things never change vis-à-vis New York teams and Michigan quarterbacks.

It is no exaggeration to say that Friedman was the player who most changed the face of professional football, from a mostly pound-it-right-at-you running game to a game that also relied on finesse and the pass. Indeed, Friedman's estimated statistics are that he threw for more than seven thousand five hundred yards (sixty-eight TD passes), and ran for more than two thousand yards during his years as a pro, incredible numbers for the time. These numbers dwarf those of any other quarterback of his era, and *Sports Illustrated* ranked him as the number twenty-nine quarterback of all time, the only QB playing prior to 1935 to make the list. In Robert W. Peterson's excellent book *Pigskin: The Early Days of Pro Football* (1997), he writes about Friedman as follows:

> In Cleveland, the new Bulldogs ... were giving a preview of things to come in the passing of tailback Benny Friedman ... who had starred for three years on Fielding Yost's University of Michigan powerhouse teams. Said Yost, "In Benny Friedman I have one of the greatest passers and smartest quarterbacks in history."

> As a rookie professional, Friedman thought nothing of passing on first down (gasp) which was heresy to traditionalists. In thirteen games he tossed twelve touchdown passes and gained more than 1,700 yards with passes—far higher figures than the league had ever seen. It was a revelation to football men, who could not believe that the fat ball of the time could be passed so successfully.

Note the word "tailback," in that Friedman played in the single wing, where the tailback was the predominant ball handler and passer.

Sadly, Friedman had a leg amputated in his later years due to a blood clot, and then began to suffer from shingles. He killed himself at age seventy-seven in 1982, leaving a note that he did "not want to be some cripple on a park bench." It is an oddity, at least, that Friedman is not in the pro football Hall of

Fame. Some journalists have suggested that Benny was not the most pleasant guy to be around, and that he tended to be a braggart about his career and a whiner about not being inducted into the Canton, Ohio shrine. Wow. This is a new one among great athletes, or humans for that matter. No whiners or boasters allowed.

The fact is there is no rational explanation for his omission from the HOF, particularly where far lesser players (think Paul Hornung, as an isolated example) are enshrined. Friedman's exclusion is particularly extraordinary because he was the head coach at CCNY for seven years and then enlisted in the Navy at age thirty-seven so as to be a part of the war effort in World War II. After the war, he was the head coach and athletic director at Brandeis for fifteen years. So Benny remained a part of the football and social scene. He did not disappear into the netherworld.

Friedman was the quarterback when Michigan lost to Illinois 39–14 on Red Grange's greatest day, the day Grange scored four touchdowns in twelve minutes and became a legend. But Benny also played (both ways) the following year, when the Wolverines stomped Illinois (well, it was 3–0) and held Grange to negative fifty-four yards on twenty-seven carries. I have been told by a fan who was at the game that the Illini decided to use some slow developing plays in the rematch just to even things up. In that game Friedman tackled Grange ten times for losses. A few years after the game, the ever-gracious Grange said that Benny was the greatest player he ever saw or competed against, claiming that "Friedman could run, pass, kick, and tackle . . . all I could do was run." Yeah, I forgot. Friedman was the placekicker, too. A very good one, kicking (among many others) the winning field goal against the Illini, and a forty-three yarder against OSU in a 17–16 victory in 1926. The kick was made from an impossible angle, the ball being spotted five yards from the sidelines in the days prior to hash marks.

Bennie Oosterbaan also said that Friedman was a "great blocker," a part of the tailback's responsibilities in the single wing. So, maybe Friedman had a right to be bitter about his exclusion from the Hall. Maybe he believed there was something else afoot. So I checked out the writings of the prominent football journalist of the time, Paul Gallico. Gallico said that Friedman, to that time, was "the greatest football player that ever lived," and that

> The things that a perfect football player must do are kick, pass, run the ends, plunge the line, block, tackle, weave his way through broken fields, drop and place kick, interfere, diagnose plays, spot enemy weaknesses, direct an offense, and not get hurt. I have just been describing Benny Friedman's repertoire to you.

Okay, but what about his pro numbers? Maybe they really weren't that great. Recently, football historian David Neft reconstructed early professional football statistics and discovered that when Friedman retired, he was one of the top five all-time rushers in the NFL and by far the top all-time passer. It was not until Sammy Baugh's seventh season in 1943 (with a different ball and liberalized passing rules) that he eclipsed Friedman in passing yards. Neft compared Friedman to the second best quarterback in his first four NFL seasons, before injuries and the decision to be a part-time coach at Yale limited his career:

	TD Passes		
Friedman		Next Highest	
1927	12	McBride	7
1928	10	Wilson	5
1929	20	Nevers	6
1930	13	Dunn	9
Total	55	#2	28

	Yards Passing		
Friedman		Next Highest	
1927	1721+	Nevers	1362+
1928	1120+	Wilson	906+
1929	1566+	Kelly	677+
1930	1246+	Dunn	825+
Total	5653+	#2	3770+

The fact is that Friedman *invented* passing, both in college and the pros, in the sense that he was the first player to use passing as an ordinary part of his offense. Aside from this, no one in the NFL has ever performed at this relative level. Not Joe Montana. Not Jim Brown. Not Bonzo.

What Neft also discovered was that Friedman averaged 5.6 yards per carry in the pros (I guarantee you no quarterback has ever done this, though Fran Tarkenton's numbers may be more spectacular), higher yards per attempt than anyone, ever. Jim Brown, at 5.22 yards, is listed as the best ever in the official NFL tomes. Plus, Friedman returned punts for an average (over his career) of 15.3 yards per return. How good is this? Well, David Meggitt, the all-time leader in the number of punts returned, averaged 10.6 yards over his career. And, among players who have returned at least seventy-five punts, only one player, Darrien Gordon from the Chargers, comes close, with a 13.6 yards per return average. So I guess it is fair to conclude Friedman was pretty good at that aspect of the game. These numbers are even better than those of another skinny, Jewish Michigan Alum from Cleveland, Desmond Howard. Beyond this, Neft points out that Friedman also punted in the pros (though only twenty-three times), routinely kicked extra points, and kicked a couple of field goals. He also caught ten passes in his career and had many interceptions as a defensive back.

I think it is likely that Jim Brown is the greatest offensive player in the history of the game. He was, by far, the best I ever saw, so much so it is hard to choose a competitor. But in arguing the point of the "greatest player ever," one's list has to include Friedman. To exclude Friedman from consideration would be akin to excluding Babe Ruth from the equivalent discussion in baseball. At the least, Friedman invented the modern game. And he is both forgotten and not in the Hall of Fame.

Given the foregoing, I assume Friedman must have been a real bad guy, a career criminal or schmo of the *n*th degree. How else can his exclusion from the Hall of Fame be explained? But the worst I could find was that some journalists thought he was a braggart. If he was, it didn't keep him from helping aspiring passers (all over the country), sometimes at no compensation and at his own expense. And the folks at Brandeis were reasonably satisfied with Friedman's role at that university. Benny essentially established sports at Brandeis and, in 1972, was awarded a distinguished contribution award "emphasizing that he had never let them lose sight of the fact that their true purpose at Brandeis was their physical and intellectual development." Friedman was an initial inductee into the Brandeis Sports Hall of Fame and, in 1998, he was recognized as one of the great contributors to the university. Aside from his athletic history, Brandeis had this to say:

> Benny is admired and respected by the athletes he coached. He committed himself to them from the very beginning, when they came to play for him in a program operating on a dream and a shoestring. His practices were not just about making them better football players. Rather, it was an environment that stressed the pursuit of excellence along with the work ethic and the character traits so necessary for success in life. And he showed them by his own deeds—securing outside financial assistance for a player who was ready to quit school in order to provide for his recently widowed mother; finding a campus room for a player who had no parents and no home to go to over the summer; maintaining scholarship aid for a player who severely injured his knee in his first scrimmage and would never play a single down in any game that year; and personally making sure that an injured player received the proper medical care before bringing the team home from a game in the Midwest—that he could be counted on to come through for them too.

In this celebration of the university's fiftieth year, Brandeis paid tribute to Benny Friedman, "a man whose personal exploits border on the unbelievable, whose dedication to his athletes during his twelve years on campus was unparalleled, and whose contributions to the university's continuing success were truly beyond measure."

Even fewer Michigan fans seem aware of Harry Newman (UM, 1930–32), another skinny (Detroit) kid who was known as an extremely accurate passer (I never saw Newman either), and as a triple-threat, since he also ran and kicked for the Wolverines. (Friedman came from New York to Ann Arbor to help tutor Newman while Benny played for the Giants.) In 1932, the Wolverines were undefeated and won the national championship behind Newman, and he was awarded the Douglas Fairbanks trophy (the precursor to the Heisman trophy), being voted the most valuable intercollegiate football player during the 1932 season. In this, Michigan actually has four "Heisman" winners. Like most players of the day, Newman played both ways, and in that year he was on the field for 437 of 480 total minutes.

Newman, like Friedman, later starred in the NFL. Indeed, Newman followed Friedman to the New York Giants and surpassed Friedman in salary, being given a ten thousand dollar salary and a percentage of the gate. In 1933, as a rookie, he quarterbacked the Giants to the NFL title game and was the leading passer in the NFL. The Giants lost to the Bears 23–21 in that game, but at one point Newman completed thirteen consecutive passes. One of these was the first touchdown pass ever thrown in an NFL championship game. Until 1934, a pass that fell incomplete in the end zone was a touchback, even if thrown on first down. Still, hadn't they ever heard of yards after catch in 1929? In 1934, his second season with the Giants, Newman lead his team to a championship win over the Bears. This was a famous game at the time, the "sneakers" game, since the Giants changed from conventional football shoes to basketball shoes at the half in an attempt to deal with an ice-covered field. Phil Knight saw this game, and now claims it was his inspiration to form Nike.

In a game against Green Bay during the 1934 season, Harry rushed the ball thirty-eight times, a Giant team record for forty-nine years. In 1935, Newman broke his back. He tried to return to the game in 1936, but he retired when he could not compete at his prior level. Newman died at age ninety in 2000 of unstated causes.

After Newman, Fritz Crisler showed up in Ann Arbor as the head football coach and the innovative Crisler brought with him the east coast offense he made successful at Princeton. This offense relied upon the single wing formation, complicated running plays out of multiple fakes, and less passing than in the Friedman and Newman years. This said, all accounts are that Tom Harmon was an extraordinary passer, though this was not a major feature of the Crisler offense. However, in the late forties, during Crisler's last years as coach,

Michigan featured the passing of Bob Chappuis. Chappuis's career ('42, '46, '47) was interrupted by World War II (Chappuis was a pilot and was shot down over Italy), but in 1947 Crisler and Michigan won all of their games with Chappuis at the helm. Crisler called him the finest quarterback he had ever coached or seen, though Chappuis was runner up to Notre Dame's Johnny Lujack in the Heismann voting. I think I smell a rat or a fixed vote. In 1947, Michigan threw for an average of 179 yards per game, the best in the country that year and an incredible number for that time. So let's check it out. Who was better in 1947, Chappuis or Lujack?

	Passes	Completed	%	Yds	TDs	Rushes	Yds	TDs	ToYds	ToTDs
Lujack	109	61	55.9	777	9	12	139	1	916	10
Chappuis	110	62	56.4	1,164	13	126	510	5	1,674	18

I admit I have found various Chappuis numbers. One source has his passing line at forty-eight for eighty-six (55.8 percent) for 976 yards, and 113 rushes for 419 yards. Regardless, the numbers are not all that close, really, and Lujack posed a mysterious choice by the voters. Well, I know, sometimes these are career awards, and it may be the case that Lujack's career numbers deserved the recognition. But these are the career numbers:

	Passes	Completed	%	Yds	TDs	Rushes	Yds	TDs	ToYds	ToTDs
Lujack	280	144	51.4	2,080	20	80	438	2	2,518	22
Chappuis	253	134	53.0	2,286	22	282	1,271	10	3,557	32

Note, again, that Chappuis's numbers are subject to some variation in various sources. The foregoing is my best bet, but the yards gained may be inflated by about two hundred. In any event, Chappuis's lifetime numbers are better. I do know, in a vague but related aside, that Michigan and Chappuis defeated the Angelo Bertelli-led Irish 32–20 in 1942.

Of course, it can be argued that Notre Dame was a better team than Michigan in 1947, since they won the national championship that year and the award has certain (undeniable) team elements. Well, Notre Dame did win the national championship. Sorta. Both teams finished the season with identical unbeaten records. They played two common opponents. The first, Pittsburgh, was defeated by ND to the tune of 40–6. Michigan beat the Panthers 69–0. Both squads also played a decent Northwestern team. The Irish slipped by the Wildcats by seven points. The Wolverines handled them by twenty-eight. Nevertheless, Notre Dame was awarded the national championship by the AP, but there was a fairly massive uproar, since ND had played only three teams with winning records over the season, and its opposition totaled twenty-nine wins, while the Wolverines played five teams with winning records, and their opponents totaled forty-one wins. There was no question the Wolverines had played a more demanding schedule. The uproar increased after the Wolverines decimated USC in the Rose Bowl by a score of 49–0 (a team also defeated by ND by a 38–7 count). At this point the AP again voted, and Michigan became the choice by an overwhelming 226–119 total. This choice has remained, for some reason, unofficial and Notre Dame still claims the title. Of course, so does Michigan.

In any event, Chappuis was likely a better player than Lujack. On the other hand, Doak Walker, Charley Connerly, Bobby Lane, and Chuck Bednarik may have been better football players than Chappuis or Lujack, though without the team success that the Irish and the Wolverines enjoyed in 1947. (I know what you are thinking. You're right. In the year Hornung won the Hiesman, the Irish pounded out two wins.)

After the 1947 season, Crisler retired as coach, and Ben Oosterbaan (of Benny to Bennie fame) took over the reins of the Wolverines. Oosterbaan continued to employ the single wing offense and the Wolverines ran it to perfection and secured the undisputed national championship in that year. But with the extremely talented Chuck Ortmann as the primary passer, the Wolverines were not a passing juggernaut. From 1949 through 1965, Michigan was a definite and sorta vaguely (and only periodically successful) pound-it-at-you kind of team. In 1966, the Dick Vidmer to Jack Clancy duo began to heat it up with Vidmer passing for a then school record 1,611 yards. Still, Vidmer completed less than 52 percent of his passes for a middlingly successful Wolverine team. Thereafter, Michigan resorted to the triple option until Anthony Carter came on the scene. Since that time, however, Michigan has had many outstanding passing years. Some of the best seasons are outlined below:

	Passes	Completed	%	Yds	TDs	Ints	Rushes	Yds
John Wangler ('80)	212	117	55.2	1,522	16	9	32	-122
Jim Harbaugh ('85)	227	145	63.9	2,729	10	11	79	139
Jim Harbaugh ('86)	277	180	65.0	1,976	18	6	96	118
Elvis Grbac ('91)	254	165	65.0	2,085	25	6	23	-103
Todd Collins ('93)	296	189	63.9	2,509	17	7	34	-81
Scott Dreisbach ('96)	269	149	55.4	2,025	12	9	60	96
Brian Griese ('97)	307	193	62.9	2,293	17	6	58	20
Tom Brady ('98)	350	214	61.1	2,636	15	12	59	-108
Tom Brady ('99)	341	214	62.8	2,566	20	6	37	-47
Drew Henson ('00)	237	146	61.6	2,146	18	4	33	-6
John Navarre ('03)	456	270	59.2	3,331	24	10	48	-91
Chad Henne('04)	399	240	60.2	2,743	22	12	55	-137

The foregoing excludes a good year by Michael Taylor, one by Todd Collins, two more excellent years by Elvis Grbac and another pretty decent year by John Wangler.

Harbaugh's 1986 season was phenomenal (particularly 2,729 yards on 277 passes), but was marred by a poor TD/INT ratio. On the other hand, Harbaugh was the most mobile (Michigan) passing QB I have seen, and it is hard to vote against his college career. After that, there is not much to choose between the best years (all shown above) of Grbac, Collins, Griese, Brady, or Henson. However, Brian Griese's 1997 season was buoyed by a good running game and a great defense, conditions that took a little pressure off of Griese in 1997. Griese's other college years, while okay, were not as productive.

Todd Collins was a great college quarterback, but his senior season was marred by a 13:10 touchdown to interception ratio. Collins, like Grbac, was backed by a very solid running game, and Collins has been nada in the pros. It is just about impossible to quibble with Grbac's record. Grbac's four years are probably in the top one percentile of all college quarterbacks, ever, and slightly better than Collins's numbers. Here are their career lines:

	Passes	Completed	%	Yds	TDs	Ints
Grbac	835*	522*	62.5	6,460*	71*	31
Collins	711	457	64.3*	5,858	37	20

Elvis Lives!!! Note that the asterisks reference the best career performance ever by a Michigan quarterback. [By the close of the 2004 season, John Navarre broke UM records for passes thrown, completions and touchdowns.] Grbac is second in completion percentage to Collins. But what about Brady and Henson? Looking to the 1999 and 2000 seasons, an argument can be made for either player. In a more comprehensive fashion, it is as follows:

	Henson 2000	Brady 1999
Passes/Completed	146/237	214/341
Percentage Completed	61.6%	62.8%
Yards Per Game	238.4	215.5
Yards Per Completion	14.7	12.1
TDs:INTs	18:4	20:6
TD percentage	7.6 percent	5.9 percent
INT percentage	1.7 percent	1.8 percent
Efficiency	159.35	142.29
Rushing Atts/Yds	33/-6	37/-47
Sacks/Yds	18/148	25/173

So, who had the better year? The argument for Henson is that his yards per completion were superior (by a reasonably significant margin), and were numbers compiled without the benefit of the Bowling Green, Rice, and (first half of the) Illinois games. Also without UCLA, a more problematic affair. With these games (consider how John Navarre fared in the first two contests), it seems likely Henson's numbers would look even better. Throw in the extra experience and the fact of his broken foot, and the answer is arguably Henson. However, Henson had a real running game behind him, a luxury not afforded to Tom Brady in 1999. And Brady's numbers include the opener against Notre Dame and (at) Syracuse (a very tough place to play, because of the noise and the fact that Syracuse was a better than decent team), games that would be tough on most quarterbacks.

Considering these realities, particularly the 1999 running game, an argument can be made for Brady. I think it is a tough one to call, that it is, indeed, too close to call. It is fair to conclude, however, that Henson played either about as well or slightly better than Brady played in 1999. Still, I favor Brady. I have watched the season a few times on tape, and his performance, in conjunction with one of the worst Michigan running games ever, is remarkable.

I think there is no single answer to the question posed at the beginning of the chapter. If the question is, "Who had the best career as a passer at Michigan from an abstract statistical perspective?" I think the answer is Elvis Grbac, followed by Todd Collins, Jim Harbaugh and, yes, John Navarre. If the question is, "Who had the best individual season as a passer at Michigan?" I think the answer is a toss-up between Tom Brady in 1999, Drew Henson in 2000, and Bob Chappuis in 1947, though an argument can be made for any of these seasons. Push comes to shove, I choose Brady, due to the absence of a running game in 1999. If the question is, "What Michigan quarterback had the greatest impact on the football universe?" there is no question the answer is Benny Friedman, followed by Harry Newman. And if the question includes the college and pro careers of players, the answer remains up in the air, though it is likely to be Benny Friedman or Tom Brady, with Brian Griese, Elvis and (yes) Drew Henson in the race. If the question is, "who was the most talented quarterback ever to play for Michigan?" I think there is no question the answer is Drew Henson, with Harbaugh in second place with Chad Henne in the mix. This said, I never saw Friedman, Newman, Ortmann, or Chappuis.

But what about Rick Leach? Wasn't he voted by the fans as the all-time greatest Michigan quarterback? Indeed, he was. And indeed, this was insane. It is certain that Leach was a very good quarterback. But no one should argue that Leach was a great passer. The career numbers of Michigan's best option quarterbacks—Leach, Dennis Franklin, Mike Taylor, and Steve Smith—are compared below.

	Passes	Completed	%	Yds	TDs	Ints
Leach	537	250	46.6	4,284	48	35
Franklin	294	153	52.0	2,285	18	12
Taylor	275	163	59.3	2,194	17	7
Smith	648	324	50.0	4,860	42	32

Of course, Leach was a strong option quarterback (as were the others), and he ran for over twenty-one hundred yards. But Smith ran for nearly seven hundred more yards and averaged more yards per carry than Leach (4.95 to 4.47 yards per carry). All four quarterbacks had great records, but Franklin's 30–2–1 is the best. The fans were wrong. Rating these four, I would call it as follows, with the inevitable caveat that some of the judgment is holistic, based upon my general impressions of their play, the strength of the teams they played on, and the orientation of the offenses at the time toward running or passing:

Steve Smith
Dennis Franklin
Rick Leach
Mike Taylor

In retrospect, maybe this is more holistic than anything else. Aren't Mike Taylor's numbers the best?

But let's get back to the original question. Who was the best Michigan quarterback? Looking at the whole picture, weighing (a) careers, (b) individual seasons, (c) the accomplishments of the team, and then throwing in (d) pro careers, (e) how the individual played in relation to his peers, and (f) my instinctive sense after watching all of the players (save four), my list is as follows:

1. Benny Friedman ('24–'26)
1. Robert Chappuis ('42, '46, '47)
3. Tom Brady ('97–'99)
4. Harry Newman ('30–'32)
5. Jim Harbaugh ('84–'86)
6. Elvis Grbac ('89–'92)
7. Drew Henson ('98–'00)
8. Brian Griese ('94–'97)
9. Todd Collins ('91–'94)
10. Steve Smith ('80–'83)
11. Dennis Franklin ('70–'72)
12. John Wangler ('79–'80)
13. Chuck Ortmann ('48–'50)
14. Dick Vidmer ('65–'67)
15. Rick Leach ('75–'78)
16. Bob Timberlake ('61–'64)
17. Don Moorhead ('68–'70)
18. Michael Taylor ('87–'89)
19. Dennis Brown ('67–'68)
20. John Navarre ('00–'03)

I admit that I fudged, ultimately not being able to decide between Friedman and Chappuis. And I admit, at this moment, number twenty should be Tom Slade or Demetrius Brown or Chris Zurbrugg or Bob Ptacek. And I am sure I have overlooked someone who is deserving. But, by the time this is printed or read, I don't want to look like a complete fool, since I believe Navarre will prove he belongs somewhere on the list. (Note: After 2001, this looked foolish and laughable to many. At the end of 2002, I think Navarre was a spot or two too low. By the end of 2003, I am foolishly low. Navarre should be in the tenth to twelfth place range. And it seems likely Chad Henne will find his place.)

But why Chappuis? The major negative is that he had a short-lived pro career, despite being a first round pick by the Cleveland Browns. But I weighed this as a lesser factor, since the question is who was the best *Michigan* QB. Chappuis's 1947 team was the best in the country, Notre Dame included. Chappuis's passing statistics in that year were beyond anything in Michigan history to that date, and his numbers held up for decades. Check it out.

Career completions? Held up as number one for twenty-seven years.
Career yards gained? Ditto.
Career completion percentage? Number one for thirty-three years.
Career touchdown passes? Ditto.
Career touchdown completion percentage? Still number two.
Career average yards gained per play. Held up as number one for twenty-five years.

Most incredibly, Chappuis's career passing efficiency number remained the best Michigan performance for forty-two years. Chappuis still rates number two all-time in this overall compilation of passing, behind Elvis Grbac. Chappuis's passing efficiency rating of 173.3 in 1947 continues to be the best Michigan season performance ever. In Drew Henson's incredible last season, Henson's efficiency was 159.4. My review of the NCAA record book only shows two better efficiency seasons by a major college passer: Jim McMahon at BYU in 1980 and Ty Detmer at BYU in 1989. And neither by very much, though both threw the ball a lot more in completely different offensive systems. Chappuis's 1947 season still dots the Michigan record book, number one in pass efficiency, number two in touchdown passes per pass thrown, number seven in yards gained per play, and number one in yards gained per completion.

To understand how good these numbers are, it is important to compare them to the passing games of the era. Lujack, the Heisman winner, wasn't nearly as good. The following chart compares Chappuis in 1947 to Michigan's opponents, Chuck Ortmann's 1948 Michigan national championship team compared to Michigan's opponents, and the same comparison for Elvis

Grbac's best season in 1991, Tom Brady in 1999, Henson in 2000, Navarre in 2003 and Henne in 2004.

	Passes	Completed	%	Yards	INTs
Chappuis '47	110	62	56.4	1,164	6
Opponents '47	156	67	42.9	806	27
Ortmann '48	87	41	47.1	836	4
Opponents '48	167	74	44.3	1,059	21
Grbac '91	254	165	65.0	2,085	6
Opponents '91	407	234	57.5	2,684	16
Brady '99	341	214	62.8	2,586	6
Opponents '99	356	184	51.7	2,546	10
Henson '00	237	146	61.6	2,146	4
Opponents '00	422	247	58.5	2,914	16
Navarre '03	456	270	59.2	3,331	10
Opponents '03	410	221	53.9	2,347	14
Henne '04	399	240	60.2	2743	12
Opponents '04	371	207	55.8	2435	16

Relatively this means:

	% Difference	Yds Per Completion Difference	INT Difference
Chappuis	13.5%	6.14	21
Ortmann	2.8%	6.08	17
Grbac	8.5%	1.16	10
Brady	11.1%	-1.75	4
Henson	3.1%	2.9	12
Navarre	5.3%	1.16	4
Henne	4.4%	-.34	4

To make sense of the foregoing, note that Michigan's team numbers are distinct, since in 1947, 1999, and 2000 (in particular), other players were also throwing the ball. Still, the numbers tend to show, in relation to the competition, that Chappuis was playing at a relatively higher level than quarterbacks who followed. I vote for Chappuis. And Friedman, of course. [In February of 2005 Friedman was elected to the Hall of Fame.]

* * * *

I am happy to say the above analysis was written prior to Tom Brady's recent success as a starting quarterback for New England, and his two Super Bowl MVPs, with the exception of the addition of John Navarre's 2003 and

Chad Henne's 2004 lines. At the time of the writing, Brady was a third string NFL QB. On the other hand, I may have undervalued Bob Ptacek, who was a pretty good QB at Michigan, and backed this up with a good pro career in the Canadian Football League, a fact I originally missed. Also, after this was written, the media proved they knew more about the unified field theory than football by awarding Nebraska quarterback Eric Crouch the 2001 Heismann. Crouch was a decent runner, but Nebraska's option attack worked because of the execution of its offensive line. And Crouch is no kind of a passer, completing 55.6 percent of his passes in 2001 for limited yards, more interceptions than touchdowns (ten to seven), and a mediocre passing efficiency (124.3). When it is considered that these numbers arose in the context of an excellent running offense, they are, at best, completely unimpressive. Indeed, John Navarre, with the worst quarterback record in Michigan's recent past (in 2001), was as good when it is considered that Navarre had zero running game to rely upon. John completed 53.8 percent of his passes—not great in today's game, but not much worse than Crouch. Moreover, John threw seventeen TDs to twelve INTs—much better than Crouch's performance. Navarre's efficiency rating was 116, slightly behind Crouch, but in the context of the offenses, Crouch was not a better passer than Navarre. Was he a better runner? Who made you so smart? (Note: By the close of 2003, it was certain that John Navarre was a much better player than Eric Crouch. Crouch's choice for the Heisman showed a complete lack of curiosity and imagination by the voters.)

Or maybe "South by Northwestern," since that's what the Michigan defense did in this contest. Granted, one can get carried away by this, but five minutes after Northwestern's stunning 54–51 victory over Michigan in 2000, the game was recognized as a classic. This is no exaggeration since, during the week following the game, ESPN replayed the contest as part of its *NCAA Classic* series. To have a better understanding of what went on in the contest, it is useful to review the basics (I couldn't do more than Football 101 anyway) of the evolution of offensive football from Yost through Warner (the Rams QB Kurt, not Pop). Admittedly, this is a book. But you'll see it here first in a few pages, lifting heavily from a variety of people who claim to know what they're talking about.

Until Benny Friedman and Harry Newman, all levels of football, even pro football, were largely "we plan to pound it at you" sort of stuff. As noted earlier, the first touchdown pass recorded in an NFL championship game was thrown by Harry Newman in 1934. To get any sense of the game at the time, think of Wisconsin head coach Barry Alvarez relying upon a mean, toothless fullback, with the dimensions of Ron Dayne, matched against Woody Hayes with an even meaner, one-eyed version of (say) Pete "I Don't Like You" Johnson. This was the NFL, mano a mano and definitely brontosaurus ball. When Hayes and Alvarez met on the sidelines prior to an OSU-Wisconsin tilt, the following was recorded:

Alvarez: This passing is just for sissies. We gonna pound it.
Hayes: Right on, Bro. We ain't playing that girlie ball. Hey, this is football.
In unison: There ain't no passing in football.

This was the NFL game until 1935. The college game was equally as brutal. The *New York Times,* reporting on the 1888 Yale-Princeton match (the best two teams of that time), noted, "It must be confessed that the spirit of unfair play was not monopolized by either side." The paper went on to explain, "The favorite methods of damaging an opponent were to stamp on his feet, to kick his shins, to give him a dainty upper cut, and to gouge his face in tackling." It isn't clear if these tactics were illegal until after 1906, when a player died in a punching melee in a pileup. Even thereafter, the game was incredibly rough. And finesse and trickery was more or less nonexistent. This began to change in the late thirties in the wake of Friedman and Newman, when a number of passing quarterbacks arrived on the scene and the NFL began to be, at least to some degree, a more "balanced" league, one where the forward pass was a part of the equation.

The change from run to pass was facilitated, in significant part, by the alteration in the shape of the ball. In 1934, an inch and a half was stripped from the circumference of the old watermelon ball, yielding to a new aerody-namic shape. This was considered, as related to me by old timers, a sort of cir-cumcision of the ball in homage to Benny and Harry. Of course, every change has its price. Gone with the watermelon ball was the drop kick, the last suc-cessful one taking place in the NFL in 1948 after a bad snap and improvisation by 49er Joe Vetrano.

Passers like Sammy Baugh and Sid Luckman flourished with the new ball, and they showed that speed and finesse could be a legitimate part of the game. The other change that revolutionized football was the addition of hash marks in 1933. Until that time, the next play began where the last one ended, whether it was a foot inbounds or in the middle of the field. If a play went out of bounds, the ball was spotted a foot or two from where the ball crossed the sideline. Given this, everyone knew the direction of the next play and, accord-ing to Robert Peterson in *Pigskin,* sometimes a "team had to waste a play just to get the ball in operating territory." Also in 1933, a rule that mandated a pass-er drop back a minimum of five yards to pass was abolished. With the change in the shape of the ball, the addition of hash marks, and the liberalization of the "drop back" rule, there was a synergistic motivation to throw.

Today, in the main, football innovation flows from the top down, that is, from the NFL to the colleges. But in the first half of the century, it was large-ly the other way around. The pro leagues were a low-rent rendezvous, and the great coaches—Fielding Yost, Knute Rockne, Walter Eckersall, Amos Alonzo Stagg, Fritz Crisler, Clark Shaunessy, and Pop Warner (to name a few), were working at the amateur level. Sammy Baugh came to the pros from a Southwest conference that was generally considered (if you liked it) "an aerial circus" or (if you didn't) "chicken football." But regardless of the standard consciousness, Baugh proved that a team could win with the forward pass (and not just in the SWC), and he became known, rightfully, as the first great pass-er in the NFL. But by today's standards, it was not "aerial" football. Baugh, in his sixteen-year career, threw the ball an average of 187 times a season. In 1999, Drew Brees (at Purdue) threw the ball 554 times. He threw it a little more in the prior season. Vinny Testaverde threw 590 times in 2000 for the Jets. Compared to Purdue recently, and all NFL offenses today, Baugh's offense was strictly three yards and a cloud of muck. And the game was still brutal.

A few years ago, I heard Alvin Wistert (the last of the great Wistert tackles to play for UM) talk about his matchups against Leo Nomellini in the late forties. Wistert was a giant of a man, in the range of six feet, four inches tall and 240 pounds, in a day when pro lineman often weighed around 200. There was a reason for this, aside from better nutrition, weight training, and people just getting bigger. At the time, it was primarily a one-platoon game, and a behemoth would tire out well before a 210-pound type. Accordingly, the huge offensive linemen of today would have been liabilities. (Indeed, two-platoon football might be the last significant innovation to flow from the colleges to the pros, an idea used by Fritz Crisler in his war year attempts to allow Michigan to compete against the powerful Army teams.) Nomellini was one of the dominant linemen of all time and at a quick six-foot-four and nearly 275 pounds (these numbers vary, this is my best guess), he could dominate a game. In Michigan's 1948 win over Minnesota, Wistert related that Nomellini, "who had a forearm like a piano leg, continually clubbed the noses of the Michigan offensive linemen." There were no face masks in those days, and Wistert claimed "most of the line" had their noses broken, and the Michigan center had "a bloody pulp" for a face before the end of the first half. Near the end of the game, when the outcome was certain, Michigan ran a play at Nomellini. The point wasn't to gain any yards. The point was to pummel Nomellini. And they did, well after the play was over, with numerous shots to his head and midsection. Nomellini seemed nonplussed. "I didn't think I was getting to you guys," was all he said.

Face masks came into vogue in the fifties. This was pretty fast work when you consider that *helmets* were not even mandatory in the NFL until 1943, and some guy named Dick Plasman played in the NFL championship game in 1940 without any headgear. Plasman is da man!!! Of course, "plasma" was also named after him. A Michigan All-American and subsequent NFL Hall of Famer, Bill Hewitt, played professionally through 1939 without a helmet (from 1931), claiming a helmet "hampered his game." To me, this sounded like the grandmaster chess player who complained he "could never play chess in England." The NFL, concerned about Hewitt's health, forced him to wear headgear in 1940.

Baugh's tenure at the top of the heap was eclipsed when Northwestern great Otto Graham showed up with bruiser Marion Motley and other Hall of Famers (Len Ford from Michigan, Dante Lavelli, Lou Groza, Mac Speedie) for the All-American Football League's Cleveland Browns. Graham signed with the AAFC upstarts and, from 1946 to 1949, the Browns were 53–4–3 (four championships), with Otto at the helm. When the Browns joined the NFL in 1950, there was general skepticism that the open Browns' offense could compete at the NFL level. They did compete. Indeed, they won the 1950 championship, beating the LA Rams 30–28 behind Graham's four touchdown passes. How good was Graham? Real good. He led the Browns to the NFL championship game for the next five years (winning two), and then retired after a 38–10 rout of the Rams in 1955. In his ten-year career as a pro, Graham's teams played for the championship in ten of those years; in other words, all of them, the Browns winning seven times. (Note. In 1943, Otto finished behind Notre Dame quarterback Angelo Bertelli in the Heisman voting. If I didn't know better, I would smell a rat or a fix. This would be like concluding Solly Hemus was a better defensive infielder than Ozzie Smith.) Graham's numbers are prodigious, and he was the best quarterback in the history of the NFL (with the possible exception of Baugh) to the time of his retirement. But how many passes did Otto throw in the Browns 1955 championship season? An average of 15.5 per game. Nothing. Even the rag arms that Notre Dame and the effervescent Ty Willingham and Bob Davie threw out there lobbed that many wobblers in a game.

I saw the end of Graham's career (and met him when I was five years old in a Cleveland Chinese restaurant), and can accurately report that (a) Otto liked dim sum, and (b) the Browns ordinarily ran a T-formation. No shotgun. Not much spreading the field. Not much throwing to the backs. The game was, "let Motley pound it at them, and when they creep up, we will let Otto show his stuff." And not much more than that. It was not a fancy offense, though the Browns were innovative in organizational elements of the game. Most of all, Paul Brown and Otto Graham brought timing routes to the game. Receivers were expected to run precise routes, and Graham was expected to put the ball at a spot at a specified moment. Until the Browns of Otto Graham, the game was "run to the hydrant and then go left and then I will look to see if you are open."

Graham was a single wing run/pass quarterback at Northwestern, but Paul Brown, the Cleveland coach and owner, could see that Graham could run his T, an offense with three backs bunched behind the QB and one or two tight ends. In other words, a formation not all that much different than a rugby scrum or the one run by Yost with Willie Heston in 1901. Still, the formation was more pass friendly than its predecessors, and it caught on like hotcakes in the NFL after George Halas and Baugh used it to dismantle the Bears in the 1940 NFL championship game by a tally of 73–0. Okay, I didn't get it at first either. How can a formation that bunched the backs together like a rugby scrum be more innovative? First, unlike the single wing (invented by Pop Warner in 1906) or double wing football generally in vogue through the forties, the T-formation quarterback handled the ball on every play and no longer had to share in the blocking load. In the single wing, the QB (tailback) had to block. This meant, half the time, he was punch-drunk from tangling with characters like Nomellini or the famed Ed "The Claw" Sprinkle. Second, Halas and assistant Ralph Jones refined the T by placing a man in motion at times, a tactic that had not been a staple of offenses in the past. Third, the motion back helped to facilitate running overloads and then counterplays if the defense overreacted to the motion. Fourth, Halas and Jones added some spreading of the field and swing passes to backs, basic trickery considered dé classé or unmanly at the time. Fifth, Halas and then Paul Brown began to spread the field by giving offensive linemen larger "splits," that is, distances between the guards and tackles. Sixth, and this was a fundamental element of the theory, Halas refined the T by putting the quarterback behind the center (instead of a couple yards back), allowing (a) the running backs to gather some steam before receiving a handoff, and (b) the QB to show his back to the defense, enhancing the prominence of fake handoffs. It worked. And others imitated. No, I haven't looked at any film. I trust the word of others for this. And my memory as a young child. (Note: In 2002, the Iowa Hawkeyes went in the other direction and reverted to line splits of next to nothing. The corn guys reinvented the flying wedge in an attempt to allow their terrific running back, Fred Russell, to dance around in small creases. It worked.)

After Motley and Graham, the Browns secured the services of the greatest player of all time (with the possible exception of Benny Friedman), Jim Brown. Even with Brown, however, the Cleveland offense did not dwarf the competition, where the Cleveland passing game died post-Graham. After Otto, it was strictly Lombardi and the Packers, the quintessential execution team, with Lombardi basing his entire offense around a few plays (notably the power sweep) and variations on the theme when a defense would overcommit to minimize the effectiveness of the Packers execution. Essentially, with everyone moving to the "innovative" T-formation, Lombardi reverted to the staple of the single wing, overloading the formation to the side of the play. Lombardi threw the ball, of course, and Bart Starr was a fine QB. But the Packer offense was strictly fundamental and vanilla to the average fan's eye, albeit the best vanilla there ever was. It was, there is no question, a very *predictable* offense, with the Packers running the single wing sweep as often as twelve times in a game.

The most significant Lombardi addition to the game was the elimination of pure on-man blocking in the Packer offense. Prior to the Lombardi era, teams were intent on moving a particular defender a particular direction. Defensive linemen at the time (typically nose guards in odd fronts) were often huge and immobile masses of poundage, just getting in the way of plays. If the Browns decided they wanted to run at the "two hole," the Lions just might put some 350-pounder there and tell him to hold his spot. Lombardi eliminated this tactic from his offense in favor of creating seals or zones where blockers would clear a lane (crease) for the back, regardless of the defender in the area. This meant that the defense dictated the blocking assignments, and it was often incumbent upon offensive linemen to communicate at the line of scrimmage. This led, of course, to defensive changes, the mountains of flesh being replaced by quick footed and more mobile defenders. Aside from this, Lombardi created option blocking, often allowing a blocker to move a defender in the direction that the defender was inclined to go. The ball carrier's role was to read the block and run against the grain of the defender's inclination. Thus was born the Lombardi aphorism, "run to daylight." (A staple of Michigan football under Bo was the "isolation" play, where the I-formation fullback would isolate on the middle linebacker and the tailback, deep in the formation, would read this block and cut away from the direction the backer was blocked or moved.)

Other NFL teams at the time tried to imitate Lombardi. But they didn't have Ron Kramer or the incredible Packer offensive line, anchored by Jerry Kramer. (When Lombardi was asked about the greatest player who ever played for him, he named former Michigan end Ron Kramer, a tight end for the Pack, and claimed, "Kramer was like having a license to have twelve men on the field.") Other teams realized the futility of attempting to out-execute the Packers. They could match neither the offensive talent nor the personnel the Packers had on defense, particularly MSU great Herb Adderly, almost without peer in the history of the game, and the philosopher Ray Nitschke. Out of this realization came an increased pace of innovation in the pro game, including the multiple sets of the Dallas Cowboys and other nuances such as the shotgun formations used by the San Francisco 49ers in 1961. Starting in the early sixties, pro coaches began to realize that there might be ways to compete with more talented teams by changing the nature of the game. Coaches knew, of course, that the essence of the game was blocking and tackling and throwing and catching. This was not and is not going to change. But they also began to realize that there were ways to minimize the impact of less-than-perfect execution on the offensive side of the ball.

Defenses began to change, too. When quick middle linebackers replaced the mound-of-flesh nose guards, smaller centers (like 210-pounder Jim Ringo) came into vogue, until the AFL brought back the bruising odd defenses and massive nose guards, like Curly Culp. With the return of the big nose guard, small centers then withered and disappeared.

The running game, to be successful, requires a semblance of execution by most all of the players on the field. One missed block, and the perfect execution of ten others can go down the drain. Plus, there is not much a coach can do about not having a great running back, except trying to find one. Running backs are born with the ability, and no amount of coaching is going to change the fact. A runner either possesses extraordinary instincts or doesn't, and coaching will not turn Jim Otis (a pretty good college but average NFL back) into Barry Sanders. On the other hand, as noted by Bill Walsh, "a passing game can be more than the sum of its parts." Kevin Lamb, in his excellent book *Quarterbacks, Nickelbacks and Other Loose Change* (1984), notes that "an average receiver can play better than a gifted one because he can be taught to maneuver better in open spaces. An average quarterback can play better than a gifted one because he can be taught better ways of finding those open spaces and delivering the ball to them. Where running backs must operate instinctively, passers and receivers can be taught what to look for." If this seems less than intuitive, think of these names—Brian Griese and Ryan Leaf. Or John Unitas and Jeff George. These couplets are legion. Leaf and George possess strong arms, stronger than most of their peers. Yet, they have had limited or nonexistent success.

Walsh's ideas have their genesis in Sid Gillman, a Paul Brown protégé who coached in the old AFL. Gillman was a believer in spreading the field both horizontally and vertically. Gillman theorized that you didn't have to run to set up the pass, and that by stretching the field, short passes would be the offensive team's option for the taking. The size of the field was Gillman's oyster.

Still, after Otto Graham, the defenses in the pros began to dominate the game, and by the mid-seventies, the game began to look like 1930 redux, *sans* the drop kick and the old "hide the ball under your jersey" ploy. (Pop Warner actually tried this idea when he coached at Carlisle at the turn of the last century. It is not a completely apocryphal history.) More than this, there was still a sense that it was somehow cheap or not manly to win games with the forward pass. As Kevin Lamb writes, "Pro football had always been a bastion of work ethic and it just didn't seem right to be able to move the ball sixty yards on one play without carrying it or breaking tackles or blocking people downfield. It was like running laps around the field by cutting across the fifty-yard line." Nevertheless, the NFL and television moguls did not like 9–7 games and, hence, in 1978, blocking rules were liberalized (pretty much putting holding on the shelf except for the most egregious instances), and the playing surface was widened by moving the hash marks closer to the middle of the field. NFL coaches took advantage of these changes, and by the mid-eighties, innovation was spinning with a new level of synergy.

Until 1978, offensive theories in the game moved at a glacial speed. After 1978, innovation was the norm. And as the rule changes trickled down to the NCAA, so did the innovation. Moreover, as the NCAA leveled the playing fields with the eighty-five-scholarship limitation, talent began to spread to places (Kansas State, Northwestern, Virginia Tech, Oregon, Oregon State, and Marshall, among others) previously barren. As the talent differentials became less pronounced, it was harder to win games on mere execution, since these differentials could be marginal. Pure chance rose to the fore as the decider of games and college football spun out of the strict control of the coaches. No fun. So coaches attempted to take control in new ways.

Two prime examples of this are found in the NFL. The first was the Minnesota Vikings of the mid to late seventies, using their wide receivers and the tight end to create space for Chuck Foreman, a fullback, to catch the ball. A "safety valve" pass to the fullback had been a part of the passing game in the fifties, and all teams relied upon screen passes. But Bud Grant pioneered a new variation of the running/passing game (take your choice) in the short toss to Foreman. The Vikings tended to use the old T formation, but with one of the backs in the "T" being spread to a wide reciever:

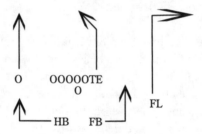

(This diagram, and the one that follows, are found in Kevin Lamb's book, as referenced.) The Vikings' theory was to clear as much space as possible for Foreman (the fullback) by pulling the defense to the weak side of the field (away from the tight end), and allowing Foreman to catch the ball in the area cleared by the flanker where, at worst, he would have to tangle with a slower and less nimble linebacker. The pass was short and easy to throw, did not depend upon great pass blocking, and was unlikely to be intercepted. It was safe and it wasn't, really, anything more than a variation on an off-tackle play, albeit one that did not depend upon perfect execution to grind out a few yards. Since Foreman was tougher to tackle in open spaces than in traffic, the play worked.

Out of this idea arose Bill Walsh's revolutionary offense (the West Coast offense), where he inverted the theory by allowing running backs to create room for the wide receivers, the latter running short routes under the coverage. It looked like this:

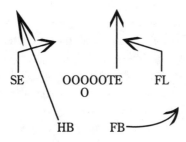

SE   OOOOOTE   FL
            O

HB   FB

In this offense, the fullback still had to catch the ball, and in the San Francisco offense, he caught the ball a lot. But the primary receivers were guys like Dwight Clark and later the incredible Jerry Rice, big possession-type guys who were tough enough to take the hits of the linebackers and safeties and still grind out a few yards. In Walsh's offense, the wideouts were not spread as wide as in the Viking or other offenses, keeping the routes short and simple with the running backs stretching the field. In this, Walsh's ideas were the Bizarro Superman version of the Viking schemes, where the wide receivers created the space for the running backs. Walsh's theory was that the flanker and split end, his best receivers, would gnaw at the weakest component in pass coverage, the linebackers. Plus, they would catch the ball about four or five yards downfield, and then try to create a big gain by running after the catch. Again, this was successful, even after defenses adjusted to eight-man coverages that left limited room for the wide receivers to maneuver.

Walsh took Paul Brown's timing passes one step further down the path of execution, demanding accuracy to one tenth of one second. This implied that the receiver's pattern and the quarterback's drop had to be in complete sync, achieved by the continual drilling on the footwork of the QB and the WRs. But Walsh and the 49ers were not satisfied. The coach recognized that the nature of the game was change, and the Niners responded by replacing their offense by 30 to 40 percent every year. That said, Walsh stressed that predictability was a key part of his offense, that a certain level of predictability was necessary for the offense to execute at its highest level. While the 49ers used multiple formations, they always started with two backs and a tight end, with either back being able to go into motion and be used as a receiver. Walsh wanted defenses to stay in their base formations so that the execution elements of his offense would come into prominence. The easiest way to guarantee a base defense was to keep his formations limited and simple, but then stem into variations by use of motion. If the offense knew what the defense was doing, this allowed Walsh's precision drilling on drops, footwork, and timing to control the game. Simply, Lombardi and Brown in a new bottle.

The most radical change by the 49ers was the use of "sight adjustments" in pass patterns, the receiver and quarterback looking at the same defensive player, and then changing a route based upon the positioning of a defender. If, for example, a receiver was running a curl route (where the receiver curls back toward the inside of the field) and the defender/defense was shading to the inside, the quarterback and receiver were to make the same adjustment, and change the pattern to an "out," toward the sideline. In the early eighties, this was a radical and controversial notion. Many pro teams completely rejected the idea as not workable. Today, all pro teams (and most college teams) make these adjustments, though for some, only one receiver has this option. For all teams this is complicated, a game of cat and mouse between the offense and defense, a game of fakes and counter-fakes.

The other radical change of the eighties was the departure from two-back to one-back offenses. Bud Grant used one back on passing downs in the seventies, and in the early eighties, the Chargers used two tight ends and one running back as a way to get the most out of their best player, Kellen Winslow, a big receiver who was most effective running patterns inside the hash marks. The Redskins won the Super Bowl with a one-back set in 1982, but color guys took little notice. Indeed, Kevin Lamb points out that in the pre-game lineup on television prior to the Super Bowl, the television network introduced two backs for Washington. But the Redskins' offense was not lost on other coaches. Legendary coach Sid Gillman determined that one back "is the only way to go." Gillman noted that it was good for passing (more receivers), good for rushing (an extra tight end as opposed to a fullback for blocking), and that it allowed an offense to design an infinite number of formations and motions out of these formations. Gillman is quoted as saying, "These coaches who are running fullback slants with two backs in the backfield have lost it."

Among present day college teams, of course, Lloyd Carr has been one of the major proponents of the one-back set, using two tight ends and a variety of motion to create overmatches (more blockers than defenders) or mismatches (big tight end blocking small strong safety) or confusion in the defense.

Until recently, Lloyd's offense reminded me of the Washington Redskins in their heyday. In 2002, Michigan reverted to two-back sets, in order to take advantage of the talents of BJ Askew, a good short receiver and a bruising runner in open spaces. While the resemblance may be superficial, UM of 2002 looked a little like the Vikings of the Chuck Foreman era. Michigan fans, in examining this, should understand that Carr is not a system coach trying to pound square pegs into round holes. Rather, Carr has altered his offenses and defenses in conformity with his personnel and the strengths and weaknesses of the opposition.

The foregoing sketch of history could fill books, but the truncated version leads us to the 2000 season and Michigan versus Northwestern. The Wolverines were 6–2 coming into the game, losing to UCLA as previously noted, and losing a 32–31 contest to Purdue and Drew Brees after leading

28–10 at the half. In the two games prior to the meeting with the Wildcats, the Wolverines had shut out a fairly good but hapless-on-that-day Hoosier offense (58–0), and an unlucky but hapless Spartan offense (14–0). My diary notes about the Wildcats are reproduced. The October 5 entry follows a 13–10 nail-biter win over Wisconsin.

October 5, 2000. The problem is that it is so easy to discount Northwestern. You think we would have learned. The Wildcats opened the season with weak sisters Northern Illinois and Duke, but ran for 236 and 259 yards in those games, about 56 percent of their offense. They could not move the ball at all on a decent TCU team, but came back with 266 yards rushing against Wisconsin, out of 544 total yards gained. Michigan, looking at the facts that (a) Duke and NIU are not relevant to the equation, and (b) Northwestern could not run against TCU, but (c) ran the ball very well against Wisconsin, might have concluded (d) Wisconsin cannot stop the run, (e) all we gotta do is pound the ball at them, and (f) isn't this the safest game and *our* game anyway? My guess is the equation went something like this. The problem is that we were playing Wisconsin and not Northwestern. Despite the fact of numerous Wisconsin suspensions, the Badgers held Western (a decent team), Oregon (a very good team), and Cincinnati (a team), to a total of 185 yards. An average of less than 62 yards per game. On this, I would suggest the idea that we could just play bubba ball with the Badgers was a little (at least) premature. If not down-right Pollyannaish. Now, I know this is simplistic. I know the coaching staff must have studied a ton of film and determined what was likely to work and what was not likely to work. But Lloyd and offensive lineman Jonathan Goodwin seemed legitimately stunned by the Wolverines' trouble establishing a running game. I am a big Carr fan. I think he and his coaching staff are as good as it gets in the college game. In this instance, however, I would not be surprised if there was some level of failure in analysis. Northwestern and that wimpy offense can run against the Badgers? Then we will murderize them. Right?

Well, we won. But, in a couple of weeks, we have the loathed and dreaded Spartans. It turns out that MSU got hammered by the Wildcats this past week, to the tune of 37–17. Again, the Wildcats gained more than five hundred yards (506), and this time, 346 of these were on the ground. This represents 68.4 percent of the Northwestern offense. So it goes something like this: (a) Northwestern pounded them on the ground, (b) we have a better running attack than the Wildcats, thus (c) it is slobberknocker time, a big relief after these weasel-like and sneaky sorta teams like Purdue and Indiana. Ah. But wait a minute here. Marshall (a good team) ran for fifty-one yards against the Meanies. And Missouri (reasonably lame) ran for 114 yards. And the vaunted team led by (as some internet poster said) "a dancing midget in a green moron suit" hammered MSU for 212 yards, sixty-three of these on the ground. And last year, MSU had a devastating run defense and a lot of these characters are back. My guesses are (a) MSU can play run defense, and (b) there is something weird and extremely fishy going on with Northwestern.

On October 22, 2000, after the MSU shutout, my diary contains the following notes about Northwestern:

October 22, 2000. And what about those pesky Wildcats? On the road. Hmm. Let me check the stats. Against Indiana, Northwestern put up 536 yards, but over four hundred of these were running yards out of a spread formation. The Cats scored fifty-two. They did give up thirty-three. They also put up 544 yards in a 47–44 win over Wisconsin, in a balanced attack. And, against the very good MSU defense, NU gained more than five hundred yards. Of these, nearly 70 percent were rushing yards. Thus, against common opponents, the NU attack looks a little more potent than our own. Their defense, conversely, is there in name only. Oops, forgot about one game. Purdue. Purdue decided to jam the receivers at the line of scrimmage and pay primary attention to the running game. Northwestern countered with an effective passing game and gained 370 yards. But they were not successful running the ball, averaging about two yards per attempt. The Wildcats still scored twenty-eight points, but this wasn't enough. Purdue won 41–28. So what do I really think? I think . . . we will score a lot of points against Northwestern, and they won't be able to keep up. I also think, as a key footnote, these passing yards are not as meaningful as the ones gained by handing the ball off. All yards are not created equal.

October 29, 2000. Michigan has the advantage of a week off between games and, given the unusual offense run by Northwestern, this seems a useful time to have the extra preparation. Northwestern won again this week, pummeling the Minnesota defense for 543 yards (334 rushing yards) and forty-one points. The final was 41–35, Northwestern scoring on the last play of the game on a forty-five-yard pass. The NU coach, Randy Walker, said he was "not surprised" about the success of the last play "because we complete that pass 80 percent of the time in practice." Yeah, sure, Coach. Maybe against your defense.

Looking at the Northwestern numbers/season, it seems the way to a win is pretty obvious. Stop the run. Michigan tends to establish its running game (a la checkers) by overloading more blockers to the onside before the defense can react. Or by running away from the overload in an attempt to catch an overshifted defense. Or, at a minimum, to make certain the defense does not have the advantage. Northwestern attempts to establish the run by spreading the field, showing pass, and then running a draw or option or inside reverse against a defense that has been spread to the edges of the surface.

So what is Carr's off-week commentary? Lloyd says on his Sunday show that having the week off came at a good time, since "we got a jump on the Northwestern game plan because they do something different from anyone we play." The coach explains that Northwestern will line up by the time the ball is marked and uses no huddle, the QB (Zak Kustok, an ND transfer) looking to the sideline to have the offensive coordinator call a play based upon (down and distance aside) the defense. Carr states that it is very difficult to substitute against such a system, which means a defense (aside from not having the advantage implied in the substitution) can get tired. Not much else in the way of pre-game information. But this one takes no genius. Stop the Northwestern running game and Michigan will win. Michigan should win anyway . . .

* * * *

The St. Louis Rams dominated the 1999 NFL and did it with no defense. The Rams decided, simply, to outscore other teams no matter what it took. Randy Walker, the Northwestern coach, took notice, since (a) he knew he could not compete on defense in 2000, but (b) he also knew he had marked offensive potential with a star running back (Damien Anderson) and a budding star QB (Zak Kustok) and some decent offensive linemen. After the 1999 season, Walker hired the Rams coaching staff as tutors vis-à-vis the NFL team's theories. The Northwestern coaches came away from the sessions with certain general ideas (or so it seems), and added a snootful of their own. Most all of these concepts had been used in the past, but I can't recall them being used in a way that was anything like the Northwestern implementation.

The Wildcat offense was unique. It relied upon the shotgun formation of Red Hickey's San Francisco teams, but NU used it one hundred percent of the time (or nearly so). In addition, Walker took Sid Gillman's advice to heart and uses a single back as opposed to the original two-back shotgun. Or no back and a complete spread of the field. Walker borrowed from the distant past of the Cleveland Browns by using a limited number of formations, three or four at most, and relied upon a small number of plays, a la Lombardi. The Northwestern running game, the heart of the offense, consisted of a QB/tail-back option and an inside counter, and not much else except for the scrambling of Zak Kustok. The passing game was mostly from Bill Walsh, short patterns under the coverage or crossing patterns under the safeties. Northwestern attempted to stretch the field vertically on occasion, but it was mostly show, keeping the safeties honest.

The key to the success of the team was a no-huddle concept, used by Gary Moeller at Michigan (and a few before him), allowing the coaches above the field to read the defense, send a play to the sidelines, and then signal to Kustok the play to be run. Moreover, the no-huddle made it difficult for the defense to substitute. Put this all together and it spelled trouble for any defense, particularly where Northwestern had the horses to make it go.

The mind connects. During the week of the 2000 Northwestern game, I was puttering around the internet looking for a DVD copy of *Blue Angel*, the 1930 Josef Von Sternberg masterpiece starring Emil Jannings and Marlene Dietrich. In the movie, Jannings plays a stuffy professor who is led to degradation and ruin by his infatuation with Lola Lola (Dietrich), a cabaret performer in Weimar, Berlin. The day after discovering there is no DVD version (there is now), I found myself hearing a real-life variation on the theme. In the case, involving, thankfully, the mere distribution of property, Mr. X tells his faithful wife of many years (her name is Lola) that he is about to leave her for his girlfriend. As it turns out, the girlfriend is also named Lola. Wife Lola, though not happy about this, still loves Mr. X and, in exchange for his not moving out, concedes to allow Girlfriend Lola to move in. Wife Lola testifies that she loved Mr. X and would do just about anything to keep the relationship viable, even allowing Girlfriend Lola convenient sexual access to her husband. After Girlfriend Lola moves in, Mr. X attempts to convince Wife Lola and Girlfriend Lola that a *ménage à trois* would be interesting. Neither Lola is enthusiastic about the prospect, but after a period of persuasion, both Lolas agree. And, it turns out, both Lolas like the sex. Hey, it worked—sorta like the Northwestern offense. But, it also turns out the Lolas like sex with each other more than sex with Mr. X. A lot more. And they like each other more than either like Mr. X. A lot more. After a period of clandestine meetings without Mr. X, the Lolas put up a united front and kicked him out of the house. At my hearing, Mr. X lamented his bad luck and ill treatment at the hands of Lola and Lola, conditions that, in his mind, justified a favorable property award. Well, of course, he got what he deserved, and I was less than empathetic to Mr. X. I suggested during my hearing there was a certain symmetry and poetic justice in the result that might be consoling to him. Mr. X didn't see it. And he was not consoled by my references to Emil Jannings, nor my thought that he might want to view a piece of abstract expressionist German art. So it goes. Lola. Lola.

In my mind, the Northwestern game is the moral equivalent of the Lola Lola case. An offensive fanatic's delight. Weird, abstract art. So odd that it couldn't exist. What the hell went on in this game? All week Lloyd had been saying that, despite the formations employed by Northwestern, it was "more of a running team" than it might have appeared from a casual observation of its games. Well, I hadn't seen anything but small pieces of two NU games and had this one figured out. And the numbers don't lie. So it was a surprise when Northwestern came out in its first series with a spread formation, and Michigan responded with a four-man front and two linebackers, with the safeties a good twelve yards away from the line of scrimmage. Michigan was playing pass! And protecting against the deep throws and mistakes by the corners. Northwestern scored in nine plays, seven runs, and two passes, neither pass beyond the line of scrimmage. Back to back running plays (the same play) went for sixty-two yards. As best as I can manage, it looked like this:

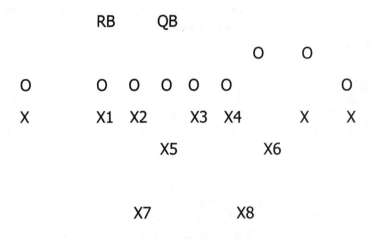

In this formation, the Wildcats had a six on five to the single wideout side of the formation, and they exploited this by running a QB/RB option to that side. Checkers!! Michigan was playing pass and Northwestern took advantage of the weak side of the formation. And when the offense flipped the running back (Anderson) to the side of the triple wideouts, Michigan made no adjustment in its defense and the Cats ran the inside reverse back to the six on five. Now, I know somebody once said (I think it was me) if you are good enough, you can line people up single file and play defense. But does the above make any sense? I admit I don't know. But the Wildcats sure seemed to.

Drew Brees, prior to the 2000 Michigan game, noted that what Michigan does on defense "appears to be fundamentally unsound" with the implication that it "looks that way, but it really isn't." Brees was saying (a) this guy Jim Hermann (UM's defensive coordinator) is a genius, and his schemes are very hard to figure out and have given me a lot of trouble, and/or (b) that weird stuff isn't going to give us any trouble this year. In fact, I think he was saying both, the latter seeming more prominent after Brees put up thirty-two points in a Purdue comeback victory earlier in 2000. But doesn't the foregoing diagram look weird? There is no pressure on the center, and he has a clear shot at X5. The receivers run their guys out of the play, X7 and X8 are too deep to help with the run at the line of scrimmage, and average blocking by the guards and tackle will open creases up the middle. I am not saying I would have figured this out, but Walker and his staff did, running Anderson inside on a seven-on-five game for long gains on the way to a score.

Michigan came right back. Northwestern loaded up on the run and played its defensive backs very soft. Since, even with the sellout to stop A-Train Michigan is still able to run, the theory is hopeless. Michigan drove sixty-eight yards for a TD. Nothing too fancy, 7–7.

Northwestern's second series buoyed my spirits. The Wildcats moved the ball to the Michigan forty-one against the 4/2 (above), but on second and nine Michigan used a three-man front and blitzed four. The Wildcats were unprepared, and Kustok tossed the ball away. On third and nine, Hermann employed a seven-man front with four corners in single coverage. Kustok again became confused and audibled out of the play sent from the sidelines. A draw. No gain. The Cats punted. Michigan started from its own twenty and then drove eighty yards in seven plays, highlighted by a fake reverse and inside handoff to AT for fifty-four yards.

It was Michigan 14–7, and I was very confident now. After all, armed with my encyclopedic (well, I looked it up later) knowledge of the game, I recognized three conditions. First, the Northwestern offense was basically Red Hickey's 49ers offense of 1961, only with a no-huddle, one back (or none), and a greater spread of the field. Second, the Hickey offense was a juggernaut for four or five games that year until George Halas of the Bears dusted off his old tapes and play books and realized that Hickey had just reinvented the wheel, the single wing (or double-wing formation) in a new guise. And Halas wasn't a hundred years old for nothing. He knew how those dinos croaked. The "odd" front. "Odd" defenses put a defensive lineman on the center's head (the old "mass of flesh" defense) and then spread the ends. "Even" fronts (unless over- or undershifted) have no one the center, as in the proceeding diagram.

Put some mean guy on the center's head, and three things happen. First, it is a lot harder making an accurate snap back to the QB in shotgun formation when you are about to get "Nomellini-ed" by the nose tackle. Second, the center can't get downfield to take on a linebacker. He has to concentrate on the noseguard. Moreover, a guard will have to help out to make certain the nose tackle doesn't "one-technique" (split the center and guard) the offense. Third, it is a lot harder to run inside. Running outside might now be easier, but since the field is spread, the tactic plays to where the defense is, as opposed to where it is not. Michigan's decision to go odd seemed sound.

George Halas or not, on the next series Michigan went odd twice, but neither time did it work, the Cats ripping off big gains. However, both instances must have involved some kind of a communication mix-up, since these formations were overshifted to the weak side of the formation:

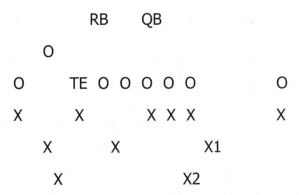

```
              RB    QB
        O
        O      TE O  O  O  O  O              O
        X      X         X  X  X             X
             X      X              X1
          X                   X2
```

Here we were odd (in a four-man front), but the defense is shifted away from the strength of the formation. On both instances, the Wildcats optioned to the strong side (the tight end side) where there were more blockers than defenders. X1 and X2 are useless and, as internet "jon" suggested, Michigan was shifted away from the only direction the option can be run. The Wildcats score a TD, but it was nullified by a holding call, and they eventually settled for a field goal. The play that stalled the drive was an odd front with the field balanced. George Halas lives!!!

Michigan continued to punish the hapless Northwestern defense for another touchdown. It took eight (all different) plays (including a holding call against the Wolverines), the visiting team using more variation than would seem necessary to keep the Cats off balance. It was 21–10.

On the Wildcats' fourth series, they went three and out, attempting to run wide on the four-on-two. They punted and, again, had no ability to stop the Michigan offense, Henson hitting David Terrell in the end zone to make it 28–10—the jinx score of the season. Northwestern seemed notably unfazed by the deficit, passing under the linebackers and running two options against the four-on-two front when it did not shift appropriately to the side Anderson was positioned; 28–17. The Wildcats then attempted an onside kick, and they recovered it. Lloyd Carr went berserk on the play, since the Wildcat who recovered the ball (caught it in the air, actually) was offside. Significantly offside, in the range of three yards. However, (a) he caught the ball twenty yards upfield, and there was no Wolverine within a couple of yards, so he might have recovered the kick anyway, and (b) if there is one infraction that is routinely uncalled, it is offside on the kicking team during kickoffs. Like offensive holding, it is not a call that one can count on. Carr was both right and wrong. In this instance, his correctness was mostly technical.

In his frustration, Coach Carr never mentioned the fact that on Michigan's prior kickoff, it appeared that Michigan was (if slightly) offside. It turned out that Northwestern fumbled the kickoff, and Michigan seemed to recover. But, like an instance in the Illinois game earlier in the year (a call that went UM's way), there was a scrum for the ball and Northwestern ended up with it by the time the play was unpiled. If, hypothetically, Michigan had recovered the ball and was called offside on that play, Lloyd would have had a major-league gripe. As it is, I found this complaint (when it continued after the game) a little weird. Especially when he had a much larger complaint to make (but didn't) about the worst judgment call in the history of Michigan football in the second half. A call that probably cost him a win. On the other hand, I suppose the guy *was* three yards offside.

Michigan continued to have no answer for the Northwestern offense, but the Wildcats stalled at the UM nine and settled for a field goal. On the kickoff, Michigan was whistled for an illegal block and, with 1:11 left in the half, the Wolverines had a first and ten at their own fifteen. Now, in a similar situation as the Purdue game, Michigan had a choice between (a) running out the half and regrouping with a 28–20 lead (Michigan received the ball to start the second half), or (b) putting the pedal to the metal to see if they could get into scoring position. I would suggest either option, in the context of this game, was viable and reasonable. But, like in the Purdue game, the Wolverines seemed to choose neither course. With Northwestern playing very soft, the only rational way of choosing (b) was "risk" passes, that is, those underneath the Northwestern corners and away from linebackers dropping into coverage. Instead, Michigan threw deep on first down, a safe play, but a hard one to complete against the defense. The pass fell harmlessly to the turf when Terrell was blanketed by the secondary and Henson was pressured. On second down, Michigan reverted to (seemingly) running the clock, and a draw play was stuffed for a loss of five. Northwestern called timeout and had one left. At this point, instead of bleeding the last timeout—and resorting to choice (a)—Michigan reverted to (b), and the Wolverines attempted to pick up the first down with a long pass. The pass was incomplete (David Terrell was double covered), and Northwestern got the ball back on the UM forty-six with forty-four seconds left in the half (and one timeout). Using the TO, Northwestern was able to move to the UM twenty-eight with a few seconds left. The forty-five-yard field goal was good, and the half ended with Michigan ahead 28–23.

In my view, the Michigan coaches never decided what they wanted to do from a tactical perspective and, in the end, this might have cost them the game. At the time, however, it seemed a minor blip. Michigan showed a powerful and organized offense in the first half. And there was no reason to believe that the offense would be less successful in the second half. The enigma was, what's going on with the defense? Again, it seemed to me that Michigan never chose what they wanted to concede. The defense in the first half appeared to be saying (a) we will not give up the long pass, (b) we will concede the short pass, but attempt to minimize the yards after catch, (c) we will try to stop the

Northwestern running game, even when it uses a tight end, with six in the box. Among (a), (b), and (c) in the first half, only (a) was a success. I think I would have made a different choice. By choosing to limit the pass over the DBs, I think we enhanced the prospects of the Northwestern strategy. I was hopeful about second-half changes, thinking that Michigan might gamble on limiting safety help on the deep throws and bring them into the running game. Plus, watching the tape well after the game, I kept waiting for odd fronts to show up in the second half.

Michigan returned the second half kickoff to the twenty-eight, and the offense continued to be effective. Northwestern stayed with the strategy of playing the run and defending the air with soft coverage. Henson exploited this choice again, with long passes to Marquise Walker and Terrell. Even when the Wildcats were in the right coverage, it didn't seem to matter, with Henson and Terrell playing pitch and catch as if no DBs were on the field. It took seven plays. Michigan led 35–23.

Michigan returned to the 4/2 on the first Wildcat series of the half, and the Cats ripped off a twenty-five-yard run on their second play. But the UM defense stiffened at midfield after a penalty (a chop block) was called on NU. My cursory review of the tape, I admit, didn't reveal the infraction. On third and twenty, Kustok could not find a receiver, and he scrambled for ten yards. As Kustok neared the sidelines UM linebacker Eric Brackins attempted to make a tackle. Brackins missed, *perhaps* touching Kustok on his right shoulder as the QB went out of bounds. It was, on the replay, a touch at most. And the replay shows that if Kustok was "hit," he was "hit" inbounds. It is the worst officiating judgment call I have seen or ever will see in my life. Danielson and Musburger (NU fans) groaned in the booth over the call, a personal foul against Michigan. It was first down for the Wildcats, and they connected on a thirty-yard pass two plays later. On third and four from inside the ten, Kustok threw a ball (probably tipped by UM lineman Dan Rumishek and thrown seven yards behind the receiver) that resulted in a pass interference call on Todd Howard. No comment. You look at the tape. Northwestern scored two plays later, but they missed the extra point. 35–29, Michigan.

At this juncture in the game, it seemed pretty likely that the Michigan defense wasn't stopping this offense. But the Michigan offense wasn't giving up either. A good kickoff return, a thirteen-yard waggle and five runs by Anthony Thomas moved the ball to the Northwestern twenty-nine. On third and nine, Henson hit Ronald Bellamy over the middle for nineteen yards, and AT scored three plays later. Not counting the drive at the end of the half, Michigan had six possessions and six touchdowns. It was 42–29. But I didn't think the Michigan D was going to get a stop.

They didn't. Northwestern returned the kickoff to midfield. On second and nine, NU brought in a tight end, and Michigan made no adjustment to the formation. Northwestern called its inside handoff to the strong side where the Cats had a four-blocker-to-three-defender edge. It became worse when the offside linebacker did not react to the handoff and the offside guard, trapping on the play, executed a perfect block on the onside linebacker. It was a foot race and Anderson won, running for a fifty-yard touchdown. It was 42–36, and there was still time left in the third quarter. For most of the world (everyone excluding Michigan fans), this was an incredible game. Even incredible for Randy Walker, since he chose to up the ante with another (and I might say dubious) onside kick. I can't say I've ever seen two called in a game (outside of endgame desperation) but the kick was poorly executed and Michigan covered the ball at the Northwestern forty. On first down, Terrell was being held on a slant pattern but broke free in the end zone. DT dropped the ball (he was rightfully pissed at himself) when he suffered an anomalous case of "alligator arms," but pass interference was called. The drop proved crucial, since Michigan was flagged for holding on the next play and they did not recover from the penalty. However, Hayden Epstein kicked a fifty-two-yard field goal, his best effort of the season. Michigan was up 45–36, still retaining the two-score edge. But there was still 2:28 left in the third.

At this moment, even watching the tape for the umpteenth time, I was steamed up about this game and I went back to try to find the hold. Okay, I admit it. If the hold had been called against the Cats, I would have assumed it was the right call. There is no way I would waste my time looking. And if the call was wrong, tough. In this, I am no different than the average fan of any school or the now constantly whining Joe Pa. But at least I admit the vagaries of holding calls, and I admit Michigan probably holds about as much as every other team in the Big Ten. My guess is the statistical data for any point of view does not and cannot exist. And, as long as we're at it, I admit that offside calls on kickoffs are made about every other millennium. But was it a hold? I don't see it. I watched the tape a dozen times. Slowed it down frame by frame. It ain't there. I can't even find a flag. Maybe a Cat fan can find it. But its gonna be hard, since the Michigan linemen (mostly) fanned on their blocks, and Henson ran for his life with the linemen either standing around or falling on their faces as Henson tossed the ball away.

After Epstein's long and accurate field goal, he expertly grounded the ball out of bounds on the kickoff. Northwestern used a tight end on first and second down, and the Michigan defense adjusted to a standard 4/3, overshifting to the strong side of the formation. On third and one, Kustok tried a sneak and was stuffed, but Michigan was called for a flagrant face mask. The replay does not show any face mask, and Danielson, also not seeing it, said, "It must have been pretty obvious, since it was called by the head referee." Hmm. A Tim Brantism. If Mr. Spock is so smart, why isn't he captain of the Enterprise? Well, I came out of the game with an enhanced opinion of Musburger and

Danielson, but this was a pretty classic non sequitur. On the other hand, I agree with Danielson as to the fact of the call. The replay was from a poor angle, and it is the sort of call that is rarely wrong.

After the penalty, Hermann changed tactics, on one instance blitzing seven with the DBs in a soft coverage. It didn't work, Kustok making a nice throw for twenty-two yards between Todd Howard and the safety. Northwestern scored on a twelve-yard scramble by the Northwestern QB. UM 45, NW 43. Almost a quarter to go. And things became desperate on the next series when Duane Missouri, maybe the best defender on the field this day (but I admit that's not saying much), beat tackle Mo Williams and caused a fumble deep in Michigan territory. Michigan jammed the line of scrimmage and gambled on second and third downs, and the Northwestern drive lost yards. But they executed a forty-three-yard field goal, and the Cats took the lead 46–45. But the Michigan offense and Henson were still breathing.

Michigan used eleven plays to score, AT stiff-arming two defenders on a sweep from the one-yard line to put UM ahead 51–46. The big plays were a sixteen-yard out pattern caught by Walker, and two twelve-yard catches by David Terrell. Michigan decided to try for a two-point conversion and was unsuccessful, a decision that was a reasonable (though not my) choice. Fifty-one to forty-six? This cannot be possible.

But there was more. Northwestern started its next drive from its own twenty-three with eight minutes remaining in the game. They threw an incompletion on first down, but Larry Foote was charged with a personal foul on a late hit on Kustok. On the next play, Damien Anderson fumbled and Michigan recovered. But the officials determined that the play was dead, Musberger stating, "Apparently he was already down." I won't release the results of my own replay. Kustok was then sacked for a ten-yard loss, Northwestern was penalized for a chop block (I can't find this penalty either) and, with 6:34 to go, Michigan had the ball with a legitimate opportunity to ice the game. (Indeed, if they had kicked the damned extra point, a field goal would also have been likely to ice it.) The Wolverines converted two first downs but, with the ball at midfield, they stalled when a deep pass did not connect, a reverse lost four yards, and Henson threw a rare poor pass on third and fourteen. The Cats, apparently, drew the line at fifty-one points. Enough is enough.

Michigan punted to the Northwestern ten, and the strength and weakness elements of the game reversed course. There was 3:36 left on the clock. Northwestern did not blow the chance. Well, they almost didn't blow it. It took the Wildcats a minute and change to move eighty-two yards for a first and goal at the Michigan eight. On first down, Michigan clogged up the run. On second down, Kustok threw an incomplete pass. On third down, an option lost two yards when Larry Foote made a nice play. On fourth down, the game riding on the play, Northwestern ran a screen. It worked to perfection, and the Cats scored. But a penalty was called for an illegal receiver downfield. On the replay, Danielson and Musburger are polite about the call, concluding that it was "very close," and noting that "almost every other close call in the game has gone against the Wolverines." Well, let me amend this. Michigan got a half dozen awful calls in the game. Northwestern was hammered on a couple of whoppers, too. And there is no question this was the worst call (for NU), since even though the lineman was well downfield, it was a legal play, since the pass was caught at the line of scrimmage or (even) a few inches behind. The replay shows the call was wrong. It should have been a Northwestern touchdown. It was a Northwestern touchdown. But, to their credit, neither Danielson nor Musberger complained (they left this up to me and the trash I left littered around the TV screen), and I came away with a revised opinion of the duo. Musburger is a Northwestern grad. Danielson's son was the backup quarterback at Northwestern. They were honest in the fact that they were cheering for the Wildcats, but they bent over backward to be fair to the Wolverines during the contest. The ability to look past a pretty crucial and awful call without going berserk portrayed their professionalism. I am a mere fan. I have an excuse. Tim Brant? He has an excuse too. He is still an idiot.

Bad call or otherwise, Northwestern was redeemed with another opportunity. On fourth and goal from the twelve, Michigan blitzed Kustok and he threw up a duck. An awful looking, wobbly, and dog-assed heave. The sort of pass that is always incomplete. Except when it is intercepted. Except this day, when the star of the game, Damien Anderson, was standing alone in the end zone. No defender was remotely close to him, the Wolverines apparently unconcerned about the player who had done the most damage. Anderson, twisting spasmodically in a sort of curlyesque pinwheel meneuver, dropped the ball. In any event, that's the game, Michigan lucky as hell, winning 51–46. But not quite. What? The end of this dratted tape still exists?

The Wolverines had the ball, and there were forty-six seconds remaining in the game. On first down, AT ran wide for eight yards. Timeout Cats. And then, on second down, with Northwestern loading the defensive front with nine defenders, AT broke through and was streaking downfield when he dropped the ball. Just plain dropped it. Northwestern recovered. Thomas, the other offensive star of the game, created a sort of symmetry with the Anderson miscue. You be good. Me too. I will create closure. There are 35 seconds left in the game. A pass for five. Another for thirteen and another for a touchdown. Northwestern was ahead 52–51 and then 54–51 when they converted the two-point attempt.

There were fifteen seconds left after Walter Cross made a nice kickoff return to the Michigan thirty-six. Michigan gained twenty-six yards on two passes and, with one play left, the ball was on the Northwestern thirty-nine-yard line. Definitely within Epstein's reach, especially with the mild wind at his back. Michigan played for the tie, but the snap eluded the holder's grasp and Epstein completed a pass downfield to the NU thirty. And time ran out. I am certain I have never seen any game quite like this. Certainly not any Michigan game. I am exhausted. The Northwestern offense shredded the Michigan defense as in no other game I have ever seen. The words came bitter the first time through but, I had to admit, I felt like the Northwestern offense had shredded me.

* * * *

As it turned out, Anthony Thomas became a major star in his first year in the NFL (2001), one of the top two or three rookies in the league. In 2001, Thomas rushed the ball 278 times for more than thirteen hundred yards. How many times did AT fumble in 2001 when no one hit him? None. How many fumbles did Thomas have over the course of the year in the NFL when he was being clobbered-by-big-and-fast-behemoths-for-chrissakes? Well, uh, none. Lloyd Carr must be shaking his head. But here is the rule, if I haven't said it before. When games are close, they are decided by fortune, chance, the randomness of events. Feel better now?

Eight *What Fans Say and Why We Are Idiots*

I am a fan. I am writing this book. I get to go first. That's how it goes in the universe of deductive logic. My diary notes follow:

November 7, 2000. In the days following the Northwestern loss, some fans excoriate Jim Hermann, the Michigan defensive coordinator, as a complete numbskull. This is almost understandable, since Michigan fans are used to good defense, especially against Northwestern, and the carnage in the game was serious, an all-time record against any Michigan team. The Wildcats put up 654 yards in the game. A record. Second place ain't close. And fifty-four points? Not quite a record, though a scan of the Michigan history book shows just how remarkable the game is. In the 120 years of Michigan football, UM has given up forty points or more only eight times prior to the most recent contest. In 1883, we gave up forty-six points to Yale. Our worst loss, in 1889 to Cornell, was 56–0, but in that game, according to one participant that I questioned, the Big Red was stomping on the naive Wolverines' toes with its very sharp spikes. My brother, also known as the Worst Fan in the United States, played for Cornell in the seventies (the 1970s), and claims that foot puncture continued to be a staple in the Big Red offensive arsenal almost a hundred years later.

After the Cornell trickery, Michigan went thirty-six years without giving up as many as forty points in a game until a weak Michigan team lost 40–0 to Minnesota in 1935. I haven't looked it up, but I hope Gerald Ford was the captain of that team. Twenty-three years later, in 1958, Northwestern scored fifty-five points against one of the worst Michigan teams ever. In 1961 and 1968, Woody ran up fifty against the Wolverines. And in Bo's debut season (1969), a pack of turnovers led to a 40–17 loss to Missouri. In 1991, FSU won a 51–31 shootout in Ann Arbor. And that is it. Nine games over forty points out of over eleven hundred. And more than fifty-three? Only twice. In 1889 and 1958. By my calculator, that is, uh, zero percent of all games played in the past forty-two years.

Putting it in another context, in the fifty-seven games in the 1901 through 1905 seasons, UM gave up forty-two points. Total points. Yeah, offenses weren't as sophisticated then. But the Wolverines did manage to eke out 2,791 points over the same period. (This is an average score of 49 to 0.75. How can it be that a team's average winning margin was 48.25 points? And think about this. A TD was only worth five points in those seasons, and the field was 110 yards long. And games were often not completed. Michigan preferred to play seventy-minute games, but often had to concede to forty-minute contests to find opposition. In the 1902 game against MAC (MSU), the MAC players walked off the field (down 119–0) after thirty-six minutes. I have passed this fact on to Tommy Amaker as a possible strategy next time we get the opportunity to tangle with the basketball Dukies or Spartans. If we can negotiate a ten or fifteen minute game it might not look quite so bad.) Indeed, Michigan has completed forty seasons when they didn't give up fifty-five points, though I admit this statistic is not particularly meaningful. But in that (a) Northwestern's scores were not (in the main) turnover predicated, and (b) the defense was not put under any sort of unusual pressure by the failures of the offense (fifty-one points and one turnover [no INTs] to Northwestern means the offense was doing its part), I think it is fair to conclude that (c) this was the worst defensive performance by any team in any game in Michigan history. I defy anybody to find another game that even comes close. The bizarreness of this is underscored by the fact that the defense was coming off of two consecutive shutouts, one of the shutouts against a team that had shown excellent offensive ability.

So the criticism of Jim Hermann is understandable, though I am certain it is not justified. Indeed, the postgame internet posts characterized Hermann to be something in the nature of Curly Howard, as opposed to the introspective and thoughtful person that he is. Carr, in his postgame comments, merely stressed that Michigan's tackling was awful. It was. But the pursuit angles of the tacklers were also awful, and that might have something to do with the structure of the defense. But was the coaching poor? I think I am asking the wrong person. It is an absolute fact that Jim Hermann knows what he is doing. It is an absolute fact that Jim Hermann did not become an idiot since he ran the 1997 defense, one that won a national championship despite the absence of an offense that could control a game.

The 2000 Michigan defense had no pass rushers, a condition that put a lot of pressure on the defensive backs. Beyond this, it was an extremely young and inexperienced defensive team. There was no playmaker on the team, no Ian Gold and certainly no Charles Woodson. Still, with the caveat that this sort of conclusion is always easy in retrospect, I think the defense played it too safe, trying to make certain they weren't burned by the deep pass or the medium route that breaks due to the lack of safety help. I think this was a strategic mistake.

Northwestern was a running team and it was crucial to stop the run first. And, or so it seems to me, this meant (against the Northwestern spread) the resort to man coverage, and forcing a safety to play run or zones that allowed the DBs to be more active in run support. I think, by trying to protect against everything, UM allowed the Northwestern offensive line to dominate the game. But could it have been a pure execution problem? Sure. It is possible that Michigan played the ideal defense against Northwestern, one that had the maximum ability to limit the NU offense, given the context of the defense's abilities. But I just can't believe Michigan was that inept. And, as an afterthought, I wonder if Michigan would have been better in an odd front (nose guard on the center), using three down linemen, three linebackers, and a "wolf." In other words, the old Michigan three-on-four, a formation that is tougher on the option than even fronts. I admit, however, that Kustok just might have thrown the ball all day, a strategy that might have been as effective. Still, this seems outside of what Northwestern wanted to do. Northwestern was imitating Pop Warner's single wing of 1906, running more blockers at the point of attack than defenders. The pass was merely a show to allow the single wing to do its stuff.

* * * *

October 17, 2001. I didn't know it at the time of my prior writing, but I think my comments about the odd front turned out to be arguable, compliments of George Halas and Red Hickey. In 2001, I saw an MSU defense with a poor secondary, great linebackers, and a fair defensive line limit the Northwestern offense to seventeen points over all but the last three minutes of the contest by staying in an odd front and pressuring the center. Having to resort to the pass when the MSU defense bottled up the Wildcat running game, the Cats were a much less powerful team. Indeed, they were more or less average. Like Red Hickey's innovation in 1961, coaches are adjusting and beginning to figure out that the Randy Walker offense is the single wing in a new uniform. Or, as it is said in law reviews, old wine in new bottles.

Michigan also divined the solution. The Wolverines opened the 2001 season against Miami of Ohio, a team that emulated (exactly, to my eyes) the Northwestern offense. Michigan continued to use four down linemen against the Red Hawks, but made certain the Miami center was occupied by a tackle on his nose, an under- or over-shifted variation of an odd front. Plus, the Wolverines pressured the line of scrimmage with their backers, forcing Miami into passing the ball. Even with a woeful showing by the Michigan offense, the Wolverines scraped out a 31–13 win with Miami gaining only 127 yards on the ground, and much of this via the quarterback (Ben Roethlisberger) scrambling against a backup defensive front late in the fourth quarter. For most of the game, Miami had no running attack. The same was true in the 2001 Michigan-Purdue contest, with the Wolverines staying odd against the shotgun spread and holding a decent Purdue running game to fifty-seven yards in thirty-seven attempts.

The Northwestern offense is anything but passé, but it will be eclipsed by some new wine in old bottles. The T-formation, perhaps. Indeed, after a bad loss in 2001 to OSU, the Northwestern coaching staff began to have doubts. OSU copied the MSU defense (odd fronts, jam the line of scrimmage), and was able to derail the Northwestern attack, at least in part, and scooted home with an eighteen-point win. Randy Walker's explanation was (as reported in the *Chicago Tribune*) that, "In an effort to make it perfect, we became cautious and inexact. In the effort to get the perfect call, the perfect play . . . we [began to] outthink ourselves. Let's not forget what we do best and let's not try to make it a perfect world." Walker's solution? Get back to basics. The Northwestern coach stated that in 2000, they had kept the playbook simple. Post-MSU and OSU, he began to think they had "too much stuff," and they were suffering from the "law of diminishing returns—that you can only get good at so much." Walker then uttered the ultimate profanity in the fan and color guy world: "I have yet to see a great offense that wasn't predictable. That's what we're going to do." In other words, Walker is harkening back to the past of Paul Brown and Lombardi. Run the offense, but keep it simple and predictable, so that execution comes to the fore.

Unfortunately for the Cats, Walker's revisionism didn't work against Minnesota in the week after these statements, as the Gophers whacked the Northwestern running game, holding the Cats to 113 yards in forty-six carries. The Gophers also shredded the Wildcat defense (257 yards rushing), but threw three interceptions and this allowed Northwestern to squeak by. My guess is, at this moment, the Wildcats will try to simplify their offense, but in the context of a new wrinkle. The defenses have been catching up, and I expect Walker, a very smart and wily customer, won't relent in the attempt to stay ahead of the curve.

* * * *

At the close of the 2004 season, Michigan fans were again (rightfully) in a funk about UM's disability to handle running quarterbacks. MSU's Drew Stanton and OSU's Tony Smith shredded the Wolverine defense out of single wing offenses. Then, in the Rose Bowl, Texas quarterback Vincent Young just free-lanced (no single wing) and juked the UM defense into oblivion in an exciting 38–37 last second win over the Wolverines. The truth is that Young is the reincarnation of Michael Vick and was just too fast and slippery for the Wolverines to handle. Still, in my judgment, the Wolverine defense would have fared better with more limited attempts to pressure Young, playing "passive" and forcing him to make throws into the creases of the defense. The attempts to pressure Young and play "aggressive" defense played to the strength of the Texas offense.

My advice is to toss the Texas game out of your equations and view it as a playmaker just making plays. But what about Stanton and Smith? Well, these guys can play, too, but in these games it was the system of these offenses that gave Michigan fits. The question for Wolverine fans in 2005 is how do we defend running quarterbacks out of the single wing? It seemed, in 2001, we had solved the problem. Maybe the solution remains vital, but OSU and MSU certainly out-executed the Michigan defense in 2004.

* * * *

I think that most cities and towns can be characterized as having an opinionated populace. Let's see. Most people are opinionated. Most residents of towns are people. I think this works. Ann Arbor has its own variations on the theme, however, with many holding force on items other than politics or religion or even sports. For those who haven't lived here, the city's quirkiness is hard to explain. It is a feel. A sense. A certain aura of something just-not-quite-on-center, like the ordinary Ann Arbor winter sleet storm where no one pays attention to that cyclist forging through the falling slush in a tee shirt and Birkenstock sandals. Many say they live here because they wouldn't be accepted anywhere else. This is followed, always, by a commentary about the positive anonymity of big cities and, inevitably, the lament that "New York is just not for me." There is a tolerance for difference in the city that does not extend to all places I have lived or other places that local denizens reference. The diversity of thought, language, dress, and being is remarkable for a town nestled between the cracks of the rust belt.

The best way that I can explain this feel is an anecdote. In the spring of 2001, my wife and I attended a performance of Mahler's Tenth Symphony as played by the Royal Concertgebow Orchestra. I am not a classical music expert. Indeed, I know less about it than football, but I thought the performance was terrific, and the majority of those in attendance at Hill Auditorium (SRO at 4,200) seemed to share my enthusiasm, since they responded with a standing ovation and numerous calls for the return of conductor Ricardo Chailly. In the midst of these ovations, a tuxedo-garbed man came stomping up our aisle with a large briefcase. His hair was askew. His face was red. He was screaming, "It sucked!" and gesturing wildly at the crowd. It was Stanley X (not his real name), a local classical music expert, critic, entrepreneur, and lecturer. I had attended a few of his lectures (they were brilliant), and I knew him slightly, though he considered me to be (and rightfully so) your basic music Philistine. On the other hand, he took my wife Sue seriously. Stan is an expert on Wagner, and he seems to have some tolerance for the variance of opinion about Wagner performances. But he draws the line at Mahler, and he takes commentary on old

Gustav as his own personal arena of ministry and vigilance. When it comes to Mahler, in the Stanley X world, there are no shades of gray. Moreover, when it comes to other opinions about Mahler, Stan believes everything you know is likely to be wrong, even if your name is Arturo Toscanini or Leopold Stokowski. In this instance, you can call me Arturo.

As Stan came up the aisle, he saw us and ranted, "This is a town of complete imbeciles. How can I live in a city where no one has *any* understanding of the *absolute* dreck that was just dished up?"

Over the continued applause, I queried, "What do you mean, Stan? I thought it was great."

"These morons just ruined one of the greatest pieces of music of all time. And I have to sit here and listen to this knucklehead audience applaud the fools. They should be booing. Any person one note away from tone-deaf would be catcalling till the orchestra scrammed out of this place and never defiled it again."

"Uh, Stan, you know I am no expert, but it seemed pretty good to me."

"Bah! Don't talk to me."

I smiled at Stan as he stalked away. I was, indeed, glad for his tirade. It was a perfect punctuation for the performance. It made complete sense to me that what most of the audience thought was great, he found to be woeful. In fact, it struck me as perversely satisfying that Stan was probably right. If he thought it was a crappy performance, it probably was a crappy performance. But we still liked it. Shouldn't this be how life is? Shouldn't we tend to be satisfied unless there is some damned good reason to feel otherwise? None of this win/lose demarcation of the sports world where, you might play great, but due to the randomness of events, you lose and become, well, a dolt as woeful as Jim Hermann. And isn't the win/lose of sports a little overrated? Hey, if somebody likes McDonald's better than real food, who am I to be a killjoy? Let them eat that horsemeat. On the other hand, I am really happy that the killjoys exist. In the words of an old hockey player (Bronco Horvath, I think), "They penetrate the homogeneous gloom." And they explain and supply some sense to an order that seems to exist on its own.

I sighed at these thoughts. After all, midway through the 2001 season, Jim Hermann became reinstitutionalized as a genius after his year of dodo-hood. Then, at the close of the 2004 season, his IQ declined again. I hope, indeed, the same fate awaits Stanley X, that he makes a triumphant return to Hill Auditorium to a standing ovation. Except for one thing. One person who dissents. Me, perhaps, yelling at Stan, "Yo, Stan! You bonehead."

But out on the evening blocks of Ann Arbor, on Washington Street this time, Sue and I bumped into Stan again, this time as he screamed at a woman in a VW . . . well-I-do-not-want-to-say. This is a clean book with obscene rants and not the other way around. As he saw us again, he began to bellow about

162

the inferiority of the performance and how the conductor was "an absolute cretin." I started to laugh. Stan began to apologize. It wasn't necessary to apologize, I told him, enjoying myself even more. I asked him to explain exactly what his objections to the performance were, when Sue tugged at me and gave me a look that told me to break it off. "Don't egg him on," she whispered. "He seems really upset." At this moment, a tall, thin, and very well-dressed man yelled at Stan from the other side of Washington Street.

"Stan, you sold me two copies of that symphony and neither one of them was nearly as good as the one we heard tonight. I think . . ."

"Blow me!!" Stan bellowed, before the man could complete his thoughts, and I burst into complete laughter, Sue whacking me on the arm. Stan apologized to me again, saying it wasn't right that we should be subjected to his outburst. I nodded but told him I wouldn't have missed it for the world. Stan turned back to the man and yelled, "It's one thing to have to endure mediocre playing of mediocre music. It's another thing to endure the complete ruination of a *great* piece of music!" I was really enjoying this now, and I tried to urge him on again, but he just smiled and stumbled off the street to the parking structure on our left.

"I am sorry," he said.

I wasn't. And neither was the tall customer of Stan's, who crossed the street, smiling and shaking his head. "The world is a better place with him," he said. I agreed, of course. Without the Stanley Xs, why be alive?

Stanley X may be one of a kind in the world of classical music, but he is strictly garden variety in sports, where fans know, or think they know, the cause of the failings of their teams. Unlike Stanley X, however, the average fan, especially the average football fan (yeah, yeah, including me—you can nominate me for the Larcom Award and I won't bat an eye), is almost always wrong. There are two reasons for this. First, football coaches tend to make their sport as mysterious and arcane as quantum physics. When asked a less-than-complex question about why a play didn't work or why a defense failed, a coach might say (as I actually heard a Purdue coach intone after the Boilermaker 2001 loss to Michigan), "Well, our tackle was supposed to be in five technique but he went into three technique, and so the defense broke down." For most of us, this is just plain, "Huh?" Kevin Lamb, in *Quarterbacks and Nickelbacks,* suggests this isn't mere churlishness by coaches. He writes that NFL players and coaches encourage the perception that football is hopelessly complicated. This perception, he argues, tends to elevate the status of the game, and makes coaches the equivalent of mystical Indian gurus if they win, or (win or lose), as sophisticated as the average MIT research scientist. As Lamb points out, the ordinary fan thinks, for example, that Terry Bradshaw should be a Nobel candidate.

Baseball fans, unlike football fans, have been educated by the players and commentators of the game, and especially by statistical analysis types like Bill

James. This has created a cadre of sophisticated fans, a very large cadre. In the summer of 2000, during an Indians-Twins game in Cleveland, I heard a sixty-ish woman explaining to another woman why pitcher Bartolo Colon's "four-seamer" was less effective than his "two-seamer." Later in the game, she suggested that Cleveland manager Charlie Manuel was stealing less this year because of concerns about the health of Kenny Lofton, Omar Vizquel, and Robrto Alomar, and the fact that "you have to steal at 70 percent to make it worthwhile, and these guys have all lost a half step. Plus, with Jim Thome and Manny Ramirez behind them, the gain is not worth the risk." I suspect this lady had read her Bill James, and she was an above-average fan. But just that. In my ordinary walks around Jacobs Field, these commentaries waft through the summer heat like dandelions. In this respect Kevin Lamb asks, "When was the last time you heard someone in the stands (during a football game) start to boo and then interrupt himself and explain that he couldn't really boo the play since he didn't understand it?"

In this regard, I hear continual invective by Michigan fans about the "stretch" play, particularly when the play is run to the short side of the field. Michigan fans just hate this play, and perceive it as a wasted down, even though, on occasion, it breaks big. What is lost on most fans is that the stretch play is the setup for the fan favorite of the past five years, the "waggle," a play where the quarterback fakes the stretch, with all of the action moving to that side of the field, and then rolls out in the opposite direction for a short toss to a tight end or wide receiver dragging across the field. This play has seemed to work since 1997 for routine and significant gains. But if you don't run the stretch (or something else that freezes the defense), no one is going to pay any attention to the motion of the play, and the waggle will be very difficult to execute. You can't make the latter effective without the threat of the former. But coaches are loath to explain this. As Lamb writes,

> Fan confusion places a maze between the public and the play-
> er or coach who deserves blame for a bad play, or a bad game,
> or a bad season. Ask a coach what went wrong on a play when
> two open receivers bumped into each other and he can always
> answer in terms of orange formations and slice techniques
> and scoop blocks, which discourages further conversation.
> Coaches and players do not like to encourage second-guess-
> ing, which is understandable since the public has a full week
> to evaluate decisions that had to be made in half a second.

It is true, of course, that all professions (even my own) speak in tongues as a way of adding some mystery, cachet, importance, and insulation to the craft. Even plumbers and used car salesmen do it. But I agree with Kevin Lamb that the game would have a broader appeal if coaches and commentators made some nominal attempt to educate the fans. Lamb states that "baseball encourages its fans to believe they know as much as any manager about when to hit and run or when to pull the pitcher [but] football encourages its fans to know nothing more than where to send checks for season tickets. " It is possible, as Lamb notes, that with a more sophisticated set of fans, "coaches might find themselves second-guessed more often, but maybe safeties would be booed less often for following a pass-catcher in the end zone after a corner blew his coverage."

Lamb sees a part of the coaching fraternity's reticence as being rooted in the fear that knowledge will yield more criticism of coaches. I would demur on this, believing the more fans understand the game, the more likely it is that the criticism that accrues may have some merit. Coaches should know by now they are going to be criticized by fans and the media when they lose, even if they put a game plan together that looked like Fritz Crisler, gave a half-time speech that sounded like Knute Rockne, and had a season-long stone face like Tyrone Willingham. So as long as criticism is inevitable, it would seem to be in everyone's interests for the criticism to be informed, as opposed to rants about "slow developing plays" or "conservative" and "predictable" play calling.

Fans are extremely fortunate to hear anything as meaningful as comparisons of "three technique" to "five technique." At least the average fan can go to the library and look up "three technique." Bon voyage, though. Most of the time, a coach will answer a reporter's question with the same sort of meaningless pablum that is spilled over the sports pages. One could cut and paste Lloyd Carr or Tyrone Willingham's postgame comments with no loss in meaning. "I think we gave great effort. We flew around at the ball. The kids never gave up. We have great integrity and I am proud to be around these kids on a daily basis." The next time a head football coach gives any real information to the public, it will be the first time.

There may be one exception to this, the annual women's football clinics at UM. These clinics (women only) are a charitable effort (cancer research) by the entire Michigan coaching staff at the end of the spring practice/player evaluation/recruiting period. My wife attended the first of these events and found it to be a riot. She came to the event a few minutes late, and was ushered into the affair by Michigan players James Hall and Evan Coleman, who yelled at her—and several others—that "Coach Carr does not tolerate coming late to practice," and that she (they) "would have to run wind sprints later." Sue said that Hall, Coleman, Dhani Jones, and Ronald Bellamy were intelligent, funny, and engaging kids, anything but bored by the show.

The first part of the event was a welcoming by Bo Schembechler, who complained, predictably, that the "last male bastion" had been destroyed. After this talk, the women were broken into groups and each position coach rotated to the groups in sequence, starting with the explanation that the position he coached was "the most important on the team." Each coach stressed technique and strategy and, according to Sue, all were approachable, personable, and amusing. When then offensive line coach Terry Malone (Sue's favorite, along with Lloyd Carr) illustrated an offensive lineman's stance, he yelled at a middle-aged woman who stood up in the midst of the demonstration, growling, "I didn't tell you that you could stand up yet."

At the end of the rotations, each participant was given the opportunity to be involved in a (very limited contact) play. Sue's group ran an ordinary isolation play out of the I-formation. The fullback in the set was one Virginia, whose job it was to block the nearest inside linebacker. Virginia, in Sue's estimation, was about seventy-five years old and not very mobile. Coach Malone, running the offense on the play, pointed to the linebacker on the defensive side and barked, "Now, Virginia, your block is the key to this play. When the ball is snapped, I want you to crash between the guard and the tackle and smash into that linebacker." Virginia's response was a very trembling, "Okay, got it, Coach."

There has been a clamoring from men, a downtrodden minority group, for this kind of show/education, but there is no inclination by the Athletic Department to cater to this demand. They prefer the ignorance of men to continue. After all, very few women are going to grouse about conservative or predictable play calling. As a general rule, only men are this stupid. Of course, it is a fact that if reporters asked an intelligent question, they might get some answer about "what went on," as opposed to the same old references that any person who didn't see the game could manufacture.

Post-Northwestern in 2000, there was not a single educated question asked of Lloyd Carr about what the hell happened to allow Northwestern to score fifty-four points and put up 654 yards. Not a single question about odd fronts. Nothing about playing pass against a run offense. Nothing about the single wing or Red Hickey. Nobody even asked whether George Halas was still alive. Nada. It is certain that coaches have very little regard for sports reporters, and rightfully so. After all, they almost never ask meaningful questions, so why the hell should coaches take them seriously? But the result of this is doltish fans and, inevitably, a sort of siege mentality by the coaches and the athletic department that is counterproductive.

Brian Ellerbe, former UM head basketball coach, found it impossible to hide his disdain for reporters. His antipathy was so profound that he would, most all of the time, quibble with the predicate of the question, even if the predicate was absolutely legitimate, if less than enlightening. I empathized with Ellerbe, but his irritation alienated those covering the team and made Ellerbe look nearly as idiotic as the reporters asking the questions. A typical Ellerbe press conference might start like this:

Reporter:	Well, Coach, you got waxed tonight 107–56. Would you say there are some problems with your defense?
Ellerbe:	Not really. We just turned the ball over so many times that we never had the opportunity to get into our half court sets on the defensive end.
Reporter:	So your defense was okay tonight?
Ellerbe:	Not really. We just didn't execute the plays the way we should have.

Or like this:

Reporter:	Well, Coach, you just lost a tight one, 46–27. Would you say there were problems with your offense?
Ellerbe:	Not really. We just didn't box out well, and we gave them too many possessions.
Reporter:	So the offense was pretty good?
Ellerbe:	Not really. We just didn't execute our offensive sets the way we designed them.

How the hell was Ellerbe supposed to answer these kinds of questions? How about, "Really? I thought we did pretty well holding them to a fifty-one-point win. After all, they have a competent but smarmy and sneaky coach, and you guys are stuck with me, a complete lunkhead. Next time those Spartans get in your face, remind them they barely eked by the last time they tangled with us. Mention that they won by a mere fifty-one points, even though the Wolverines had a Pet Rock at the helm."

I suspect and admit that Ellerbe was never asked a meaningful question by any reporter in his career. And, indeed, he was in an impossible situation, with the university refusing to deal with the Ed Martin matter in any rational way. That said, the best part about losing Ellerbe has been the absence of "not really" to the answer to any question, regardless of how dopey or obvious.

Push comes to shove, I blame the coaches and the athletic departments for making the fans and reporters a pack of cretins. And I include myself in this, by the way. But the second group of culprits is reporters, who would seem to have some vested interest in attempting to lift themselves and their clients (readers) out of the ooze. Fat chance. I can't resist another example: Jim

Cnockaert's column after Michigan's 24–10 football victory over Purdue in 2001. In this writing, Jim suggested that the 2001 offense, despite dire predictions to the contrary, was doing "about as well" as the 2000 offense. Cnockaert concluded that the 2001 offense, without Drew Henson, Anthony Thomas, David Terrell, Mo Williams, Jeff Backus, Steve Hutchinson, and David Brandt (the last four, as of this writing, are all starting on NFL offensive lines) was playing pretty close to the 2000 level. Jim opined:

> Heading into Saturday's game against Purdue UM ranked second in the Big Ten in total offense, third in both scoring and passing offense and sixth in rushing offense . . .

> These rankings are pretty amazing [since] last year's offense, with all of those future pros, had slightly better per-game averages in those four categories, but really didn't rank any better in terms of the Big Ten except when it came to running the ball.

I would suggest the phrase "except when it came to running the ball" is like saying, "In their primes, Jesse Owens and former pro rassler Haystack Calhoun were about the same in running the one hundred-yard dash, except that Jesse ran it a whole lot faster." Let's look at the 2000 offense as compared to the 2001 offense as of the time of Jim's writing.

	Yds Per Rush +/-		Yds Per Completion +/-		Passing Efficiency +/-	
2000	4.8		14.6		159.4	
2001	3.6	-25%	12.7	-13%	134	-15.9%

I guess if Jim thought these numbers were equivalent, the *Ann Arbor News* should have cut his paycheck from 13 percent to 25 percent to see if he noticed. And note that the above numbers are understatements in the differences in the offenses.

In 2000, the offense got almost no help from the defense when matched against any two-dimensional attack (UCLA, Purdue, Illinois, Northwestern, and to some extent Auburn and OSU). This meant that, despite the efficiency of the 2000 offense, it ran about nine fewer plays per game than the 2001 version. Plus, there was pressure on the 2000 offense to be perfect, since any mistake was magnified by Michigan's defensive failures. In 2001, the defense allowed the offense to sputter and self-destruct (four turnovers, for example, in the Purdue game), not move the ball at all early in other games (Purdue, Illinois, Washington), and still come out on top by eventually executing (Purdue, Illinois, not Washington) as the game wore on.

The fact is that the 2000 offense was about as good as a college offense is going to get. It was in the top one percentile of college offenses in my lifetime. The 2001 offense, through the MSU game, was downright nasty, excluding the miraculous play of Marquise Walker. The run blocking was marginal, and the pass blocking decent (but just decent). BJ Askew ran hard, but there were not many creases available. John Navarre played intelligently and rarely made a panicked play. But, in QB performance over the past twenty years, I would call Navarre's 2001 season below average, at best, though in the context of Michigan QB play, average is pretty good. (By the end of the season, I would have revised this down to well below average by Michigan standards and about average by historical Big Ten standards. In 2002, Navarre was decidedly above average, even by Michigan QB standards. In 2003, Navarre was damned good by any measure.)

I have had my say. What do the fans say? The most common complaint about the Michigan team is that the Wolverines are "too predictable" or "too conservative." My guess is these are the most common complaints among fans nationwide except, perhaps, at Northwestern in the fall of 2001, when Randy Walker was complaining that the Wildcats had to get back to basics and run a less complicated and more predictable offense. To be honest, I found Walker's statements in this regard to be either pretty funny or compelling since the 2000 Northwestern offense was one of the simplest I saw all year. Very few formations. Very few plays. What Northwestern did was (a) run a "high concept" idea of playing to the weakness in the defensive formation by a sequence of signals from the skybox above the field to the sidelines, to the QB, and then to the team, (b) use a running offense out of what was generally perceived as a passing formation, and (c) spread the field horizontally. By the middle of 2001, when teams realized that (a) the Cats really didn't spread the field vertically, (b) it was a running attack, and (c) it was the single wing in a new wrapper, the offense struggled, except to the extent they could execute and win. Hence, Walker's lament is that they had to get back to execution and keeping it simple. At the time, I predicted only moderate success, absent Walker's ability to make midseason infusions to his ailing running game. As it turned out, the Wildcats lost their last six games of the season. Most of the time the offense was pretty good, but it wasn't 2000. The Cats could still pass, but the running game was sliding. After the NU offense got stoned by Indiana, it seemed the jig was completely up. Meanwhile, the Cat defense was doing its ordinary thing, giving up points faster than they could be counted. Walker either needed to revamp his offensive thought or, easier, find some kids who could tackle. This didn't happen in 2002, the Cats getting creamed by cream puffs early and often. Northwestern did slide by Duke in 2002, proving that the Blue Devils are the complete yin and yang of the major men's sports sponsored by the NCAA. [In

2003 and 2004 Walker continued to prove he could coach, but not enough talent left the Cats with middling success.]

* * * *

Is Michigan predictable? As Randy Walker pointed out, all good offensive teams have some element of predictability. The Browns got the ball to Motley, and then Jim Brown. The Packers ran the power sweep, and then adjusted as the defense overcompensated. The Cowboys ran an infinite number of formations to set up isolation plays for Tony Dorsett. But it was still the same old isolation play. The 49ers threw the ball to the wideouts under coverage, and Bill Walsh insisted on the predictability of the offensive structure, in order to ensure the predictability of the defense. The Vikings threw the ball to Chuck Foreman in the flats. Over and over. They did what worked, and when it worked, they did it again. Glenn Rice could shoot the J. He did. Magic Johnson could take it to the hole, like nobody ever saw, in that big body. He did. No one has ever criticized either tactic as predictable. Yeah, right, Jabbar should have abandoned the sky hook and taken up twenty-foot jump shots. That hook shot was just so irritatingly predictable. As I noted previously, in 1999, a year of complete grousing by Michigan fans about the UM offense, Michigan coaches called pass plays slightly more than half the time. In 2000, with a very strong running game, it dropped to the 40 percent vicinity. Through the first six games of 2001, with the running game slightly better than (and the passing game not as good as) in 1999, the Wolverines returned to a balanced attack, calling running and passing plays evenly. Carr and then Michigan offensive coordinator Stan Parrish responded rationally to the abilities of the team. If they had a running game, they went with it. If they did, they balanced the attack. In 2002, the Michigan running game was again erratic and unimpressive, and the Wolverines continued in a balanced attack, calling passing plays about 53 percent of the time. In 2003, the Wolverines could run and pass, and the run game dominated by 52 to 48 percent.

When I have mentioned the foregoing to passionate anti-Bo and anti-Lloyd fans, they suggest that Michigan uses very few plays and formations, and they "can always tell what's coming." And, it goes, "If I can tell, then certainly Purdue coach Joe Tiller can tell. And so can Wisconsin's Barry Alvarez, and even OSU's (deposed) John Cooper." Well, maybe. But what exactly was John Cooper's record against the Wolverines? I know OSU must have been pounding us over the past fifteen years, given the fan criticism I have heard. And the fact of the matter is that the Purdue guys and Badger guys hardly ever beat the Wolverines, ever. Let's do a decade by decade scan:

	Purdue Wins	Cheesehead Wins
1870s	0	0
1880s	0	0
1890s	1	1
1900s	0	0
1910s	0	0
1920s	1	1
1930s	0	1
1940s	0	0
1950s	0	1
1960s	5	2
1970s	2	0
1980s	1	1
1990s	1	2
2000s	1	0

The most predictable thing here, aside from the fact that this looks more like machine language than anything else, is that Michigan generally beats these teams, except in the 1960s, when Purdue just happened to be better than the Wolverines. But overall, Michigan has beaten Purdue and Wisconsin eighty-seven times to twenty-one losses. I guess that's not what the critics mean. They mean that in those games that Michigan loses, at least those of recent vintage, the Wolverines were too predictable, meaning the Wolverines did not run enough variation in formations or the variations gave away the plays. Or something like that. After all, why the hell should the Badgers or the Boilers ever win a game? Right?

A formidable, recent example is the 2000 Purdue game, where the Wolverines blew a 28–10 lead at the end of the half, and lost 32–31. The fan grousing was, essentially, that Carr was "too predictable"; that Michigan went into a shell in the second half after being a perfect four for four (four possessions, four touchdowns) in the first half. I went back to the tape. What the Wolverines did in this game, as they generally have under Carr in big games, was show a new formation, run a primary and variant play out of that formation and then move into variations on a theme as the game progressed, depending upon what worked and what didn't.

There was much fan praise for the first half performance, and rightfully so. It is hard to complain about twenty-eight points on four possessions. But the truth of the matter is, it was a more shell-like offense than in the second half. In the first two possessions of the game, the primary Michigan set was an off-set I-formation, sometimes with motion by a second tight end, sometimes with no motion, sometimes with both backs resetting their positions before the snap.

On these early series, when there was motion, Anthony Thomas ran behind the H back (tight end). On those plays without motion, Michigan ran simple zone blocking and attempted to spring AT through the middle of the defense. When the backs reset, the play was a pass into the flats. These plays were balanced by (a) short passes in the flats out of a three-wideout, one-back set, (b) an occasional waggle, and (c) a wild card play in each series. The Wolverines also ran ordinary split backs, sometimes handing off to A-Train on a sort of inside reverse, and sometimes showing play action and throwing downfield.

Watching the tape, by the third series, it would seem the Boilers would have figured it out. In this series, on third and two from the Michigan thirty-eight, the Wolverines were in the offset I. There was no motion. Based on the game history, one would predict that AT would be running the ball up the middle. No trap blocking. He did, and he cut to daylight for a sixty-eight-yard touchdown run. So predictable. But I didn't hear anyone on the maize and blue side yammering about the call. Nor did I hear any complaints about the commencement of the fourth series, when, out of the offset I (no motion) Michigan threw in its first wrinkle, a screen pass to BJ Askew for forty yards, the predicate for another touchdown drive.

After Purdue took the second half kickoff for a TD, the first second half Michigan possession went as follows:

1. (First and ten, UM twenty-five) One back formation. Motion by the H back (TE). AT runs behind the TE. No gain.

2. (Second and ten, UM twenty-five) A new formation in the game, AT split wide. Henson tosses a short pass to AT, and he gains nine and a half yards.

3. (Third and a foot, UM thirty-four) The offset I. No motion. AT runs up the middle, and Purdue is waiting. But AT gains the foot for the first down.

4. (First and ten, UM thirty-five) For the first time, UM runs play action out of the offset I. The pass is incomplete.

5. (Second and ten, UM thirty-five) One back. Dropback pass to Ronald Bellamy over the middle of the field. The gain is eight.

6. (Third and two, UM forty-two) At this point Michigan adjusts to play number three. Michigan shows the offset I. No motion. But as the Purdue defense pinches in, Michigan runs a sweep. On televi-

sion, it looks like there is no one between AT and the goal line, but the play is whistled down due to early movement by the tight end.

7. (Third and seven, UM thirty-seven) Shotgun formation. The Wolverines throw over the middle of the field in a fifteen-yard route. Incomplete. Punt.

So, in this series, the Wolverines showed two new plays out of an old formation, but one did not work, and the other went in the tank due to an execution mistake. Not counting the aborted sweep, the Wolverines passed on four out of six plays. I wouldn't call this going into a shell, or anything close.

By the time the Wolverines got the ball back for their second drive of the half, it was late in the third quarter. Again, Carr and Parrish showed a varied and balanced offense. And they moved the ball.

1. (First and ten, UM twenty). One back. Motion. Screen pass to AT for three.

2. (Second and seven, UM twenty-three) One back. No motion. Reverse to wide receiver Ronald Bellamy for thirteen yards.

3. (First and ten, UM thirty-six) Offset I. No motion. AT up the gut for three.

4. (Second and seven, UM thirty-nine) Offset I. No motion. Pass over the middle to David Terrell. Complete for an eighteen-yard gain.

5. (First and ten, Purdue forty-three) Split backs. Inside handoff to AT gains six.

6. (Second and four, Purdue thirty-seven) Same formation and play as number five. Gains two.

7. (Third and two Purdue thirty-five) Offset I. No motion. The blast up the middle. Purdue is waiting. No gain.

Now, it is fair to criticize play number seven. Indeed, since Purdue seemed to have picked up on the probabilities of the formation, I think the call could be questioned. But it also worked, under similar circumstances (down and distance), for a sixty-eight-yard TD in the third series of the game. Even if it was an unwise play, doesn't the offensive coordinator get the right to a clunker every now and then? In any event, it seems irrelevant, since Michigan continued the drive by punting to the Purdue five. The Boilers were three and out, and Michigan returned a punt to the Purdue twenty-five. It was, in a real sense, the same drive. At this point, it was early in the fourth quarter.

1. (First and ten, Purdue twenty-five) One back. Toss to BJ Askew goes for nine yards. A holding call nullifies the play.

2. (First and twenty-one, Purdue thirty-six) Shotgun formation. Short pass to AT for twelve yards.

3. (Second and nine, Purdue twenty-four) Shotgun formation. Pass to Marquise Walker for seven.

4. (Third and two, Purdue seventeen). Split backs. Play action pass to sideline. Incomplete.

Michigan kicked a field goal to go ahead 31–23. Again, there was nothing to criticize in the play selection. The drive was killed by a holding penalty, and the failure to convert the third and two. Purdue drove the field, scored a TD, and missed the extra point. It was 31–29. There was a little over six minutes left in the game. Michigan got the ball at its twenty. It continued:

1. (First and ten, UM twenty) One back. Motion. Wide receiver screen gains five.

2. (Second and five, UM twenty-five) Offset I. No motion. Here it looks like Purdue is guessing AT up the gut. It appears that Henson checks off to run the play to the strong side of the formation and wide. Askew blocks the wrong guy, or so it seems, and the play blows up. Minus six.

3. (Third and eleven, UM nineteen) Shotgun. Henson has all day to throw, but the receivers seem covered. Incomplete.

Michigan punted and Purdue drove the field again. This time they missed a chip shot field goal, and Wolverines had the ball with 2:11 on the clock. The Boilers had two timeouts left.

Here, as in the Northwestern game later in the year, the Wolverines cannot seem to choose between bleeding the clock and chancing the pass that could lead to the first down and win the game. This was a difficult choice and one that, if it went wrong, would subject Lloyd Carr to second-guessing. One first down by the Wolverines and they would close out the game. Given Carr's and Michigan's historical tendencies, it was a lock that Purdue would commit to stopping the run. Did Michigan run the clock? Or did Michigan gamble that Henson could hit a receiver in man coverage and end the game? It appears Coach Carr chose the former, running Thomas into a stacked defense on first down for a gain of one. Purdue called a timeout. On second down, Purdue completely sold out to the run, every defender within four yards of the line of scrimmage. Michigan ran a reverse to Ronald Bellamy. It lost two yards. Timeout. There is 1:56 left on the clock, and Purdue has no timeouts. Michigan, presumably, had chosen the course of bleeding the timeouts and running the clock. Indeed, if they continued with the plan (and, assuming that a draw play gains three to five yards), Purdue would get the ball back with 1:03 at its (approximate) thirty-five with no timeouts. And a field goal kicker who seemed unlikely to make anything beyond forty. This means Purdue has about forty-eight seconds to drive the ball forty-five yards. This would allow them a thirty-seven-yard field goal attempt, probably a fifty-fifty for Dorsch.

On third down, Purdue came out with a standard four-man line. They were playing pass. And Michigan did pass, Henson throwing into coverage on a roll out. Incomplete. Michigan then punted, Epstein booming the ball to the Purdue forty with 1:41 left. Brees scrambled for ten, threw an incompletion and then a completion for nine yards. The clock was running, and there was about a minute left in the game. Third and one. Brees throws a short completion out of bounds for four yards to the Michigan thirty-seven. There were fifty-three seconds on the clock. Assuming the "conservative" strategy, there would be fifteen seconds left, and Purdue would be in a bind, since it takes about ten to eleven seconds to get the field goal team out and ready. They would have had one logical option, a (minimum) twelve-yard out pattern with the receiver getting out of bounds. Instead, they threw short and out of bounds to the thirty-two, and fifty seconds remained. Purdue completed a pass to the twenty-three and, on a ball thrown into the ground to stop the clock, Michigan was caught with too many players on the field. With a few seconds to go, Dorsch tried another thirty-five-yard field goal. Again, the kick was pulled wide. Gary Danielson in the broadcasting booth and the Michigan team thought the attempt might be wide. It wasn't, the ball sneaking through by a few inches of the left upright. Purdue won 32–31.

Looking at the second half of the game, Michigan threw on twelve of twenty-two plays, and ran a reverse on two of the ten runs. The problem here was obvious and it was that Michigan had eight ordinary running plays in the second half. Eight. The failure was not predictability or that the Wolverines went in a shell. It was that the defense could not control the Purdue offense or the clock, and that the offense made two key execution mistakes (penalties) that killed or hampered drives. Fans, tempered by years of being told nothing about the game by those whose job it is to inform, are little more than instinctive. We scored three points in the second half. We must have gone in a shell, because the offense was so good in the first half. The mind connects.

Early in the 2001 season, I was dismayed by the Michigan performance against Miami of Ohio, since the Michigan running game looked woeful. However, as the season wore to the midpoint, the running game improved, and the run defense began to look like a rock pile. After the Western Michigan game, a game where the Wolverines gave up 374 yards passing, an editor from the *UM Press*, an astute fan, called me, expressing her thought that our pass defense was going to be our downfall. She might have been right. But at the time, I was not concerned about pass defense, since passing yards are often empty in terms of the ultimate outcomes, and (aside from this) the Western QB was damned good. I was still worried about the running game.

As a salve to my instinct about the relative emptiness of passing yards, I went back through my database and examined the impact of who won the running and passing games. Looking to either team, it showed that the team that rushed for more yards won ninety-three and lost twenty times, a winning percentage of 82.3 percent. The team that won the passing game won fifty-seven and lost fifty-six, a winning percentage of 50.4 percent. But what about those instances where a team won these wars by more than one hundred yards? On the running side, it made little difference, the hundred-yard winners going 46–9, or 83.6 percent. But the hundred-yard passing winners were 27–18, or 61.4 percent. Evaluating this in the context of those games where the one hundred yard passing winners lost the running game, however, the number fell to 12–17, or 41.3 percent. The inverse situation (hundred-yard running winners that lost the passing yardage game) was 24–8, or 75 percent. All roads seem to lead to Bryant and Schembechler and Hayes. I think it is reasonable to conclude that the hard-won yards, the running yards, are of greater currency than passing yards. All yards are not created equal.

The foregoing became painfully obvious in the 2001 MSU game where Michigan threw two interceptions to none, and the Spartans outrushed the Wolverines. These two conditions almost guarantee a loss, and the Spartans won, 26–24 on a touchdown scored in the last second of the game when a friendly timekeeper may have awarded MSU an extra play. (It was actually worse than this, since the umpire, contrary to NCAA procedures, sprinted the ball from the sidelines to the hash to set up the last play, with no regard for an accurate spot or the fact that the Spartans had eight men on the line of scrimmage on that play. There are other problems with the play, including a blatant hold allowing Spartan QB Jeff Smoker to avoid Larry Stevens, and the fact that the snap on the next to last play happened after the clock hit the one second mark.) But the truth is—despite numerous (three to five) brutally bad calls against Michigan in the first half leading to 14 MSU points—that Michigan did not deserve to win (I am not certain MSU deserved to win either) where

Michigan made key mistakes (interceptions, dopey penalties correctly called), and could not run the ball. MSU, with a marginal (okay, awful actually) passing game, and Smoker getting sacked twelve times (I don't recall ever seeing this many), ran three running plays at the Wolverines. One of the plays, a standard (and hated by UM fans) stretch, was stopped exactly one time by UM. It was as predictable as could be that the Spartans were going to run TJ Duckett on this play, but the Wolverines seemed powerless to stop it. MSU executed the play almost flawlessly (and almost no other at all) again and again. Indeed, it is fair to criticize the MSU coaching staff for not running the play enough, since MSU only got into trouble in the game when it attempted to pass.

This MSU affair illustrates how games are won and how they are lost. Say these mantras: The team that throws more interceptions almost always loses; the team that is more effective in running the ball almost always wins. Put these two together and you gotta be real lucky to come out with a win. So, sure, it is a fact that MSU got some home cooking by the LaPetina officiating crew, a crew that should be drummed out of the Big Ten and the human race. But Michigan dug its own grave in this one and, if we had won, we would have backed into a game and we would have been so damn lucky I (almost) would have preferred the loss. Three years later, in retrospect, I want this loss, I want to own it since I know in my heart we deserved to lose, yet it still gives me something to grouse about.

The LaPetina crew also gave us a hard game in the 2002 OSU affair, two pass interference calls (both wrong) giving a substantial edge to the Bucks. Lloyd Carr also thought these calls were wrong, but felt the game was otherwise well-officiated and didn't really complain about the refs, believing UM should have executed and won anyway. So, at this point, I only suggest LaPetina and his cronies be tortured and given another chance.

From an abstract perspective, my only criticism of Lloyd Carr's biases relate to the end game. As noted previously, I believe that Michigan mishandled the end of the Northwestern and Purdue games in 2000, not because they lost, but because they never seemed to decide what they wanted to do. In trying to play both ends against the middle in those games, Michigan ended up with the worst of all worlds. My criticism with the end of the MSU contest in 2001 was a call that no sane coach would make, yet I think it was the correct choice. With 2:40 left on the clock, Michigan had a fourth and (maximum) one foot at the Michigan sixteen. The Wolverines were leading 24–20. The standard choice is a punt, and no sane coach would do otherwise. None. But I think the logical and rational play is to attempt the first down. The predicate for my belief is that it is fifty-fifty (at least) that Michigan can make a foot on the play. If they run a play and make the first down, with MSU having only one timeout, the game is over. If they don't, Michigan still has the opportunity to stop MSU from scoring a touchdown. While it is less likely the Spartans will score a TD from midfield than the sixteen-yard line with 2:40 left, the difference in the probabilities between these scenarios is well less than 50 percent. That is, the thirty-four-yard differential does not decrease the MSU scoring chances by 50 percent. Plus, if the Spartans do score from midfield, the clock is likely to be erased. Michigan has no final opportunity. If, conversely, MSU does score from the sixteen, there is likely to be a minute or so left, enough time for the Wolverines to move the ball into field goal range. Note, in this respect, that Michigan still had three timeouts remaining. They also had Hayden Epstein, who had kicked a fifty-seven-yard field goal earlier in the game.

The point is that in punting the ball away, Michigan gained (as it turned out) twenty-seven yards in field position. The losses were (a) the opportunity to win the game on one play with a fourth and a foot, and (b) the loss of the opportunity to tie (or, less likely, win) the game with a last minute drive. Essentially, the Wolverines traded three opportunities for one.

I have a friend who is good friends with an MSU football coach. He posed this issue to the coach. The coach responded that "whoever came up with this one might have a point. But I suspect any coach who tried this would be fired in about five minutes if the first down wasn't made." I would say this is true, in the main, only because there is so little public thought about the game.

I posted the foregoing theory on the internet. No one bit on it, save for a very sophisticated fan named Craig Weston who conceded that a measurement to ascertain the distance was worthwhile. My point was that the measurement didn't matter, since the spot was no more than eighteen inches short of the first down, and it was more likely in the nine-to-twelve-inch range. Assuming UM is fifty-fifty on such a play, it seems to me that going for it (even by pass) would be the right choice. In 2001, Michigan was seven for twelve on fourth down attempts. The Michigan opposition was seven for eleven. In 2000, the Wolverines were seven for nine. The opposition seven for twenty-one. In 1999, it was five for ten and nine for fourteen. From this, I think, it is not a stretch to conclude that fourth and a foot had (at least) a fifty-fifty chance of success. Let me try to quantify this. Assume (I think this is conservative but fair) that Michigan's chances of making the first down were fifty-fifty. Assume that MSU's chances of scoring a touchdown from the sixteen were fifty-fifty against that Michigan defense. Assume that MSU's chances of scoring from the fifty (assume an ordinary thirty-five-yard turnaround on the punt) were only 25 percent (probably low). And, assume all other variations on the theme (fumbled snap on the punt, punt being fumbled or returned for a TD) are equal. Assume, if MSU scored, Michigan had a 10 percent chance of scoring a field goal to tie the game. With these predicates, by deciding to punt, Michigan grabbed hold of a seventy-five percent chance to win. By not going for the first down, they lost (a) the 50 percent chance on the first down, plus (b) a 25 percent chance (0.5 times 0.5) of stopping MSU, plus (c) the 5 percent chance of tying the game and winning in OT. On these numbers, UM traded an 80 percent chance for a 75 percent one. Not a good trade. Of course, I don't think these numbers are right; my guess (after looking at NFL numbers from the 1997 season and some recent NCAA data) of the reality is this:

Making the first down=0.6
Scoring a TD from midfield=0.3
Scoring a TD from the sixteen=0.5
Scoring to tie the game=0.15

Given these numbers, Michigan traded a 84 percent chance for a 70 percent opportunity.

As a fan, this is my primary criticism of Carr and his coaching brethren. Not the general tactical calling of plays, but the strategic notions of when to hold 'em and when to fold 'em. Unlike other fans, I think play calling as a reason for winning or losing is well overrated. Rather, what drives me crazy is the boilerplate decision making in going for one or two points after a touchdown, or deciding to kick on fourth down and a few inches, when the context of the game provides great opportunity for working against the grain. I think, more than Spartan Bob, the outcome of the 2001 MSU game was decided by Carr's failure to run a play with 2:40 left. His decision, regardless of how ordinary or seemingly rational, put all of the Wolverine's eggs in one basket and kissed two opportunities good-bye.

If this seems wacky, consider similar circumstances in the 1999 Michigan-Illinois game. In that game, Michigan was leading 27–7 with six minutes left in the third quarter. The Michigan defense chose to blitz and actively pressure Kurt Kitner during the rest of the game (decisions I don't necessarily disagree with), and this led to quick scores by the Illini, with Ron Turner's team taking a 28–27 lead with a few minutes left in the contest. (I found it odd that no Michigan fan complained, after the game, that Michigan should have been in a prevent defense. The message to coaches is clear. Style points count.) Tom Brady then led a Wolverine march down the field in the waning minutes but things unraveled when, with a second and three from the Illinois twenty-eight, the ball was snapped over Brady's head, resulting in a third and thirty and moving the Wolverines out of field goal position. On fourth and thirty the Illini intercepted and ran the ball back to midfield.

At this point in the game, the Wolverines had two timeouts. There was 1:15 left on the clock. By snapping the ball and taking a knee, Illinois could have left the Wolverines with the ball at the Michigan twenty with no timeouts and at most twenty-five seconds left to play. Instead, on first down, Turner chose to hand the ball off. The play fizzled, and Michigan used a TO. After the play, I turned to my brother and suggested that if Illinois handed the ball off again, Michigan should let the guy run the field and attempt to tie the game from a position of relative strength, the Michigan offense versus the Illini defense. They would be, after all, only down by eight points with Illinois kicking off with a minute left to play and a timeout in hand. Bizarrely, Illinois did hand the ball off. And Michigan did whiff on its tackles, and the Illinois running back, instead of falling down, turned it into a TD. Illinois was now ahead 35–27 with fifty-nine seconds left.

The ball was knocked through the end zone on the ensuing kickoff and the Wolverines started at their own twenty. Five plays later, with twenty-nine seconds left (and still one TO!), the Wolverines were at the Illinois sixteen with a first and ten. At this point, they had taken an impossible situation to one where they had a legitimate chance to win.

It didn't work for Michigan, Brady throwing into coverage on the next play, resulting in an interception, a fumble, and a safety. Illinois kicked off from the twenty with ten seconds remaining (ahead 35–29), and Brady was left with one attempt into the end zone, but the play was defended well and unsuccessful. I have no clue whether the last Illinois touchdown was the result of intentionally not tackling the ball carrier. My guess is it was fifty-fifty whether this was a Michigan strategy. Nevertheless, it is a strategy that is often ignored (admittedly, Illinois and Turner were paying no attention), costing a team the best opportunity left on the board. And I see these opportunities go by the wayside in game after game, with coaches relying upon the historical choices they have witnessed versus the choices that allow the greatest opportunity to win. If Carr decided to have his defense whiff on the final Illini TD, he was bold and a genius and he should be applauded. He will never (and should not) tell, of course.

Aside from the endgame, I think most coaches tend to see the "small" picture in football, asking the question, "How do we make first downs?" as opposed to, "How do we score points?" I find this very odd, since I think most coaches, on the defensive side, think in terms of points allowed, as opposed to yardage allowed or first downs rendered—something that seems lost on fans. Otherwise, you wouldn't hear fans responding crankily about soft or prevent defenses. But I would argue these defenses have their legitimate place, particularly if they encourage the point of any defense: not allowing points. But on the offensive side of the ball, in my opinion, there is just way too much short ball played on third and a yard. Ignoring the time and score elements of a game, I would prefer to see an offense that makes it clear that it might try to play big ball on the small plays. The point of this is (a) sometimes it will pay off big, particularly as the defense plays man and brings the linebackers and a safety in to run support on play action, and (b) making it clear that one (if a minority) tendency of the offense is to take the big play, allowing easier opportunities to make the small ones where a defense must defend against all alternatives.

In this same vein, I think there is both too much and too little attention paid to ordinary notions of field position, at least in terms of recognizing offensive opportunities. It is a 0–0 game early in the second quarter, and it is fourth and a foot at the offensive team's forty-yard line. Assume, for purposes of the example, the teams are even. I think that 99.9 percent of the time, a college (or pro) coach will choose to punt the ball away. But, assuming the offensive team has, say, at least a 50 percent opportunity to make the first down, I would argue the opportunity favors the risk. Or, at least, taking the risk some of the time is an even proposition with long-term value to a team. Why? First, in my opinion, it puts an incredible amount of pressure on a defense when they know the offense is playing four downs and not three. Second, all yards on the field are not equal. Yards at the end of the field (either end) are harder to gain than yards in the middle. In the above example, if a coach is confident his punter can place the ball inside the ten, then punting is an offensive tactic of value. But if not (and if he doesn't have Ray Guy, which he doesn't, the answer is "not"), the yards where the ball is likely to end up (the twenty-five) and where it was punted from (the forty) are the easiest on the field to gain, where the defense has more field to protect. I can't prove it, but I know that every coach in the country would hate to play against a team that said, "We are going for it on any fourth down (absent other, obvious, and better choices, like kicking a field goal down a point with ten seconds left on the clock) where we have a yard or less to go, even if it is our own ten-yard line." I know I don't want to play against this team, particularly if it is MSU or OSU.

I admit the coach using this fourth-and-one-or-less philosophy would last about one season before being pilloried and thrown on the scrap heap. And I can't prove my notion that fourth and one or less (field position be damned) is the right strategic philosophy. That said, in the *Hidden Game* the authors studied the results of fourth down and short plays, and determined that "any time a team is faced with a fourth and one or even a fourth and two, it should go for the first down . . . Actually, this even applies to punting but the coach who will call for a run in a close game with fourth and two at his own ten has never been born. Statistically, we can prove that a team would come out ahead, but we can't factor in a coach's ulcers."

Nine *John Orr and Things Coaches Have Told Me That I Promised Never to Tell*

L isted below are some of my favorite coaches, in no particular order, and excluding many others, such as Lloyd Carr, Tommy Amaker, and Carol Hutchins.

John Orr. John Orr never got his due in Ann Arbor, partly because he created rising expectations with his early success. When a supposed-to-be-great team in 1972–73 went into the tank (13–11 overall), fans clamored for Orr's hide, and—honest—burned him in effigy on campus. This was part of a widely publicized "Dump John Orr" campaign organized by the usual suspects. Expectations were high for the Wolverines that year with the return of All-American Henry Wilmore (a senior), sophomore phenom Campy Russell, a great rising point guard in Joe Johnson, plus a six-foot-eleven center (Ken Brady), and a deep bench. But even with this talent, Orr was faced with a major problem going into the season, since Wilmore's posse had convinced him he would never be a high draft pick in the NBA playing his natural position (power forward) at six feet, three and a half inches tall. Orr went along with Wilmore's demand and moved Henry to the back court, a decision that did not seem especially problematic given the presence of Brady, Campy, and senior Ernie Johnson. The problem was that Wilmore, an absolutely great player, was not a true guard. Indeed, he wasn't a guard at all. He couldn't handle the ball. He wasn't much of a passer. Henry was an early version of Charles Barkley without the extra fifty pounds of girth. As pointed out by Jeff Mortimer in *Pigeons, Bloody Noses and Little Skinny Kids* (1978), if Wilmore "had stayed at forward, some professional team would have had to spend a lot of money to find out" he couldn't play guard. Mortimer concluded, "As it was, Henry showed them for free."

Wilmore's back court play caused the team to suffer. Worse, sources close to the program at the time told me that the team split into factions over jealousies arising between Wilmore and Campy Russell. Against Illinois, in a spiteful snit over Orr's attempts to get Wilmore and Russell to cooperate, Wilmore refused to shoot the ball until late in the game. Apparently, Wilmore was trying to make a point to Orr, that he should be the main wheel and not Campy. With the Wolverines trailing until the last few minutes of the contest, Henry thought he had demonstrated the reality of his position, and he started to turn aggressive in his offensive game. Wilmore scored thirteen points in the last five minutes, but Michigan couldn't pull the contest out.

Orr went nuts after the game and was particularly furious since he believed he may have compromised his team's interest, if in part, in deference to the interests of one player. Orr confronted Wilmore in the locker room and (again by rumor), the confrontation became physical. Orr thought athletic director Don Canham might fire him over the incident, particularly when the public clamoring for his removal was palpable. But Canham didn't. Things righted when the coach took a harder line with his players, and when his players rallied behind the coach in the next season. In the following year, without Wilmore, Brady, and Johnson (a combined fifty-three points a game of scoring), the Wolverines won the Big Ten championship and made it to the Elite Eight in the NCAA tournament. In the NCAAs, the Wolverines lost to eventual champions Marquette (and Al McGuire) by a score of 72–70. After this season, Orr was always held in reasonable regard in Ann Arbor, though not in as high a regard as he deserved.

Early in the summer of 2000, I had the opportunity to talk with Coach Orr. He looked fit and healthy and he retained a very quick wit and powerful sense of humor. I talked to Orr at a small gathering of his acquaintances and friends, but he was as friendly and cordial toward me as he was toward those with whom he shared some history. I was warned, prior to being introduced to Orr, that he had an "incredibly colorful vocabulary." This turned out to be a major understatement, though Orr was never offensive (in my consciousness) in his use of language. It seemed, rather, his way of establishing a certain order of emphasis, like dictionary markings for syllabic construction. The greater the obscenity, in both quality and quantity, the more Orr wants you to know that he means it. Or, alternatively, that you should understand the places in his stories where emphasis is appropriate and where it is not.

I asked Orr about a statement I read in *Sports Illustrated* many years ago, attributed to Bob Knight. The quotation was (something like), "John Orr's idea of defense is to beat you one hundred to ninety-eight." Orr laughed when I mentioned this and said that he remembered Knight's comment, but thought the score referenced was "102 to 100." He then said, "Let me tell you about that [three obscenities in a row]. That [obscenity] bad mouthed me every chance he got, even though he had a winning record against me and I was always civil to him. So after I retired, the [five obscenities in a row] calls me up and asks if I will come to talk to his [obscenity] team, since the [obscenity] claimed he was having some difficulty convincing them to play any [obscenity] defense. I said to him, 'You [two obscenities], why the [obscenity] should I help you with your [obscenity] team when you always treated me like [obscenity], you [seven obscenities in a row].' The [obscenity] always said I didn't know a [four obscenities in a row] about defense, and here he is asking me to help his [obscenity] team." The truth is, through this tirade, it was obvious that Orr both respected and liked Knight, if in some perverse way. Most of all, Orr recognized good irony and humor when he saw it, and he wanted his listener to get the point, and the points of emphasis. And, in fact, I think Orr may have spoken to the Indiana team and/or worked with Knight at some clinics.

I expressed my frustration to Orr with today's college game, a game verging on the clutch and grab of the NBA, and one that showcases more individual talent than team play. The coach responded, "I'm not sure the team play is any different, but I always believed the game of basketball should be fun, for both the players and the fans. I don't enjoy watching a game with a lot of holding and shoving, and I never enjoyed playing in those kinds of games." Coach Orr went on to explain that he thought the fun of basketball was the up and down nature of the game, the speed, athleticism, and elegance of the players. Orr said, "I believed in defense, I just didn't believe in holding the ball for thirty seconds or slowing the game into some variation of soccer or football. And I never believed in playing defense by grabbing onto people." Yes, I have cleaned this up. There were a few obscenities in the comments.

Orr's commentary about the state of the game, as far as I am concerned, was right on the mark. The game *was* more fun when he coached, until the control freaks and the four-corner offense came to dominate the contests. By the mid-80s, before the shot clock, as many games as not consisted of just standing around.

John Orr was never fully appreciated in Ann Arbor, but he became something close to an icon in Iowa. He took on a long-standing, awful program at Iowa State and turned it into a successful one. He recruited Steve Grayer out of Flint, and thought he had also landed Glenn Rice, until his old buddy Bill Frieder wiggled Rice away to Ann Arbor. Even though Rice was Mr. Basketball in Michigan, he was not a national recruit (it is a question whether MSU recruited Rice very vigorously, if at all), and Michigan only pursued Rice (at least aggressively) when it became clear that Roy Marble was headed to Iowa and T. Greene was tendered by DePaul. Indeed, Frieder told Orr that Michigan was not recruiting Rice, and Orr was stunned when Rice chose Michigan. Orr felt a sense of betrayal, and still feels that Rice and Grayer would have given him a real shot at a national championship. Of course, this also eluded Frieder until Steve Fisher and then athletic director Schembechler took over the Rice-led Wolverines in 1989.

I have watched all of the Michigan basketball teams since Dave Strack in 1965 and, in my judgment, Orr has been the best bench coach at Michigan. His teams just plain overachieved. He was underappreciated in Ann Arbor, but the folks in Ames seemed to understand what they had.

After I spoke with Coach Orr, I heard him interviewed on the radio. The amazing thing to me about the interview was the absence of a single expletive. How does he do this? His private conversations are predicated on obscenity. It is how his speech makes sense. In public, he turns on another switch. He is still funny. He still tells a great story. Not as good, but still good. But I can't figure out how he can shift so seamlessly between styles. The radio interviewer asked Orr about some game against Providence many years ago (that Michigan lost). Orr not only remembered the game, but he recalled in detail how Michigan lost, that his team had, in particular, trouble making free throws. A few days after this interview, I stumbled across internet rumblings that John Orr had offered to coach the Wolverines after Steve Fisher was fired, that Orr volunteered to be a one-year interim coach. The rumor went, and I could not believe this, that Michigan (or then athletic director Tom Goss) turned Orr down.

I checked the rumor out with two of Orr's best friends, guys who still live in the Ann Arbor area. They told me the rumor was true, but worse than whispered. Apparently, Orr offered to coach the team for a year at no salary, as a way of showing his loyalty and love for Michigan. (Though, to be fair, he probably has a greater loyalty to ISU, and rightfully so.) Orr made this offer to Tom Goss through the athletic department. It is amazing to me that the offer was turned down in deference to appointing Brian Ellerbe the interim coach. It is beyond amazing. After all, Ellerbe had not exactly burned up the college basketball world to that point in time. Ellerbe's record, in his three seasons as a head coach at Loyola of Maryland, was 9–18, followed by 12–15, and then 13–14. Okay, maybe he was improving. But it is hard to understand why Michigan would have wanted a young, unproven coach with a career winning percentage of 42 percent and zero winning seasons, as opposed to the Orr solution. Even worse, the story is that the athletic department refused to acknowledge the fact or generosity of the offer, never calling Orr back. That's the story at least.

The Orr story, if true (and I believe it is), speaks to the incredible ineptitude of the Goss administration, or someone at UM. I would like to lay it on Bollinger, but such shameless speculation is beyond (even) me. John Orr, the best coach in Iowa State and Michigan basketball history, offers to coach Michigan for a year with no compensation, due to his love of the game and the university. He offers Michigan a way out of the box it was in, the impossibility of finding an adequate replacement for Fisher, given the timing of the firing. Moreover, Orr's plan avoided the downside that was inherent in the appointment of any other interim coach, the possible temptation to hire the "less than best" candidate after a satisfactory year with a veteran and talented team with several NBA prospects. Even better, after a year in the program, Orr would have been the ideal consultant to help hire the new coach. He would know, more than anyone, what was needed in the program. And his understanding of the college game and of the rising young coaches on the horizon (he might have coached against some) would position him perfectly to allow Tom Goss to make the best possible choice.

This is not a revisionist theory. After Fisher was fired and the rude and boneheaded offer to Cal (and former EMU) coach Ben Braun went nowhere, there was talk about hiring UM guard Robbie Reid's father (Roger Reid) as the UM coach. The elder Reid had been a successful coach at BYU but had been fired, a condition that precipitated his son's transfer to Michigan. Apparently, Roger Reid offered to take the job, but only if there were conditions attached to the interim label, that is, he would become the permanent coach if his team did x, y, or z. This is, again, largely newspaper and internet rumor, but it was the rumor. And the story was that Michigan had some interest, but only if Reid would concede to be a purely interim coach, that is, he would not be a candidate for the permanent job. Either that, or there would be no thumb on the scale due to his prior performance. In any event, the deal could not be worked out satisfactorily, and Ellerbe was hired as the interim leader.

But while this was all going on, here was John Orr on the sidelines, making the perfect offer to save Michigan's scalp. It would have been retro. And cool. Orr's hiring would have received a cornfield of positive publicity. And even those in Iowa would have loved it. It would have created a media circus, at least a local circus, and was exactly the sort of PR Michigan needed. The media loves John Orr. And they should. The games would have been fun. Orr would have loved it. And it would have shown. Plus, with a good team, Mo Taylor (name to be banished to parts unknown), Jerod Ward, Robbie Reid, Louis Bullock (name to be deleted), Robert Traylor (name to be changed to Benedict), and Maceo Baston, Orr could have left town, at last, the way he should have, with a successful season and everyone feeling the afterglow of you-really-can-go-home-again-sometimes. Instead, apparently, Michigan treated the offer with disdain, not even responding. If this story is true, and I believe it is, it speaks of a denseness that is impossible to fathom. As long as I am on this topic, I reproduce my diary notes from early February of 2000 vis-à-vis the candidates for the Michigan basketball job. I think I deserve a C+ for my analysis. When Tommy Amaker takes the Duke job (who knows?), some of these names will crop up again.

1. *Rick Majerus*. Forget it. Ann Arbor folks complained about Bill Frieder being a lousy dresser and a slob and a weirdo. They didn't like the fact that he walked around with a towel over his shoulder, a sort of two-boxtop-and-end-panel version of Jerry Tarkanian. Maybe they wanted the real thing, Jerry T and

his traveling probation show. Ann Arbor denizens didn't like it that Frieder was such a monomaniac and not the A-squared ideal, a sort of charming and urbane-but-grown-out-of-it Holden Caulfield with a slightly rusting MG stashed out back, just in case the party breaks up. In this context, Majerus is impossible. Coach Rick alternately lives out of his car (pizza boxes spilling out) or a fleabag motel with magic fingers. Majerus dresses like Clara Bell, and I don't mean Steve Smith's mom. He makes Frieder look like a model in *Lipstick Vogue*. I like Majerus. He can coach. He is funny. He is incredibly weird. Yeah, I would support the choice. But I like Ellerbe. Sorta. And in a weird and less than lucid way, I love the fact a guy so ill-suited for the job could endure. So what do I know? Chances of Majerus being the next Michigan coach? Less than the possibility of current AD Bill Martin hiring an Elvis impersonator to lead the football Wolverines once Lloyd Carr hangs it up. In other words, less than zero.

2. *Rick Pitino*. At the present moment, he is the people's choice. The Celtics gig is over, with Rick taking his parting shots at Boston, focusing his comments and energy on all of the "negativity" in the town. I lived in Boston. And Brookline. And Jamaica Plain. And New Bedford. I worked in Brockton, and I went to law school in Boston. I liked law school. It was a reasonable experience. And I hated Boston. Boston is just not a livable place, and there is nothing in the town compelling enough to justify the hassles and downsides, unless you get lunch privileges with Red Auerbach. No Flats. No Jacobs Field. Fenway is a rotting rat haven. I would much rather live in Cleveland or Pittsburgh or Chicago or name anywhere. The moon. I draw the line at Lorain, Ohio.

But Rick P's comments about the negativity in Boston seem churlish and bizarre to me. Yo, Rick, the Celtics were not winning any games and you put together a team with no discernible future in the period of your tenure. A bunch of ex-Kentucky guys who seemed to get in one another's way. He traded a lottery pick for Vitaly Potapenko to man the middle. Please. He obtained Walter McCarty, whose only understandable credential was that he stumbled around the court for Pitino at Kentucky. He acquired Kenny Anderson, as if this guy has ever shown any point guard abilities, and absorbed his gigantic contract. He acquired Chris Mills and Travis Knight, and paid these two forty-seven million. He did, however, pass on Tracy McGrady. Mills? McGrady? Pretty even, right? The Celtics were 35–47 last year, and are 21–26 as of this writing. In '97–98, Pitino won thirty-six games. In '98–99, they won nineteen games. The Celtics roster includes Tony Battie, Chris Carr, Walter McCarty, Eric Williams, Bryant Stith, Chris Herren, Adrian Griffin, Mark Blount, Randy Brown, Jerome Moiso, Kenny Anderson, and Milt Palacio. Yeah, Paul Pierce and Kenny Walker can play, when they are not in each other's way, which is most of the time. But doesn't the rest of this roster look like it was lifted right out of the CBA? Or my Thursday night game? And, Pitino has managed the amazing feat of having no center, no point guard, and no two guard, unique in the NBA.

So Pitino hasn't won any games and has put together a team that has no potential to win any games in the foreseeable future. Despite this, Pitino is complaining about the negativity in Boston. I think, as a matter of positive spin, this is naive. Pitino, instead of complaining, should be apologizing to Bostonians for putting together such a crappy team. Rick's naiveté is particularly strange in relation to the universe of professional sports fans, a cosmos he should understand. Pitino won nineteen games two years ago. And got paid millions. Isn't it reasonable to assume that the average rotisserie guy perceives that he could have done as well? It seems possible that some might have done as well. Hell, Brian Ellerbe might have done as well. And shouldn't Pitino know this?

The foregoing said, Pitino has been a very successful college coach, but much of this success came at Kentucky, a place where it is very difficult to lose. Or, at least, no one has managed to lose there yet, even a brain surgeon like Joe B. Hall. But Pitino was also successful at BU and Providence, much more problematic venues. Bill Simmons, *The Sports Guy,* stressing Pitino's ineptitude as a pro coach, thinks that Pitino is "the best college coach I've ever seen (and that), like John Blutarski, Rick Pitino was meant to stay in college." Pitino is an extremely sharp dresser. No question. And he is charismatic. No question. And he is very smart and very glib. No question. Moreover, Pitino is an extrovert and likes to hang with other basketball junkies. He isn't a snob or above having a beer and some buffalo wings with some loaded fans he bumps into at the local watering hole in, say, Tipp City, Ohio. Pitino brings a very aggressive and exciting full-court style that fans love and (if it works) generates excitement for casual observers, and compels high school recruits. Pitino would bring instant credibility for the Michigan program, and would balance the MSU-UM playing field, at least as a matter of general perception. Pitino would put fans in Crisler, at least for a while, and be an instant fix.

So what are the negatives? First, Michigan will have to pay for Pitino. A snootful. And this means they may have to make adjustments for Lloyd Carr. But Pitino will generate some revenue, and the Michigan financial situation continues as a smoke and mirror show, at least as far as I am concerned. Michigan might pull the financial trigger for Pitino.

The second issue is the perception that Pitino is a carpetbagger, that he moves from job to job based upon the lure of greener pastures, and Michigan should not have to endure the specter of continuing speculation about a return to Kentucky or the Los Angeles Lakers when Phil Jackson finally decides he is the second coming of the Swami Satchadanada. But I see this as a small price or, indeed, a small benefit. This kind of focus on a program makes it higher profile, confers some cachet. The implication is that no one will be too embarrassed to follow in Pitino's shoes, the spurned position will be perceived as anything other than dé classé by the "hot" candidates. Moreover, think about the names "Tubby" Smith and Billy Donovan. Who are these guys? The present coaches at Kentucky and Florida, both highly regarded, were assistants for Pitino. The man has a sufficiently healthy ego, and he has been able to recognize and develop coaching talent. If Pitino would leave, it would seem probable that (a) he was "hot" because he had turned Michigan around, and (b) he would be leaving competent assistants in his wake.

So I would take Pitino. Most everyone would. But (assuming Ellerbe is gone) will Michigan offer Pitino? I would say this is 80 percent likely. And would Pitino accept? About a one in four chance. I think it is 90 percent that Ellerbe will be fired. So 0.9 times 0.8 times 0.25 yields eighteen percent. There is an eighteen percent chance Pitino will coach the Wolverines next season. Neither more nor less. You can't look this one up.

3. *Bob Knight*. If Bo were still the AD, there would be an incredible power struggle within the university, since you know that Knight would be the Schembechler choice. This would be, in itself, a lot of fun for everyone, especially those who live in East Lansing or Columbus. The plusses and minuses of Knight are so well-known as to be banal. Would Knight take the Michigan job? In a flash. The thought of sticking it to Indiana must keep him awake nights, heart racing. Hell, the thought of him sticking it to Indiana while at Michigan keeps me awake nights. Will Michigan offer Knight the job? Well, the price would be right, and Knight would bring fans into Crisler. From a financial or program perspective, hiring Bob Knight would be the best move. It would be as (reportedly) deranged as Bob himself, but it is the right move. The guy is *the* Coach Bob. He has gotten obsessed, and he is gonna stay obsessed for the rest of all our lifetimes. So what if he is a paranoid schizophrenic? (In fact, he is probably only a borderline personality.) He would be *our* psychotic, and the amusement value of locking horns with the more-or-less sane world would be worth it. It would push any Tom Izzo news next to the obituaries and the weight reduction testimonials. But it seems highly unlikely Bill Martin would tether his future on the hiring of Bob Knight, even if Knight promised to see three therapists, five faith healers, a snake handler, Drs. Ruth and Laura, and be monitored as to his Prozac ingestion.

Would I support the hiring of Knight? It is too amusing to say anything other than an incredibly enthusiastic "yes." Will he be offered the job? No. Not until he coaches somewhere else for two or three years and becomes the kinder and gentler Bob. In other words, not in anyone's lifetime. Call it one thousandth of one percent. No realistic chance. Bill Martin will hire Knight only (a) if he goes insane and senile at the exact same moment, or (b) if he turns over control of the athletic department to someone with a truly warped sense of humor (me). But maybe this already happened in the past, and this explains the Orr/Ellerbe scenario. And, like smallpox, we are over it.

4. *Perry Watson*. No way. Perry has been a successful coach and anyone who has seen his University of Detroit teams knows that Perry can put a team together. But, does Bo know football? Yep. And does Perry know Ed Martin? Only for twenty or so years, going back to Perry's high school days, when Martin was Antoine Joubert's neighborhood valet and/or other flunky. Perry may be completely innocent of any wrongdoing surrounding Mr. Ed and the Michigan program. If I had to bet on it, I would contact Ed and play the pass line. Innocente. But the appearance of impropriety is the key here. Michigan can't afford to even think about Perry. Zero chance. But who knows? Perry's revisionism is so heavy that maybe he believes, he really believes, that his prior identity was Wilbur Post.

5. *Jay Smith*. He was a restricted earnings coach while at Michigan. Plus, he was (a) great with the media, (b) great with alums and kids in the Michigan camps, and (c) extremely visible as a coach on the sidelines, specializing with the post players. Jay did well at Grand Valley, and after a couple of weak seasons at Central, turned the Chips around. He groomed a big kid (Chris Kaman) who will go in the first round of the NBA draft in 2003. There is a very limited probability that he had anything to do with Ed Martin. None of this matters. He was around when Ed was around. End of story. No chance. Jay might have the opportunity when the next job opens up. Maybe in another decade if things go well for Jay from Mio. I admit, however, that it is rumored that Jay rubbed certain key folks the wrong way during his stay in Ann Arbor. I am not certain how. Or who. And I heard this from a very credible source not named Tony Soprano. Hey, I don't know. I just report the rumors behind the news.

6. *Tommy Amaker*. I believe he will be one of the finalists. Amaker is a young and attractive person with a Duke pedigree. He is now the coach at Seton Hall, and I think he would perceive the move to Ann Arbor as a step up, especially since he has had two frustrating seasons at SH. This is also the problem. Amaker has put together back-to-back .500 seasons, despite leading teams with talent. They were young teams but, nevertheless, he has not shown he can win. Plus, Amaker has had off-court struggles this year with, among other things, fights between players. The rumors are that his team was not exactly a cohesive group, to say the least. Still, Amaker may be it. Call him a 20 percent shot, even though he has no proven history of actually winning games. I would predict, if the Pitino Circus does not work out, that Amaker will be choice number two. He has an Ann Arbor "feel," a saner Holden Caulfield not yet gone to seed. He will have a very long rope after the Ellerbe fiasco and the fact that UM may well take a major hit from the Ed Martin saga.

7. *Kelvin Sampson*. The Oklahoma coach has been rumored so many times for the Michigan job that he seems as old as veteran character actor Walter

Brennan. In 1979, Sampson talked Jud Heathcote into allowing him to hang around the MSU program as a grad assistant. Sampson bounced to power-house Montana Tech, and then was a minor success as a young coach at the moribund Washington State program. But, take note, Sampson's first three years were anything but spectacular at WSU, the team compiling a 30–57 record, before turning it around in the next four years to a pretty impressive 73–46. This is a winning percentage of 61.3 percent, not bad for a doormat in the PAC 12. Sampson then moved to Oklahoma, where he has compiled con-sistently good results, his worst year at 17–13. At the moment, his team is 19–4. So Sampson has a positive history. His rep is pretty good. But Sampson has done most of his damage with junior college players at Oklahoma and, at the moment, JCs make up half of his roster. This isn't going to happen at UM, but it may not need to happen. My guess is that recruiting at Michigan will prove more satisfying than at Oklahoma, assuming Kelvin would retain some of the present staff.

The big question mark re: Sampson relates to graduation rates. Last time I checked, it was pushing zero. I put very little stock in graduation rates. I think they are not meaningful, at least in the context of what is attempted to be proven. But I think there is an appearance of respectability in these numbers that make them relevant in predicting a theoretical successor for Ellerbe. Call Sampson a 7 percent solution. And by a hair. But would he want to bump heads with old cronies? Uncertain. Heathcote despises Michigan, and the depth of his loathing has yet to be plumbed. He still thinks Michigan cheated to get Michael Talley (for real), even after his whining was investigated and it turned out to be completely unfounded. And my guess is that Jud's boy Izzo loathes Michigan too, though I have yet to see another coach who can get up much animus for TA. Anyone telling you anything different (including Tom) is unlikely to be telling the truth. Does Sampson want this particular role?

8. *Skip Prosser*. The Xavier coach. Unlike Sampson, Prosser graduates near-ly all of his kids. But this is, most likely, reflective of the kinds of kids likely to want to play at Xavier, as opposed to those attracted to Oklahoma. Regardless, Prosser's graduation rate history works in his favor.

Of course, as in most of these things, it cuts both ways. Let's say Prosser graduates 50 percent of his players at UM after hitting it at 85 percent at Xavier. Won't this difference then imply something negative about the AA/UM environment? And, given this, doesn't it make more sense to hire someone who has never graduated anyone? Kelvin Sampson graduated no one at Oklahoma. And he graduated 50 percent of his players here. This proves the academic superiority of the university. A lawyer's trick. Ignore this.

Prosser also has a reputation as a good teacher and a good person. Those within the Xavier community speak highly of him. What about Prosser's record? Pretty good. Prosser was Pete Gillen's assistant for many years until

Pete left for a higher paying position at Providence. Since then, Prosser has won more than two-thirds of his games, winning twenty games or more in five of his six seasons, coming into this year. This year (as of this writing), Xavier is 18–5. There is no real negative about Prosser. Except perhaps that he is seen as sort of a blah choice. Well, sorry folks, but at this point in our history, Prosser may be close to a perfect choice. But any flirtation with Pitino puts this choice in the can. It would be too much of a letdown for the lowest-common-denominator fan. Call it 0.92 (Ellerbe's revised chances of being fired; it went up in the last page or two) times 0.85 (the chance of Prosser taking the job if offered) times 0.1 (chance of the job being offered) equals 7.82 percent. As an aside, Prosser is rumored to be a possible for other jobs (Pitt, for example), but he seems pretty loyal to Xavier, and I believe it will take something a lot more interesting than the Pitt job to pry him away. (Prosser eventually ended up leading Wake Forrest's very successful program.)

9. *Ben Braun*. The rumor is that Tom Goss wanted to scoop up Braun at the time of the Fisher firing but, apparently, Goss misunderstood the depth of Braun's longing to return to this area. Ben Braun is a fine coach and a good man. He would be near the top of my list. Maybe at the top. But all indications are that he wants to stay at California, that he is happy at Cal. Moreover, there is noise that Cal might up the ante to keep Braun. I think it is unlikely Braun will return. Very unlikely. I would put the percentage at less than one.

10. *Rudy T.* Rudy can't fail, of course. He is one of the greatest five or six players ever at Michigan. He was a successful pro. He has been a fine NBA coach and has won two NBA championships. Rudy grew up in the Detroit area. He is a natural choice, except for one thing: he don't want the job. Forget it. He has made this clear for some time.

11. *Cazzie Russell*. Same as the above. Except Cazzie is from Chicago, and absolutely wants the job, and would take it fast and on the cheap. Cazzie has coached at the CBA level, and is now coaching for a Division III school in Savannah, Georgia. He has been relatively successful in these endeavors. Cazzie is an intelligent man. He is well spoken. Very well spoken. He cuts an impressive figure, and is an icon in Michigan basketball. He recently finished his college degree (in the last five or six years, I think), an issue that had been raised about him in the past. The problem is that Cazzie is not exactly a young guy (about sixty), and has zero history of recruiting or running a program at the Division I level. For these reasons, I would place Cazzie as a very long shot. But still a wild card. Who thought, after all, that Larry Bird would be a successful NBA coach? Call it 3 percent.

12. *Gary Waters*. The head coach at Kent State was a Braun assistant at EMU. Waters was an integral part of EMU's success, and may have been primarily responsible for evaluating and recruiting players like Earl Boykins and Derrick Dial, big-time talents that others passed on. At Kent, a basketball

doormat in the MAC, Waters completely turned it around, winning unheard of numbers of games for that program. In 1998–99, KSU won a record twenty-three games and the MAC championship. He was voted coach of the year in the conference. This was (a) the first MAC championship ever won by Kent, and (b) the school's first NCAA appearance. The Flashes lost in the NCAA first round to Temple, but only by seven, and KSU proved they belonged. Waters followed this up with another twenty-three-win season (and another coach of the year award), but this time lost by a point in the MAC tournament. Kent played in the NIT and beat Rutgers at home and Villanova on the road (by fourteen) before losing to Penn State by seven at Happy Valley, a game where PSU outscored Kent by fifteen from the line.

Coming into this season, Kent was predicted to finish last or near last in its division of the MAC. Despite this, the team is 18–7. And it is a team of midgets, the starting back court at five-eleven and six-one and the starting forwards at six-three and six-five. There is no usable size on the bench. Waters has played pro basketball (in Spain). He is from Detroit and has recruited the Detroit and Saginaw Valley areas for years. He also knows/has recruited the Cleveland and Pittsburgh areas, places where Michigan should be strong. (Nate Gerwig, a six-nine top 150 recruit from Pittsburgh will attend Kent next year.) Waters has an undergraduate degree in business and a master's degree in education. And he wants the job. Waters, from what I know, would be my first or second rational choice. I would call him about a 15 percent possibility. He lacks the name recognition of Pitino or Majerus or Braun or Amaker. But I think there is a reasonable chance he is the best coach available. The downside here, from a Bill Martin perspective, is that he creates little excitement. Indeed, many would complain that Michigan had gone cheap and not hired a "name" coach. If Waters is not hired at Michigan, he will move up the food chain. His record is just too impressive to be ignored. If Pitino and Amaker do not work out, Waters should be the favorite. After that, your guess is as good as mine. (Waters is now the head coach at Rutgers.)

* * * *

Joe Paterno. (Most commonly referred to as "Joe Pennsylvania.") Everyone loves Joe Pa, and I think it is more than just the fact that he is an old guy coaching in a young guy's game or the fact that his teams have gone in the tank the last couple of years, making Paterno a lot more lovable to everyone except the Nittany Lion loyalists. This is how these things go. If Lloyd Carr started taking it on the chin from the Sparties every year, I guarantee you that he would be perceived as a much more sympathetic and lovable character in East Lansing. I know, for a fact, if the basketball Wolverines routinely beat on MSU by thirty to fifty the next few years (in other words, more or less balance the recent scales), I would have a much higher opinion of Tom Izzo. (In this vein, I heard a lot of Spartan fans complaining that Brian Ellerbe got a "raw deal" from Michigan, that in another fifteen years, he might have come close in a game or two against the Spartans.)

The foregoing admitted, I think Joe Pa is a legitimate icon, even if he comes back to life, Lazarus-like, and actually ties the Wolverines in one of his last thirty or so games against Michigan during his Penn State tenure. I know as of this writing it is hard to believe, but Michigan is rumored to have actually lost a game to Joe Pa and the Nittanies at some time in the last century. Few may remember it, but I am old enough to recall. After this particular loss, I took my ten-year-old nephew, Sam, to an open basketball practice at Crisler Arena. After a few minutes, Sam said he was going for a Coke. When he did not return in ten minutes, I went to look for him, and panicked when I could not find him in the arena. I went outside to the rim around the arena and noticed a limo parked at the base of the Crisler steps. Near the bottom of the steps sat Sam, being tended to by an older man. Joe Paterno. As I recognized my nephew, Paterno stood up, patted Sam on the shoulder, and got into the limo. Sam later said that he was wandering around the arena, saw Paterno, and decided to congratulate the coach on the PSU win "even though I told him I was rooting for Michigan and hated to lose." Paterno told his ride to wait, sat down with the kid, and talked to him about the meaning of games, the nature of winning and losing. Paterno told Sam something like, "Losing is a hard lesson. But so is winning. And the truth is that none of it is all that important. And that's the hardest lesson of all."

On the eve of the 2000 PSU game, I wanted to say, "Joe Pa is my hero." He is. But instead, I said, "I hope we kick Penn State's ass again." We did. And also in 2001. We eked by in 2002. The sneaky Lions pulled a conniving trick and got UM off their schedule in 2003 and 2004. I think my diary notes shed some light on this:

November 12, 2000. Penn State comes in pretty much as I thought, a poor man's version of Wisconsin or MSU, but without the steam and vinegar that those teams showed against the Wolverines this year. Joe Pa's pregame talk, from a reliable Penn State fan who was in the locker room, went something like this:

Joe Pa: Well, men, I know it has been reported that our quarterback has a rag arm, but let's go out there and show them what is really meaningful in life. It's not winning. It's not losing. These things are illusions and transitory.

Player: Coach? Sorry to interrupt. But didn't Spinoza once say that nothing follows from following?

Joe Pa:	No. That was Hume . . . or maybe Beano Cook.
Player:	Doesn't that imply one cannot grasp the meaning of things?
Joe Pa:	What do you mean?
Player:	See what I mean?
Joe Pa:	How could I?

In the other locker room, Lloyd Carr and Jim Hermann were likely to be saying something like, "Let's go out there and just kick the shit out of them." At least that's the way the teams presented when they came onto the field. To me, Michigan seemed jacked up, eager to put the embarrassment of the Northwestern game behind them. Penn State seemed kinda reflective, as if to say, "Gee, there's a lot of folks here today. Do you think they know Newton's Second Law has been suspended for this game?"

* * * *

During the 2002 season, Joe Pa complained so much about officiating in the Big Ten, mostly with no cause, that many began to love him a lot less. Especially Randy Walker at Northwestern, who complained, after getting waxed by the Nittanies 49–0, that Paterno's season-long whining about officiating had caused innumerable holding and clipping penalties against the Lions to go uncalled in the PSU-NU game. Who knows? Walker might have been right. But if I were he, I would save the counterattack for closer games. Penn State could have played that game in handcuffs and won.

Paterno went ballistic over a bad call in the PSU overtime loss against Michigan in 2002, and it is true that he had a point. Sorta. With less than a minute left in regulation and the Nittanies at midfield, Zach Mills threw a thirty-yard pass down the left sideline. Wide receiver Brian Johnson fought off the DB and made a fine catch, but was ruled out of bounds. The replay showed that Johnson was inbounds. So Joe was right. Except that with 1:45 left and PSU facing a third and twelve at its own seventeen, a thirty-four-yard incompletion (the ball bounced about a foot from the receiver) was ruled a completion. Had this been ruled upon correctly, Michigan would have had the ball at midfield in regulation with 1:30 or so remaining, and the complained-about play would never have happened. The Big Ten office reviewed the Paterno complaint and agreed the Johnson incompletion call was an official's error. They also found the prior completion call to be an error. The Big Ten office found there to be five blown calls in the game, three favoring the visitors. In the abstract, I would take this on the road any day. (As an aside, the Big Ten reviews show an average of 4.8 blown calls per game, according to *Detroit Free Press* reporter Michael Rosenberg.)

* * * *

Indiana Coaches, Keady and Cameron. Yeah, Indiana endured the (probably deranged unless he accepts the Michigan coaching job someday) Coach Bob, but it also has had the benefit of Cam Cameron. My impression is that Cameron did a terrific job with Indiana football, with teams that were nearly bankrupt of talent. The fact is that Indiana is not a hotbed for high school football, and the state is trolled by Notre Dame, Michigan, Illinois, MSU, and Purdue, making it a mandate for Cameron to look elsewhere. I know, for a fact, that Cameron's ability as a coach while in Ann Arbor was highly regarded by those within the program. And I know that his teams, despite the talent problems, seemed organized and focused. But I have my own little story about Cam, in his very young days as an assistant coach at Michigan.

As diehard fans might know, Cameron was a basketball player at Indiana. He was a solid player, but not much of a scorer. Indeed, my recollection is that he was the perfect system player for Knight, one without any ego. In the first year that Cam was a coach at UM, I found myself checking him in a pickup game at the old IM building. My team, in that game, was comprised of a pretty solid group of playground players, if one discounts the level of athleticism that one might find in the average intramural building. Cam's teammates were all worse than me. In other words, they stunk. My team was scoring, but so was Cameron and the game was close. Now, I had seen the guy play on many occasions and the one thing I recalled was that he couldn't shoot the rock. I mean, not at all. So I gave him room. He hit a seventeen-footer. And then he nailed another. So I checked him to eighteen feet. He hit again. And then once more from twenty feet. My team was giving me the fish eye. Check that chump!!! So I did, getting in his face, knowing that he could drive around me with little effort. But I knew this, and I knew he knew this, and that I would have to guess his move to have any chance. As Cameron dribbled to his right, I thought he might try the red-headed version of the Earl Monroe reverse dribble and, a miracle and a fluke, I admit, I timed his move right, stripping the ball. I headed the other way for a layup.

Now, I had been there before. I have seen many instances of extremely skilled players picked clean by some ham-and-egger. And I know what happens. Every time. As the hack goes to the basket, the skilled player comes over the top to attempt the block, and either (a) humiliates the player by slamming the ball off the board and taking it back the other way on a five on four, or (more likely) (b) makes the block and pummels the poor sucker who made the strip into submission, often with the breaking of appendages as the hack is driven to the floor or stanchion (pick one or two). Well, I was waiting for this,

197

and I heard Cameron chugging up behind me. I thought about using the basket to come up and under on the left side, but this could be even more dangerous, since (a) he could have killed me anyway, and (b) I might have looked like a fool if I didn't time the shot. I would also be lying if I denied that, at the moment, I felt it would have been a sort of weasel-like play.

I decided to play it straight. And Cameron came after me. Until the last step, when he relented. The ball rolled through. He never touched me. Except when he patted me on the back and said, "Nice play," as we returned up the floor. This was not only a shock to me but, I am sure, a rarity in street ball. Cam Cameron is da man, regardless of his golfing prowess (be da ball) or if he never wins another game at Indiana. And, at Indiana, he might never win another game, unless he gets to play Penn State a lot.

At the end of the 2001 football season, Indiana went on a veritable tear in the Big Ten, finishing 4–4 in the conference. In Indiana football terms, this is a definite winning season, an upset equivalent to the basketball Wolverines going 8–8 in some future Big Ten war. Not that winning these games did Cam any good, since the fools at Indiana canned him after winning four of his last five with a defense that had slow and small guys and an offense consisting of more or less one guy. I rooted for the poor Hoosiers to lose a lot next year, and they didn't let me down, winning three games in 2002. Post-Cameron, the Hoosiers are the doormats of the Big Ten. Meanwhile, Cam was hired as offensive coordinator at San Diego (NFL), where he and Drew Brees have turned the Chargers from nothing to something. Nice move, Hoosiers.

Keady is a whole different animal. There is no way he would have given me an uncontested layup, even if I were in a wheelchair and I was his grandmother. Not that that fatso could play at Cameron's level. Or maybe even at my level. Opposing fans generally don't like Keady because he wins a lot of games with a style that is, well, some place between intense and brutal. To put it politely. Keady is an ex-pro football player who recruits an occasional genuine basketball star (Glen Robinson, Brad Miller), but he has had primary success with guys no one ever heard of, and guys he turns into brutes by the sheer force of will, theirs and his. Does anyone really think a team should be able to dominate games in the Big Ten with guys like Ron Rowinski or Steve Scheffler or Brian Cardinal or the passel of other slow gorillas that Purdue generally throws out on the court? Keady does and has. Keady is the most intense coach in the country and his teams play with this intensity. Bill Buntin and Oliver Darden and Cazzie Russell might have invented "bloody nose lane" in the Big Ten, but Keady has taken it to a high art. Everyone hates to play Purdue. Even if they stink, you're gonna get hurt. And there is a good chance you will lose, too. No fun.

Spring workout time at Purdue? Six AM. Fall workouts? Seven AM. If you are late? You run fifty "Mackeys" from the top to the bottom of Mackey

Arena. If you are not? Maybe twenty-five. Mackeys. Then what? Maybe pulling a pickup truck up a hill. Or carrying players piggyback around the arena. Drills? Well, according to *ESPN Magazine*, "Loose Ball" is a favorite. Two players stand at the baseline and then have to dive for a ball on the floor. They must hit the floor and each other. Any others? "Bull in the Ring" is another fave detailed by *ESPN*. In that drill, the "bull" stands in the key and has to take five charges from guys starting at the three-point line. Any lines drawn? Yep. An assistant coach suggested the Purdue players try steer wrestling. Keady vetoed the idea. Out of this atmosphere, the Purdue teams are always as tough as any team in the country.

The odd thing about Keady is that he doesn't seem to be an icon among Purdue fans, proving that it is not just Michigan fans who are snot-nosed, spoiled brats. Purdue fans act like Keady is a poor man's Brian Ellerbe, for chrissakes. (That admitted, UM fans are still a hell of lot more pleasant than Buckeye football fans, who are more or less an ordinary coterie of rampaging Cro-Magnons after a Sterno binge. On the other hand, I admit that UM fans might lead the league in whining, with Penn State fans giving us a run.) Keady has a sort of John Orr status (Michigan, not Iowa) in Indiana, and I routinely hear the Boiler faithful complaining about the guy. First, of course, he can't recruit. Of course he can't recruit. Have Purdue fans actually ever been to the campus? Have they ever been to South Lafayette? Enough said. And, while Indiana is a great high school hoops state (though not as rich as Michigan in talent), the Boilers have to compete with the prestige basketball school, Indiana, plus MSU and Notre Dame and others who are willing to spend their energies in Hoosierland. Even Michigan pulled one of the top two players out of Indiana for the class of 2002, (near) seven-footer Chris Hunter. And out-side of Indiana (or maybe Ann Arbor), no one gives a rat's ass about the Purdue basketball program, so dragging guys into Nowhereville is no small trick. Second, somehow Purdue fans seem to think they ought to win a lot of games with perceived top stars who are strictly minor league talents. The truth is, it is only Keady's force of will and incredible ability to make his teams more than the sum of their parts that has kept his program at the top of the Big Ten.

I admire what Keady does with his teams, but I also admit to a certain irra-tional bias for the guy. It's not just the hair (the "pur-do"). It's not just the scowl. It's not just the ill-fitting clothes. It's not just the fact that no call made against Purdue has ever been right. Though these things add up. Ultimately, I am compelled by his incredible array of courtside expressions. And the fact that, as an opposing fan, you just can't get mad at a guy who looks exactly like the school mascot. Keady must be the only creature on the planet who is the offspring of an inanimate object.

Game in and game out, the Purdue coach is the most fun to watch. Win or lose, postgame, Keady is always a gentleman. He is a good winner and a good loser, at least in his public persona. And as a chronic basketball watcher, even the late night ESPN73 post-midnight tilts from Boise, I believe Keady gets as much out of his teams as anyone, regardless of what Purdue fans think.

The only coach close to Keady in on-court animation was Tom Young, when he coached the Youngstown State Penguins. I recall a game at Crisler Arena when Young became very upset over a series of poor calls (the Penguins were getting jobbed), and the coach began to jump up and down while flapping his arms. Young was spindly, and he reminded me of a runaway Ichabod Crane being chased through the Halloween darkness by some headless demon. In the midst of this weird and awkward ballet, Young's sport coat split up the back, all the way to the collar. Am I not a mad coach? Am I not Nureyev? Yes! And he continued in this fugue, flapping like a frustrated dodo trying to get off the runway, until he was exhausted beyond caring. I like to think of Young as the inventor of the now-banned tear-away sport coat.

Most of all, I like the fact that Keady wears his heart on his sleeve with no pretense of anything else. His face always says it all. None of this Coach K sneakiness. A classic example, for me, came in the 2000 Michigan-Purdue game in West Lafayette, when Purdue center John Allison executed the conference's first and almost successful quadruple dribble.

The ball is tossed into the post. Allison looks around. He puts the ball down for a single dribble and picks it up. Fine. The center then looks around again. He decides not to kick the ball out. Instead, he decides to dribble it again. The violation is not called. The camera pans to Keady. A small smile curls at the edges of his lips. Allison looks around for a third time, but still seems disinclined to give the ball up. This ball be mine. He decides he wants to dribble again. He does. Two dribbles this time. This is fun! The camera pans to Keady. There is now a complete look of disbelief on his face, a look that can only emanate from his visage. The camera pans to the referee. No call. I am watching on TV. I am yelling at the screen. Is this a weird time vortex? Has Big Ten ref Ed Hightower been cloned into threes? Is Jim Bain still alive? Did Spartan Bob just become a ref and convert to Boilermakerism? Allison has just successfully executed a triple dribble, something I have never seen. But Big John is not satisfied with the accomplishment. He wants more. He wants to be immortal. Allison looks around again. He searches for an outlet. Maybe he is feeling guilty. Maybe he is lost in some cosmic void. Maybe he spent the day with Joe Paterno, and has decided that something weird is going on. Like a momentary failure of gravity or the absolute knowledge that his hands had turned magnetic. Hard to know. But we do know that he starts to dribble again. The fourth dribble sequence. The camera moves to Keady, and the look on his face is completely indigenous to the real Coach K, the only person on the planet who can create the right look for the wrong moment. Oh yeah, I forgot. The violation gets called this time, by the ever-vigilant Big Ten zebras. Justice is served, and Keady leans back into his seat, an ironic and satisfied look on that face.

Keady's team, stinking out the joint completely, managed to eke by Michigan by twenty in the "quadruple dribble" contest. In 2000, if you beat Michigan by twenty, I guarantee, it was just barely getting by. I knew Michigan was bad, but I felt Keady's team had almost no ability. Except that they were tough and disciplined and organized, a lot more than what they should have been. The rematch in Ann Arbor showed the marked juxtaposition between the coaching in West Lafayette and what endured in Ann Arbor (Brian Ellerbe). Purdue came into the game on a six-game losing tear, its team completely decimated by injuries. Both of Purdue's inside starters, the six-ten Allison (Keady probably whacked him with a two-by-four for dribbling so much) and power forward Rodney Smith (gored by a real bull when the Purdue coach felt he wasn't getting enough action from human chargers in practice), were out for the season with ankle injuries. Keady was forced into a three- and four-guard rotation, playing against a Michigan team with two seven-footers (the Joshes; Asselin and Moore) and one six-foot-nine player (Chris Young). Plus, Michigan had Lavell Blanchard, an excellent jumper, at six-foot-seven.

Michigan, playing better over the course of the year, was 10–13 prior to the Purdue game, and had an opportunity to make the NIT. Ellerbe might even save his job with a season on the plus side. This, and the injuries to an already marginal Purdue squad, should have implied a fired-up home team against a disconsolate visitor. Not even close. The Boilers came in determined, and the Wolverines were flat and emotionless, just going through the game with little energy. But the contest did show the home court value of Crisler Arena, since the Wolverines cut the twenty-point deficit on the road by a 78–59 nailbiter loss at home, despite the fact that Bernard Robinson was hot, hitting eight of ten shots from the floor. After the game, Brian Ellerbe noted the matchup problems caused by Keady's use of four guards, and implied, somehow, it was a major advantage (no fair!) for the Boilers. My diary notes follow. One more thing—the Purdue guards were not big guards. They were all in the six-foot to six-foot-three range. Purdue's inside guys were both freshmen, the very unknown and marginally recruited Jed Buscher and Kevin Garrity.

February 28, 2001. Uh, Brian. Usually when a coach complains about matchups, it is due to one-on-one size or quickness issues and not because "my team is a whole lot bigger than your team and, hence, you had the advantage." Indeed, it is the first time I have ever heard a coach use this particular explanation or excuse. Not that Ellerbe is (necessarily) wrong. I know, from my own experience, that playing a guy quicker than you is worse than playing a guy bigger and slower, at least within some reason. But usually when you have a size differential, you try to take advantage of that by pounding the ball in, getting to the line, forcing the other team into foul difficulty, and zoning (or quasi-zoning) to minimize any quickness issues. Most of the time, it is the smaller team complaining. Think, for example, if Michigan came out with a lineup of Earl Boykins and Avery Queen and Muggsy Bogues and Spud Webb and Eddie Gaedel. Would the other team be whining about quickness issues, or might they not decide that, say, their seven-footer had an inside advantage against a five-three guy? And if it is such an advantage to be smaller and quicker, why isn't Michigan beating the bushes to recruit small, quick guys? Hey, Brian, the basket ain't on the floor. News flash. *It is an advantage in basketball to be tall.* I know this because Beano told me. And if you are really convinced of this new reality, I suggest you check out some jockeys, for example. At least one of these guys must have a deadly crossover dribble.

Last time I hunted around, Ellerbe wasn't recruiting midgets, but was searching every corner of the planet for a big guy who could actually catch the ball. Meanwhile, Michigan got thirteen total shots from Josh, Josh II, and Chris Young, and zero trips to the line from this trio. Coach Ellerbe noted that "a lot of times they had four guards on the floor, and it is hard to utilize both your post guys because it hurts you on the defensive end." This can be a fact, in straight man defense. But this ain't the pre-2003 NBA, and there is no prohibition from throwing up a zone. Moreover, I like the chances of either Chris Young or Josh I against a six-three guy. Hell, I like *my* chances inside against a five-footer, even if the guy can jump out of the gym. He's gotta come down, right? And I don't like my chances of stopping most six-six guys in the post, even if they have the finesse of a gorilla and I play as dirty and as sneaky as my heroes Brian Cardinal, Ron Rowinski, and Steve Scheffler combined. Fact of the matter is, I am gonna get crushed.

In any event, with Purdue's three- and four-guard rotation, one would think that Michigan had some edge on the boards. Nope. We got clobbered 38–30, with the starting Purdue guards pulling down sixteen caroms, compared to our total of thirteen for our two centers and power forward. Maybe the ball bounced weird. It happens. Josh I pointed out, and he had a point, that Michigan was hurt by using "unusual" lineups to matchup with Purdue. I suggest (with all deference to the Michigan staff) that the Wolverines, instead of trying to play Purdue's game, should have tried to play their own game and taken advantage of the other side of the coin. I think, indeed, this is what most would have tried, using one's own advantages, as opposed to playing the other person's game and taking one's stronger team off the court. Even the average flub-a-dub coach would have tried this out. Maybe we would have lost the game by more. But at least we wouldn't be complaining about being *bigger* than the other team.

* * * *

Jim Carras. Carras, the Michigan golf coach for many years, may have the lowest profile of all of the coaches on the Michigan staff but, somehow, everybody in town knows who he is. For the first twelve years of his tenure, Jim never asked for nor received any salary. In his thirteenth year, Carras set up a meeting with then AD Jack Weidenbach, who assumed Carras was going to ask for a raise. Weidenbach now jokes that he was prepared to "double or even triple" Carras's salary, but "I was prepared to draw the line at that." It turned out that Carras only wanted to ask for something more than the two scholarships he was allotted at the time. Weidenbach, a more than decent man (and in my non-expert judgment, a competent AD, contrary to Don Canham's more expert evaluation), granted the request, and then noticed that Carras wasn't getting paid. Weidenbach offered some money, but Carras turned it down, only asking for help with his health insurance. Eventually, Carras was paid a nominal salary.

Early in August of 2000, I spent a morning with Coach Carras. I met Jim more than a decade ago while playing tennis with my wife. Playing on the court next to us was Bill Frieder and (as it turned out) Coach Carras. Jim was in his mid-fifties at the time (he is now in his seventies), but was (and is) an obvious athlete, quick and instinctive. Frieder was a hopeless tennis player, but he was having fun, taunting Carras and anyone in earshot. As Jim took Frieder apart, I yelled at Frieder (I admit to a certain similarity in personality), "You better bend your knees, Coach, or that guy will continue to kick your ass." Frieder yelled back, "Okay, tough guy, me and her (pointing at Sue) will take on you and him (pointing at Carras), and I guarantee we will kick your asses even if I don't bend my knees." The choice of partners was no big concession by Frieder since, even to the untrained observer, it should have been obvious that Sue's strokes were superior to my own. So we played, with Frieder expanding and contracting the lines to ludicrous proportions. We played with them again that summer, but we never became anything more than vaguely casual acquaintances with Frieder. We became friends with Jim Carras, a man who has more friends than anyone I know.

Jim is the kind of person who remembers everyone's name and occupation and personal history and pet's birthday, even if he has only met the person briefly at some distant time. He also has the gift of making you feel important, as if your well-being has been on his mind over the past, say, two years since you last ran into him. And the truth is, maybe it was. Jim is warm, funny, and compassionate. He always has time to talk. I have seen Jim, for example, at the hardware store with a receiving line of every-person-in-the-joint wanting to shake his hand and say hi.

Coach Carras and Bill Frieder were good friends, and I imagine Jim being a perfect companion for the basketball coach. Frieder is all frenzy and edginess. Always looking for the angle. Carras is always up. And he seems forgiving, if not impervious, to the faults of others. Jim is a basketball fan, and Frieder often dragged him to see players that Frieder was interested in recruiting. Jim tells a story about one such trip, through a blinding snowstorm (Frieder always made Carras drive), to see a tall, gangly sophomore point guard. Jim found the kid to be slow and awkward. He could not jump and his shot was ugly and erratic. He had, indeed, no jump shot at all. Jim's opinion was to forget about the kid, that he had a limited future as a Division I player. Indeed, when I first saw the kid, in his senior year of high school, I was almost as pessimistic, and was confused by all the hoo-haw about him. It turns out that Frieder's eye was a little sharper than Jim's (or mine). Earvin Johnson.

Michigan cannot be a national player in golf. The weather conditions make it nearly impossible for the program to compete at such a level. This said, Jim has coached some very respectable teams, teams that have competed in the NCAAs. The program has produced several pro golfers, most recently Michael Harris, who participated in the Masters' Tournament in 2000. A major advantage of the Michigan program is a beautiful course (the Blue Course) created by the legendary Scottish designer Alistair McKenzie. McKenzie designed a few prominent courses in the United States (five or six), most notably Augusta (yes, that Augusta) and Cypress Point, but he was primarily a European designer from the early part of the twentieth century. The Michigan course is difficult, beautiful, and quirky. The greens are huge, rolling and (for me) impossible to read. (I admit I am a complete hack. I consider myself a sort of "black box" golfer, unless in-the-rough-or-in-a-trap-or-out-of-bounds-or-in-the-water defies all ordinary notions of randomness.) A second advantage Jim had was the Michigan golf building (though Jim may not see it as such), a Frank Lloyd Wright prairie-style structure that is classic in design and comfortable. The major competitive disadvantage the Michigan program faces is that Jim only has four scholarships to divide, a condition that made it nearly impossible for him to offer a prospective recruit a full ride. Jim did so on two occasions, but both of these kids went elsewhere. And neither has turned out to be Jack Nicklaus or anything close. Indeed, both have proven to be disappointing to their respective schools, at least as golfers.

Jim had to juggle his four scholarships and parse them together, based upon the vagaries of his team and promises he has made. And the failure of the golfers to whom he has offered full rides made the dangers of such offers evident. The full-tendered golfer who does not perform would be alienating to the team and a drain on Jim's ability to otherwise structure his program. In any event, and most of all, Jim is proud of the kids that have graduated from his program (something in the general range of one hundred percent) and proud of the fact that most have gone on to success at all levels of professional endeavor. If you get a chance, stop in the golf building and say hi to Jim Carras some day. He will remember your name. Your wife's name. Your kids' names and birthdays.

While the media spotlight on Lloyd Carr and Tommy Amaker is red hot, the heart and soul of Michigan sports is coaches like Jim Carras and Dick Kimble (diving) and Newt Loken (gymnastics) and Carol Hutchins (softball) and Jim Richardson (women's swimming) and Red Simmons (women's track) and many others. These coaches bleed Michigan. It is their lives. And when they retire (Carras, Kimble, Loken and Red Simmons are now all retired), they remain in the consciousness of UM sports by their presence and support. This is what makes the program what it is. They are why people care.

Ten *What Referees Say and Why We Are Mean to Them*

Well, I admit that I really don't know what referees say. I know what fans say, and it is something like, "I'm blind. I'm deaf. I wanna be a ref." But officials don't seem to write very much or often about their profession or experiences, though an uninformative work shows up occasionally. Jim Markbreit in football and Ron Luciano in baseball come to mind. I think the best writing about officiating is Earl Strom's book outlining his life in the NBA (*Calling the Shots: My Decades in the NBA*). My favorite stories in the Strom book concern the venues and quality of arenas that the league used to play in. Unlike the big, glitzy arenas of today, the NBA was a low-rent show for most of its existence, games being played in second-rate gyms in Hershey, Pa., or Rochester, Syracuse, or Fort Wayne. Strom talks about a game played on a floor that was rotting, and when a big center came down with a rebound (it might have been Wayne Embry, and if it was Embry, he didn't go up very far), one of his feet went through the floor, the wood splintering under his weight. Not certain what to do, the center tugged his foot through the debris and passed the ball up court. Strom blew his whistle. Traveling. It was not a popular call with Wayne.

I suppose it is not surprising that little is written by officials. It is their role, after all, to be anonymous. But many may find it surprising that referees will sometimes talk to fans, sometimes during games. Many years ago, a Big Ten ref turned to a beefy fan at Crisler Arena who had been on the ref's case over the course of the game and said, "Did I get that one right, fatso?" I cheered the ref on this one, as did others in Crisler, even though the guy was blowing calls. And since that time, when I have been fortunate enough to be near the court, I have heard officials get into it with fans.

Once, in an exhibition game between UM and the Australian National Team, the Aussie coach was on the refs mercilessly, to the point where I began to loudly defend the officials. Midway through the second half, the coach walked over to consult with me about the officiating. By late in the game, the coach would walk over to me and ask, "Was that one right?"

In the fall of 2001, during a preseason scrimmage, I complained to long-standing (and pretty good) Big Ten basketball referee Tom Rucker about a quick three-second call he made against Lavell Blanchard. I yelled, "Tom, if you're gonna give us that sorta call during the season, we are in real trouble."

Rucker held the ball and delayed the scrimmage. He walked over to me and explained, "You know, that was really Leon's [Jones] fault. Lavell thought he was going to shoot, and he got stuck in the paint too long. You better tell Tommy to make certain Leon takes his looks when he has them." Rucker was right, of course, both in his analysis of Leon's mistake and his sarcasm about my level of influence on his shot selection. It was a fortunate day for any team when Rucker, now retired, called their game. He made mistakes, of course. It is impossible not to. But Rucker always tried to call an even game, and I never saw him work with his thumb on the scale. Unfortunately, aside from Rucker and some others, officiating in the Big Ten (in basketball, not football) has a pretty woeful history. A part of this, perhaps a major part, is a Michigan perspective, since Crisler Arena has a long history of providing almost no home-court advantage.

There are about two thousand diehard Michigan fans. And that counts the ebb and flow of four hundred or so students. Michigan basketball fans are late-arriving and early-leaving types, and there must be at least upward of (let me count them) several venomous ones, that is, those who know the history of, say, referee Jim Burr and that game he gave us in 1987. And most of these fans have been banished to the depths of the gold section, far from the court, the blue seats primarily occupied by big-wheel donors, mostly not there or mostly asleep. There are a few good fans down low. Local insurance man Clem Gill is worth an entire section of fans recently released from an institution. The problem is there are not very many Gills (or lungs), and Crisler presents something closer to a library than any of the various snakepits in the conference. More than anywhere else, visiting teams (particularly in conference games) are likely to get a fair shake at Crisler. The intimidation factor is next to zero. Aside from Crisler, Bryce-Williams (PSU), Welsh-Ryan (Northwestern), and (mostly) Williams Arena (Minnesota) you can see some very funny stuff, though this has mitigated in the past few years.

A number of years back, Bill Frieder attempted to encourage/embarrass Michigan fans by installing his own (de facto) "Fried-o-meter," his subjective evaluation of the fans, the amount of ruckus they created during games. Frieder saw the disparity between the home and away environments and the obvious implications in close games, and he attempted to *shame* the fans into cheering. It worked. A bit. And when the Five were around, they caught the imagination of the fans, particularly the young fans, and this made Crisler a more active environment. On the other hand, the Fabs seemed to piss off certain referees, most notably Ed Hightower, and Crisler was still not a major league advantage for the team. Fisher was never able to engage the fans in the way that Frieder tried, except with the Fab Five, and Brian Ellerbe just alienated fans with his aloof style and disregard of all ordinary public relations. It is no exaggeration to say, for most of the past thirty years, that Crisler Arena has been a "home away from home" for the rest of the teams in the Big Ten, that it is rare for a visitor to get hammered by officiating at Crisler. Of course, in the past half decade, the fact that the Michigan teams have not been very good (okay, they basically smelled until 2002–3) has also been prominent in making Crisler a very friendly venue for visiting teams. When you are getting cranked by twenty on your own court, officiating don't mean squat.

Will Tommy Amaker change Crisler? I thought, initially, that Amaker would bring competent and then good basketball back to Ann Arbor and that he might, out of the ashes, build some excitement. In Amaker's first year, this turned out to be a false hope. But Amaker understood the importance of PR, the importance of reaching out to anyone who might have any interest in his program. Despite his terrible 2001–2 team, Amaker was tireless in trying to build something, if only in others' belief in him and in the future. Voila, in 2002–3, the Amaker-guided Wolverines became quite respectable. And, very weirdly, Crisler became a more or less, if quasi-legitimate, basketball venue, with the Wolverines shooting 55.7 percent of the free throws taken at Crisler, as opposed to home teams getting 54.5 percent when the Wolverines were on the road. This was skewed, I admit, by the fact that PSU brought its football team to Ann Arbor. Take that game out of the equation, and toss out the Indiana game on the road, and the Wolverines shot 50.6 percent of home free throws, versus 51.9 percent for home teams when on the road. In 2002–3, Crisler looked like a fairly typical Big Ten venue. It was the same thing in 2003–4. Indeed, in the 2004 NIT tournament Michigan was a snake pit, something I had never witnessed in my thirty-seven years of watching basketball at Crisler.

Now, it would be unfair of me (big deal) to give others the impression that there are no crazy fans at Crisler. Going into the 2001–2 season, in fact, there were almost *no* fans, and that tended to limit the craziness quotient. But there was a time, even prior to the Five, when a few wacky fans could be found lurking around. During the 1990–91 season, for example, I sat near the court with the most bizarre group of fans I have ever seen, at least at Crisler. I am the first to admit that Michigan is at the bottom of the totem pole in fan weirdness. Now and forever. Most of the fans are asleep, suffering from narcolepsy, or have died in their seats and are just decaying from season to season. In fact, this seems almost a matter of pride among Michigan fandom. We may be as dead as doornails. We may show up only now and then. And we may show up ten minutes late and leave ten minutes early. But, hey, we are here, every now and then, even though we don't know a damned thing about the game. Well, we are here. We might applaud a bit. But only if Michigan is up by twenty and our stock portfolios haven't taken a beating in the past week. Pass the cappuccino, will you? (Diary note pre-Amaker: "Hey, Bill Martin, will you drop the puck on these characters? Fat chance. What is likely is that ticket prices will increase in a sort of Chivas Regal theory. No one wants to drink this rotgut? Well, just jack up the prices and give it some cachet—hell, put some antelope piss in it—and the price increase will convince people you can actually drink the stuff. Somehow, though, I think this is unlikely to bring fans into the arena. If Knight or Pitino had been named the new coach, a combined 18 percent chance as analytically demonstrated in a prior chapter, Michigan fans would have shown up for the spectacle, the soap opera of the show. Basketball would have been the mere vehicle for the circus, until Pitino started whining about all the "negativity" in Ann Arbor or Knight was institutionalized. That road forsaken, Michigan needs a radical idea—like winning a few games—before people actually wander into the mausoleum.")

But during the 1990–91 season, I sat in row one, and a guy behind me, he looked more or less normal, started and continued a mantra for the entire year. It went exactly, "You eat it, ref. You know you eat it. I know you can hear me. Don't pretend you can't hear me. Don't deny it. Everybody here knows you eat it." There would be a thirty-second pause. And then the cycle recharged. Now, this guy didn't just say his mantra once a half. Or twice. Or twenty times. It was continuous. I timed him. Thirty seconds between cycles. Game after game, ahead or behind. Good calls or bad calls. I admit I thought the guy was both hilarious and bizarre, and would have paid significant dollars to the athletic department to have him sit near me every game.

This shtick was punctuated by his partner, a guy who (I never knew why) always showed up in a long blue terry cloth bathrobe. Under the bathrobe was food: Twinkies, Girl Scout cookies, or Big Macs. Chocolate Yoo-Hoo drink stuff and Ding Dongs, Snowballs. He was the Harpo Marx of Crisler. And, I don't know why, the guy would offer the snacks around to designated folks, but mostly the officials. It was, "Mr. Referee, would you like a Ding Dong? Fresh today."

Next to these two guys was a man who never said very much or cheered. But he always wore a giant, plastic Wolverine head. I have no clue where he got it, since I have never seen one before or after. And I am certain there was or is no other Michigan fan around willing to wear such a dopey ornament on his or her head. The man had red hair and horn-rimmed glasses. In his forties. Probably an accountant. But he made a noise periodically, in what he told me was a "decade of serious study of the Wolverine growl." It went something like "aroo-aroo-grawww." Personally, I wanted this guy as far away from me as possible. I am reasonably certain I saw this guy at a Michigan practice in 2001. He had aged, but it was the same ratty plastic hat. And who else would wear this sort of a contraption to a *practice*?

In the first row was another guy I considered dangerous. A youngish man who always wore a Batman costume. Don't know why. Was too afraid to ask. But I once heard him refer to himself as the "Bat Wolverine." His cheers, though often sporadic, were laced with superhero jargon. Often in a French accent. "I weel keel zees cheating referees wis my bat rope and feed ze remnants to de bat hound." Uh. Right. I kept my distance.

And then there was my group, headed by the Worst Fan and the Hex King, Jim B. The Worst Fan is my brother John. John is an MD. He has a master's degree in public health. He is one of the kindest and most thoughtful persons I have ever met. Until he attends a Michigan sporting event. John thinks Michigan has never gotten a fair shake from the referees in any game *ever*. It doesn't matter if we just beat Panhandle State (the Vagrants, you can look it up) by fifty. We still got hosed by the refs. John and I once attended a Frieder-era Indiana-Michigan game and we managed to get seats about ten feet from Bob Knight. Michigan won the game (in double OT, if my memory is right) with my brother having a running commentary *at* Bob for much of it. It was, "It was a bad call Bob. His name is Referee Rucker. I think you should point that out to him," and "Mr. Knight, there is a process server in row two. I would scram outta here quick after the game," and "Mr. Bob, that is such a nice sweater. It really does make you look thinner," and "Don't worry, Coach, that chair isn't nailed down," for two and a half hours. More or less nonstop. And loud. Foghorn loud. And the truth is that the other fans in the area were either (a) actually paying attention to the game (rare enough for Michigan fans), or (b) being their normal, polite selves. Now, I admit, when Bob would stand up and attempt to intimidate the refs, some fans might suggest that Mr. Knight "sit down," but that was about it.

In the following week's *Sports Illustrated,* Knight complained that the Michigan fans were "the worst fans in the United States." Initially, I was pretty shocked by this. The Michigan fans, given the game, were as meek and polite as any fans would have been. But then I remembered one exception. And I knew that John had been dubbed, by Coach Bob no less, as The Worst Fan In The United States.

The Worst Fan yammered about every call and tortured the opposing coaches (they were in earshot, especially since John has a prodigious capacity to make noise). The Hex King was sui generis, one of a kind, convinced that he held the secrets to a sort of sign language that would put the ultimate kibosh on the opposition. Now the guy was educated. At Oberlin College and Michigan. And he was a ballplayer himself. A good one. And he was a computer engineer with some sort of high security classification. A bright and more or less normal person. But at Crisler, he was a human highlight film of body runes. Chokes. Finger crosses. Eye poking gestures. Bizarre gyrations. So, for example, the Indiana-Michigan game would go something like this:

211

"You eat it, ref."

"Would you like some pink Twinkies, Mr. Referee?"

Choke sign from the Hex King.

"You know you eat it."

"Aroo-aroo-grawwww"

"Hey, Mr. Knight. Take some Twinkies from this guy, you look a little peaked."

"I know you can hear me, ref."

Eye gouging motion from the Hex King.

"I weel feed zee intestines to de bat weasels, Bob Knight."

"Aroo-aroo-grawww."

"Don't pretend otherwise, ref."

"How about some nice Yoo-Hoo, Mr. Knight?"

"Drink the guy's Yoo-Hoo, will ya, Coach? You look too scrawny to me."

The Hex King drools, saliva rolling down the front of his shirt.

"Don't deny it, ref."

"Aroo-aroo-grawwwwwwww."

"I weel rip out ze eyeballs and let ze goldfish nibble on zem."

"You meatball, Knight. Why are you insulting this guy? Take a Twinkie, will you?"

"Everybody here knows you eat it, ref."

"Aroooo-arooo grawwwwwwwwwwwww"

Well, did any of this work? I think I can answer with a categorical "yes" on this one. After all, when Michigan played the Hoosiers in Bloomington that year, the free throw differential was 43–13, a mere spread of thirty. And the fouls were 29–14. After all, Indiana was a very clean team and thus, in Jemele logic, shouldn't be called for the six hundred or so moving screens it threw out in that and every other game. Or the perpetual two-handed checks on the perimeter that were a Hoosier staple, even after being outlawed in the NBA. But with our little corner of fans doing their stuff at Crisler, Michigan was a stellar one of five (yeah, I think it was Dr. Ed Hightower on this one) from the line, while Indiana shot fifteen of twenty-four. So the difference in free throws attempted plummeted from thirty to nineteen. I think we should take personal credit. We did, I am sure.

The best basketball referee in the Big Ten at the present time is Steve Welmer. Welmer is somewhere in the range of six-eight-plus, and my guess is he actually played some organized ball. Welmer has an unusual feel for the game—what should be called and what is okay to let go. Welmer's inclination is to let the players decide the game, and he tends to call the obvious stuff and let the little things slide. Welmer is so far ahead of the curve that it is hard to designate second place. A few years back, I would have named Jody Sylvester as number two, an official I used to think was hopeless, but who improved, year after year, until his only peer in the league was Welmer. Sylvester, like Welmer, was not intimidated by the ravings of coaches and fans. Unfortunately, as soon as Sylvester got to be any good, he quit or retired or turned to pro rasslin'. I didn't see him call any games after the 2001–2 season. After these two, the drop off is severe, though Tim Higgins can call a good game. For the past two years, though I can't believe I am writing this, Ed Hightower called good games. Indeed, Hightower was as consistent as anyone I saw during the 2003–2005 period.

My own paranoia about Big Ten officiating began in the '75–'76 season, and focused on road games (within a week or two of each other) at Illinois and Indiana. The incidents are outlined more extensively in Jeff Mortimer's fine book *Pigeons, Bloody Noses and Skinny Little Kids*. The Illinois game was a monstrous affair, a home job to the *n*th degree. Michigan's star guard Rickey Green fouled out with more than four minutes to go in the game, but the Wolverines were holding a 75–72 lead with less than a minute to play. Illinois hit a jumper, and an imaginary foul was whistled on UM guard Dave Baxter, but UM was given a reprieve when the Illini missed the free throw. However, UM forward Johnny Robinson did not box out; Illinois got the putback, and secured a 76–75 lead with forty seconds to go. Michigan missed an attempt for the lead, an Illinois player got the rebound, was fouled, and went to line with roughly fifteen seconds left in the game. There was no double bonus at this time, and after the Illini missed the free throw, the Wolverines hustled the ball down court. With a few seconds left on the clock, Phil Hubbard missed a short jumper, Wayman Britt missed a tap, and then Johnny Rob dumped the ball in for a seeming 77–76 Michigan win. Official Art White waved the basket off, even though the ball was shot prior to the end of the game, with the explanation that "Robinson did not have control" of the ball. Apparently, according to White, the shot was a "tip," and a tip, unlike an ordinary shot, must be in the basket (as opposed to in the air) when the game concludes. Now, nobody had ever heard of this rule or had ever seen it called this way. And I have never seen it called this way since. But John Orr did not contest White's explanation, and only said (essentially), "If that's the rule, I got no argument." Later, Orr was steamed when he watched the replay and saw, indeed, that Robinson did have "control" of the ball.

The matter came full circle a week or two later against number-one-ranked Indiana in Bloomington. The Hoosiers would go undefeated that year and eventually win the national championship—against Michigan—after the Wolverines demolished undefeated and number two Rutgers in the NCAA semifinals. No serious fan can dispute the fact that Indiana was the best team in the country that year. They deserved the national championship. But on this

213

day in Bloomington, Michigan was the better team, a conclusion even Bob Knight admits in his (allegedly) lucid moments.

Michigan was leading the Hoosiers by four and had possession of the ball with thirty seconds left in the game. Phil Hubbard attempted to dribble the clock out, but Indiana guard Quinn Buckner leveled him. Buckner, years later, told Tom Hemingway he wanted to foul Hubbard because he was the worst free throw shooter on the team, but was concerned because "I hit him so damn hard I was afraid they were going to call an intentional foul." But they didn't call an intentional foul. They didn't call a foul at all, choosing to call Hubbard for traveling. Buckner then hit a basket at the other end, cutting the lead to two with fourteen seconds left in the game. Steve Grote, a good free throw shooter, was then fouled, but Grote missed the front end, Indiana got the rebound, and came down court. With three seconds left in the game, All-American Scott May took a jump shot from the corner. He missed (an air ball) but Jim Crews got the rebound for Indiana and threw the ball back up. The ball clanked away as time expired, but Kent Benson made a final swat at the ball after the buzzer sounded. It went through. The replay showed that Benson never even touched the ball until after the game was over, but the officials let the basket stand, concluding the ball was in the air as the buzzer went off. This was wrong and, in addition, the "tip" rule authored by Art White disappeared for the game. The contest went into overtime, and Michigan took an early four-point lead. But Hubbard and then Grote were hit for their fifth fouls and the Hoosiers pulled the game out.

By the early seventies, it was certain that basketball officiating in the Big Ten was pretty inconsistent. To be honest, it was wretched. I felt some anxiety in saying this, but then I reviewed (the legendary) Tom Hemingway's *Life Among the Wolverines*. Hemingway has been watching games for longer than I have, and he knows basketball. In his book, written in 1985, he claims that officiating was so solid in the Big Ten in the sixties that it went (largely) unnoticed. He writes that many fine officials retired in the early seventies and, at the same time, college games began to be officiated by three-member crews. At the time, John Orr saw no advantage in adding an official, and said, "It just gives them a 33 percent greater chance to be wrong." Aside from Orr's homily, the increase in the number of officials diluted the number of quality referees.

Everyone acknowledges that officiating skill is a very unique talent, even more unique as applied to basketball games at the college level and above. It is, I guarantee you, harder to be a competent referee than it is to be a competent player. I have tried it. I sucked and found it to be difficult beyond comprehension, as hard as consistently hitting a one iron from a tight lie. With this as a predicate, adding more refs to a pool of talent that was likely to be thin in the first place meant it was certain the caliber of officiating would decline. Hemingway claims that by the mid-seventies, officiating in the Big Ten had transformed from the extremely competent to the horrible. That, in the sixties, "you might see a bad call every game" but by the eighties, "it was more like one bad call per minute."

From 1975 through the mid-nineties, I felt that many Big Ten games were officiated little differently than pro rasslin' matches. The crowd yells at the ref. The ref goes over to see what all the brouhaha is about. A foreign object is pulled. More yelling by the fans. More distraction for the referee. More foreign objects. But it has gotten better, much better, in the recent years. In the main, I think the present generation of referees within the conference are just more competent or have improved, lead by Steve Welmer and Gene Monje and Dan Chrismann (who disappeared in 2002–3), to name a few. And others, like Dr. Ed and (particularly) Jody Sylvester (also gone, but in 2001–2), have improved their games. Yeah, Phil Bova still might be around, and Tom O'Neil, once very solid, seems to get worse each year. But all in all, as Michigan teams got worse, I felt the officiating seemed better. So what is going on? I surmise it is possible that officiating gets less relevant when the teams are not close in ability. When the teams are even or almost so, any bounce or call can make a difference. At this point, we all know, announcers aside, that "good teams don't win close games." Fortunate ones do, and then only in the short run, over a limited number of trials. Still, in watching and reviewing many close games, I think the Big Ten has cleaned up its act.

It is probably a fact that all fans, even Duke basketball fans, think the refs screw them. (Year in and year out, Duke gets the most favored officiating that I see—so, yeah, Tommy, you made your point. A stray example is the '91–'92 season, the Fabs frosh year, where the Wolverines managed to get into the NCAA title game [against Duke] shooting forty-five *fewer* free throws than their opponents over the course of the year. Duke? They shot a trifling 460 more freebies than their competition, pretty amazing considering the Duke defensive theory that year was to clutch and grab on the perimeter, to make up for the fact they were so damned slow.) So anything I say on this point is suspect. Like most fans, my bias is manifest. Still, in the 1975 to 1997 period, Big Ten basketball officiating was awful beyond comprehension. It was so bad that in 1993 even the governor of Minnesota, Arne Carlson, got into the act, complaining that the Gophers had been mistreated in a game against (who else?) the Hoosiers. Incredibly, Carlson wrote Rich Falk (the Big Ten director of officials) to complain about the game. He wrote, in part,

> It was not a question of an occasional bad call here or there, which all basketball fans can expect. It had all the earmarks of a deliberate plan to simply take the game away from Minnesota. In all of my years watching basketball, I can't say I have ever seen worse officiating.

Indiana was physical, strong, and aggressive. Yet they were rarely called and almost never in the second half. On the other hand, every time Minnesota applied pressure, the whistle blew. Whenever Calbert Cheaney drove for the basket and used his left arm to push a defender out of the way, the defender was called for the foul instead of Cheaney . . .

My take is that the governor was most likely right. Cheaney and Indiana did reap the benefit of favorable officiating in the early nineties. Very favorable. And Minnesota received some awful officiating on the road (even at Crisler)—the Gophers rarely seemed to get the benefit of any doubt. But the governor misunderstood a few things. First, everyone gets jobbed at Indiana, even Keady. The benchmark is the juxtaposition of home and road officiating. The truth is that home cooking goes on everywhere, sometimes even in Williams or Crisler arenas. Analysis can only occur in the comparison of games at home and those on the road. Second, it seems unlikely Calbert pushed the Gopher defenders away with his *left* arm on anything other than an isolated instance, since Calbert is decidedly left-handed and was likely to be using his right arm to create space. Third, Cheaney was a complete finesse player. He didn't have any kind of a physical game. This makes me wonder whether Arne actually saw the game or even if he knew jack about hoops. Aside from this, I would have advised the governor to keep his own counsel, since his comments probably ceded control of the state to Jesse Ventura, a guy who really knew about bad officiating. My surmise is this was not lost on the voters in the state. I would have also advised old Arne not to use government stationary to make his complaint. It would seem that this kind of expression is more in the realm of ordinary fan angst as opposed to government business.

The governor of Minnesota was not singular in his dismay. I know that Steve Fisher did not believe he always received reasonable treatment at the hands of Big Ten officials. Fisher never complained in public. The worst he might say (as in 1993, when Iowa shot thirty more freebies than UM en route to an eight-point win, and three of five Wolverine starters were in deep foul trouble by the middle of the first half) was that "we have to do a better job of getting to the free throw line." But in private, Fisher felt there was more than one official in the conference who was terrified of Knight, making it tough for any opponent to get a fair game against the Hoosiers. Moreover, Fisher expressed in private that Ed Hightower "loves Knight" and "hates Michigan," and he could not figure out how to approach the Big Ten or Dr. Ed in the attempt to balances the scales. Fisher complained to his friends that Hightower was very hard on the Wolverines and that Hightower had his own (mysterious) agenda. [Notice: This is pure rumor, hearsay, and innuendo. I wasn't there. But it is really reliable hearsay.]

My recollection is that Michigan was routinely hammered by two referees prior to 1998, Ed Hightower and Phil Bova. In my mind, we just never got balanced or consistent games from these two. But how could I prove this? And how could I check my own subjective impressions? I started by sorting through my old basketball tapes, looking for games not in the written records and cursing the fact that I had not saved more. But I did find three games in my collection from the 1992–93 season officiated by Ed Hightower, the season where Arne Carlson went ballistic and the Wolverines had their most talented team of all time. It would seem, given the team Michigan put on the floor, that they would never have a game where officiating made a significant difference. Chris Webber, Jalen Rose, Juwan Howard, Jimmy King, and Ray Jackson were sophomores. Three All-Pros. King and Jackson were each voted as MVPs in the CBA, and King had some minor time in the NBA. They had great shooters off the bench in James Voskuil and Rob Pelinka. Voskuil and Pelinka were smart, tough, and experienced players. The Wolverines also had senior Eric Riley, a seven-footer who hung around the NBA for a number of years. The ninth man was Michael Talley, who was a starter prior to the Fabs at the point position. He was also a former Mr. Basketball in Michigan. The team had strength, depth, power, and the ability to shoot the ball. King and Jackson were extremely athletic and excellent defenders. Chris Webber played defense and allowed the rest of the team the unusual tactic of funneling to the baseline, with Webber able to cut off easy access to the basket. The Wolverines played team defense and were able to double the post as well as anyone ever in college basketball. One would think that this team would draw fouls by the buckets against its opposition since, the fact is, there have been very few college teams ever (maybe none) with this level of athletic ability.

Sometimes the Fabs did dominate the foul stats. But not as often as one would think (actually, it was pretty rare), and never like Indiana, and not at all when Dr. Ed officiated. The Wolverines were 31–5 in that (Arne's) season, losing in the NCAA finals to North Carolina (George Lynch and Eric Montross) after sneaking by the Tar Heels earlier in the year. Ed Hightower presided over four of the five losses that year, somehow missing out on the fun in the 93–92 loss at Bloomington. In the tapes that I have Hightower officiated in the 76–75 loss to Indiana at home, a win on the road against Minnesota, and the national championship loss. In the Crisler game (called with Phil Bova), the Wolverines shot six free throws to Indiana's ten. Hightower was reasonably invisible in the game, calling four fouls (three against UM and one against Indiana) leading to two UM fouls shots. Now if this game had been on the road, I would have been ecstatic about the officiating. But it was hard to get worked up about a game at home against a significantly inferior team where the home team gets to the line for six shots. Moreover, there were two awful calls against Chris Webber (Bova) down the stretch that made the difference in the game. Not that Indiana didn't play great, because they did. To be fair, I would label this a pretty well-officiated contest, if it had been on the road or even a neutral court. The problem was the juxtaposition with the road games.

One week after the Indiana game, Michigan played at Minnesota (Voshon Lenard and a reasonable but non-NBA cast), and the Hightower foul count (his alone) skyrocketed to twenty, with fourteen being called against the Wolverines. While the game was in doubt (the Wolverines had won it at the four-minutes-to-go mark) Hightower had made eleven of his fifteen calls against the Wolverines, with the Gophers going to the line for ten shots on his fouls and the Wolverines shooting zero. At this point in the game, the foul shot total (all refs) was 18–3 in favor of Minnesota. The end total by Dr. Ed was 16–4. What is most interesting about the Minnesota contest is that it took place after a Wolverine loss at Iowa City, a game presided over by Jim Burr, Tim Higgins, and (again) Ed Hightower. At Iowa, the Wolverines lost 88–80 when the Hawks shot forty-two tosses to UM's twelve. In that one, Howard and Webber fouled out, and both of these players (and Ray Jackson) had three fouls before the first half ended. Rob Pelinka was whistled for four fouls in ten minutes and Eric Riley for four fouls in fourteen minutes. Iowa had limited (none, really) foul issues in the game, allowing them to play defense as hard as they wanted.

The Iowa game had been the subject of commentary by Patrick Reusse in the *Minneapolis Star Tribune* by way of Reusse's support of Arne Carlson's complaint about Big Ten officiating. Reusse commenced his column with the caveat that he would vote for Harold Stassen over Carlson, since Reusse perceived Carlson to be a complete dope. However, Reusse admits that Carlson finally "stumbled onto an issue with which I agree. The refereeing in the Big Ten men's basketball games was a disgrace." Reusse's column went on to outline some of the Gophers' woes with the officiating in Bloomington:

> That was the night when the basketball ricocheted off a couple of players, then went out of bounds next to the Indiana bench. The referee nearest the play rushed to the spot and pointed that it was the Gophers' possession. The well-known Indiana coach then leaped from the bench, put his face in front of the official's and described him with a two-word noun that was prevalent in Redd Foxx's comedy routine.
>
> Did the referee slap the well-known Indiana coach with an automatic technical? Not exactly. What the guy did was hustle to the area of the Minnesota bench, tell [Minnesota head coach] Haskins that he was reversing his decision and would give the ball to Indiana, and to request that Haskins help him out by not complaining.

Right then, Haskins knew the referees did not control the whistle-blowing inside Assembly Hall, but that it was controlled by the well-known Indiana coach.

Reusse continued:

> Last week Haskins swallowed his disgust and gave credit to Indiana for its comeback, tainted as it was. Privately, Clem's friends say the coach is still fuming about the twenty-four fouls called against his team, compared to fourteen for Indiana, the team that was trying to come back. Clem is also said to be unhappy with his friend Carlson's letter; the coach is worried that referees—angry with Carlson—will take it out on the Gophers.

Reusse then suggested that Carlson should have attempted a different tactic to bring his point to the fore; that Carlson should have complained about a non-Minnesota game. Reusse's choice? "The treatment Michigan received from the referees Sunday at Iowa City."

> It is noble that the Hawkeyes and their loyal fans are dedicating their play and their enthusiasm to Chris Street, the student and basketball star who was killed in a car crash on Jan. 19. I'm just not sure the referees are supposed to join in the wave of the emotion by shafting the opposition, which is what Ed Hightower, Tim Higgins, and Jim Burr did to Michigan.

In a rare example of sports reporting, Reusse concluded with the attempt at some analysis:

> The Gophers have played four Big Ten games in Williams Arena this season. They have been called for fewer fouls three times and an equal number of fouls the fourth time. The totals are eighty-one fouls against opponents and seventy against Minnesota.

> The Gophers have played three Big Ten games on the road. They have been called for more fouls in those games. The totals are forty-nine fouls against opponents and eighty against Minnesota.

> People who are of the opinion that Big Ten men's basketball referees are something more than a collection of weak-kneed weenies are invited to offer an explanation.

I don't know if Reusse and Haskins had reason to fear reprisals from the

Big Ten zebras for the rest of that season. I do know that Reusse was a little myopic when viewing the big picture, since Ed Hightower and company did everything they could to keep Minnesota in the game at Williams, something he must have known, since he looked at the numbers and must have witnessed the contest. Not that I deny Reusse's primary point. And I concede that Minnesota, in general, has gotten jobbed in Bloomington and on the road at times in the conference. On the positive side, I believe and hope that it has gotten a little better over the past five or six years.

As it turned out, the Wolverines also got stuck with Dr. Ed in the national championship game that year, a fact that must have put Steve Fisher someplace between livid and disconsolate. The Wolverines lucked out here, since Hightower only called six fouls in the game. Unfortunately for the Wolverines, all six were called against them. Well, what can I say? I like Carolina. I liked Eric Montross and George Lynch. But the truth is, they were fouling in this game as much as the Wolverines. So in three games with three future NBA All-Stars, the Hightower foul count was UM seven, Opponent twenty-three (really, to be fair, more like UM five, Opponent twenty), and the foul shot total UM six, Opponent twenty-four. (Or, more accurately, UM two, Opponent eighteen). In other words, in three games, when the outcome was yet to be determined, Hightower sent the Wolverines to the line a total of one time for two tosses. (I rewatched the Carolina game again in the summer of 2004. To be fair, only two of Hightower's six calls in that game were obviously wrong. He did make one call against Carolina in the game, traveling, and missed two grossly obvious offensive fouls against Carolina and a plain-as-day offensive goaltend.)

I no longer have a tape of the Duke loss that year, but I remember going into the game with the hope that Michigan might get at least an even shake from the Big Ten officials in Cameron, since Michigan got hammered at home the prior year by the ACC crew. (In the earlier game, Michigan outscored the Blue Devils by fourteen from the floor, but were outscored from the foul line by seventeen en route to an 88–85 OT loss to an excellent Duke team with Grant Hill, Christian Laettner, and Bobby Hurley.) But Dr. Ed showed up for the 1992 game in Durham, and UM lost to the Blue Devils by eleven in the process of again being outscored from the free throw line by seventeen. Chris Webber did not get to the line in that one, probably because he wasn't as strong, nor his skills as refined, as the guys who checked him, Cherokee Parks and Eric Meek. (Check Cherokee out these days. He now has more tattoos than Dennis Rodman. Poor Cherokee, stuck under the dubious tutelage of Christian Laettner, has never seemed to get it together.)

The good news is that most of the referees in the Big Ten, guys like Tom Clark and Sid Rodeheffer and Jim Burr, had (by 2004) graduated from pro rasslin' to a sort of random and benign impartiality theory of calling games. It is as if the magic eight ball is now the arbiter of Big Ten basketball, an anarchistic generator that tends to move to the middle over the long haul. That said, Ed Hightower really graduated in the past two years, even calling the block/charge correctly (the hardest call) as often as would seem humanly possible. Dr. Ed is a referee with a very good reputation, at least outside of Ann Arbor. In the mid-eighties through the mid-nineties, however, I thought Hightower had the potential to become the reincarnation of the legendary and never-to-be-surpassed-in-awfulness Jim Bain, an official who seemed intent on getting in players' faces and hoping, just hoping, he might piss one off sufficiently so that he could call a "T" (it often happened) or take a slug at him (too bad I never saw this). Hightower had this seeming propensity, but he has mellowed over the years and, I hate to admit, he has improved. But it has been a weird and quirky improvement. For years I thought that Hightower missed one hundred percent of all block/charge calls. It was uncanny. If Hightower called it a charge, the replay showed otherwise. I never saw any official (even including Jim Bain) so consistent in his ability to blow it. But Ed began to get a lot better, though stranger. Sometimes it seemed like he was only going to make traveling calls. Other games, he only made calls on offensive players. Some games, he made no calls at all. I began to perceive him as a sort of Major Major, excising all verbs, then all nouns. Then, I had to admit (though I hated it) that Hightower morphed into being about average among Big Ten refs, though this may only have spoken to the level of the officiating in the conference, sort of like being intellectually about average as compared to the set of Jesse Helms, Gomer Pyle, and Lassie. Then, Hightower actually got pretty good. Well, we will see. (In the 2002–3 season, I had no gripe with Hightower. Indeed, he was so consistent I almost hoped he would be calling games, as opposed to some others in the conference. *Almost*. In 2003–04, he was even better. No complaints in 2004–5, though we were 1–2 when we drew Dr. Ed, losing the road free throw battle 32–56.)

In 1998, Hightower got into a physical altercation with fellow referee Ted Valentine at halftime of an Illinois-Indiana (of course) game. Jim Arehart described the incident in the November 1999 issue of *Referee Magazine*. In the game, near the end of the half, Bob Knight, after a protracted period of ranting, called Valentine a "fucking liar." Arehart then wrote about the halftime exit as follows:

> At the half, Valentine immediately went to midcourt and waited for his partners so they could leave the floor together. At Indiana, teams exit via center court. Hightower was speaking with Knight nearby and when they finished, the coach veered toward Valentine instead of going straight to the locker room. "I see him coming out of the corner of my eye," said Valentine. "I made my mind up that if he says something,

then it's going to have to be a technical foul. He walks to me and he walks as close as he can to me without touching me. He starts walking around me and I can see from my peripheral vision that his eyes kept getting bigger as he's walking around me. He's not saying anything, but this whole show is to bring the crowd down on top of me. We're always taught as a crew that if one person called a technical foul, the next guy has got to call the next one. Nobody on my crew called a technical foul. It disappointed me because I would look out for my crew."

Valentine, cheesed off by the lack of support from fellow refs Tom O'Neill and Hightower, then got into a fight with Dr. Ed, a physical altercation that was broken up by O'Neill. After halftime, Knight continued to berate Valentine. Arehart writes,

The second half picked up right where the first half left off, with Knight trying to intimidate the officials. "I go right where I'm supposed to go [shortly before the half began] and Coach Knight is across the court in his bench area," said Valentine. "I'm kneeling down and I'm trying to stretch. I looked over and there are these size thirteen shoes standing right in front of me. I look up and there he is [Coach Knight]. He starts hollering and screaming at me: 'Why in the f— didn't you do this and why in the f— didn't you do that, and f— this and f— that!' I looked up at him and said, 'Coach Knight, you need to go to the other side of the court.' The referee on the game [Hightower] is standing nearby and next to him is O'Neill but nobody is doing anything to get Coach Knight away, which by right is a technical foul. I put my hand up and he goes to say something else. I say, 'Coach Knight, you better go to the other side.' He said something else and I said, 'Bob, you better go to the other side because I'm going to put my whistle in my mouth.' At that time, he turned and the referee on the game [Hightower] put his arm around him and walked him to the other side."

Valentine was still dissatisfied with what he perceived was his partners' lack of willingness to step up and take care of business. "I felt we passed too many times," he said. "I passed after the first technical. Then, when he walked around me, I passed again. Now, it's the third pass."

With ten minutes left in the game, O'Neil called a tech on Illinois when a player hung on the rim. Knight began to argue this call, complaining that, in addition to the tech, a foul and/or goaltend should have been called. Knight was in a complete rage, according to Valentine, and after giving the Indiana coach more rope than he should have, teed him up twice more. The Big Ten ended up suspending Valentine, concluding the second "T" should not have been called (unreal). Ultimately, Valentine felt betrayed by O'Neill and Hightower in not "having his back," and said he would be fine if he never worked with Hightower again.

Well, despite my satisfaction with Dr. Ed's officiating in the past few years, I remain wary, and my Valentine's Day present might be the same as Ted's. Now let me say this again. I am the first to admit that basketball officiating has to be one of the hardest skills on the planet. It is a harder skill than playing the game or arbitrating domestic disputes or calling balls and strikes in a criminal trial, and I ain't kidding. But how come women's games in the Big Ten are almost always well-officiated? Indeed, I can't recall seeing a Big Ten women's game decided by officiating, while this is a common occurrence in men's ball. Okay, I admit it. The answer must be "speed," the relative paces of the games. But then, how come the officiating in the ACC has been so much better than in the Big Ten? Well, I know the answer to this one. Better officials. Somehow, the ACC has cornered the market. Am I as good a ref as O'Neill or Hightower? You really don't need to ask. In my experience, I was awful or maybe worse. And I also admit, if you actually know the referees' names, there is something wrong with you. Even worse than knowing the answer "Beano."

As long as I am at it, the next time Michigan gets a neutral game from Phil Bova on the road (in the Big Ten at least) it will be the first time. Okay, maybe the third or fourth. My favorite recent Bova game was a few years ago (1998) when a weak Michigan team completely outplayed a good Indiana team in Bloomington, outscoring the Hoosiers by eighteen points from the floor. But Luke Recker, shooting mostly jump shots, went to the free throw line twenty-five times (not a typo), and Indiana shot twenty-seven more free throws than Michigan en route to a two-point win. Indiana *did not score a basket for a nine-minute period* in the second half and still won the game. This was the most brutally officiated (Michigan) game of the year, a game where the officials seemed completely intimidated by the presence of the (possibly and allegedly, unless he is hired by Michigan) deranged Bob Knight. It wasn't the first time, of course. And it was far from the most blatant example of timidity by officials in the land of Bob Oz. (Checking the Kentucky record book, a choice made at random, the most free throws ever shot against a UK team was eighteen, by Pete Maravich for chrissakes. But in that game, where Maravich put up sixty-four, UK had six more attempts than LSU. Well, we know Recker is right there with Maravich.) I want to put Bova (in my memory) at the fifty-to-eight free throw game in Iowa City a few years back, but I can't recall who did that one. I hope I never remember. But if I do remember, I hope it was Bova. Okay. Bova is probably a loving husband and a good father and an altogether decent man. I hope not. But I have reason to believe he probably is. And I have to admit the guy seems to try hard. He breaks a sweat in games. And, when we are out of conference, we have gotten fair games from Bova, even if these have been against Mojo State or some other stiffs that Brian Ellerbe brought in to guarantee that UM would not whiff for the entire season. Moreover, in the last three years of the Ellerbe tenure and the first four years of the Amaker regime, officiating was a primary nonfactor for the Wolverines. The Wolverines found plenty of ways in five of those years, sometimes pretty inventive ways, to lose on their own, and they didn't need any help from the referees, thank you. So I apologize. We just always seem to get hammered by this guy, and I hope to never see him again in my life. I guess I could live without Hightower too, at least in any important game played by Michigan. But that probably means well after Dr. Ed has retired, when the grand jury reconvenes and then concludes its two decade long work on the rumored ghost of Ed Martin's illegal bingo and chuck-a-luck games over at St. Cecilia's, so I have little concern. Moreover, I definitely had a long run of enjoyment watching Dr. Ed in games not involving Michigan. Always an adventure. No fouls and seventy-four three-second calls. No problem, the guy has big feet. Or just no calls at all. No autopsy, no foul. Or a call every five seconds. Hey, hang loose, I gotta control this game, that guy is as mean and intense as Mo Taylor. (By the 2001–2 season Luke Recker had transferred from Indiana to Iowa and was a much stronger player than he had been at Indiana during his twenty-five-free-throw days. But when Iowa went in to play Indiana at Bloomington Luke got to the line once. I guess this was just random.)

In reviewing my warm and fuzzy feelings toward Hightower and Bova, I found the following sense-impression in my diaries, just to make certain I don't get too revisionist in my own thoughts:

February 13, 2001. Meanwhile, Ellerbe's team gets whacked at Indiana by thirteen. The jig was up when the officials were assigned, since Ed Hightower got the game, and it may be a fact that Michigan has never won any game on the road (ever) when Ed (or Phil Bova) was in the officiating crew. I have no idea whether this can be looked up, but my surmise is the Wolverines record is no better than 10 percent on the road with Dr. Ed, and this might well be generous. In any event, the first-half free throws were fifteen to four and the final tally thirty-five to seventeen, with some fake Indiana fouls at the end making it not look that bad. I guess the difference arose because Kurt Haston, the Indiana center, is such a clean player, and Indiana has now abandoned the continual and never-ending illegal screens since Knight was banished to

Palookaville or Waco or El Paso or wherever the hell he is. But more than this, the Wolverines turned the ball over twenty-five times to the Hoosiers ten, and only a few of the turnovers were the result of bad calls. Well, we stunk and we lost to a mediocre but very superior team. But if Michigan were the Lakers, I would guarantee you Shaq would foul out with Dr. Ed as quick as Josh Moore, in other words, in about eight minutes. (Josh Moore fouled out in a game in five minutes in the 2001 season. At the time, I thought this had to be a record for a player not actually trying to commit fouls. I remarked to other fans that this had to be as fast as anyone could *conceivably* foul out without trying. Wrong again. In Josh's next game, he fouled out in four minutes.)

* * * *

So why should anyone pay any attention to the ravings of a complete homer, even if the homer is the Minnesota governor or a perceived-to-be-wronged coach who plays the game in public or the second-rate innuendo of some biased fan? Good point. Make that excellent point. So I went back and checked the box scores. This is no easy feat, even in the age of the internet, since (a) internet data does not go back that far, (b) some box scores are hard to find or just don't exist on the various school sites, and (c) sometimes the referees are not designated in the boxes. These limitations aside, I thought it might be useful to test my impressions of Hightower and Bova, that, in general, they seemed to be putting their thumbs on the scale in Michigan games. I got nervous before I began to look this up, so I was ready with two caveats. The first, in case the records seemed pretty neutral, would be (after all) that these refs always worked with others and, indeed, sometimes with very good referees. The second was that I don't pretend to say that Hightower or Bova are fixing games or even have any bias. In this implication, I think Arne Carlson was well out of bounds in his analysis. There is not a chance in a billion that these guys were on the take or directing the outcome of games. And I admit I have no logical reason to believe either official has or had any conscious animus toward the Wolverines or the Gophers. Both these things said, it sure seems to me that these two, more than any other current officials, have given us many bad games, games where I felt that officiating was the difference in the outcome, games called with distinct sets of rules for the teams on the court. Regardless of the record, I know two things. The first is that I am right about this. The second is that the failures of these officials were not intentional or conscious.

So what does the record look like? Unfortunately, the sources I have looked at do not designate the officials in the box scores. Except in the last few years, in the period where I believed the officiating was generally pretty good in the Big Ten, I have found it almost impossible to attach officials to games. Okay. What about in the post-1999 period, the time you are not really whining about? In this period, as to Phil Bova, there are sixteen games against non-meatball teams, that is, Big Ten or legitimate D-1 competition. The Michigan record in those games is five wins and eleven losses. The record is 0–8 on the road, 1–0 on neutral courts, and 4–3 at home. In these games, Michigan shot 47.9 percent of free throws awarded. In Ed Hightower games, the Michigan record is 12–14 (since 1999), with UM going 1–8 on the road, 1–1 in neutral games, and 9–5 at home. In the Hightower road win (at Purdue in 2003), Purdue shot twenty-nine free throws to UM's nineteen. Overall, Michigan shot 46.1 percent of all free throws in Hightower games. The totals are 48.6 percent at home; less than 41 percent on the road. But this is not the period I am grousing about.

Prior to 1999, my results are limited and, absent a complete record, I am reticent to post a partial record. Suffice to say, I was not surprised by what I did find, a combined Bova/Hightower result of one win on the road (Minnesota, as referenced, with a big Minnesota FT advantage), about fifty-fifty at home, and about 43 percent of all free throws taken by UM. It is hard to draw conclusions, however, on the partial evidence I have found. (The UM 1991–92 media guide, for example, does contain box scores from the prior season. It shows @ Indiana favoring the Hoosiers 43–13, and @ UM favoring the Hoosiers 24–5. It shows @ Iowa favoring the Hawks 36–16 and @ UM favoring the Hawks by one. It shows @ Wiscy favoring the Badgers 39–10 and @ UM favoring UM 14–12. But what it doesn't show is who the officials were. My memory is just not that good.) I do not suggest, by the way, that foul shot differential is the sine qua non of judging whether a game was reasonably officiated. To the contrary, such a differential might be an indication of a well-officiated game. After all, guys like Mo Taylor and Eric Riley and Maceo Baston and Jarod Ward were a lot meaner, more intense, and physical than, say, Brian Cardinal and his predecessors at Purdue or Mateen Cleaves or Kirk Haston (substitute Brian Sloan or Quinn Buckner or Kent Benson) or Kowskie or Vershaw or Smakiyu at Wisconsin. That said, my impression remains that Michigan has often not gotten a fair shake from these guys. The record, such as I could find it, does not disabuse me of my impressions.

Incidentally, how come Wisconsin always has players named in onomatopaeia? Okay, at one time Michigan had Steele and Sword and Irons. But these guys were on the football team. Vershaw and Kowskie and Smackiyu? And on the women's side in the 2000–1 season, the cheesehead guys had Leah (but not very) Hefte and Jessie Stomski and Rachel Klongland, and, I ain't kidding, they played very hefty (except for Hefte) and stompski-like. But in that year, the real Wisconsin force was Nina Smith, a six-seven bruiser who was not just the "Nina" of the women's game, but also the Pinta and the Santa Maria as Smith shredded the Wolverines at Crisler. Nina was not, however, the biggest player Michigan faced that season. In the first round of the NCAA tournament, Sue Guevara's team faced Virginia and six-ten center Elena Kravchenko. Could Kravchenko play? Well, think about Pete Vignier. Then put him in cement overshoes and make him wear a cheesehead or a wahoo hat. Then get him drunk and blindfold him. Make him wear handcuffs and a straightjacket. Now you have Kravchenko on the court. That said, she would be a force in my Thursday night game.

A final note on this is that the University of Michigan did a recent survey of officials. One of the questions asked was whether referees gambled on games. 2 percent of those responding to the survey said they made illegal bets themselves, and knew of games in which gambling had a definite influence on the officiating in a contest. So next time you hear a fan yelling "fix" or "pay-off" (I know this fan, incidentally, and he scored a sixteen hundred on his SATs and an eight hundred on his law boards [no, not me]), who knows, he might be right.

* * * *

Okay. I will admit it now. Desmond Howard caught the ball. Maybe. And as long as I am at it, I think it is useful to clarify a few other rules in football.

1. Does the timekeeper have the discretion to stop the clock?

   No. Not until the official on the field signals that time is out (or in). A timekeeper has no discretion. He is to act in a purely ministerial fashion as based upon the directions from the field. At least under the rules. Apparently, the policy is to allow the timekeeper some discretion. So the answer is, who knows?

2. So the clock doesn't stop when the ball hits the ground?

   No. Under the rules. Under the policy, it isn't clear. Not that it should have made any difference, since the clock was stopped when the ball was snapped, not when it hit the ground.

3. But the stadium clock is not the official one, right?

   Wrong. It is the official clock. Officials have the discretion to adjust the clock after a play if they think it is wrong, but the stadium clock is it.

4. Shouldn't MSU Coach Bobby Williams have been given his timeout back when Michigan had twelve men on the field?

   Probably. Assuming he asked for it. But it isn't clear that he asked for the timeout to be rescinded. This said, it is hard to predict this made any difference. If he asked for the TO back, the entire fabric of the game would have been altered. As astute MSU fans have pointed out, if the correct call (pass interference) had been made in the end zone on Desmond Howard (assuming it wasn't a catch), it is only about a fifty-fifty chance that Michigan would have won that game. Aside from this, if the TO had been restored, the clock would have restarted when Williams changed his mind, since the play had been a sack of the MSU quarterback. MSU might not have gained any time by rescinding the timeout.

5. Was the timekeeper truly known as "Spartan Bob?"
   Yes.

6. What are the rumors about him?
   The rumor is that he is an MSU employee. He is also rumored to have been removed from a UM-MSU hockey game when, after repeated warnings, he refused to stop beating on and shaking the glass. The rumor continues that he was dragged out of Yost "kicking and screaming." I have no idea if these rumors are true. They are persistent, and MSU has refused to release the guy's name. Not that I blame them, since I wouldn't release it either.

7. Didn't Michigan really "deserve" to win this game?
   You must have been up all night drinking some very hard stuff. I have no clue what "deserves to win" means in the context of this particular game. I am certain I have said things like this myself, certainly even in this book, but I have no clear idea what I meant. Michigan played a woeful second half. MSU stunk up the joint in the first half, but got by with some marginal pass interference calls. I can't honestly say Michigan deserved to win, whatever that might mean. Indeed, I know we didn't deserve this one. And, since Michigan didn't deserve to win, we have to start hunting around for some other viable candidate. And that candidate would not usually be the Buckeyes, though I am certain some OSU fans would love to get credited with a W in an MSU-UM game. But look at it this way: Michigan definitely sucked dishwater at Wisconsin two weeks later, and came out of that game with an incredibly lucky win, despite one of the most pathetic offensive efforts I have ever seen played by the Wolverines against one awful and completely meatball defense. Not to be nasty, but the Wisconsin 2001 team evinced one of the worst defensive teams around, a team that gave up sixty-three points to Indiana and forty-two to the Spartans and lots of points to every

body else. Did we deserve to win that one? Hell if I know, but Lloyd Carr seemed to indicate that we didn't. I do know that we were awful on the offensive side of the ball, and I would have been embarrassed going into OSU with an undefeated record in the conference. As it turns out, OSU would have shared the embarrassment, given the Michigan offensive showing in that game.

There, that's what the rules say. Assuming I'm not wrong.

* * * *

After the majority of this chapter was written, Ed Hightower called the Wisconsin-Michigan (2002) basketball game in Ann Arbor. Wisconsin stunk as bad as limburger in this one, and even an officiating crew of Phil Bova, Jim Bain, and Barry Alvarez couldn't have given the Badgers the game. But, I have to admit, Hightower worked a pretty damn good game, neither calling too many or too few fouls, letting the game go when he should. And not guessing on plays too close to call. It was a Welmeresque game in terms of officiating, if not the play. And after this one, Dr. Ed presided over the Michigan loss to Illinois at Crisler, a competently officiated game where neither team got an edge. But these were neutral games at home. If we get games on the road like this from Hightower, I promise to take it all back. Almost all of it, anyway. My instinct has been that Hightower, a school principal and definite straight arrow, never really appreciated the Fabs and was inclined to give them zero benefit of the doubt. As these guys have receded into the Michigan past, and (especially) as Tommy Amaker demands the best behavior from his players (no technical fouls in three years), we have received reasonable officiating from Hightower. [So far in 2004–05, UM is shooting 44 percent of all freebies taken in Hightower games. No gripe.]

There must be someone else out there who shares my dismay at the changes in college basketball. The games have more of a pro look and feel every year. But my guess is that many in the seventies thought the same thing, geezers complaining about jump shots and dunking and the increasing speed and athleticism of the players. I desist. But one thing I can't quite shake is the change in the college fans, particularly over the past five years. I admit that I think random, rowdy, and anarchistic fan behavior is well inbounds, so long as it isn't violent or doesn't stoop to personal diatribes directed against individual players or opposing fans. Indeed, the involvement of the fans makes the game. After all, Indiana versus Michigan, even at Crisler, is not intended to be a trip to the opera. (One year, sitting in Bo Schembechler's Crisler seats [don't ask and I won't tell], a fan complained because I was "yelling in her ear.") However, what has evolved is this dopey group taunt, a way for the masses to lay it on the opposing team and/or its fans in a very personal way.

I blame Duke (who else?) for this. The Cameron Crazies are Duke students who have pioneered the group taunt, and have been lionized in the electronic media, particularly by Dick Vitale. I am certain Michigan (and many other schools) envy the level of student support given to Duke's team. I know I do. And there is no question the Duke fans can be clever. But it seems to me they go overboard and are more often mean than clever. Worse, all fans (including Michigan) emulate the Duke partisans, though rarely with the cleverness of the Cameron crowd. The Cameron Crazies spawned Northwestern's rancid Purple Haze and MSU's cretinous Izzone and the awful Michigan (help us) Maize Rage and some crappy thing called the Nut House (OSU), all student groups with the laudable intent of creating excitement at the games, but with the ultimate result of organized trash talk. Hey, I don't care if the Rage wants to yell at the opposing team's coach or the referees. This is expected and in bounds. But I think the line is crossed when one attacks the opposing players and begins to create an environment during a game that borders on the dangerous.

In my judgment, these student groups have brought an ugly and mean-spirited tinge to college basketball, one that I don't think existed prior to the most recent rise of Duke. I admit, however, it is a fine line, one perhaps best relegated to the footnotes of a tome on some medieval and arcane legal doctrine, like the Rule Against Perpetuities. Let me explain my inconsistency.

During the 2000 MSU-UM game at Crisler, as MSU went on a run to put away the hapless Wolverines, Spartan point guard Mateen Cleaves gestured at and taunted the Michigan crowd. Mateen then became the object of the group taunt by the Michigan students (in the form popularized at Duke) of "al-co-ho-lic." This, regardless of Mateen's taunting (it was possibly responsive), was out of bounds. Cleaves did not deserve this. He was a college kid, for chris-sakes. I don't care much for Cleaves, based upon stories I have heard from other MSU athletes and based upon his reported (and some nonreported) troubles at MSU. But aside from anything else, there is no question Cleaves was a team player and a fierce competitor, a player whose game demanded admiration. It was demeaning for the Michigan fans to act so boorishly. The matter was not made any better when an MSU family member or friend (in her fifties, I would guess) stood up and gave the Michigan crowd the finger. This heart-on-the-sleeve and adolescent behavior made an ugly crowd uglier. The Sparty fans, as MSU pulled away, started chanting, "Why so quiet?" They got back (rightfully so), "Why so stupid?" And then the MSU fans chanted, "We own Crisler." And the Michigan fans chanted back, "You own trailers." The "Go green. Go white" cheer was then matched by a "Can't read. Can't write" cheer. The problem is that none of it was fun. It was on the edge of dangerous, a miniature Bosnia. The Spartan fans at that game were provocative and in the face of Michigan fans. Finger pointing. Stuff thrown. Near fights and skirmishes. The Michigan fans, in some sense, started it. And I see more and more of this. Root for your team. Have fun. Be clever. Be Boilerplate and *Rocky Horror Picture Show* rude (hockey fans). And be happy if you win. But don't taunt the opposition or its fans. Okay. Blaming Duke for this is a stretch. Nothing follows from following and, more likely than not, it is a mere symptom of the culture. You are what you eat, and blah blah blah. But I still blame Duke. They started it. (In the 2002–3 season, I felt these student groups improved dramatically, with the trash talking taking on a much more benign edge. By 2003–4, they seemed a completely positive force, with little of what behavior I would call "mean-spirited" going on in Ann Arbor or elsewhere as far as I could tell. I was wrong. Again. Maybe.)

When considering the best game ever in Ann Arbor, a Duke graduate who is a friend of mine suggested the December of 2000 UM game against the basketball Blue Devils. Two problems with this choice. First, the game was at Duke and, last time I checked, the Duke campus has not moved to Ann Arbor. Second, it wasn't a very good game. One normally thinks of good games as being competitive, and I don't nominate the Michigan total of two points out of the first thirty-six scored as qualifying under the normal meaning of the word. Here are my diary notes on this game:

December 10, 2000. I should have spent yesterday with football statistics as opposed to watching the Duke and Michigan game. A good friend of mine (from Ann Arbor) went to the game since his wife was being recruited to teach at Duke's law school and he got a weekend trip out of the ratty AA weather. (Getting out of the AA weather turned out to be an attraction, but more relevant was the following juxtaposition of former students: Clarence Darrow [Michigan] and Richard Nixon [Duke].) Regardless of the merits of teaching at UM law versus Duke law, the present valuation of the states of the Michigan and Duke basketball programs is not exactly a contest.

Neither was the game. My friend was initially pissed, since he was given an obstructed seat in Cameron and was unable to see the basket that Michigan was shooting at in the first half. This turned out to be a minor disutility, since Michigan chose the unusual strategy of not actually making any baskets in the first half, racing to an early two to thirty-four deficit. From that point on, it was all Michigan as they finished the half down only 16–25, resulting in a 59–18 Duke margin at the intermission. It could have been worse, since Duke shot eleven for eighteen from the free throw line, and had eight turnovers, an uncharacteristically high number for the Blue Devils. Meanwhile, Michigan turned the ball over twenty times in the half and shot five for twenty-three from the field. Lavell Blanchard was one for eight from the floor, and center Josh Asselin managed to get one rebound and four fouls in five minutes of play. And no Wolverine scored more than one basket in the half, a stat I am sure has not happened in fifty years to any team in the Big Ten. It wouldn't surprise me if, in the history of the Big Ten, this is a singular event. Chris Young, with five points and five rebounds (and no turnovers) was the best Wolverine on the floor, assuming this concept has any meaning in this kind of a game.

Duke has as good a starting five as anyone in the country and little depth, but they substituted liberally in the first half. My friend, wearing a Michigan jersey, took a moderate (but reasonably moderate) amount of grief from the Cameron fans. However, he concluded that even the Duke students felt more sorry for the Wolverines than anything else, and couldn't muster the energy for any significant antipathy. Even their chants ("Gary Coleman" toward midget point guard Avery Queen) were pretty tepid and uninspired.

Michigan played better in the second half, but I can't imagine there was any other possibility. The Wolverines actually started on a 14–4 run and, with the officials giving UM the benefit of the doubt (to say the least, it was a complete act of charity), and Coach K calling off the dogs in the last eight minutes, Duke ended up winning the second half 45–43. Not embarrassing at all. But the final score of 104–61 made the game one of the worst losses in Michigan history. Michigan continues to break new ground. Searching around for good news, most Michigan fans will be surprised to know we are 3–3 in our last six games with Duke, and one of those losses (last year in Ann Arbor) was underscored (if not predicated) by some dubious ACC officiating. And despite Michigan's all-time 7–15 record against the Blue Devils, the Michigan pregame press release points out (after this loss) that the Wolverines are 30–26 (all time) against the ACC. This means, against other ACC teams, Michigan's record is 23–11.

But the dark side isn't all that hard to find. First, the Michigan press release seems to contain an arithmetic error. Either that or some MAC team used to be in the ACC.

Second, Michigan has lost its last three games to Duke and the road games were losses by forty-three and forty-four points. Third, this loss was the fourth worst in Michigan history. Two of the other three also belong to Ellerbe-coached teams. Fourth, this game started out 34–2 and could have been (easily) a fifty-point loss (Okay, maybe sixty, okay, okay, maybe eighty), if Coach K had wanted it that way.

How much worse can a major college team do than 34–2? Michigan had twenty-nine turnovers and Duke scored forty-five points off of these turnovers. I have never seen numbers at these levels. During half time, Jeff DeFran (doing the broadcast on WJR with Dugan Fife) said, "You would not believe the phone calls we've been getting here," with no further explanation. Gee, I wonder what these calls sounded like. But I will guess it wasn't "I think we should extend Brian Ellerbe's contract." Assuming the calls came from Michigan fans. My suspicion is the attitudes in East Lansing and Columbus might have been slightly different. At the end of the game, DeFran complained about the calls, saying, "Look, folks. Don't take it out on me. I didn't hire the coach, and I didn't teach the Michigan team how to play defense."

* * * *

So the best game ever seen in Ann Arbor was not the waxing in Durham. And, for some of the same reasons, it was not the Michigan-OSU football game in 1969. This is, I admit, my all-time favorite game, since I suffered through the demolition the Buckeyes laid on us in the prior year, Woody going for two at the end of the game with the Buckeyes ahead by thirty-four. Woody, when asked why he went for two, said, "Because I couldn't go for three." And I endured the taunting and swearing (and later the rioting) of the drunken and Skol-spitting OSU fans, looting and tearing up High Street in Columbus in a sort of postapocalyptic frenzy. For me, 1969 had the purity of revenge, if only in my own heart.

Michigan-OSU in 1969 is a favorite for many others, since it was so unexpected, the Buckeyes on a long (twenty-three games) winning roll, and many extolling the Bucks in that season as one of the greatest college teams of all time. Well, the Buckeyes were terrific, but I am not certain they were one of the greatest teams of all time. Indeed, Michigan was more talented in 1969. The Buckeyes did have the dubious icon Jack Tatum. But the Wolverines had All Pros Dan Dierdorf (Hall of Famer) and Reggie McKenzie (HOF), Jim Mandich, Jack Harpring, and Tom Darden. Don Moorehead was a better QB than Rex Kern (Kern had no ability to throw) and the Wolverines were stronger at running back and at the skill positions. When one scans the rosters, Michigan looks a little more talented.

Other Michigan fans choose this game as a favorite, since it was Bo's first season, the year when Michigan came back on the football map after almost two decades of very up and down play.

But the Wolverine pounding of the Buckeyes in 1969 was a lot worse than the twenty-four to twelve score, since the Wolverines missed at least three short field goals in the second half. The Buckeyes threw six interceptions and, after the first quarter, they were completely dominated. It wasn't the 2000 UM- Duke basketball game, but it was still completely one-sided and not really a great game, at least in the abstract. In my subjective mind, it remains my best experience as a fan, an experience that was magnified by the quiet and introspective Ann Arbor that accrued after the stomping. We shared, mind you. But the sharing was private and house-by-house. Pass the Cuervo Gold, will ya? And would you mind some Coltrane on the stereo for a while? (The truth is that the highest quality football game I have seen in Ann Arbor, albeit one of my least favorites, was the loss to MSU [28–27] in 1990—the Desmond Howard game—the blown last call *adding* to the quality of the play on the field and the coaching on both sidelines. The most exciting game? The 2005 UM win over MSU. An impossible contest with Braylon Edwards proving to be among the greatest players in UM history, probably the greatest since Benny Friedman.)

The best game in any sport that I have witnessed in Ann Arbor was actually two games. A hockey doubleheader in 1998. Before I get to this, I admit that I know next to nothing about hockey and refer all interested persons to John Bacon's fine history, *Blue Ice*. I am a fan, however, and the Red Wings are one of two professional sports teams (the other is the Cleveland Indians) that routinely capture my interest. Aside from this, I confess to being an ignoramus. I know the rules, more or less, though I don't understand the differences between, say, charging and boarding. My brother Roger, sharing this mystification, suggests a more fan friendly set of definitions for hockey penalties. He recommends anything in the vein of "roughing" be redefined as "roughhousing." This would be, in his world, a two-minute penalty. And anything else that isn't quite as bad as "roughhousing" would be called "horseplay," a one-minute penalty. Then there would be three-minute penalties for "smearing" or "clobbering," four minutes for "mayhem," and five minutes for "beheading," and so on.

Michigan plays hockey at Yost Arena, an old and minimalist structure holding about seven thousand fans. It is the antithesis of dull and lifeless Crisler Arena, an environment designed for sleeping. Crisler is dark and quiet, the sound absorbed by the cushioned seats and the domed ceiling. Yost, even when it is quiet, is loud, the sound bouncing from the bright metal benches and corrugated roof. At Yost, a little bit of clapping sounds like a ruckus. A lot of yelling is palpable, concrete, a matter of touch. Yost can be so loud, in fact, that some bring earplugs to the games, particularly if they are near our seats, below the Michigan Pep Band, the ringleaders of the hockey ambience. Yost is, there is no doubt, the Cameron of college hockey, if I do not vitalize Duke too much in the comparison. And if this doesn't sound too inconsistent or a lapse into complete self-loathing. Did Coach K take Red Berenson's place? No? Good deal.

In basketball, the players wear little clothing and their faces and emotions can be seen. They are vulnerable to the crowd, a part of the crowd, and there is a symbiotic relationship between the turmoil on the floor and that in the seats. Because of this, and because of the major role played by referees in basketball (and the inevitable influence of the crowd on referees), the home-court advantage in basketball is profound. It also exists in hockey, but not nearly to the same level. Hockey players wear pads and helmets and have weapons. They are insulated from the fans by the glass. Fights, intolerable in basketball, are accepted as a part of hockey, no big deal really unless the party goes well out of bounds. And this level of insulation from the fans changes the nature of the rules. Everything goes. For example, a few years back in Detroit, after a Red Wings game, some players from a visiting team climbed the glass and went after a few fans. God help them, some of these yo-yos in the stands tried to fight back. But even this didn't seem like such a big deal. A basketball player going into the crowd to fight fans would be banned for life. A hockey player might only be banned from a good sportsmanship award or the Lady Bing Trophy. (The foregoing was written prior to the Pacers-Pistons brouhaha of 2004. If this had been a hockey fight, it wouldn't have rated a footnote.)

I attended my first hockey event at age nine, a game between the Cleveland Barons and the Hershey Bears of the old IHL. I sat next to a graying woman in the first row. As soon as the puck dropped (She yelled, "Drop the puck, you dickhead."), the woman began to pound on the glass and scream at a Hershey player to "hit him with your purse, Maurice." She yelled this a lot. A precursor, in my life, of the "You eat it, ref" guy. And near the end of the game, the player (whose name was not Maurice, but something like "Hatchet Face" Seidel) "hit" the woman with his middle finger, sending her into hysterics over the rudeness of people from Pennsylvania. And this goes on at Yost, like all other venues, with the goalie becoming the primary object of the fans' derision and attempts to influence the game—yeah, you worthless sack of dung, you really are a sieve. "Sieve," of course, being the operative term of art in hockey, though Michigan has borrowed from Cornell (and added some of its own invective) in labeling the goalie a "vacuum" or a "black hole" or mentioning that he "just sucks," even if the guy has just made twenty great saves in a row. And, in fact, his mother thinks so too. And through all this, the officials seem oddly unfazed or uninfluenced, with officiating at Yost being not much different than officiating at Munn in East Lansing or any other place in the CCHA.

This "separation" of the game from fans makes the home ice, regardless of how crazy things are in the stands, a more level playing field than exists in basketball. At the least, you won't see any fifty to eight free throw games in college hockey. Indeed, the penalties in hockey are most always balanced. But who would know anyway? Not one person in forty in the stands has a clue whether that particular clubbing was mere horseplay or roughhousing or some other transgression. Or, indeed, no transgression at all.

Michigan was a top seed in the NCAA tournament in 1995, but it lost in the semifinals (4–3 in overtime) to Maine. In 1996, UM was again one of the favorites and, in fact, it won the national championship. Michigan was a heavy favorite in 1997 and the team compiled a 35–3–4 record over the season. This was the best Michigan team that I have seen. However, it faltered in the NCAA semifinals, losing to Boston University (3–2) in a game where they were outmuscled by the Terriers. Michigan was still very good in '97–'98, but they lost eleven games in the regular season, and Michigan State played better over the course of the CCHA schedule. Michigan was considered a longshot to win the national championship, and MSU came into the regionals as a top seed. The Spartans had a bye in the first round, waiting for the Yale-Ohio State winner. And North Dakota, rated in the top three in the country, also had a bye and would play the winner of Michigan and Princeton. On the first night at Yost, Ohio State took care of Yale 4–0 in a game that was a matter of abstract interest to the UM fans. However, the MSU fans joined a small Yale contingent in rooting for the Ivy League school. Some OSU folks were pissed. In the second game, the Michigan team struggled with Princeton. The OSU fans that remained in attendance seemed objective observers. But some were rooting for Michigan, and many kept their mouths shut. And many in the Michigan crowd noticed this. A sizeable MSU contingent was present for the game, cheering for Princeton and taunting the Michigan fans.

At the time, I thought this was truly crazy. You can admire the MSU legions for their honest sentimentality and romanticism, but you don't crap where you sleep. On the following night, the Spartans would be playing the Buckeyes, and the majority of fans were likely to be wearing maize and blue. OSU would be an underdog, and there is some inclination among all fans to root for the perceived-to-be lesser team. So, given this (they must have been cognizant), the MSU fans said, "Hey, fuck it," and chose to alienate the majority of the crowd for their key game of the season. This, as an aside to a certain segment of fans, is what "arrogance" means in the real world.

The folks in my part of the arena were mystified by MSU's behavior and expressions of passion. Even if you despised Michigan, wasn't the better plan to be quiet or (if you could stomach it) even root for UM in order to build a neutral environment for the following evening? I thought so. After all, it is not a natural state of affairs for Michigan fans to be rooting for an OSU victory. Michigan fans are ordinarily indifferent to ambivalent about OSU-MSU contests, but many say they support MSU out of home state loyalty. In any event, the MSU romanticism came home to roost when Michigan snuck by Princeton 2–1. The Princeton game was an even affair, Michigan winning on a lucky goal and terrific goaltending by Marty Turco as the game concluded. I didn't give Michigan much of a chance against the NoDaks, but I sure as hell planned to show up and root for the Buckeyes and the Wolverines on the following evening.

As it turned out, I was on the same page as other Michigan fans. MSU was a significant favorite over the Buckeyes, who had never been to an NCAA Frozen Four. MSU scored the first two goals, and it looked like they would cruise. But the Buckeyes would not give up. By the time the underdogs had tied the game at 2–2, the crowd was in a complete frenzy, with the vast majority pulling and going crazy for OSU. Michigan fans sang "Hang On, Sloopy." They attempted to imitate Brutus the Buckeye. They dotted the "i." They tried to spell "Olentangy." It was, indeed, a weird scene, an OSU lovefest at Yost Arena. MSU went ahead by a goal late in the second period but the Buckeyes tied the game midway in the third. After this, it was aggressive and hard-skating hockey by two outstanding teams, Chad Albon (for MSU) keeping the game alive with an impossible save in the last minute of regulation and OSU goalie Jeff Maund then turning back good MSU attempts in overtime.

With eight minutes left in the first overtime period, Andre Signoretti scored on a slap shot for OSU and Yost seemed pushed to the breaking level. Ordinarily, after such a game, the crowd would wander into the night, with the elation and despair of the contest dispersing into soft expletives and explanations on the sidewalks of the city. But this time, only the vast majority of the MSU fans and a small portion of the OSU fans left Yost. It was already getting late. I was tired. And we were just getting ready to roll.

At ten-thirty, or maybe a little later, North Dakota and Michigan squared off. My impression, from the first game, was that there could not be two better hockey teams in the country than OSU and MSU. Indeed, I didn't know if I had ever seen two better teams in the college game. But North Dakota disabused me of the notion, skating fast and strong en route to a 2–0 first period lead. One goal was scored by Mitch Vig, presumably the real notorious one, and no relation to the former Michigan center Pete Vignier or point guard

238

Anna Thorius. Can Mitch Vig play? I have no clue. But I know what I thought at that moment. The second period started with the NoDaks on a five-minute power play, and prospects appeared dismal for the Wolverines as the pressure on Marty Turco was unceasing. But Turco made a terrific save to relieve the pressure and then fed the puck down ice to Matt Herr who scored a short-handed breakaway goal to cut the lead to 2–1. From this point on, the Michigan fans did not relent, and the Wolverines seemed to extract energy from the crowd, including the many Buckeyes who stayed to root for their newfound allies. The NoDak power play continued, and a minute later, Michigan scored another short-handed goal, but this time the goal was waved off, the referee determining that the linesman had blown the whistle when two players were tangled up at mid-ice. Not that anyone could hear a whistle. The Michigan crowd went berserk over this and, indeed, this is the sort of deflat-ing event that can kill a comeback. And it seemed to, for after Michigan skat-ed off the long penalty, the NoDaks scored on a four-on-four and the 3–1 lead seemed insurmountable. North Dakota was just too solid. Too big. Too fast. Too Vig.

But the crowd did not give in, and North Dakota seemed to wear down. Michigan responded to the crowd's energy and regained the inertia when Bill Muckalt scored his thirty-second goal of the year to cut the lead to 3–2 with eight minutes left in the second period. It was now after midnight. Perhaps well after. Many fans had been there for more than six hours. And the level of intensity in Yost, impossibly, continued to mount. My head pounded. My ears rang. The band, a few rows behind me, was gaining energy. And, in some sense, it was just starting.

The second period ended 3–2, but Michigan came out feisty in the third period and scored a quick power play goal to tie the game. At this point, my ears were numbed and barely functional. The band kept pouring it out. The fans continued to exude energy and noise. The arena was a wall of sound, no letdown, despite the fact it was early in the AM. After the tying goal, both teams had their chances, but each goalie was sharp and kept his team in the game. Then, with less than three minutes left in the period, Justin Clark created a turnover that engineered a Matt Herr and Bobby Hayes two-on-one with Herr passing to Hayes, who buried the shot. Michigan then held on, Turco making a huge save with a few seconds left on the clock. Matt Herr had a goal and three assists in Michigan's 4–3 win. It was the middle of the morning. Many fans had been at Yost for eight-plus hours, and even those did not seem anx-ious to abandon the afterglow of the surprising win, or the high-fiving with the many Buckeye fans who stayed to root for the Wolverines. "The Victors" was sung. Sung again. Then "Varsity." And then "The Yellow and the Blue." The fans demanded encores from the team, and no one seemed to want to go home. It was a timeless and naive experience. Something from a simpler time.

Until finally, we wandered home from Yost, in the middle of the morning, with our ears ringing and the triviality of the experience filling our souls.

Michigan won the national championship that spring, dominating New Hampshire in the semifinals 4–0 and sneaking past Boston College 3–2 in overtime in the finals. In retrospect, I think either MSU or North Dakota might have been the best team that season (OSU, UM, and BC were very close), but the fact of the location of the games at Yost, with the incredible fan support, may have been the edge that propelled Michigan to the Frozen Four. And it didn't hurt OSU or UM when the Spartan fans turned uncharacteristically simpleminded and Yost became a home venue for the Bucks.

In 2001, the NCAA regionals were also played in Ann Arbor. Michigan beat the two most highly regarded WCHA teams, top-rated Colorado College and Denver, in very high-quality games. The Wolverines lost in the semis to eventual national champ Minnesota. The environment at Yost was extraordinary in those two nights of hockey, but they could not compare to the 1998 event. The 2002 regionals, again at Yost, saw Michigan win close games over number nine Maine and number two Colorado College before losing (again) to Minnesota in overtime in the semis. The Wolverine fans showed up in full force again and Yost saw incredible playoff hockey for the third time in five years.

Michigan hockey fans are excellent, but they were rivaled by the Iowa softball faithful in 2001. These fans (a small cell group) eclipse any I have ever encountered in enthusiasm and loyalty, regardless of game score. A portion of my diary notes from Michigan softball in the spring of 2001 follow:

Softball. The Wolverines started the season slowly, losing close games to many of the top teams in the country on their February-perpetual-road-game. By the time the Big Ten schedule got rolling, the Wolverines were hot, winning eighteen in a row before a 3–2, 11-inning loss at OSU. In the last week in April in Ann Arbor, Michigan played Iowa in a crucial two-game series, the Wolverines needing to win one game to sew up the Big Ten regular season championship and a home-field berth in the Big Ten tournament.

It is a hot weekend, perfect for softball, and Iowa has a sizeable contingent at the game. And they seem more numerous than they are, since they are loud and enthusiastic, pretty much the antithesis of the relatively quiet and introspective Wolverine legions.

The Iowa fans are great. They sit on the grassy knoll along the left-field line about a hundred feet from the plate and grouse about every single ball and strike call. It is like sitting in a crow convention. One guy complains when a ball is bounced to the plate, "That was a strike, ump. What game are you watching? How much are you being paid? You dummy. If you had one more eye, you'd be a Cyclops. You stiff. Idiot." I turn to the guy and ask him if he saw the ball bounce in front of the plate. He says, "So what?" Exactly. This guy understands the core of being a fan. Objectivity or fairness has nothing to do with it. You take up the cudgel of borderline reality and it all happens from there. The Iowa fans remind me of a cadre of the Worst Fan, and I wish Michigan had about fifty of these types to pester the umpires.

In the Saturday game, pitchers Kristi Hanks of Iowa and Marissa Young of Michigan are basically unhittable. Neither team can make contact, and most of the base runners are the result of walks or bunts or marginal defense. Indeed, Iowa manages exactly two hits in the game that aren't bunts, but both come at propitious moments. The umpiring in the game *is* particularly weird, including a walk given to a Michigan hitter on three balls in the first inning. The Hawkeye fans are (rightly) incensed and harass the umpires for the next two hours. But more than this, and to their credit, they cheer on every play for their team. No, make that every pitch. These fans are as good as I have ever witnessed. The game is tied 0–0 at the end of regulation. In the Iowa eighth, the Hawks get their first nonbunt hit, but still only have a runner on first with two outs. The runner attempts to steal and is thrown out (it is not even vaguely close), but the umpire, having been bombarded by the stream of Hawkeye invectives and complaints for the past seven innings, calls her safe. The Hawks feel as if they got their due, and they are quiet now. No complaints. "We be good now, thank you." And an Iowa hitter knocks a seeing eye single to center for a lone run. It holds up as Kristi Hanks demolishes the Wolverines in the bottom of the inning.

In the rematch on Sunday, Iowa led off against Michigan pitcher Marie Barda with a solid double. But with two outs and the runner at third, clean up hitter Katy Jendrzejewski hit a hard grounder at first baseperson Marissa Young and it looked like Barda was out of the inning. The ball took a weird hop, however, and it handcuffed Young. She could not make the play and it was called an error. The run scored. And it held up for another 1-0 Iowa win. Michigan put a runner on second with one out in the last three innings but could not drive the base runner home, though twice the Wolverines hit shots that were flagged down by the Hawkeye outfielders.

The results were disappointing, particularly since it seemed to assure Iowa a home field berth for the Big Ten Tournament and a probable tie for the regular season championship. But on the following weekend Michigan swept MSU while Northwestern upset Iowa. This left the Wolverines with the regular season championship and home field in the playoffs.

* * * *

The Iowa Crows (fans) make the daunting trip to Ann Arbor for the Big Ten tournament for the second weekend in three. This is a long trip, and I am mightily impressed and decide to sit with them for the first two days of the tournament. Both teams have byes (as the number one and number two seeds), and both teams win fairly easily in the second round, though Kristi Hanks looks very hittable in a 6–1 Iowa win over Wisconsin, and the Wolverines look like they will never hit anything in a 2–0 win over Penn State. The good news for the Wolverines is that ace pitcher Marissa Young is very sharp, the toothless Lions barely able to touch her offerings in the contest. Hanks, conversely, is hit hard, but tends to bear down and get out of jams when Wisconsin puts runners on base. On the other hand, the Hawks pretty much demolish the Wisconsin pitching with one well-hit shot after the next. The Hawkeye crowd is calling out the Wolverines. "Bring them on. We can beat them again," one geezerette caws.

But the Wolverines are prepared. Hutchins starts Marie Barda (the ordinary rotation), and Barda has no trouble with the Iowa bats in the early innings. Hanks is throwing hard in the first inning for the Hawks, but she also throws hard and wide on a comebacker to the mound. Iowa commits a second error later in the inning, and this creates a 1–0 Michigan lead on no hits. Iowa can barely touch Barda and in the fourth, the Iowa defense again comes unglued and Michigan takes advantage with a double off the fence by Marissa Young for one run and a home run (her first ever) by catcher Kim Bugel for two more. Iowa coach Blevins removes Hanks in deference to freshman Sarah Thomson, a fine pitcher who was effective against Michigan in a prior contest. But the Wolverines hit Thomson harder than Hanks, and Iowa is lucky that Michigan only adds two more runs, even as the Wolverines hit solid shots that are picked off by the Iowa defense. In the bottom of the sixth, down 6–0, Iowa puts together its only offense of the day when All American second baseperson Kelsey Kollen does not get her glove down and commits an error, and the Hawks begin to put some pressure on Barda. Despite the fact that Marie looks like she is losing it, Hutchins leaves her in the game and she works out of the problem, albeit with the bases loaded. In this inning, though down by six, the Iowa fans are energized and alive, screaming and snorting (honest, real snorting) for their team. I am (again) impressed. The Wolverine fans would have been quiet until there was some legitimate chance. We would have cared, mind you. It's just that this caring wouldn't come with much in the way of screeching or noisemaking. Crows? More like barn owls. And on the Michigan side, it is the ordinary, "Any Camembert left? Oh, thanks. De nada." Michigan wins 6–1 and moves to the championship game.

* * * *

Oh yeah. Just to be fair. If I think it is arguable that the Spartan fans hurt their team in the 1998 hockey playoffs, I think it is a lock that Michigan fans cost the Wolverines a win against Jimmy Johnson and the number one (football) Miami Hurricanes in 1988. With the Wolverines leading 30–14 with six or seven minutes to go in the game, the Wolverines had a first and five near the Hurricane thirty-five-yard line. The Michigan fans, thinking the game was over, started a loud and noisy and moronic "wave," creating enough ruckus so that the ball was snapped early by the Michigan center and fumbled by quarterback Michael Taylor. Then, with the Wolverines playing the clock and Miami coach Jimmy Johnson playing the angles (I won't get into it), Miami came back for a 31–30 win. The fact is, without the Michigan fumble, Miami had no chance to win the game. And the fact is that the fumble was caused by the fans. You don't believe me? Watch the tape on ESPN Classic one of these days. So, if I think MSU fans can be self-destructive, I also think UM fans can match them. We have the capacity.

The oddity of the Miami affair is that it is just about impossible to get UM fans to make noise to help their team. But we found a way to make noise to hurt the team. Maybe this is our particular brand of arrogance.

Twelve *Jamal, Drew, Josh Moore and Jim Corbett. Also, Henry Heskowitz.*

Jamal. It may be very hard to believe, but it is a fact that in the 1999–2000 season the Michigan basketball team, then coached by Brian Ellerbe, got off to a 9–2 non-conference start, and this included a very tough loss to Duke at Crisler by the score of 104–97. In the Duke loss, Jamal Crawford scored twenty-seven and dished out six assists, while only turning the ball over once. His Duke counterpart, Jason (now Jay) Williams, scored seventeen, had eight assists, and four turnovers. I don't insist that Crawford was as good a player as Williams, who was the top college pick in the country by the time he left Duke. But he was in the same general league, and it was certain that Jamal was a major league talent, a lock for the NBA.

The Wolverines were up and down in the early part of that Big Ten season, but had a good road win at Purdue and a win over top-twenty-five Illinois for a respectable 3–3 record, not bad with four of the six games on the road, including tough games at Iowa (a close loss) and Indiana (a blowout by the Hoosiers).

Michigan seemed like it had an outside shot at an NCAA bid in that year or, at least, a home court run in the NIT. But then the NCAA stepped in and declared Crawford ineligible, and the Ellerbe ball of wax completely melted down. The NCAA intervened due to the fact that Crawford had received benefits while in high school from a nonrelative. In understanding what happened here, one has to know that Jamal's father had little involvement with him as a child and his mother had significant issues, aside from being poor. While attending high school in LA, Jamal's best friend was shot and killed, and Jamal and his mother decided to move to Seattle. After this move, Jamal was supported, at least in some part, by a man named Barry Henthorn, a family acquaintance. The Crawford issue was weird in a number of respects. First, while the NCAA initially suggested that the Henthorn connection was the problem, this later shifted to the fact that, while in high school, Crawford wrote a letter of inquiry to the NBA about being drafted. This letter was not responded to by the NBA and, shortly after being written, was rescinded. This would have been completely within the rules for a college player but, according to the NCAA, it was not okay for a high school player. Or, at least, there was a gap in the rules for high school kids. Because of this, and the fact that the rule was in the process of amendment to make the procedure the same for college and high school players, the NCAA gave Crawford the supposedly lenient penalty of an eight-game suspension to go with a six-game suspension for the Henthorn activity.

The suspension arising from the letter to the NBA was universally decried as ludicrous. The drafter of the rule was especially critical, since when the rule was changed to allow such activities by college players, he stated that no one ever considered the change as it might apply to high school players. From the drafter's perspective, the NCAA was enforcing a provision that had not covered high school students by mere oversight. In this context, the drafter went on to say that if the committee would have considered the question, it would have also changed the rule for high school kids. After the Crawford suspension the rule was changed, Crawford being the only fish caught in this net.

The Henthorn suspension was even worse, since it involved a person (Henthorn) who was neither a Michigan booster, an agent, nor a wannabe agent. The NCAA never suggested that Michigan did anything wrong in the recruitment or tendering of Crawford, since Henthorn played no role in Crawford's recruiting. Nor has it ever been implied that Henthorn did anything wrong, save for supporting a kid where no other adult was able or willing to pick up this role. Moreover, Crawford, unlike some at UM and all other schools, was at least a vaguely legitimate student, someone who had an interest in going to school and being involved in a college environment. He was not involved in any criminal activity and, from all accounts, was passing his classes. Indeed, Crawford seemed a polite and ordinary kid while on campus, at least according to numerous students who knew him. All of this said, I would have no issue with the NCAA not bending the rules for Crawford or with the six-game (or greater) suspension. Except for one thing. This is a rule that has been applied to Crawford and almost no other player in the country, despite the fact that all teams, or most all, have a player who has received benefits from non-family members while in high school. This isn't just my snot-nosed opinion. The following excerpt came from Bryan Rosenbaum in the *Arizona Daily Wildcat,* a not atypical report of the affair:

> The way the NCAA handled Michigan's Jamal Crawford, who saw his best friend killed in Compton, Calif. and then moved to a family friend's house in Seattle, a year ago was despicable. Of course, by doing so, Crawford broke the rules because he accepted benefits from a Seattle businessman, Barry Henthorn, and was suspended for the rest of the season. Had

it not been for Henthorn, the man that saved Crawford from the streets, Crawford might have been the next person murdered at a Compton bus stop.

I'm not saying this was a clean, legal, and right thing to do, but if this story was about anybody else, you would be praising this "booster" as a hero, a person who saved another human being from a wretched life.

As it is, he was helping an athlete, and the rest of that athlete's life will never be the same. The Crawford suspension must have stunned the Michigan athletic administration since the NCAA, until this time, had ignored pre-college benefits being paid to players so long as there was a "pre-existing" relationship between the nonrelated adult and the athlete (student). However, this must have been the "vogue" area of enforcement in that season (it hasn't seemed to crop up since), in that the NCAA also suspended Dermarr Johnson (your basic Bob Huggins one year and out star) at Cincinnati when it was learned his AAU coach paid for $7,500 of Johnson's tuition at prep school. Johnson's suspension? One game.

Crawford jumped to the NBA and was a lottery pick with the Bulls. He had some success at the end of his rookie year and then injured his ACL. In the 2002–3 season, he began to make progress. By the end of the 2004 season, it was clear he was a player on the rise, a middling hot property in the NBA. There is no need to feel badly for Crawford. He is a millionaire. But the sad part of the story is that Crawford expressed continued unhappiness in the pros and felt cheated out of a college career or, perhaps, a college experience. The Chicago papers have reported that Crawford only left UM because of a mandatory condition imposed by the NCAA for his return to Michigan, that he repay fifteen thousand dollars of benefits conferred by Barry Henthorn. Apparently, Crawford had to repay the money by the commencement of school in 2001, or he would be permanently banned from NCAA competition. Since he was also barred by NCAA rules from (a) working during school, (b) taking out loans (against future earnings) to repay the money, and (c) looking again to his only legal source of cash (Henthorn), Jamal had no way to comply. He could have borrowed from his family of course and, if he was the average Princeton or Duke player, this might have been possible. But if he were such a person, he wouldn't have been in his circumstances in the first place. Crawford was a child who was economically abandoned by an impoverished family. The NCAA imposed a penalty that he could not comply with. Yet, it was imposed for circumstances that exist for hundreds of high-profile high school athletes.

It appears that someone at the NCAA (or some of the member institutions) realized the hypocrisy and venality of the Crawford ruling, since this element of NCAA rules is about to be changed. And it could be changed in a pretty radical fashion, allowing for athletes to secure bank loans by imposing the collateral of future earnings. High school students could engage in any variety of activities heretofore viewed as professional (such as accepting prize money) and still be eligible for NCAA competition. The most controversial element of the proposed change would allow kids to compete professionally (even in their chosen sports) for a year after high school and retain three years of college eligibility. This one, of course, will completely overrun any notions of amateurism. Once this cat is out of the bag, the blurring between professional sports and amateur sports will be completely nugatory. Who knows? Maybe it is already. Whether this is good or bad seems problematic to me, but the changes seem in tune with the culture, a society that suggests all persons market themselves in the real world of opportunity costs. Time will tell on this one, but it is now a near certainty that Crawford will be the only athlete caught in this trap. Of course, Crawford could be creating a revisionist history, now having realized that he has repaved paradise with his own parking lot.

All of the foregoing said, I will be the first to admit that there may be facts surrounding the Henthorn activity that made the NCAA action reasonable. Maybe there was evidence that Henthorn was on the road to agent land, though this would be belied by the fact that Henthorn did not and has not acted as Crawford's (or anyone's) representative. Maybe there was something else. It is always naive to assume the media will figure out what is going on, where the NCAA is pretty tight-lipped about its decisions. But the treatment of Crawford is very difficult to rationalize in the cauldron of the NCAA's inactivity with regard to other players. Who? Okay, how about Duke star Carlos Boozer? Boozer, according to Dan Wetzel, the (then) editor of *Basketball Times*, moved from Alaska to California to live with his AAU coach during his high school career. This coach reportedly had ties to shoe companies and agents, unlike Barry Henthorn. Unlike Henthorn, the coach derived some potential direct benefit from his caretaking of Boozer. And what was Boozer's penalty? Who are you kidding? Wetzel attempted to approach the NCAA with this (seeming) anomaly, and the best answer he could get was that Michigan reported the Crawford issue. Duke did not report the benefits received by Boozer. So Wetzel wrote a column about this. And the NCAA's response? None. And did Duke then report? No. Hell if I know, I am just reporting the rumors. But, as Wetzel stated, "If you are going to apply the Crawford standard, there are hundreds of kids in this country who should be suspended immediately."

The irony of the story, of course, is that Michigan somehow got a black eye out of it. This was so despite the fact that (a) there was no question of improper recruiting (b) there was no implication of anything untoward while the kid was at Michigan, and (c) Michigan reported a "problem" that is routinely ignored by other schools, even Duke. Yet, the university came out of the affair looking bad, leading (or so it seems) to the firing of Athletic Director Tom Goss, maybe the patsy of this one for all I know. But the punishment was its own virtue: Michigan ended up with Tommy Amaker as coach and Bill Martin as AD, as opposed to Goss and Ellerbe.

The victim of the story, if he was being honest with us, was Crawford. And, it would seem, Crawford was the person the NCAA should have wanted to protect. Oh, silly me. What the NCAA really desires to protect is the window dressing of a successful Duke (or Michigan or Notre Dame) program that does not get upstaged by the so-called renegades on the block. The level playing field is the ultimate basis of NCAA activity, so long as it is imposed in a way that gives the big-timers (even or particularly Michigan) the edge. The interests of the individual athlete are a footnote in the equation. A near irrelevance.

Drew. Unlike Crawford, Drew Henson came to the University of Michigan from an intact, middle-class family. By chance, I sat next to Henson briefly at a Michigan baseball game when he was in high school, and he seemed an intelligent, kind, and thoughtful kid, not particularly impressed with himself. He also came to Michigan as a millionaire, a top draft pick by the Yankees, another in a continuing line of Michigan recruits/players (think shortstop Derek Jeter and David Parrish, among others) picked off by George Steinbrenner. This oddity in the NCAA rules is almost impossible to understand, at least when measured against the Crawford suspension. It is okay for a kid from a middle-class family, like Henson, to be under contract in one pro sport—indeed, to be a millionaire—and play in college as an amateur in another. It is not okay, however, to be a poor kid from a broken home who receives trivial subsidies while in high school from a nonparent or nonrelative and still be allowed to play as a scholarship athlete. When one looks at these rules and their applications, it is certain it is not the interests of students or athletes that are being protected. It is, rather, the interests of the institutions and their phobias about level playing fields, and what would happen if Podunk U was allowed to funnel benefits to a point guard with a crossover like Tim Hardaway. We would all be offended by this, I am sure, as offended as we were by the Sam Gilbert scams at UCLA (nobody cares, now or then), or those of Ed Martin (please), whatever amount of cash there might have been in addition to the birthday-cakes-in-the-dead-of-night-in-the-parking-lot-at-Crisler-Arena. (The more I think about this, the crazier it seems. What if Crawford, as a six-year-old, had been picked up off the street by a do-gooder-bleeding-heart-liberal who then went on to take an interest in the kid and helped provide him with food and

249

clothes? Presumably, this would also keep the kid from playing at the college level and receiving a scholarship, absent some guardianship action.)

The juxtaposition of Crawford and Henson is made poignant by Crawford's lament about his lost college experience versus Henson's choice to chuck his senior year for the honor of playing with the New York Yankees instead of (as was the fact at the time) the pathetic Cincinnati Reds. Prior to Henson's decision to leave Michigan in order to play full time for Steinbrenner, I had predicted there was no way Henson would leave before his senior year. I argued it would ruin a reputation that could not be repaired, and that Henson had already passed on the Steinbrenner inducements in the past. Plus, at the time, I could not see Henson leaving Michigan in the lurch for a quarterback. If Henson had determined to put his name into the NFL draft, I could understand it. But I could not understand how he could abandon his senior year for a month or so of extra practice time with the Steinbrennerite cult of evil, Derek Jeter or the reincarnation of Lou Gehrig or otherwise. I could not have been more wrong. My diary from the week of Henson's defection follows:

Drew Henson. Call me Beano. Feel free to. But how the hell was I supposed to know that the lowlife, convicted scum-sucking pile of decaying Buckeye nut dung (aka George Steinbrenner) would pull the stunt of reacquiring Henson and then making him a godfather offer? Let's start with the obvious. First, there is absolutely no chance that Saint George would have made the offer to a Buckeye quarterback (or maybe any other quarterback) under the same circumstances. Assume, for example, that Henson had one more year with the Bucks. Is there one chance in a million that George would have made the same offer? Well, of course, George might have been concerned (as would have been likely) that Henson would be the first choice in the NFL draft and he might have wanted to forestall this option. (My guess is that Henson will still go in the first two rounds of the draft in the not-distant future if his baseball career looks anything other than solid.) But George could have done this and still allowed Henson to finish his final year of eligibility. In other words, if Steinbrenner's concern was the competition posed by professional football, he could have made his offer and still allowed Henson to finish his college career. In not doing this, it is certain that a part of what Henson is being paid for is the renunciation of his football eligibility. This is axiomatic. Otherwise, it would have been a part of the deal.

Think about this. What if Steinbrenner, OSU's biggest booster, decided to pay Drew Brees (while in college) three million dollars to play baseball with the Yankees, on the condition of the repudiation of his Purdue scholarship, even though Brees hits the curve ball about as well as George does. Ed Martin and Sam Gilbert aside, one cannot pay players to play for the team you support. But it is okay, apparently, to pay players to lure them away from your opposition. Now, I admit, this is an unusual case. And I admit that the primary element of Steinbrenner's motivation was to secure Henson's services for the Yankees. But get this straight. It is one hundred percent fact that a part of what George was paying for was Henson's termination from the Michigan program, regardless of Drew's status as a baseball prospect. (Incidentally, Drew is a fine baseball player. But, from what I have heard, he is not yet ready to play third base for the Yankees. And he is likely to be two years away under any circumstances, best case scenario.)

You don't buy this? Well, apparently, neither does Drew, quoted as saying that "I know he is an Ohio State guy, but he is running a major business . . . I don't think his personal issues would affect a business decision." Well, Drew, listen to yourself. Henson's comment about the negotiations with the Yankees is that "in a perfect world, I would have finished my football career here and gone on to play third base . . . Unfortunately, it has been made clear to me that the opportunity that presented itself at this time will no longer be there next January . . . ." And the difference is? Well, about two weeks of spring football (Carr would have let him slide on this) and a few weeks in the fall, the difference, no doubt, between Willie Mays and Willie Mays Hayes. In other words, the Yankees were willing to forego their offer to their brightest future star over the matter of roughly one month of practice/playing time? Right. They would trade him back to the pathetic, drunken Reds for Harry Chiti and a player to be named later because of a lost month. (By the way, did I mention that Chiti was the only player ever traded for himself? I did mention it?) How about this quote from Henson: "The discussions [about coming back to UM] did not go very far." Oh. Gee. I am stunned. Steinbrenner did not concede this was a negotiable item? Wonders will never cease. And why wasn't it negotiable to George? Because the condition had no value to him? Right. Conditions without content are always the ones that you will never bargain away.

Michigan fans are almost one hundred percent (well, 80 percent) pissed at the Hensons. This is (for a change) something other than fan myopia. When Tim Biakabutuka left Michigan early (he had graduated, though) for the NFL, no one, I mean no one, criticized the choice. And Tim B had as good a third season as Henson. And the same was true of Charles Woodson, who had a better junior season than anyone since Alvin Wistert and Germany Schultz combined. No one criticized David Terrell for not playing in his last year of eligibility. Moreover, save for the defections of TE Milt Carthens to the USFL or Eric Turner to the NBA (completely idiotic choices absent private data), I cannot recall any significant criticism by Michigan fans of a Michigan player who left early for the dollars of professional sports. There was no criticism of Chris Webber or Juwan Howard or Jalen Rose in their choices. Michigan fans recognized the legitimacy of these decisions.

When Tyrone Wheatley stayed for his final year, amidst speculation he would leave, there was great admiration for Wheatley. But there was also a sense of wonder and some comment on the lack of wisdom in the decision. Wasn't he, after all, giving up a lot? Particularly where (unlike college quarterbacks) running backs are subject to some risk of career-ending injuries? But in the Henson case there is little empathy, since a part of what he has sold is Michigan. There is some sense, a legitimate sense, that Henson has sold *us,* an asset he does not own. If, for example, Henson had decided to sign with the Reds because it was time, there would be some wondering about the waste of his senior year. But Michigan fans would still have a high regard for Henson and would have respected the dilemma of his choice. If, for example, Henson decided to enter the pro football lottery, we all would have lamented, but understood the choice. And, in either case, Henson's status within the Michigan community would have been secure and intact. Of course, the Reds would not have made such an offer. And neither would anyone else in major league baseball. Only Steinbrenner. And no one would have bargained for Henson's senior year, because it only had value to one person in his circumstances. Only Steinbrenner.

Out of this, what the Hensons do not appear to realize is that Drew has sold more than his senior season to the Buckeyes. He has sold his good name and his universal admiration among those who loved him. He has sold out, but it is not the money that matters. Ultimately, what he has sold will be worth more, much more, than what he has gained.

And then there is the timing of the matter. If Henson had decided to take the Yankee offer in January, Lloyd Carr would have had some opportunity to recruit a quarterback who would want to compete for a four-year starting slot. Indeed, it is a certainty that the top high school quarterbacks in the country would have been intrigued by such a possibility. The March decision tied Carr's hands and left the program high and dry to this alternative. It is possible, of course, that the March move was just how it worked out, just the timing as designated by Herr Sturmbahnfuhrer Steinbrenner. But would Steinbrenner actually have made such a transaction with the Reds if Henson were going to blow it out of the water? Isn't it more likely that the Hensons had some clue as to Steinbrenner's plans and some communication with the Yankees about what was going down? Reds? Yankees? Give me a break. Who do you want to play for? The fascist-riddled enemies of the people or a team with a nickname reminiscent of humanism and social progress? Okay. I relent. I am raving now. Is Marge Schott still alive? She is? She isn't? Either way, I take it all back.

Of course, if John Navarre turns out to be an adequate replacement, all might be more or less forgiven in Wolverineland. But if Navarre goes in the tank and/or the Wolverines lose to the Buckeyes in 2001 with less-than-stellar quarterbacking by UM, you can bet that the resentment among the Wolverine faithful will be thick and indelible. At least for a while. If Henson turns out to be Roberto Clemente then, maybe in thirty years or so, the incident won't rate an asterisk. After all, who remembers what Madonna or Clarence Darrow or Iggy Pop or James Earl Jones or Cathy Guisewite or Lawrence Kasdan or Raul Wallenberg or William Mayo or Branch Rickey or Arthur Miller or Gildna Radner or Frank Murphy (the best Supreme Court justice, ever) or Jessye Norman did as students at UM? Some of us probably want to forget about Gerald Ford. Most all of us prefer to not recall Ted Kaczynski and (either) Leopold or Loeb and the wretched, smarmy cryptofascist Anne Coulter. And who remembers what the racist, anti-Semitic, and insane Richard Nixon did in his student days at Duke? Nixon's presence, so far as I can tell, didn't hurt Duke's basketball program. But so it goes. Duke, hopefully, will never forgive Nixon. I hope to forgive Henson.

One of the other oddities to me is that Henson left money on the table. Len Pasqurelli, writing for *CBS Sportsline*, points out that Henson would have been able to command as much money as Peyton Manning (or Tim Couch), about twenty-five million dollars over three years, as opposed to the seventeen million over six given by the Yankees. Pasqurelli's guess is that Henson left at least half of what he would have been able to command if he had finished his Michigan career. This is in football, of course. But even if Henson's first love and choice is baseball (this must be true), the leverage of the football potential/reality could have been worked to secure a contract in the ballpark of the Steinbrenner offer. Or so it would seem to the casual observer. Henson's agent, of course, must have been concerned about this reality, and I am willing to suspend judgment that the agent (former UM baseballer Casey Close) knew better. I hope Henson is successful. I hope he becomes Clemente and Babe Ruth combined. I take that back. I hope he becomes Clemente and Raoul Wallenberg combined, but without the tragic demises. But I fear for my own ability to forgive unless Drew (a) graduates from the university, and (b) pulls a Steve Smith with a huge endowment to the U as a sort of "my bad." We'll see. Without this, I fear there will be no midrun salvation for Henson. Hosanna.

On the *Wolverine Den*, poster "gulo gulo vorax" writes for many in saying, "Some players have disgraced the Maize and Blue in the past. Some have stolen, some have gotten into fights, some have caused property damage, but none has sunken to your depths, accepting a bribe not to play football from a Buckeye . . . Let there be no mistake, that is exactly what happened here." Is this way too harsh? Probably. But this is what many think, and his analysis of what happened is on the mark. There is no other honest spin.

Eric Lanai, another poster, wrote that Henson sold out for "Luis Sojo money" and "left his teammates in the lurch [by] selling his integrity for peanuts . . . ." Well, not quite peanuts of course, unless Eric is one very wealthy dude.

Brian Griese recently signed a six-year, thirty-eight million dollar contract with twelve million up front. Griese, a fine quarterback, was not as good in 1997 as Henson was in 2000. And Henson, in my judgment, has vastly greater potential as a pro quarterback. As a QB, I think Henson could be Benny Friedman or Sammy Baugh or Joe Montana or better. Henson could be, and I ain't kidding, the third best offensive player to ever play the game (after Jim Brown and Friedman). As a baseball player, I doubt if Henson will ever be as good as Joe Adcock. Indeed, Adcock, or maybe Max Alvis, would seem the pantheon for Henson. I hope I am wrong about this. I surmise there is a good chance, since I always seem wrong about Drew Henson. (By the summer of 2003, as it turned out, it became clear Henson had no future as a big league baseball player. Henson continually struggled at AAA, hitting in the .220 to .230 range with some power, not enough walks, and a passel of strikeouts, about one in every four at bats. Plus, rumor had it he was far short of ML quality as a defensive player, at least at third base. By 2004, he was out of baseball and headed for the Dallas Cowboys, the naive Houston Texans trading his rights for a midround draft pick. My guess? By 2007, Henson will be recognized as the top QB in football.)

Josh Moore and Jim Corbett. As noted earlier, Josh Moore was a brief-term center on the Michigan basketball team with a world record ability at committing fouls. Moore, an affable and intelligent kid, was forced from Michigan due to his marked lack of academic interest and, in the past few years, he has stumbled from China to the Clippers (2004) as a basketball vagabond. Nice work if you can get it, since I assume Moore received the league minimum for zero minutes played in 2003–4.

But as long as I am into juxtapositions (Jamal and Drew), I know that Josh Moore, at seven-two and Jim Corbett, at five-five are the relevant local basketball icons for old guys. I would have assumed, as I got older, that pick-up games would get cleaner. Post-forty years old, one would think participants would have less ego invested in the sport and, hence, playground ball would be a reasonably urbane affair, devoid of cheap shots and bad fouls. Nothing could be further from the truth. Swimming against the current and stuck in the past, confronting the present reality is too harsh for most to endure. The older the game gets, the slower it gets, and there is a direct correlation with game speed and both advanced and not-so-subtle clutching, grabbing, holding, choking, elbowing, and basically just plain Luscatoffing your pals. Essentially, Dirty Play 501.

I think this was the story with Josh Moore, an honorary old guy, who just couldn't seem to move his feet, despite the fact he seemed much more agile than the average seven-two guy, assuming the notion of "average" can apply to such persons. At Michigan, Josh never learned to use his legs on defense and this led to his never-to-be-surpassed record of two foul-outs in nine minutes of playing time. This is something we will not see again, about as likely as a

150-home-run season by Detroit Tiger Brandon Inge.

Over the course of the 2000–1 Big Ten campaign, Moore was whistled for forty-eight fouls in 129 minutes of play. Converting this to forty-minute games, this is almost fifteen fouls per game. Yep. Three foul-outs for every complete game played. Michigan opponents, not the cleanest guys in my estimation, were called for 3.92 fouls per every forty minutes played, compared to 4.28 fouls per forty minutes for the Michigan team as a whole. It is a fact that Moore got more than his share of bad calls. Not Eric Riley bad, but still a number of calls where the refs saw Josh's size and mobility as a convenient scapegoat. Moore was more. Conceding this, JM's high regard, indeed his legendary status among old dirty guys, arises from the chasm between four and fifteen fouls per interval. This is a lot of space, more space than anyone has ever seen at this level of play.

The operative words here are, of course, "at this level of play." At the old guy pick-up level, there are guys who would foul out in one or two trips down the court. Of course, these are very slow trips, but still . . . The most notorious local guy is Jim Corbett, the perfect complement to Josh Moore since he is almost two feet shorter and two hundred pounds lighter than Moore. If one could write a formula that could compare size to fouls per minute, use Josh Moore as a benchmark, and then inverse the correlation, you would then have Corbett. In other words, multiply Moore's fouls by a factor of eight or nine and you have an idea. Once again, I know I will be criticized for being subjective and exaggerating. Not so. I consider Jim a friend and, for many years, I played with him on a team in the five-foot-nine divisions (you could be up to five-ten) of the university intramural leagues. I played center on this team for roughly fifteen years and, I admit, the team was, by and large, clandestine and "illegal." We won a few more games than we lost against kids who were, by the end of our run, twenty to twenty-five years younger.

"You guys are still students here?"

"Yep. Slow learners."

"But how come half of you guys are bald?"

"Just high testosterone levels."

"And weren't you here ten years ago?"

"You got us confused with someone else."

We won some games. Well, maybe we won half. And in this fifteen-year period, Jim Corbett was often a very effective shooter in these contests. Indeed, on more-than-isolated occasions, Corbett's ability to shoot the ball from distance broke games open. But he also fouled out one hundred percent of the time. Every single game. Like the sun in the east. Like Ripken showing up. Always. Now, Corbett is about Earl Boykins' size, and he could move his feet. So I leave the rest to the reader's imagination. Clue: think about the concept of "choppers" in the Italian basketball leagues.

The five-nine games often resembled land wars. Since a number of games would be scheduled at once, a running clock was used and the officials were loath to call shooting fouls unless it was a particularly brutal one. Didn't matter, of course. Corbett still fouled out. And, in comparison, I consider myself a pretty average old guy player. In other words, dirtier than Ricky Mahorn or Jeff Ruland. How many times did I foul out in these games? Well, my highest foul total was three.

The foregoing said, it would be unfair of me not to mention that Corbett is one of the cleanest ten guys I play against. Come on. Nope, he is. I said Jim was notorious. He is. And, taking the heat off others, he has earned a perverse sort of legendary status. I don't think he is as physical as most of the people who complain about him, including me. And, save for minor bruises, he has never hurt me in a game, something I can't say about myself toward others.

I can't leave this team without mention of another Ann Arbor celebrity. A prominent member of the five-nine team was the famed Henry Henry. Later to become known as Herskey Herskey and, dust to dust, Henry Herskowitz. Now, Henry was nearly five-foot-eleven, but was never challenged in these games, I think because Henry was a finesse player who rarely fouled, and no one wanted to squawk about his presence—a rare and legitimately clean player—as compared to, say, the more physical guys on the team (the rest of us). The five-nine games were played with a running clock, and the procedure was that a player could be challenged at any time in the game for being over the height limit. One year we were in the second round of the playoffs, leading by three points with about six minutes left in the game, when Henry was challenged. I am not certain what the penalty was for a successful challenge, but I assume it was a forfeit. And the penalty for a bad challenge was two technical free throws. The game stopped and the clock ran as Henry sauntered to the measuring stick on the side of the IM wall. I assumed we were done and began to gather up my gym bag, but Henry returned smiling, having been ruled legal. I then milked the next minute or so off the clock by sinking both free throws with some of the slowest foul shooting in the history of the game. We won. The other team was steamed and fought among themselves.

We went to Fraser's Pub after the game, and Henry explained that he "knew that slumping wouldn't work. I was certain that had been tried and they were on to it." But Henry is an engineer, and he used his training to come up with an alternate plan. "I just made sure my feet were a few inches from the wall, and I leaned back slightly." Apparently, this technique worked, since he cruised in at five-nine and fifteen-sixteenths. I wonder, though he denies it, if money changed hands. Maybe this fell into the 2 percent category of basketball fixes as admitted by referees in the UM study. Or maybe the refs, seeing that Henry was the only guy on the floor who hadn't maimed someone during the game, were pissed that our opponents challenged him. Or maybe it pissed them off that our opponents were challenging a college undergraduate who looked forty-five years old. Poor guy. Who knows?

We actually made it to the finals that year—six guys in their forties in an undergraduate league—but Henry made it clear that we had to tank the final game, since none of us were legal, and we didn't want the game to be up. This is what Henry called a "must lose" game. Never fear. In the finals, the team we played had two guys who could dunk. They could all run and shoot. It was a legitimate "must lose" game (they were too good, we "must lose"), and we didn't need to put the fix in. We lost with ease, maybe by thirty-five. Maybe by more, trying as hard as we could.

In the season following the "Henry lean," we were playing against a dorm team, a team with pretty limited ability. We were up by thirty or so early in the second half, even though Corbett had already fouled out and we had only started with five guys. Still, four on five, we were increasing the lead, mostly because the Hex King, Jim B, was on fire. With about twelve minutes on the clock, I tipped an errant pass to Jim B and ran like hell to fill the lane. The Hex King had scored enough during the contest, and I wanted to make certain he gave me the easy shot in the open court. Or, at least, to make certain that he felt damn guilty about pulling up with an open guy on the wing. As I hustled down the court, I felt that my left hand was numb. I looked down and saw that my index finger was bent in a ninety-degree angle at the middle joint. Dislocated. I was pissed. The Hex King would get another easy look.

Running hard, I decided to pop the finger back into its rightful place. I had seen this happen to others and assumed it was no big deal to just pull the digit back into its socket. I tugged at my finger. Nothing. Then again. It exploded. Exploded into an incarnadine fission of blood on my face and chest and onto the court. I kept running and looked at the finger again. I had split the skin over two-thirds of the finger's circumference, and I could see bone and tendon. I stopped. The Hex King, of course, nailed the jumper.

The game had started at ten PM, and I went over to the emergency room at the hospital. The place was quiet and I received priority care, a young resident putting the finger back into place, irrigating it tirelessly with salt water to minimize the chance for infection, and then sewing it back together. It was about three AM. I wandered out to the waiting room. Odd noises. Laughing. There sat the Hex King, some hospital staff, and Kelly W, a guy who plays ball but was not even on the five-nine team (way too tall), who were cracking a case of beer and partying. In retrospect, I am certain it was the nonalcoholic type. The resident wandered out and asked for a brew. No problem. The security guards looked the other way. Hey. It's the middle of the morning. The place is almost empty. We are it. The doc asked whether we won. We did. Finishing three on five (remember, Corbett had fouled out), the Hex King, (our point guard) and best athletes Paul Shapiro and Henry had managed to hang on for a forty-two-point win. I am even more pissed now. They *stretched it out* without me. And I was pissed that I was going to miss the rest of the season. I looked at the resident. He scraped five-ten.

"You got any game, Doc?" I queried.

"Some," he replied. "Think John Bagley."

The resident took my spot on the team (everyone said it was a step up in ability), but I felt better when they lost in another legit "must lose" game in the semis.

Events came full circle when the basketball doc suggested I hang around the hospital for the next couple of hours to see a specialist who came to work in the AM. He said it was a dangerous injury and the chance for infection was pronounced. So I waited at the hospital, records in hand, until the specialist showed up at around nine o'clock.

"Who are you?" he asked, from the other side of the room.

I pointed to my hand.

"How did you do that?"

I told him.

"That's not possible. A finger won't split open that way. To me, it looks like you sliced your hand on some kind of metal."

"No, it really happened the way I said."

"Or maybe you caught your hand in a bear trap or some other sort of trapping device."

I told him again what happened and explained that I was a vegetarian and wasn't hanging out trapping bears. I mentioned I hadn't seen a lot of bears lurking in the Ann Arbor alleys lately.

"So you must have done something to your hand with a sharp or pointy object."

I noted that usually, when playing basketball, I don't carry a lot of metal objects around, especially if they are pointy or have edges or are sharp. I told him, "It kinda puts a crimp in the game to have people bleeding all over the place."

"It still looks to me like you cut it on the edge of a tin can or something."

"They don't make cans out of tin anymore."

"You know what I mean. And I don't understand why you would come into my office and lie about an injury. How am I supposed to give you competent medical treatment when you just come in here and lie to me? When you are ready to be truthful, why don't you come back and see me." The doc skittered away from my presence.

Yeah, this pissed me off. To the point where I began having dreams about this guy. Night after night for a few weeks, I found myself in a child support

258

enforcement hearing as a neutral, with this guy owing a snootful of dough. And every night this dream ended at the same place, with me ready to lower the lever of the thousand-pound shit hammer on him. But, I thought at the time, this is just more tricks of the mind. Just one more variant way for the mind to connect and to make sense out of things that really make no sense. Or, at least, to put closure on the craziness of existence. But I just couldn't get rid of the dream.

Except this time it came true. I didn't know the guy had a child support case. And I never handled these hearings. No more than three or four hearings in twenty years. But a few weeks after my injury, a clerk in the court system asked me if I would hear an order of income withholding case, a hearing where an OIW is either entered or adjusted due to an accumulation of arrearages in child support. All of the attorneys who ordinarily handled these cases were unavailable. I said I would do it. As the parties and the county official charged with taking care of these matters (called a JSO) came into my office, I was working on an opinion and did not immediately look up. The JSO handed me the court file and the cardboard began to take on a weird glow around the edges. At first, I swear to whatever, I thought the damn file was on fire. Then, I realized it was something else: the file had taken on some mystic proportion. I knew before I knew.

I looked up and made eye contact with the guy. His face turned pasty. "How's your hand doing?" He smiled.

I paused, at this point, for what seemed like minutes. For a brief flash, I was angry and thought I had better pass the case on to someone else. But there was no one else. For a moment, I considered making the guy's life miserable by, if in no other way, humiliating him for his failure to pay his child support as ordered by the court. But I knew I couldn't do this. Then, I thought of *House of God* rule number two. It is, "In case of cardiac arrest, the first pulse to take is your own." I did. I calmed down. My bias desisted. I asked the payer/doc what he thought should happen. He told me. It was reasonable. His failure to pay was neither vengeful nor mean-spirited. It was, more or less, a clerical error. He was willing to do the right thing. I thanked him for his presence and candor and entered an order in conformity with his suggestion. He smiled and said that he hoped that my finger healed well. I thanked him for his concern. My dreams went away.

Is there a point here? Another good question. There are a lot of them actually, though most may seem a little attenuated to the focused mind. I will let others sort it out. For me, the moral is this: never carry sharp or pointy objects onto the basketball court. It puts a crimp in the game.

Twenty years ago, Bill James revolutionized the way people look at baseball by pointing out that a simple formula will project, to a high degree of certainty, the number of games a team will win over the course of a major league season. The formula is: runs scored by a team squared, divided by runs scored squared plus runs allowed squared. In other words, if the Indians scored six hundred runs and gave up five hundred, their projected winning percentage would be this:

(600)*(600) divided by [(600)*(600) + (500)*(500)]

By the application of Pythagoras, the Indians would be projected to win 59 percent of games played, or ninety-six wins in an ordinary 162-game season. As a real world example (choices at random, I swear), take the 2001 Indians and Tigers. The Indians scored 927 runs and allowed 821 in that season. The sum of the squares formula suggests the Indians would win 90.79 games. They won ninety-one. The Tigers scored 724 runs and allowed 876. The formula states that the Tigers would be expected to win 65.75 games. They won sixty-six. These came out too good. So I tried another. Anaheim's numbers suggest it should win 76.6 games. It won seventy-five. Try it out yourself. This is a pretty damn good formula.

The formula can be applied with success to other sports, though one has to adjust for the fact that (a) the large number of trials in baseball allows the formula to work with minimal degrees of error, and (b) in games (football/basketball) where there are a lot of points, the formula needs to be cubed or quadrupled to realize meaningful results. The formula, in its Jamesian form outside of baseball, seems to work best in hockey, since the trials are reasonably large and the scoring is reasonably low. I ran the numbers against the Michigan hockey team results over three years:

Year	Goals	Goals Allowed	Predicted Wins	Record	Adjusted for Ties	Error
'98–99	140	99	27.99	25–11–6	28–14	0
'99–00	161	104	28.93	27–10–4	29–12	0.07
'00–01	167	110	31.38	27-13–5	29.5–15.5	1.88

As the above shows, Pythagoras allows one to connect scoring and records over large numbers of trials. But what's the point? Well, there are at least three. The first is a partial proof that offense and defense are equivalents. A team can be successful by scoring a lot or by not giving up very many. There is no mathematical way to conclude that "defense wins games" any more than "offense wins games." The truth is, it is best to be better than your opponents in both, but it is equally as good to be a lot better than your opponents on one side of the ball/ice/equation.

The James/Pythagoras model implies it is logical to build a team (a la Northwestern in 2000) by putting all of one's talent on one side of the ball, as opposed to spreading it out. At least where there is less than enough to go around, or if you are building a team in, say, the NFL. The second point is that if the projection tends to be out of sync with the team's actual record, it might be useful to hunt around at the details of the record to see if a team was just plain unlucky over the course of a year. (The 2000–1 UM hockey team, despite underachieving in relation to the formula, was anything but unlucky. While the Wolverines were 1–4 in two-goal games, they were 7–2 in one-goal games, a much higher percentage than their overall record would have suggested to accrue. I think the answer lies in the GLI tournament, where the Wolverines lost twice while being significantly depleted by the world junior tournament. Moreover, the error is only 6.4 percent, probably little other than ordinary error over the course of the number of trials.)

The third obvious use of the formula is as tea leaves for the future. In the 2000–1 basketball season, I made a prediction about Michigan's Big Ten record as based upon its nonconference schedule:

December 28, 2000. It didn't get better against Towson University, an opponent in the same general cut of competition as BGSU and Morris Brown. Towson was 6–5 prior to the UM game but had losses at Drexel and at Delaware State (by eighteen). It also had losses to UMBC (???) and Morgan State on neutral courts. With back-to-back wins prior to the Towson game I expected the Michigan team to show some improvement, some indication that it was getting ready for the Big Ten tests. But it did not happen. Towson stayed with Michigan the entire game, leading by eight with fifteen minutes left on the clock. The game was tied with nine minutes left, and UM led by a mere point with a minute to go. But the Wolverines cruised in the final minute, crushing the Tigers by a final tally of 73–71. The game might be called a "thrilling victory," but it was more like "sorta relieved and pass the bottle." Towson outscored us from the floor, and the free throw differential was the game difference (a nine-point UM advantage), but some of this might have been justified, since Michigan had a decided advantage in the paint. Though, who knows, the Towson coach (Mike Jaskulski) may have seen it otherwise. No one was truly outstanding for the Wolverines, but I did like Avery Queen's seven assists to one turnover. After the game, Ellerbe said, "We beat a solid team." Coach Jaskulski agreed, labeling his team "pretty good."

Well, if this is true, maybe things aren't so bad after all. But, according to Pythagoras, Michigan's first ten games do not portend good things in the future. The numbers suggest seven or eight Big Ten wins (out of sixteen games), but this is on the hypothesis that the teams we played are roughly comparable to Big Ten opposition. Well, Duke is the equivalent of MSU, but maybe not as good. And Maryland is the equivalent of Illinois, but maybe not as good. And St. Johns might be about the same as Iowa or OSU, but maybe not as good. Wake Forest corresponds to Indiana, maybe a bit better. These four teams would seem pretty typical of Big Ten competition. Then throw in Towson as more or less equivalent to Northwestern, though probably not as talented and a lot more fun than playing against Bill Carmody's grinding Princeton offense. Assuming these five teams are more or less equivalent to an average Big Ten schedule, the theory projects Michigan at 6–10.

The problem here is that there are too many points to project accurately by squaring. Probably, for the idea to be useful as a predictor, the relationship of points scored and allowed will need to be cubed or (more likely) quadrupled. Without any attempt at application to prior data, the five-game hypothetical "Big Ten equivalent" projects a 4–12 record (via quadrupling) for the Wolverines. This assumes, of course, that in these five games Michigan was what it will be, something that would seem (hopefully) unlikely. But then I took a look at the Michigan schedule. What games do we have a reasonable chance to win? Indiana at home. At Northwestern. At Penn State. Iowa at home. Minnesota, Purdue, and Northwestern at home. Seven games. Assume we can win 70 percent of these and one someplace else. That's six and ten. Split the difference. I predict five wins. Assuming a win against (very, very bad) Eastern Michigan University this week, that makes UM 11–16 going into the Big Ten tournament. Call it 1–1 in the tournament That makes it 12–17. And that makes Brian Ellerbe and his staff where? You got it. Palookaville. Or at least throwing himself on the mercy of Bill Martin's court with some sort of a Faustian plea.

But just how demanding has the Michigan schedule really been? This is a tough one, since some of these schools aren't on anyone's radar. Eventually I found a rating, by some guy named Erik Packard, that tracks 906 schools on a single scale. And that includes #695 Panhandle State University. Honest. You can look it up. And if you did, you would see that OPSU (the O is for Oklahoma) has a six-six forward named Siesta Pettiford and a six-nine, 250-pounder, one Richard Whitfield, with a definite game face and mean-looking tattoos. I checked out the OPSU schedule. Never heard of a single college that it plays. But it is 7–4 at the moment, and Siesta is averaging more than twenty points and seven-and-a-half rebounds per game. And the school nickname? I wanted to romanticize this one, thinking that "Hoboes" would be nice. Or "Moochers." Or "Oklahoma Sponges." Or the "Spare Changes." But then it came to me. Exactly what it must be. The Panhandle State Vagrants. Elegant. Catchy. It must be true. I was certain, but was then disappointed when it turned out OPSU is one of innumerable "Aggies." But I would be remiss if I didn't mention that the Aggies have won the national rodeo contest three of the past four years. This would mean, in terms of rodeo programs, OPSU is number one. And, to be honest, I would want to bet serious money that OPSU would-n't give the current basketball Wolverines a tussle. Aside from OPSU, the Packard ratings (12/26/2000) for Michigan's opponents are as follows:

Duke #2

Wake Forest #3 (too high)

Maryland #21

St Johns #108

Towson #238 (apparently not in agreement with the post
                      game assessments of both coaches.)

Wagner #241

BGSU #259

Western #270

Oakland #328

EMU #355

Morris Brown #402

All of the Big Ten teams are rated in the top fifty, with the exception of Indiana at sixty-five (that will change) and Northwestern at #111. Michigan is listed at #196. This is in the same vicinity of Salem International, Wisconsin-Stout, and William Carey. No, I didn't have the heart to look up Salem International (#194). The "Witch Trials"? The "Menthols"? Or Wisconsin-Stout (#179). The "Guinnesses"? The "Hearted Fighting Guys"? Or even William Carey (#209). The "Nations"? The "Me Back to Old Virginies"? In any event, assuming Packard is right, this means that, aside from Duke, Wake Forest, Maryland, and St. Johns, Michigan (if they beat EMU) will be 6–1 (losing the only game on the road) playing against the (as an average) #299 team in the country. Ouch.

December 29, 2001. I was close in my 2000 projection (above) as based upon the nonconference action, but my holistic 5–13 was not as good as Pythagoras's 4–12 (the exact record), and he didn't see, according to rumor, a single game of the preseason. So what about the year of the present writing? In Tommy Amaker's first year, Michigan's nonconference record was 4–5. This looks worse than Ellerbe's record last year (6–5). But when you run Pythagoras against the scores that are representative of a Big Ten schedule (via Sagarin), you find that Michigan has scored 336 points and allowed 386. This corresponds to a 36 percent winning percentage (via quadrupling), and suggests Michigan will be 5.76–10.24 this year. So call it six wins in the conference. (As it turned out, the Wolverines finished the Big Ten at 5–11. Pythagoras was off by .76 of a game.)

* * * *

How to Get Rich. As any stat freak with a passing interest in the NFL knows, some numbers geek is always trying to make sense of NFL stats and put them into an equation that predicts wins and losses. Most of these are betting types, trying to find the hidden secret to the big-point-spread Nirvana. No more snake eyes. No more hitting that hard sixteen with a jack. No more tracking the roulette wheel to find, well, Major Strasser has been shot. Round up the usual suspects. Mostly these guys are on the internet, advertising that for just three-ninety-five (hundred) dollars, you can own their ironclad secrets: their secret statistical links will provide you an 80 percent winning edge against the point spread. Well, first of all, no one picks 80 percent against the line. And no one picks 70 percent. Anyone telling you that is not telling you the truth. What about 65 percent? I dunno. There may be someone out there who, by discarding most all betting opportunities, can pick 60 percent-plus. But if there is such a person, he ain't giving it away. He is laying it on the line himself. Truth is, if a gambling service can pick 55 percent-plus and (maybe) 60 percent on its best bets, it is probably a pretty good service. Probably real good.

In the nonbetting world, *The Hidden Game,* the book mentioned in chapter three, makes a valiant attempt to find some statistical truths about the NFL using multivariant linear regression. In other words, they make an attempt to cook the data to fit the results. Their after-the-fact formula for predicting points scored by a team, as based upon other stats, is

Points Scored = (Yards)/(14.07) + (Net Turnovers*2.02) - 38

In the words of Groucho Marx, "I thought I was a corpuscle." First of all, any equation attempting to prove a reality that uses a constant (thirty-eight) in this fashion seems a dubious prediction of reality. It is reading history through the rearview mirror with no attempt at the future. Second, the authors relate that most teams "will come within twenty-five points by use of the equation." They then try out an example, and note that the team in question scored seventy more points than predicted, in this case 472 versus 402. Assume the same variation on the other side of the equation, in other words that the team will give up 332 versus 402. The difference here is profound. A team scoring 402 and giving up 402 is likely to win eight and lose eight in the NFL. A team scoring 472 and giving up 332 according to Pigskin Pythagorus, is likely to win thirteen and lose three. In other words, the difference between a team that might win the Super Bowl and one that won't make the playoffs. Even the (admittedly) ordinary variance of twenty-five is somewhat less than useful, where this is the difference between 5.7 and 10.3 wins, assuming an average of 332 points per team over the season, as was the case in 1997. The variance is too much. And too useless.

But what the heck. I tried the formula out on 2001 data for twenty-two teams chosen at random and their competition over the year. And then I compared it to my guess of the average number of points usually scored in a season, 332. (We can rewrite the equation as 332 + 16 - (17/17) + 1 - 16.) The distribution of error is shown in the chart below, where the column on the left represents how far off (the variance between) the prediction and the realities were vis-à-vis points scored by the team being analyzed.

Point Variance From Formula	*Hidden Game* Formula Number of Teams	Ross Formula (332) Number of Teams
0–10	6	3
11–15	2	4
16–25	1	3
26–40	6	3
41–60	4	4
61–80	2	1
81+	1	4

Okay, so *The Hidden Game* did better, but not so much better to get worked up about it. Indeed, the Ross formula (points scored = 332) had ten out of twenty-two teams within twenty-five points, where *The Hidden Game* hit at nine out of twenty-two.

But is there some secret to picking against the spread? I dunno. I can't do it. But you can try this one out and, I promise, there is at least some level of utility if you are serious about making the attempt. Let me preface the following with the note that I don't know any bookies and I have made only two or three football bets in my life. But I do play in the occasional office-type pool, and I do pay attention. For a long time, I have noticed an odd little stat that seems to correlate with winning in the NFL. Not against the spread, but winning. The stat is yards per passing attempt. This has been little more than a curiosity for me, until recently (devoid of ideas), I tracked 140 NFL games to see if my instincts were right. In those games (all in 2001), the team that averaged more yards per passing attempt (YPPA) won a hundred and two and lost thirty-eight times, a winning rate of 73 percent. Now I know some smart guy is going to say, "Big deal. The correlation of winning with interceptions is that good or better." And, continuing the argument, "How does this help anyone beat the freakin' spread? This is just a win percentage."

Two good points. However, unlike interceptions or turnovers, elements that are mostly random and nearly impossible to predict, it seems possible that YPPA is relatively predictable. It is not, unlike turnovers, something that is only clear after the fact. Second, since there is or may be this element of predictability, some smart guy or computer whiz should be able to create a power rating using these numbers to reverse-engineer an equation that will apply to future events. I am not that person, but I did try out a simple formula for week seventeen of the 2001 NFL season. Here is the formula:

(1) Calculate Team A's YPPA, less yards allowed per passing attempt.
(2) Perform the same calculation for Team B.
(3) Subtract the difference between (1) and (2) and multiply by five.
(4) Apply (3) to the superior team and adjust for the home field (2.75 points).
(5) Compare to the point spread.

One caveat or axiom to the equation: Never make the play when a team that is negative in calculation (1) or (2) is favored over a team that is positive in the calculation. And, as a corollary, my surmise is the best plays will be those that cover the spread (in the equation) arising out of a positive and negative calculation in steps (1) and (2). It would seem that teams that are both positive or both negative pose tougher predictions, and pose games more likely to be decided by chance. Two defined examples follow, both from week seventeen of the 2001 season:

<u>Green Bay @ NY Giants with the Giants getting three points</u>
(1) Green Bay's YPPA is 7.51. The defensive number is 5.95. The difference is 1.56.
(2) NYG numbers are 6.63 and 7.00. The difference is minus .37
(3) The total of 1 and 2 is 1.93. Multiply by 5. The result is 9.95.

Under the theory, (3) calculates the difference in the abilities of the teams, almost ten points. Compare this to the spread and adjust for home-field advantage. So, under the theory GB is plus 9.95 points, less home field (2.75), 7.2 points in favor of the Pack. The line says, to bet the Packers, you must lay three points. This leaves 4.2 points, a pretty substantial number. Plus, it is a positive versus a negative play. Put every cent you own on the Pack.

Who won? The Packers won by nine and covered the spread. Now, I admit, I think most would have liked the Packers anyway. The game was more meaningful for them. The Packers were, even to the casual observer, the better team. The line was not too heavy. I think, outside of the New York area, the money was likely to come in more heavily on the Pack. But what about the next game on the list, the struggling Denver Broncos on the road against the struggling Indianapolis Colts? Unlike the Green Bay game, I would have suggested this to be a good game to pass. But if I had to bet it on instinct, I think I would have picked Denver, feeling that the Colts defense was so weak that the Denver offense would be able to control the game. Plus, Denver was getting two-and-a-half points. But the theory said otherwise.

<u>Denver @ Indy with the Broncos getting two-and-a-half points</u>

(1) Indy's YPPA is 7.66 less 7.77 or minus .11
(2) Denver's YPPA is 6.38 minus 6.95 or negative .57
(3) The relative weight is .46 favoring Indy. Times 5 is 2.3 points favoring Indy.
(4) Add the home field to the team difference and Indy is 5.05 points preferred.

Since the spread is only two and a half points the formula suggests Indy. Indianapolis won easily (by nineteen), and this game made me begin to think (since it was so counterintuitive for me) that there might be some predictive utility in looking at this statistic.

So what about the rest of the week? Not all that bad. The total for the week was 10–4 (one no-play) against the spread. In games where the formula covered the spread and the projected winner was 0.2 YPPA (net) to the positive, and the other team was at least 0.2 YPPA to the negative, the projected winner was 6–0 versus the line. Okay, I am the first to admit this was a very limited trial, and I know the long-term prognosis cannot be that good. But it seems there is a chance the rule of thumb might push the average better to 52.5 percent against the line, covering the vigorish, and limiting some suicides.

For the price of this book, it seems that adding some years to your life expectancy is on the plus side of the ledger. Of course, the best advice I can give is to strictly limit your betting to the amount you can comfortably afford to lose as an entertainment expense. But I understand the fascination. Having a backed opinion and putting one's instincts on the line, even for twenty cents, makes the beer taste better and, otherwise, why the hell should anyone care about the fortunes of a bunch of millionaires and their billionaire owners on a quest to rip off the citizens and taxpayers of the towns they defile? Yeah, I love it. I hate it.

As of this moment, it is the day before the pro football playoffs (2001–2 season). The wild card games. Let's try the formula prospectively. You will just have to trust that I am being honest about this and I won't cook it after the fact. In order of preference, it looks like this:

Tampa Bay @ 6.12 - 6.54 = -0.42
Philadelphia @ 6.57 - 6.09 = + 0.48

This appears to be the sitter of the week. The difference is 0.9. Times five is four and a half points. Add the home field, and Philly is 7.25 points better. The line is plus three Tampa Bay. Plus, you have a negative/positive game. On the soft side, Philly has one of the rising stars of the league in Donovan McNabb, and Tampa Bay has why-is-he-in-the-league Brad Johnson. If the formula flops here, it ain't no good. Maybe. As an aside, this game (versus the spread) seems a near-tossup for commentators. A number of TV talking heads are taking Tampa Bay straight up. In *Pro Football Weekly*, three of their five analysts like Tampa Bay. I don't get it.

My second favorite game is Oakland over the Jets. It looks like this:

Jets @ 6.19 - 6.14 = + 0.05
Raiders @ 6.98 - 6.23 = +.0.75

Using the formula, the Raiders are plus 6.25 against a four or four-and-a-half point line. Enough fat to make it a worthwhile game. The problematic aspects of the game are threefold. First, Vinny Testaverde runs hot and cold. Very hot and very cold. He is hard to predict. Second, so does Rich Gannon, the QB for the Raiders. Third, the Jets, Jets, Jets can play pass, pass, pass defense, and the Oakland YPPA may be a little bloated against this defense. Still, it looks like a good play on the Raiders.

My third pick would be Green Bay over San Francisco, giving three and a half points. The line opened at four and has dropped a half-point, implying a lot of smart money has come in on the 49ers. I can understand this, since I like the 49er QB, Jeff Garcia, over Brett Favre. Both are excellent, to be sure, but I think Favre is more likely to throw the INT under pressure, more confident to make the low-percentage play than Garcia. I also think the teams are pretty even, but with a significant edge to the 49er wide receivers. Still, the formula calls it Green Bay.

San Fran @ 7.03 - 6.35 = +0.68
Green Bay @ 7.69 = 6.01 = +1.68

The difference is 7.75 points against a three-and-a-half point (or four point, if you got GB late) line. Magic eight ball says, take the Pack. But where both teams are so positive, my guess is the difference is razor thin.

The last game is Baltimore at Miami, the road team getting two and a half points:

Baltimore @ 6.48 - 6.11 = +0.37
Miami @ 7.36 - 6.55 = +0.81

The total is plus 4.95 Miami, less the spread of two-and-a-half. I like this game about the same as Green Bay (Miami, but not by much), balancing the Ravens defense and their defending-champion status versus my judgment that Miami quarterback Jay Fiedler is now playing at a higher level than Elvis Grbac. Close, but I go with the Fish.

So what happened? Well, the Eagles won by twenty-two, easily covering the spread. Oakland had a little more trouble, but still won by fourteen. The Packer game could have gone in either direction in the last minutes (at least against the spread), but the Green Baysians recovered in the waning minutes of the game. And the Fish? Well, in the words of someone (PJ O'Rourke?), the Dolphins looked as dead as a carp in a tub of motor oil, with the Ravens running a predictable and boring offense consisting of just about one play, pounding the ball up the gut of the defense over and over. So the formula was three and one for the weekend, 13–5 since I began to use the theory. But most of all, in the positive/negative matchups where the positive team was predicted, the theory was 7–0. I don't know for sure, but I guess this means there is a high degree of certainty that the theory is arguable. I will let you do your own revisions and adjustments, but I probably just saved you enough money to justify buying another copy of this book. (The theory was 5–1 over the next two weeks, and 1–0 in games where it looked real good. So the totals were 18–6 and 8–0. This is enough for anyone to break even.)

Is there any application to Michigan football? In 2001 there was, with the team throwing for more YPPA winning nine of eleven games. The exceptions were Iowa and Wisconsin, games where Michigan either (a) should have lost (Wisconsin), or (b) could have lost (Iowa). The twelfth game? That was MSU, a dead heat in YPPA. On the other hand, the game was also a dead heat or, at least, I still don't know who won. In 2000, Michigan beat the opposition in every game in YPPA, and Henson and company put up a remarkable 8.6 yards per attempt. This beat every team in the NFL in 2001, with the exception of St. Louis and its incredible 8.9. In 2001, Michigan's number fell to a very less than stellar 6.4, and this resulted in a negative 0.2 YPPA (in relation to the defence) over the course of the season. The decline in points scored was consequential, adding up to a difference of 102 from the prior year. Trading in the woeful defense of 2000 for the generally pretty good one in 2001, the Wolverines managed to lose one more game than in 2000. But let's not be deceived by this. Michigan was extremely lucky to win eight games in 2001, a fact that I really like to stress, since I picked UM for 7–5 on the year, ultimately winning in a meatball bowl game as opposed to getting hammered by the Tennesseeans. And they were extremely unlucky to only win nine games in 2001. With a healthy Henson and any kind of a half-assed defense in 2000, the Wolverines would have run the table.

As an afterthought, New England covered in the 2002 Super Bowl, a condition predicted by the formula in the last chapter. The numbers did not work miracles. They did not predict a win against the Rams. They did, however, suggest the Patriots were the better play against the huge line, particularly looking to the numbers over the playoffs.

I tried the theory out in 2002–3, and it was only slightly better than flipping a coin until the playoffs, when it again kicked into high gear, winning eight of eleven games. It seems the database for the theory must be pretty significant before the numbers have much meaning. Or, at least, that was my rationalization. In the following season, it didn't seem any better than flipping a coin.

The theory was so random in 2003–4 that I thought it was just plain worthless, albeit no more worthless than my ordinary choices. But I checked it out in the playoffs anyway. How did it do in 2003–4? The italicized teams are the system picks. The numbers in the parentheses represent the system's point call.

Den (+3) at *Indy* (+5.65) Indy 41–10 W
Seattle (+7.5) at GB (+3.60) GB 33–27 W
Dallas (+3) at Caro (+2.9) Caro 29–10 L
Tenn (-1.5) at Balt (-2.15) Tenn 20–17 W
GB (+5.5) at Phil (-0.15) Phil 20–17 W
Indy (+3) at *KC* (+5) Indy 38–31 L
Tenn (+6) at NE (+2.90) NE 17–14 W
Caro (+7) at StL (+1.25) Caro 29–23 W
Caro (+4) at Philly (+0.60) Caro 14–3 W
Indy (+3) at *NE* (+3.40) NE 24–14 W
NE (-7) and *Caro* (-1.25) NE 32–29 W

Nine-and-two is as good as anyone did. The problem is, over most of the season, I doubt if the theory was better than fifty-fifty. It might have been worse. Hold your tickets.

Middles.

Gary Moeller. Bo's best boy's weird and mysterious journey at Michigan continues to feel tragic to me. Moeller has bounced from team to team in the NFL and had a short trial as the Lions head coach, one that was markedly more successful than his predecessor, or (especially) his successors, but not good enough to land a permanent job.

In 2001, after being dumped by the Lions, Moeller was hired as the defensive coordinator for the Jacksonville Jaguars. In the prior year, the Jaguars had scored 367 points and given up 327. Pythagoras predicted these point totals would yield a 10–6 record, exactly the record the team achieved on the field. So Jacksonville management looked at these numbers and decided (a) our points scored were well above average in the league, (b) our points allowed were in the middle of the league, or maybe a little below average, so (c) if we can decrease our points allowed by about forty, we will be a 12–4 team, a team ready to compete for the pantheon. Not a bad theory, so far as it went.

Jacksonville hired Moeller to patch up the defense, and in 2001 the Jaguars decreased their points allowed by exactly forty-one. The promised land. However, the Jags managed to cruise in with a 6–10 record, not exactly what management had in mind. The problem? Despite the fact that Moeller's defense was fourth in the AFC in points allowed, and despite the fact that only one team (Pittsburgh) had a markedly better defense in the AFC in 2001, and despite the fact that the Jacksonville defense allowed nearly as few points as considered to be very good defenses like Tampa Bay and Baltimore, the offense scored seventy-one fewer points than in 2000, putting the kibosh on management's plan. The solution? Fire Gary Moeller, of course, the *defensive* coordinator. And they did, kicking Moeller's keister into football oblivion or some other assistant's job somewhere else. Meanwhile, the legendary John Cooper took Moeller's old job with the Cincinnati Bengals.

Why did Moeller get the hammer? As far as I can tell, the problem was that the Jaguars had no pass rush, few sacks, and did not intercept a lot of passes. They didn't give up points, but it didn't look like a good defense because it wasn't "aggressive" or "attacking," and reminded everyone of the dreaded "bend but don't break" football loathed by football fans the world around and, more importantly, by those in Jacksonville management. Plus, sometimes Moeller went into a prevent defense, the absolute bane of all football fans and color guys. The fact that the Jacksonville defense improved by 12 percent in points allowed, the bottom line, after all, became less important than style points.

What got really weird at Jacksonville was that the Jags were unable to retain their offensive coordinator, Bob Petrino, who left and took less money to work at Auburn. Management tried to lure Tom Clements to run the offense and offered him huge dollars to take the position. Clements turned the offer down, despite the lack of any equivalent opportunity. So what's the point? Well, mine is that if the management of a team or franchise makes it clear it is less interested in what wins and loses games (scoring points and not allowing them—in other words, how fast did you go down the hill?) than how a defense or offense looks (were you graceful in going down the hill?), it might be a hard sell to hire and keep the coaches that can actually accomplish something. In other words, if you wanna turn football into figure skating, my guess is you will end up with tight ends that can't knock down a linebacker, though they might look good turning a double axel. I say this with emphasis to all Michigan football fans, including myself, next time we yammer about a play call or a defensive theory.

Now, I admit, there may have been an offensive/defensive symbiosis in Jacksonville that is less than apparent to a person just looking at the season from the outside. And it may be that Tom Coughlin, the Jacksonville head coach, is such a pissant (he reportedly is) that nobody wanted to work for him. I don't know. But I do know Moeller's journey has been a strange one. He won more than 78 percent of his games at Michigan, and was a successful coach with the Bengals and then the Lions, including a reasonable stint as interim head coach. He then performed a miracle by taking a crappy Jacksonville defense and making it respectable. No pass rush, though. Not "aggressive" enough. Bye. You be out on the streets because the obsessive Romanian judge gave you a zero in style points.

Ends.

Lloyd Carr. Style points were also becoming an issue with Lloyd Carr. At least to the fans. Going into the 2002 season, Carr had made major changes in his coaching staff. Bobby Morrison, ill with cancer, was on an extended leave of absence. Quarterback coach and offensive coordinator Stan Parrish resigned, after (apparently) a dispute with Carr over either (a) the direction of the offense, or (b) (more likely) Parrish's role on the coaching staff. Carr replaced these two with coaches who had been on the Michigan staff in the past, Bill Sheridan, a well-regarded coach, most recently at Notre Dame, and Scott Loeffler, a QB and grad assistant under Lloyd who went off to CMU when Mike DeBord took the head coaching job with the Chips. (DeBord also came back in 2004 after being dumped by CMU, and was put in charge of special teams and recruiting.)

In 2002, Sheridan worked on the defensive side of the ball and became the recruiting coordinator. Loeffler coached the quarterbacks, a place where he has had some marked success. Since the Wolverines could have hired Jim Harbaugh (he applied), Carr must really have thought Loeffler could coach and recruit. Offensive line coach Terry Malone became the offensive coordinator.

Many UM fans viewed the 2002 changes as a sort of desperation by Coach Carr, that this fourth offensive coordinator in eight years represented a sort of crossroad for the coach. The laments were, of course, we are just so "predictable" and "not aggressive" and "not imaginative," unlike that varied

Nebraska option attack. There were two camps on this. One was that Lloyd had won 76.7 percent of his games, slightly above the historical average for Michigan football and, hence, there was no reason for any concern. Lloyd had proven he could coach. He seems a good person. We will be just fine. And, if our worst seasons are 8–4, well, we can live with that, so long as no football Ed Martins or other such characters show up on the radar screen.

Others pointed out that Lloyd was eighth among all Michigan coaches in winning percentage, lower than the lowly Gary Moeller and, hence, he represented plain old mediocrity, at least in Michigan terms. Of course, Lloyd was also only three percentage points lower than Bo, and was coaching during a time when he didn't get an automatic six or seven wins a season against vastly inferior competition. In some sense, Bo only had to win half his games to go 9–3. The eighty-five-scholarship limitation means that most teams in the Big Ten are now able to compete. The rollover quotient has declined by a marked degree, and even the top half of the MAC, in any given year, can compete with most of the major schools.

The anti-Lloyd or Lloyd-is-at-the-precipice camp pointed out (a) the offense sucked for most all of the 2001 season (true), (b) the offense really smelled against Ohio State (true again), (c) we lost to MSU when the Spartans outplayed us in the second half by a significant margin, even though Jeff Smoker got smoked out of his hole as much as the Taliban (basically true), and (d) Tennessee pretty much demolished Michigan in 2001 in all facets of the game, except running the ball, where both teams were ineffective (absolutely true). With these predicates and the fact that since 1997, Michigan's record had declined from 12–0 to 10–2 to 9–3 to 8–4 . . . well, Michigan fans did the basic arithmetic (7–5, 6–6, 5–7) and the football Wolverines were on the verge of transformation into Notre Dame or Penn State, used-to-be big guys on the block who now have sand kicked in their faces on more-than-isolated occasions.

And then there was the style point issue that dotted the landscape of fan critique. To these fans, the coaching changes were a signpost that Lloyd was on the verge of a flame out. Worse, Lloyd's perceived desperation was seen as misguided since, with the ascension of Terry Malone, we were likely to get even more conservative. That is, it was hypothesized a line coach would likely want to win via smashmouth and was unlikely to "throw over the middle" or whatever other (I would say idiotic) mantra happened to be popular at the moment.

It was an interesting time for Carr and his staff. In 2002, the Wolverines had an absolutely great secondary and a terrific defensive line. There were some moderate issues at linebacker, but that was it. This left Terry Malone and Carr in the offensive hot seat. Would they play it like 1997 (worked pretty good, I would say) and let the defense dominate the games with a no-mistake offense, or would they, as the clamoring among fans seemed to argue for, let it all hang out, with some sort of an offensive apocalypse? The four horseman, but throwing intermediate routes over the middle on every down. Personally, I had no clue. But I did know why the Wolverines were sluggish in 2001. I thought it was pretty obvious really. It was (a) awful offensive line play on the running game, allowing teams to play both safeties in the passing game, (b) inconsistent quarterback play against defenses playing pass, (c) some inability of the Michigan offense to stretch the field (in either direction), and (d) some problems with the receivers creating space against pass defenses thick in coverage.

So would Carr/Malone open it up? I thought they might. And if they did, I thought we were likely to be in real trouble. It meant either the defense was not as good as it appeared to be or the offensive line had not improved, meaning the pressure was really on Navarre, but this time without Marquise Walker. All I had to add to the enigma was that Terry Malone was my wife's favorite coach at the women's football clinic. She reported Malone is smart, funny, approachable, and definitely not full of himself.

Malone did not pursue the offensive coordinator's job; it was not in his plans. Accordingly, he scrambled to learn and, two weeks into the position, had already met with offensive coordinators of more than one NFL team. Malone's comments about the offense were,

> I really believe one thing: with the way that football is played today, you can't just say you're going to do one thing or another. No one has done it. Even the teams that are totally one-dimensional, you never see those teams as being really successful programs. You have to be able to execute the entire game plan. You've got to be able to pass the ball and complete passes when defenses dictate that, and yet you have to be able to have a physical attitude that you're going to be able to punch people out and move the ball on the ground. The nice thing about Michigan in 2002 is we have players at all the positions that you can run a balanced offense.

And so, at the time, I wondered. What if the 2002 Wolverines run the ante down to a 9–4 or worse season? What will we think of Lloyd if this happens? And what will we think if he does it with no style points? Does it matter if we go down in an offensive flame, throwing the ball all over the field (and all over the middle) in an aggressive and unpredictable red-hot imitation of spuriousness? Spurrierness? Essentially, whassup?

I posted a variation of the foregoing paragraphs in the form of question on the *Wolverine Den*. The general tenor of the responses was that Carr is at the end of his rope, not necessarily with the university or in relation to his job, but a metaphorical end in his "relationship to the masses." And, or so it seemed to me, much of this end is predicated on style points, the "fact" that Carr has a "predictable" offense, or that Michigan has tended to play "two one-dimensional" offenses, the predictable running game and then (when desperate) the predictable passing game. I think, in the main, the responses were nuts and showed little attention to what actually happened on the field. But I also think they were honest displays of frustration arising out of the probable reality that expectations were higher than obtainable in 2002. I thought 2002 would be a key year for Coach Carr, at least in terms of the clamoring by the hoi polloi. To ensure his place, Lloyd needed a good year. He needed this more, at least from a fans/media perspective, than in any of his prior years as head coach.

* * * *

As it turned out, UM was able to scrape by Washington with an unlikely field goal after a probable wrong call (a fourth down pass called a fumble, as opposed to incomplete) and a bonehead UW mistake (twelve guys on the field). UM won a very close game and, as in most close games, they were very fortunate. The Wolverines then handled a decent Western team before traveling to Notre Dame. Michigan played well enough in South Bend, but an array of fumbles (mostly unforced), real penalties, incorrectly called penalties (Big Ten refs), a phantom TD for ND (fumble two yards prior to the end zone à la Charles White), and a complete blockhead penalty at the end of the game (a pointless late hit) led to a two-point Notre Dame win. The game was the counterbalance to the Washington victory.

Utah then traveled to Ann Arbor. While most UM fans didn't appreciate it, Utah had a good defense, one of the better defenses Michigan would face in the year. Utah was quick and able in the secondary and very tough against the run. Michigan controlled most of the game, since the Utah offense had no running game and little ability to stretch the field, but a fumble at the Utah goal line and two missed field goals (one a long extra point) kept the Utes in the game until the end. UM again scraped by, 10–7, though this was a game that Michigan dominated.

At this point in the season, the serious Wolverine fans were all over Carr, his coaching staff, and John Navarre. Despite the fact that the Wolverines had given Washington its only loss, Notre Dame was undefeated, and Utah and Western both showed ability in other games, many Wolverine fans were pissed. It seemed to me that 3–1 was okay against the level of competition (probably as tough as anyone played) but others, probably the majority, were less satisfied as the Big Ten season commenced. UM traveled to Champaign to play the Illini, and the UM staff had to be surprised to find Coach Ron Turner's team abandoning its zones in exchange for eight or nine guys jamming the line of scrimmage and the Illini secondary playing man/bump and run in order to maximize pressure on Navarre and at the point of attack. Turner let it all hang out, a complete sellout to the aggressive, blitzing defense that won style points with fans. It also won points with the Wolverines, Michigan putting up forty-five in three quarters when the Illini turned the ball over five times and could not control the UM receivers in man coverage. Still, in the bye week prior to a showdown against Joe Pa, many of the UM followers were cranky.

The crankiness subsided as Michigan eked out an overtime win against PSU and then handled Purdue on the road. John Navarre played very well in both games and, after three consecutive good performances, the critics were more or less silenced. But they were waiting, I was certain, and ready to pounce. And they did when UM got hammered by Iowa, probably as bad as any Michigan team has looked in the past forty years (with the exception of the Donovan McNabb bruising), by a score of 34–9. The score was 10–9 Iowa midway through the third period with Michigan receiving a punt that would place the Wolverines in reasonable field position. Michigan had been outplayed, badly outplayed, but had held on in the game (somehow) and seemed destined to come back. But the punt was fumbled, the Hawkeyes recovered the ball deep in Michigan territory, and they never looked back.

The oddity about the Iowa game aftermath was that the criticism of Carr became very muted, because the game seemed to suggest the possibility that UM was just plain overmatched. And after the Wolverines clobbered MSU (49–3) and then won against Minnesota and Wisconsin, Carr had a redemption game against the undefeated and number-one or number-two ranked OSU. Very few in Ann Arbor thought Michigan had more talent than the Buckeyes. Those few predicting a UM victory relied upon karma, or the past, or the instinct that Michigan just tends to win these games. As it turned out, the talent level seemed not that disparate as the Wolverines controlled the ball, stopped the Bucks on all but two occasions, won the kicking game, had twice the number of first downs (twenty-six to thirteen), easily dominated in yards gained (370 to 260), and ran more than 60 percent of the plays in the game. But the Buckeyes dominated in turnovers, penalties, and the scoreboard, turning in a hard fought and elegant 14–9 victory. It left Lloyd with the same two camps of followers though, oddly, with the more vocal camp moving to the pro-Lloyd ledger. It also left the OSU minions with their ordinary riots and car burnings, etc.

But all turned out well in Mudville as the Wolverines finished the year with a 38–30 win over a Florida Gator team that Michigan matched well against. Lloyd escaped. But, as is the present nature of the game, the Wolverine faithful were convinced they were sitting on a juggernaut next year. The heat is always on. And it was really on for Lloyd in 2003. My diary notes for 2003 are reproduced below:

August 23, 2003. Expectations shape perceptions. Most fans were not expecting much from 2002 Wolverines and, hence, the Wolverines' 10–3 record, with close losses at OSU (badly outplayed by UM) and Notre Dame (a toss up) tended to overshadow the Iowa blowout at home, the OT win against PSU, and the fact that UM "deserved to lose" at home to a not-all-that-good Washington team. Plus, the beating UM took from the Hawkeyes left the impression that UM wasn't overmatching good teams with talent. The bowl win against Florida left a good taste in everyone's mouth, especially when OSU beat Miami in OT in the national championship game. Many thought, "How far away were we?" when all but one game over the course of the season was in the Wolverines' grasp. The truth was, between stretches of brilliance, we struggled.

Fan expectation is quite different heading into the 2003 season with UM having a deep and experienced team and, indeed, no notable weakness. The depth on the team seems profound. A typical fan commentary is reproduced below, found on a Wolverine football posting board.

> I am just so confident that we will run the table, that I am seriously going to have a breakdown if we lose a game. It is really weird, like I am totally not worried about losing to anyone, because I'm that sure of our team, but there is always that chance. Before anyone says it, yes maybe I am a little overconfident, but that's my job as optimist of the board, right?

I can understand this poster, but it isn't as if there are no clouds on the horizon. The Wolverine running game, not very good in 2001, got worse in 2002, dropping from eighth to tenth in the conference in yards per attempt. And, while the Michigan passing game was potent in gross production, the Wolverines were also tenth in the conference in yards per pass attempted (as noted), a statistic having a more than tepid correlation with wins.

In Big Ten play in 2002, Michigan threw the ball more often than not, passing an average of thirty-six times a game. The weakness of the running game left little choice, but trying to overcome talent with guile is always problematic. The only conference teams that threw more often than the Wolverines (Illinois, Northwestern, and Indiana) went a combined 6–18 in the Big Ten. By contrast, undefeated Big Ten co-champs Iowa and OSU threw less than one third of the time. Iowa and OSU combined threw only five more passes a game than the Wolverines. Michigan fans, in their optimism, seem to be missing the connections. I know what the roster looks like this year. Deep and good. I also know what we looked like last year, inconsistent and fragile.

September 29, 2003. The season started weird, with CMU's running game pummeling the UM interior line for more than two hundred yards. I was distraught, thinking that if the Chips hammered us this easily, well, what happens with the powerful Notre Dame running game? Still, the Wolverines eked by 45–7. The Michigan running game was hot and continued so in the following week when a hapless Houston team came to town. The Wolverines demolished one of the too-many-to-count Cougar teams 50–3. It wasn't that close, and the Wolverine run defense was remarkable. (Houston, as of today, is 3–1, actually finding three teams they could beat.) Plus the offense looked unstoppable.

Then Notre Dame showed up, if the phrase "showing up" doesn't express more vigor than the Domers actually had. Tickets were selling for a one-hundred-dollar minimum, and the game was witnessed by more than any other contest in college football history. Michigan turned the ball over near its own thirty-eight early in the game, but the defense came on the field fired up, and Notre Dame did not gain an inch. And, as it turned out, this was the deepest penetration of the day for the Irish, who couldn't run or pass the ball in a complete imitation of a west coast offense or, for that matter, a football team. The Domers couldn't play defense either, as the Wolverines shredded ND with subs coming in the game late in the third quarter. The final was 38–0, but the score was deceptively close. Postgame, the Wolverine faithful were on the verge of declaring the national championship on the spot. I understood this feeling. But I also understood that, despite the Irish's last minute comeback win at home against a pretty good Washington State team, Notre Dame looked worse than either CMU or Houston. Indeed, I thought this was the feeblest ND team I had ever seen. But this was a fleeting thought. Mostly, looking back at the tape, I watched unheralded fullback Kevin Dudley pound and pancake the Irish linebackers into submission—thinking, damn, we look pretty good.

Reality returned in the next week when Michigan traveled to Oregon. Actually, I sat down that afternoon to watch the Sparties and Irish prior to the late Michigan start. Watching the MSU defense dismantle the Irish offense at South Bend, I began to have a queasy feeling in my stomach. Notre Dame is not very good! Not only that, they categorically stink. They can't block or throw. They are pretty slow on D. The Michigan winning streak of CMU, Houston, and Notre Dame now felt a lot less impressive and comforting. (The Domers completed their second Big Ten hat trick in three years by losing the following week to Purdue. It ain't just money keeping Notre Dame out of the Big Ten.) And this impression made a more indelible mark when Michigan, in the first quarter at Oregon, managed to possess the ball for a total of fifty-six seconds, probably a world record. Still, UM blocked a short Duck field goal and returned it for a TD, leaving the Wolverines with a 6–0 lead (missed extra point) at the end of the quarter.

With the Michigan punting game going in the tank (one meatball liner returned for a TD, another TD for Oregon was facilitated when a fake kick went awry after a snap hit the ball carrier in the head and reversed the field by forty yards), it was a miracle the Wolverines were down only 24–6 late in the third quarter. At this point, John Navarre led the Wolverines on a sustained comeback, completely through the air. Midway through the fourth quarter, the

Wolverines were behind only 24–21 and twice had the ball. The first time, the Ducks intercepted a Navarre pass deep in their territory. The second time, the Michigan punting game again failed, a punt blocked and a run back for an OU touchdown. Down 31–21, the Wolverines scored on a spectacular Steve Breaston reception and run, but the UM kicking game bit them again, missing the extra point.

Michigan executed a successful onside kick and, down four with two minutes to go, drove to the Duck side of the field. With less than a minute remaining, a long reception to Stevie Wonder was called incomplete (wrong call, but we had one of significance in our favor, too), and then a fourth down pass barely missed connection inside the Duck twenty. For the game, Braylon Edwards had thirteen receptions for 144 yards, the aerial show blunting fan criticisms, but not the kicking game.

Salt was rubbed into the wounds of the more-depressed-than-howling UM fans when, in the following week, the Wolverines sleepwalked through the worst team in the history of the Big Ten, Indiana. The Wolverines, again, had a punt blocked and returned for a touchdown. Coverage on special teams looked particularly shaky, though Indiana didn't make us pay. Indiana is so bad, everyone in the MAC would hammer the Hoosiers. And it would lose by a minimum of forty-two at the hands of Bowling Green or Miami or Toledo. The Hoosiers lost by twenty-four to Connecticut, a school I didn't even know had a football program. It got even worse later in the day (for Michigan fans), when the Oregon Ducks lost to Wazoo, the incredible losers to Notre Dame (probably the only team Indiana can beat), by the score of something like 79–4, when Oregon committed seven turnovers in the first half and then had two punts blocked for touchdowns. The Ducks finished with nine turnovers, not counting the blocked punts and, despite gaining 414 yards (to 399 for Wazoo), still managed to lose by seventy-five. (Okay, it might have been thirty-nine.)

The benchmark game of the season is this week, when the Wolverines tangle with the Hawkeyes in Iowaland. Iowa won its first four against middling competition but then lost 20–10 in an evenly played game in East Lansing. MSU started hot, with Spartan QB Jeff Smoker tearing up the Iowa defense early. MSU lead 14–0 halfway through the first quarter when Iowa brought in All-American safety Bob Sanders, nursing an injury from the season opener. Sanders and the Iowa defense shut down MSU from this point forward, with MSU gaining less than one hundred yards in the next three and a half quarters. Sanders aside, a good Spartan defense and five Iowa turnovers kept Iowa from any serious attempt to win the game. The UM-Iowa game should be an emotional game for both teams. I am anything but confident about the outcome, since UM couldn't move the ball on Iowa (at home) last year and the Hawkeye defense seems at least as competent this time around, especially with Sanders healthy. I expect a close, funky Michigan loss, highlighted by a bizarre penalty.

October 5, 2003. Damn, I am good at this. Though it was about ten times funkier than I could have imagined. My lingering and growing suspicion that Michigan lacks some organizational core in the kicking game (duh) was given impetus in the late-week Oregon at Utah game. Utah, now coached by ex-BGSU mentor, Urban Meyer, is the most focused team I have seen since the early Schembechler teams of the seventies. One difference is that Meyer seems less dogmatic in his visions, though Bo's dogma was the right one (run the ball, don't throw interceptions). Meyer's team seems organized and on the same page. They present as seamless. The offense is crisp and Utah, with about one-tenth the team speed and athleticism of UM, pounded Oregon by seventy-four. Well, by four, actually. Utah has also beaten a good Colorado State team, California, and Utah State, with a two-point loss at Texas A&M. How many Utah starters would start at Michigan? You must be kidding, but my guess is (maybe) two or three at best. Meyer was passed up by MSU in deference to paying John L. Smith the largest contract in the universe. Smith looks like a very good coach, but I think Meyer might be the best college coach on the planet right now.

Meyer's team, I know this is hard to believe, can actually cover kickoffs and punts. Even against Oregon. And, on occasion, it can actually punt the ball without it being blocked. And, watching Utah, I was envious and sickened by the fact that I knew my original thinking about the Iowa game was right. Yeah, Oregon at Utah is an easier game for Utah than UM at Oregon. A lot easier in the context of the seasons. Still, Meyer was playing with a very different deck, and it made me think we were going nowhere.

At first, it didn't look like my anxieties were justified, and I was relieved as the Wolverine defense stuffed the run and the measly Iowa passing game. The Michigan offense was able to move the ball pretty easily, especially in the air, and with four minutes remaining in the first quarter, the Wolverines were ahead 14–0, with John Navarre blistering hot. Then it all caved in. On the kickoff, Iowa took advantage of continuing weak special teams play, and returned the kick thirty-one yards and added fifteen on a (weak) personal foul penalty called against the Wolverines, their second of the game. Starting on the UM forty-six, the Hawks marched the ball in. 14–7. But Navarre was still hot and led the Wolverines to their third score in three tries, this time a Garret Rivas field goal. 17–7.

Again, however, the Wolverines couldn't cover the KO, and the Iowa guys started from midfield. This time, the UM defense stiffened and limited Iowa to a field goal. 17–10. In the following series, Navarre threw to Jason Avant for seventy-one yards, but the drive stalled at the Hawkeye nine. A Rivas field goal pushed the game back to 20–10. Late in the half UM special teams broke down again and the Hawks returned a punt for forty-three yards. A third UM personal foul pushed the ball to the Wolverine nine and, on third down, the Hawkeyes passed for a TD. 20–17 at half.

The second half stayed close, but the Hawks took a lead on (what else) a UM blocked punt. Late in the game, Iowa drove the field, and led 30–20 with five minutes left. The Wolverines didn't give up. Navarre threw well on an eighty-six-yard drive, and the game was 30–27 when the Wolverine defense got the ball back with over a minute left to play. The Wolverines moved to the Iowa forty-four, but three incompletions ended the game. Oh yeah. As in the Oregon game, a long pass to Avant in this last drive was caught, but incorrectly called incomplete. Michigan gained 463 yards to Iowa's 295, but Iowa won the rushing game (one hundred to seventy-four) and the special teams game (a shutout here).

It surprised me that the UM fans didn't seem that worked up about the loss (excepting the special teams play), but perhaps it shouldn't have, where Carr's team won on style points. John Navarre passed for 389 yards in the game (a UM record), and this seemed to rub some of the tarnish from the result. Weird.

January 5, 2004. By halftime of the Minnesota game, the paint was gone with the tarnish. Michigan was down 14–zip and, while the Wolverine offense had a little smoke (no fire), the Gopher running game was shredding the Wolverine defense. Minnesota, relying upon a small, quick offensive line, angle blocked the Wolverines into nothing and the fine Minnesota runners, especially Marion Barber the twenty-seventh or twenty-eighth, exploited the open spaces. Michigan scored on the "alligator" pass (backward toss to wide receiver Steve Breaston followed by a cross-field pass to Navarre) early in the third quarter, but the Minnesota offense kept the UM offense off the field. Starting the fourth quarter, the Wolverines were down 28–7 and the game was over. But the Wolverines scored quickly, and then the Gophers threw an ill-advised pass, intercepted by safety Jacob Stewart, and returned for a TD. The Gophers, incredibly, went ahead 35–21 on a fifty-two-yard QB sneak, but the Wolverine passing game was not stoppable. UM scored thirty-one points in the fourth quarter to eke out a 38–35 win. The game was destined for OT when, on the last drive, Chris Perry fumbled the ball into traffic. Somehow, TE Tim Massaquoi scrambled between defenders for the ball, saving the UM opportunity for the winning field goal.

Minnesota rushed for 423 yards against Michigan, an all-time worst for the UM defense. Still, the excitement of the win—the way it was won—overshadowed the problems in the run defense. When the Wolverines outplayed and/or pounded Illinois, Purdue, Northwestern, and MSU, the Oregon and Iowa losses were relegated, in fan-think, to the road bump of the kicking game—improving as the season wore on.

Michigan worked OSU over in its annual showdown, winning 35–21 in a game that wasn't that close. And when UM lost 28–14 to USC in the Rose Bowl, the consensus was that the Wolverines were just overmatched by the USC talent level, a probable fact. Lloyd Carr comes out of the season as good as it can be, a 10–3 season where fans believed it to be a "real" 12–1 year spoiled by the kicking game. Plus, the Wolverines beat the Spartans, Buckeyes, and Irish, extra points for these wins. The style points earned over the year, losing while letting it all hang out, covered the problems. And, good news for Lloyd, fan expectations are more muted in 2004 than in the past. For a change, maybe, Lloyd will get breathing room.

February 11, 2005. Lloyd did get breathing room in 2004 from the media and the fans, except for my overly optimistic article in the *Ann Arbor Observer*. Based upon my estimate of QB Matt Gutierrez's performance in the spring, I thought the Wolverine offense would roll in 2004, and that the defense would be good enough. As it turned out, Gutierrez tore a pectoral muscle during the final week of fall practice—was out for the season—and, surprise, freshman Chad Henne got the nod for the opener against Miami (Ohio). Henne played about as well as any freshman could play in the opener under the circumstances, which was, to be honest, not very good. Still, even with a measly 274 yards of total offense, the Wolverines won by 43–10. Seven turnovers (five INTs) by the Red Hawks told the story.

The trip in week two to South Bend was much less hospitable for the Wolverines and Henne. The Irish were steamed about losing to an average BYU team the prior week and were steamed about losing 38–0 to the Wolverines in 2003. Still, the Wolverine defense took the heat out of the Notre Dame kettle as Michigan held a 9–0 halftime lead. It was a deceptive advantage, however, where a vanilla Wolverine offense (there was no other choice under the circumstances) sputtered and gasped in the first half, letting a lot of points fall off the board. Henne, confused by Notre Dame's coverages, was well too eager to throw to his check down receivers and the quick ND linebackers cleaned up on these passes. In the second half, Notre Dame discovered the edges of the UM defense to be soft, and freshman runner Darius Walker exploited this weakness as ND controlled the ball and, eventually, the scoreboard. Notre Dame won 28–20, with the Wolverines scoring their only TD late in the game. The Wolverine total offense of 313 yards was unimpressive, with many of these yards accruing after the game was decided.

The Wolverine offense was again woeful at home against San Diego State. But UM got by 24–21 when Carr inserted midget running back (freshman) Mike Hart into the game and, for the first time in the season, UM showed some ability to move the ball on the ground. Henne had another tough outing, throwing twenty-eight passes for just 179 yards and three interceptions.

After three years of treating poor John Navarre like the second coming Mussolini, the Wolverine fans had wised up to their prior wretched behavior and fell in love with Chad Henne. Nobody was happy to lose to ND or scrape by San Diego State at home, but nobody was blaming Henne, either. To the contrary, most seemed assured of his potential and expressed satisfaction with the young quarterback's play. On the other hand, few weren't wary concerning the Wolverine's re-match with Iowa. The party line, those pessimist Stalinist UM fans, believed it to be unlikely that Henne would play at the level we needed against a team that had whacked us in consecutive years. But Henne made a great leap forward, throwing for 236 yards and no interceptions, while the Wolverines stoned the vaunted Iowa running attack for a negative fifteen yards. Mike Hart ran for over one hundred yards for the second straight week, and it looked like the Wolverines were on the verge of becoming a complete team. They cruised in, 30–17.

The Wolverines were a little flat on the road at Indiana, but Henne's learning curve was still on an upward cycle as he completed seventeen of twenty-one passes for 313 yards. Minnesota came to Ann Arbor the following week. The Gophers were undefeated and rated one slot higher in the national polls than the Wolverines (thirteenth to fourteenth). Michigan dominated the action, but turnovers and a couple of big Gopher plays left UM in a 24–20 hole with three minutes to play and the ball on the UM thirteen. Henne then showed shades of Tom Brady as he led the offense on a six-play-eighty-seven-yard drive, highlighted by a spectacular thirty-one-yard TD catch and run by tight end Tyler Ecker. The Wolverines won 27–24.

Then came the Michael Hart show, the freshman running for 234 yards against the Illini defense, playing like cigar store Indians with a bad case of termite infestation. The Wolverines won 30–19, and this set up a showdown at Purdue against (again) a team one spot higher in the polls (twelfth versus thirteenth). Purdue All-American QB Kyle Orton was overshadowed by Henne, and Mike Hart ran for 206 yards as the Wolverines again snuck by, 16–14. The Wolverine defense stymied the rascally Purdue running game.

Thereafter, the season got weird in a way that no one would have predicted. In the Wolverine's bizarre and unlikely win over Michigan State, coach John L. Smith, the Hunter Thompson of the coaching world (I love John L.), decided to run the old single wing against the Wolverines. Not that psychedelic and souped-up Northwestern horizontal-passing fake out with the single wing as the prize inside, but the real deal. The Spartans came into Ann Arbor with some straight Old Crow and old smashmouth single wing football. Overload the formation to the tight end side, bro', and then here we come. Dudes, big old QB Drew Stanton (and then Damon Dowdell) is gonna pound it right at you. It was, indeed, little more than a game of Red Rover. Just to keep the defense honest, though, Smith left speedy running back DeAndra Cobb in the formation to show the hand-back draw—in case Jim Herman's defense wanted to over shift just a little too much. The Spartan plan worked. Drew Stanton and Dowdell ran for 120 yards and passed for 167 more. But the hand-back draw to the weak side of the formation was the killer, with Cobb taking two for 138 yards and two TDs. On the day, MSU gained over five hundred yards and lead 27–10 with eight minutes left in the contest. About five thousand or so disconsolate Wolverine fans made their way to the aisles, cursing the low-life Sparties and their sneaky attack. Problem is, Henne and Braylon Edwards and the UM offensive line didn't know the game was over. A forty-six yard pass to Edwards led to a stalled drive and a short Wolverine field goal. Six minutes and twenty-seven seconds were left on the clock. Michigan recovered an onside kick and it took Henne fifteen seconds to find Edwards again, this time with the receiver making a startling thirty-six-yard TD grab by pulling the ball away from a defensive back in perfect coverage.

Now the Wolverines kicked off, but penalties against MSU aborted their drive and the Michigan offense had the ball again. This time it took Henne fourteen seconds to find Edwards in the end zone. It was pretty loud in the darkened stadium. Both teams scored field goals in the first OT period. Both scored touchdowns in the second OT period. In the next OT Henne found Edwards for his third TD of the day (eleven catches for 189 yards). Michigan held and won, 45–37. Mike Hart ran for two hundred plus yards for his third straight game, the first time this had happened in Michigan history. This was, no question, the most improbable game I have ever seen in Michigan Stadium. And maybe the most exciting.

The following week the Wolverines handled Northwestern 42–20, but the Wildcats' running game, out of a more stylish single wing, (switching from Old Crow to single malt) taxed the Wolverines. And, again, the hand-back draw proved nettlesome, Noah Herron taking one sixty-eight yards to pull Northwestern to within one point midway through the third quarter. By this point in the season, the cat was well out of the bag in planning an attack against Michigan—run the single wing and, if you can, run the QB out of the single wing. Ohio State had the ingredients to make this go, with a fine running QB in Troy Smith. But Michigan fans knew—they just knew—that the Wolverines defense would solve the equation.

Coach Jim Herman's troops didn't. The Wolverines lead early, 14–7, as both teams showed the ability to move the ball. But the OSU defense began to stagger the UM running game and this forced Henne into too many passing downs, with the Buckeyes making key interceptions. The mystery for Michigan was the single wing, the Buckeyes stealing John L. Smith's offense and, with better receivers than MSU could put on the field, Ohio State cranked the Michigan defense. OSU won 37–21 and the OSU offense—pretty inert for most of the year—was dominant. Still, Michigan finished 9–2 and headed off to the Rose Bowl to play #4 rated and 10–1 Texas.

Michigan fans howled about the defensive performance after OSU, and there was a general clamoring for Jim Herman's hide. The howling was worse when UM played a terrific offensive game in the Rose Bowl but lost, 38–37, when Texas quarterback Vincent Young ran for 192 yards on twenty-one carries. Texas didn't need any freakin' single wing or fruitcake handback draw to flummox the Wolverines. They merely needed to put Young in space and let this slippery-as-an-eel character do his thing. Young was, truly, miraculous to watch. Fast and elegant and impossible to tackle.

Michigan comes into 2005 with a set of mixed expectations. But most of all, the question is, how does UM stop running quarterbacks? With Troy Smith and Drew Stanton back, Herman's crew will get his chance. My thoughts are that Troy Smith was good, Stanton was real good and Young was from another world. Sometimes, you just have to give the other guy credit in his ability to execute. My guess is, in 2005, this won't be any solace to Michigan fans—should the pattern continue.

By early 2005 the media was already chomping at the bit about the coming season. One late March afternoon I witnessed a tense press conference where Lloyd Carr and Jim Carty crossed swords, with Carty insisting that his readers had a right to know "what happened" (defensively) in 2004 and Carr insisting he would only speak to the future, not the past. To his credit, the (perhaps unfairly) reviled-by-me Rich Thomaselli took up the cudgel of peacemaker, and lobbed a softball to the coach to ease tension in the room.

To be fair to Carr, it didn't take much to know what happened against Texas; Vincent Young was just better than the Wolverine defenders. This one, I think, should have been apparent to anyone whose job it was to pay attention. The dude just was elusive as Michael Vick, and even the pros can't tackle Vick. This wasn't a coaching failure. It was a tackling failure.

To be fair to Carty, I think Carr could have explained some generalized observations about the styles of attack used by OSU and MSU. The future is the past and it wouldn't have hurt Carr or the program for the coach to act a little less defensively and explain some Football 101 to the hoi polloi. As I have argued previously, a more educated media and fan base is a more rational one.

As it stands, Carr's defensiveness, whether tactical or otherwise, makes him a sitting duck for Carty and other less thoughtful writers if UM's defensive woes against running QBs continue. (The talk is that Carr and new DL Coach Steve Stirpling [late of MSU] will use more 4–3 fronts than in the past year as a defensive staple. This seems in accord with fan-think, which makes me real nervous. My thinking, after some serious channeling with John Edward via George Halas, is that UM should stay odd and zone as a primary defense against single wing teams, allowing the LBs and DBs to keep sight of the QB and forcing the QB to make throws in the seems. Let's face it, if a QB (Stanton, say) can threaten the defense by running and passing, any defense is in trouble. But what the hell do I know? Lloyd isn't enthusiastic about talking to me, either.

Tommy Amaker. (October 2002). Most of the Michigan basketball faithful, and yeah, that probably means about sixty-five out of the ninety-three or so, are more than willing to be patient. But even in Amaker's first year, some of the patience was wearing funky by the middle of February, when the 2001–2 version of the Wolverines didn't look any better than the group Ellerbe pitched out on the floor in the prior year. I think the realization point came after a truly bad Purdue team (Keady's worst, no question) waxed the Wolverines by thirty-six points in Lafayette by a final of 79–43. This game followed a loss against Colorado State at Fort Collins. Okay, anyone can lose a nonconference game on the road. But CSU was a woeful team, last in its conference. It finished 3–11 in conference, and that included a twelve-point loss against San Diego State (at home) a couple days after the Michigan game. Yeah, Steve Fisher coaches the Aztecs. Hell, I can't even remember the name of the conference CSU plays in, though I think it's something like the Midwest-Mojave Loco Weed Division of America Mountain West. Or something pretty close.

After these two very bad losses, UM came home to play a good (but just good) Indiana team. It was a contest for more or less five minutes, until the Hoosiers started to play, and socked the Wolverines by a 75–55 final, despite the fact that the Hoosiers' best player, Jared Jeffries, had an injured ankle and was limited in time and effectiveness. How many twenty-point wins do the Hoosiers have on the road this year? Indiana was pretty good on the road (4–4), but they have only hammered one team by worse, the hapless Penn State Nittany Lions, the one team Michigan has been able to beat away from Crisler. And how many wins does Purdue have by thirty-six points? You don't need to ask.

The Wolverines couldn't right the ship and got blown out by twenty points twice more before playing OSU respectably at Crisler, but still losing by nine. Michigan's run of losses by thirty-six, twenty, twenty and twenty represented the worst four-game stretch of any team in Michigan history. So how about Amaker's team? Setting the bar as low as possible, how did this year's team compare with last year's team? Neither sight is pretty, but here it is.

	Ellerbe	Amaker
Record	4–12	5–11
Pts Scored	70.5	61.6
Pts Allowed	78.1	72.2
Differential	-7.6	-10.6
Turnovers	262	233
Opps. TOs	181	214
Rebounds	33.4	29.4
Opps. Rebounds	34.6	34.0
Shooting %	42.6 %	41 %
Three-Pt %	29.7 %	30.3 %
Opps. Shooting %	43.6 %	48.6 %
Opps. 3-Pt %	35.7 %	43 %

Of course, both teams finished the season by getting worse, Ellerbe's team losing eight of nine, including five complete blowouts, and Amaker's losing six of seven, five by twenty points or more.

Much like the Carr situation (only to a much lesser degree), fans are splitting into camps on Amaker. One camp, and that includes me, doesn't care if he is a great or mediocre coach. What Amaker brings to the university is more important than wins and losses and, where it seems likely he is at least competent as a coach that is enough for me. Michigan has gone a year without any significant incidents in the program, and that should come as a huge relief for most of us. Plus, he has recruited his first class, probably a very good one with at least one certifiable star (point guard Daniel Horton), and he is likely to back this up with another good year, since high school basketball in Michigan remains pretty loaded. The best thing about Amaker's first recruits is that they are all legitimate students. All have GPAs over 3.0 (some much higher), and all have scored in the one thousand range (some much higher) on the SAT test. We can keep losing for all I care, painful as it may be. But we won't. It will turn around.

The fans' taking more negative Amaker positions just don't see how barren the talent cupboard is at the moment. They think, for example, that Lavell Blanchard is a good player, a potential pro. They think the same thing about Bernard Robinson. Why they think this is beyond me. Blanchard is not an NBA player, at least at the moment. Indeed, it won't even be close (he won't be drafted next year), absent the cure for a (theoretical) psychological impediment (being more or less normal) or some miraculous change in his abilities or a weird growth spurt to six-nine so he can play the position most suited to his skills (power forward). Robinson has more athletic potential, but his future in the NBA is problematic at best. He is an NBA athlete, but his skills have a long way to go.

A second camp, the majority view, believes that Amaker should be given time and, as frustrating as that may be, they argue it is just way too early to tell. They believe that Amaker should be given the opportunity to be evaluated in light of a history where he has brought his own guys into the program. Most of these fans like Amaker, but would be willing to pitch him to Panhandle State if, in another two years, there is still no light at the end of the tunnel. Still, these folks shake their heads when they see what appears to be the obvious, that Amaker's first team was no better than Ellerbe's last team. Maybe worse.

The third camp, still a vast minority, thinks Amaker can't coach. They look at the juxtaposition of the past two years, see no improvement, and perceive nothing but darkness in the future. They say Amaker couldn't coach at Seton Hall and he can't coach here and Michigan should have hired someone else, preferably Pitino or Knight or Waters. Some might even think we got rope-a-doped by the Coach K illusion. The hard thing for Amaker, at least in relation to these fans, is that Michigan may not be not all that much better in 2002–3. He will probably start a freshman point guard and be faced with the certainty of using a freshman at center and maybe power forward. This team could be very hard to watch (or it could be great fun), and it is not impossible that the Amaker laments could get pretty thick, with those in camp one moving to camp two, and camp three becoming audible. But Bill Martin will hang with him and, in 2003 and beyond, this will be a real team again and the kudos for Tommy will emanate from all corners. There will be much revisionist history. You can call me and torment me if this isn't true. But my view is and will be, even if we lose the next fifty games in a row, that Amaker should be the coach here for as long as he wants. My surmise is that AD Bill Martin takes the same view.

But what about the numbers in 2001–2? Don't they truly stink? They do, of course. And I would argue this year's version of the Wolverines was the worst since (at least) 1962, slightly worse than last year's model. But there are a few glimmers of hope in the numbers once it is realized that Ellerbe's team had two huge bodies, Josh Asselin and Josh Moore, that were not replaced on the Amaker team. Now, it is true that Asselin was not a star. And it is true that Moore was even less so, and that his expected time to foul out was about ten minutes. But these two guys allowed Michigan, and especially the tough and admirable Chris Young, to play hard in the middle, to fight for rebounds and contest shots. Michigan was a less than average rebounding team in 2000–1, but it was just barely below average in the Big Ten, a good rebounding league. In Amaker's year, they were as bad as it gets, and this was predictable since (a) Chris Young was forced into tentative play, since there was no backup center and no other player over six-six on the team, and (b) when Young was out of the lineup, the rebounding carnage was brutal, and (c) Young was often in foul trouble. The fact that Michigan had exactly one player on the roster who qualified as a power forward or center meant that there was little way Michigan could compete, unless, say, it had Jason Kidd and Kobe Bryant in the back court. I checked it out. They didn't.

So what could Amaker do? Well, one thing that seemed possible, despite the fact that his guards were either not very good or not very tested, was to limit turnovers by controlling the pace of the game and encouraging the Wolverines to be careful with the ball. Add this to more defensive pressure, or at least better defense, and you have a recipe for improvement. Amaker was at least partially successful in this, the Wolverines decreasing their turnovers and increasing the number of TOs created, moving from the woeful to the mediocre in this element of the game. To this end, Amaker said (in quasi-private) that his goal was "to win games with the principles we are trying to establish and not on the momentary consideration of who can make a basket." In other words, in Amaker's first year, he was looking at the long run and making it clear he had bigger fish to fry than winning twelve versus ten games. Amaker's primary goal was to establish the nature of his program, that those who played will be those who follow the mandates of the coaching staff and those who demonstrate, in practice, that they are on the same page with Tommy. Ultimately, or so I think, this will pay dividends.

One other thing that stands out in the numbers is the three-point shooting. Not so much on the offensive end, since it was equally as lousy in each of the past two seasons. This is an arena, and I think most would agree, that has little to do with coaching. Either you can shoot the three or you can't, and coaching is likely to make little difference. (Okay. I agree a coach can have an impact on the quality of shots taken, but that is a long and convoluted topic in relation to the comparison of Amaker to Ellerbe. You will just have to take this minor point on faith. The Wolverines did not get worse looks from beyond the arc this year as compared to last.) Michigan's season-long percentage placed it at #209 in the country, according to the official NCAA stats. Looking only to Big Ten games, it would fall into the #303 range, out of the 323 teams listed. Of course, UM was last in the Big Ten in this category.

The defensive three-point percentage is what really stands out at 43 percent allowed. This percentage is off the charts, last in the Big Ten. And not just last by a bit, since the tenth-place team (Purdue) was 5.6 percent better than Michigan. This is truly astounding, since the difference between the first place team, Northwestern (32.3 percent), and Purdue at number ten (39.4 percent) is only somewhat larger than the gap between UM and Purdue. In that the best team in the country only shot 43 percent (Oregon, Marshall) from beyond the arc, my guess is Michigan was just about the worst team in the country in defending the three. From a relative perspective (43 percent allowed/30.3 percent shot), this has to be some sort of a record. To say it is off the charts is to understate the fact. Check out the following chart, the relative difference between three-point shooting percentage achieved and allowed in 2001–2:

MSU	+ 10.5
Indiana	+ 4.0
Minnesota	+ 3.1
OSU	+ 1.1
PSU	+ 0.5
Wiscy	+ 0.4
Iowa	-0.5
Illinois	-0.7
Northwestern	-1.5
Purdue	-1.7
Michigan	-12.7

This defies belief for me, and I watched all the games, please have mercy. For seven teams in the conference, three-point shooting had a nominal impact, about (up to) a point per game, one way or the other. For two teams, it was a significant (but not overwhelming) positive. For MSU, it seems to have been the best thing it did on the season (except for its terrific rebounding), but the Spartans actually scored twenty fewer three pointers than their Big Ten opposition, since they shot relatively few threes (Izzo must have insisted on only high-quality looks) and allowed a snootful (the MSU interior defense was tough). MSU was very positive in the three-point element of the game, but the above number may overstate how positive. As for Michigan, well, what can anyone say? This is impossible.

My guess is there are at least five reasons for Michigan's woeful showing. First, the Wolverines were lousy shooters, especially when Chris Young wasn't shooting. Second, the Wolverine point guards were midgets. It wasn't that tough to get a good look against Avery Queen or Mike Gottfredson, hard as they might have tried on defense. Third, the Wolverine guards were either slower than snakeshit on the perimeter or clueless on defense. Fourth, the Wolverine small forwards were either slow in adjusting to the perimeter or so focused on providing inside help (or both) that small forwards who could shoot the three got a lot of open looks. The fifth reason is pure random luck, maybe as prominent as any of the above reasons combined. The Wolverines did not defend the three any better in 2000–1 than in Amaker's first year. The ball just went in more this year.

Looking to the MSU anomaly, it is fair to ask whether the percentage difference in the above chart translated into points. It did. A lot of points. If Michigan had managed to shoot 33 percent from beyond the arc and hold the opposition to a similar percentage, the Wolverine point deficit in the Big Ten would have fallen from a negative 170 to a negative 61. In other words, much of the difference in separating the Wolverines from the abyss, and near-mediocrity, was shooting and defending the three, something I find hard to lay at the feet of Amaker, at least to any significant degree. Push comes to shove, I think this year's version of the Wolverines had a snootful of ill-fortune in this element of the game. That and the fact that they couldn't shoot the ball for shinola.

One more thing, though I admit it may not be relevant for many. After Michigan had lost to Purdue, Colorado State, and Indiana, I attended one of Amaker's Monday luncheons with the expectation that the coach might be just a little cranky or testy or (at best) short with his audience. Nothing could have been further from the truth. The coach was his ordinary polite, kind, and thoughtful self, never bridling at questions that covered (a) the "senselessness" of his substitution patterns, (b) why the PA person announced the Michigan team the way he did, (c) thoughts about putting the words to the national anthem on the scoreboard, and (d) (I swear) how to improve Chris Young's free throw shooting motion (I guess the 79.4 percent that Young shot for the season just wasn't quite good enough for a center in the Big Ten). Not only was Amaker kind and polite to all of the questioners, he answered every question the audience had, staying for seventy minutes to unravel every single nutball theory in the universe (from hypnotherapists to dietary supplements) to improve the Michigan team.

It got so crazy I considered asking him who he thought shot JFK but, in a rare moment of thoughtfulness, I desisted. When no one had anything else to ask, Tommy prodded the crowd for more. Nothing? Well, thanks for being there for the program and being the great fans you are. No irony intended. I guarantee.

To those who are basic bottom line types (just wins and losses, baby), Amaker's patience and demeanor might not mean very much. But to me, on the decade-long heel of Ed Martin, Amaker seems the right bromide. I noticed, in the Big Ten this year, a change in the sideline coaching demeanors of previously polite and controlled coaches. Mike Davis and Jim O'Brien, in particular, became incredible whiners after (collectively) many years of being urbane on the sidelines. And Tom Izzo, always animated but picking his spots to go after the zebras, became a constant referee baiter and complainer. None of these guys are dumb, and they must believe that to get a fair shake, they have to attempt some level of intimidation. But Amaker did his thing. Always polite. No techs. And his team was polite. No trash talk. No technical fouls during the entire season that I recall. They went about their business. And Michigan came away with reasonably called games from the refs this year, shooting only twelve fewer free throws on the year than its opponents in the Big Ten. Indeed, I felt that Michigan got decent to great officiating in every game it played, with the exception of the first half at MSU, when Phil Bova took Chris Young out of the game with ludicrous and nonexistent fouls. That said, MSU was all of the twenty-seven-point difference better than Michigan. Okay, maybe twenty-four. Or thirty.

June 14, 2004. After a brutal start to the 2002–3 season (0–6 against not very stellar competition) there was some level of grousing about Amaker. The Wolverines then rolled to thirteen straight wins (this seems like it should be a typo), including a 6–0 Big Ten start. Well, the schedule was favorable and the Wolverines came back to earth, but the 10–6 Big Ten finale (and 17–13 over-all record) was considered a big success in all quarters from a team with three freshmen starters and four freshmen playing prominent roles. All fan grousing had stopped dead in its tracks by the end of the season.

By the close of the 2003–4 season Tommy had been named Saint Izzo in Ann Arbor. Everyone was on the bandwagon and rightfully so. The Wolverines were 9–2 in last year's preseason, beating a good NC State team at home, a bad UCLA team at home, and losing to a very tough Vandy team on the road. The Wolverines also lost to BU at home (Phil Bova). But ten games into the Big Ten season, it looked like business as usual for Michigan, the Wolverines standing at 4–6 in the conference and the fans at Crisler behaving in their ordinary blasé demeanors. When number twelve Wisconsin came to Ann Arbor, the athletic department listed the crowd at 12,153 but, to be sure, there were fewer than ten thousand on hand. What few fans or media persons seemed to recognize at this point in the season was that the Wolverines were playing reasonably, they just couldn't shoot the damn ball. Lester Abram was at 50 percent (and 44.1 percent from beyond the line), but Daniel Horton was as cold as is possi-ble, at 31.4 percent (27.6 percent from beyond the arc) and Dion Harris, the freshman guard with a sweet stroke, was not better, 28.2 percent from the floor and 32 percent from beyond the arc. The Wolverines were shooting 41.7 per-cent as a team, as compared to 45 percent for their opponents, a huge differ-ential. But as I watched the games, I kept thinking, "This team is not that bad, we just need to hit a couple of shots to prime the pump."

Daniel and Dion then started to pick it up. The Wolverines won four of their last six in the conference and split in the Big Ten tourney. In the NIT tourna-ment, they ran off five straight to win the title. The Wolverines finished their last thirteen games at 10–3, and ended up 23–11 for the year. Two of the final three losses were close, by three to MSU and five at Indiana (the new Hightower). A big step up from the post-Fisher past. But the weird thing was that Crisler went crazy for a tournament of also-rans. In the NIT opener against Missouri, 5,500 first-come-first-serve fans created more noise than I thought was possible at Crisler. It put at least a sliver in the heart of the notion (expressed by me, among others) that the building, somehow, is a priori quiet. Bernard Robinson and Daniel Horton both commented on the strange atmosphere in Crisler. And Tommy Amaker expressed his appreciation of the level of enthusiasm from such a small crowd. AD Bill Martin should have taken the names and addresses of this group. And the word spread. The games could be fun!

A few days later, another first-come crowd of 11,241 screamed and ranted the Wolverines to a second victory, this time over Oklahoma. A real crowd at Crisler. Amaker took notice and again tipped his hat to the UM partisans, saying, 'It is really a nice atmosphere. Our players are talking about it. I am hoping that maybe this can be a springboard for the program in the future." Two days later, a slightly smaller crowd helped the Wolverines to a victory over Hawaii. Graham Brown called the Crisler crowd "amazing" and, more telling, Hawaii forward Julian Sensely said, "We kind of let the crowd get to us." I guarantee you these words have never before been spoken about a Crisler Arena game from a visiting team.

At Madison Square Garden, it was strictly no contest in the semis as Amaker's team crushed Oregon. In the finals, the Wolverines struggled in shooting the ball, but defeated an also cold-shooting Rutgers. In the wake of the late-season run, it is now a given that Amaker and his staff know what they are doing. And when the coach struggled through two strange recruiting decommitments (Al Horford to Florida and Joe Crawford to Kentucky) and a third snub from a local kid (Malik Hairston to Oregon) who was a perfect fit (minutes, position) for the 2004–5 Wolverines, the fan response was, "Well, maybe we are better off without them." Sour grapes, perhaps. But the right rationalization.

Amaker has a problem in 2004–5. He has four scholarship players to play three spots (the one, two, and three), and one of these, Ron Coleman, is a freshman who may be (my guess) or may not be (the experts' guesses) ready. Tommy may have to zone more than he likes and "go big" with Brent Petway or Chris Hunter taking some minutes at the three. Given the fact that a back court injury may mandate this, it is axiomatic that a "big" theory has to be a part of his hand. To this point, this has not been an Amaker preference and, as fans, we will see how flexible the coaching staff can be. It will be fun.

February 18, 2005. It hasn't been fun, or it hasn't been to this point in time, at least. Lester Abram hurt his shoulder and went down for the count by the third game of the season. This meant that Ron Coleman graduated from (at most, as it appeared) ten minutes per game to being a major cog in Amaker's plans. With no scholarship players left to pick up the slack, walk-ons John Andrews, Sherrod Harrell, Doni Wohl and Ashton Bell got minutes. Sometimes significant minutes. And these guys all had injuries of one sort or another over the first two months of the season. Then Graham Brown had surgery and was out for six weeks. Chris Hunter injured his ankle and missed most of December and early January. Brent Petway suffered from shoulder problems that limited his time and play for much of the season. Worst of all, point guard Daniel Horton injured his knee and missed a month, but made a quick recovery and was back for the Big Ten opener. It was an injury epidemic like none I (or anyone else) had ever seen, forcing Amaker to use two walk-ons, Dion Harris and Ron Coleman, on the perimeter for the majority of the season to this point in time. As of today, in scholarship players, UM has no point guard, one two guard (Harris) and a freshman small forward. Ouch.

Somehow, Amaker kept the ship floating and the Wolverines were 12–5, with a 3–0 Big Ten record after upsetting Iowa on the road. Many felt that this was "Tommy's best coaching job, ever" and I had to agree. Some even talked about making the NCAA tournament if the Wolverines could just hold serve at home. But then Horton was charged with domestic assault (his girlfriend) and the misdemeanor charges led Amaker to suspend the point guard. The Wolverines lost the next nine in a row (a school record), some badly, as opponents targeted Harris with their best defenders, double and triple teamed in the post, and took their chances with less skilled players. Turnovers became an epidemic, especially when teams pressured the Michigan ball handling in the backcourt. Once the ball got beyond the time line, with only Harris able to hit from outside, the Wolverine offense was worse than anemic.

The pressure on Tommy was profound. Horton's criminal case was the first non-basketball "incident" for any of his players and it hurt him deeply. Some Michigan fans, thinking, somehow, the Wolverines should be able to compete using kids out of the student body, went after Amaker. Such attitudes, to me, were beyond comprehension, when it was obvious the Wolverines were trying—they haven't given up yet. As of this week there are rumors that Amaker will take the job at Virginia next year, something that I can't see as realistic for anyone involved.

The problem might be nothing other than a one-year setback, due to an epidemic of injuries. Next year, the Wolverines bring in three perimeter players so there should be plenty of depth. But it isn't a lock that Daniel Horton will be back, though it looks at the moment that he will return. And it isn't a lock that Lester Abram will return with no ill effects from his injury. With Chris Hunter flat-lining at a pretty nominal level of play, Courtney Sims in complete retrograde, and Brent Petway looking too often for highlight plays, Tommy may have to start all over.

March 21, 2005. MSU is making a run through the NCAA tournament. (The MSU women are too, both teams now in the Final Four). Many UM fans, including myself, are rooting for the Spartans, hoping that Izzo's guys carry the supposed-to-be ragged banner of the Big Ten.

MSU's success has created pressure on UM's basketball programs, bare shadows of what MSU puts on the floor. Tommy Amaker, in particular, is now subject to a scrutiny that did not exist last year. MSU will remain powerful in the mid-run, at least, and I think this is a good thing for the Big Ten and Michigan. But can UM compete? Since I have no doubt about TA's abilities, and where the state is rich in basketball talent, I vote/predict "yes."

Fifteen *Means*

Iam a real fan. I am a lifetime member of the loosely formatted Real Fans Club, as real, mind you, as the Elks or Kiwanis. And who are these fans? What is their secret handshake? Their sign of distress? There is none, of course. But all real fans know and are known by the pseudo-Zen of Roger Angell's baseball prose and what Saul Bellow calls that "why did you kill my dog?" look when waxing serious about some element of some random game. All real fans know this, have experienced these minor humiliations on as many occasions as one can count. And, as a real fan, when a law student, I would plan my Cleveland to Boston all-night trips to start when the Indians came on the radio (losing to the Twins again, for chrissakes), and traveling east across Pennsylvania or New York in a caffeine-induced high and trying to dial my beater's radio into the Pirates or the Cardinals or the Tigers or even the dog-assed Red Sox in extra innings on the west coast through the obtuse and humid night air of late summer. This is what fans know. It is the games, of course. It is the games.

And the games go on. This is, after all, the point of sports, the we'll-get-them-next-year seamlessness that mocks the finality of the "real" elements of our lives. And it used to be the only point, at least as far as one could tell from the landscape of the media or the talk on the street. Things have changed. In my childhood, in the fifties, the games were child-driven and child-organized, no parents needed or wanted, thanks. These games, the games of kickball, dodging cars on the streets, and the random field sports organized by scavenging the stray kids in the neighborhood, are things well-dispersed in the past. To kids today, assembled into organized cadres of leagues and schedules and uniforms and travel teams, it is a past as alien as secret decoder rings for two boxtops and an end panel, plus that dime you found, hunting for stray bottles down by the tracks.

Our childhood games were free flowing, one participant pulling up with his bike as one left, and never ending, bats and gloves littered around the field for the return the next day. The game morphed from baseball to football to basketball with the change of season, with no discernible leader or decision being made about the change. It was like a flock of birds, moving north, then west in unison, at some mystical aura of the wind. On Saturdays, the games began after we delivered our papers, or did our chores (or often both), and ended well after dark, with the voices of parents echoing from blocks away, the sadness of the two-minute warning. Sometimes we had to mow the field, hand mowers being pushed to a vacant lot not being used by older kids. We measured the base paths by steps and cut bases from cardboard till the grass wore bare at the anointed spots. Sometimes, playing basketball on cold winter evenings, we had to shovel the snow from the court and run some lights with long extension cords from an accepting neighbor's outlet. Sometimes we hung nets or chains, a hand-cupped ladder facilitating the chore. "Will ya hurry up, Ronnie? My hands are freezing and you are as fat as an ox." Other times it was a complete improvisation with the elements at hand, whether natural or human. Right field, of course, was often out. Or, stuck with a bunch of marginal defensive players, I would suggest everyone bat wrong-handed to speed the innings up.

We did whatever was necessary to make the game go, to make it not end, even if it was only my brother John and me, one on one, struggling to master the nuances of throwing the electric-taped whiffleball. Over the fence was out of bounds. Through the window was a week's wages from the *Plain Dealer*. Gone. And, inevitably, we threw the high hard one at one another when the game got close. Chin music was definitely not over the fence.

It was not, I admit, a kinder or gentler world. Perhaps it was less so, though, without question, it was a more trusting time. Gloves missing from the detritus of the field did not mean an accusation of other kids. It meant a search for Ralph, a dog on the loose with a fetish for glove leather. And it was a time when athletes were revered beyond ordinary reason and a world where athletes' owners (at least in the pro world) exploited them in the context of the market structure. This exploitation, however, made them more like us. Athletes were not rich people. They were just like ordinary adults, no different than Mr. Dominic, who could throw a mean curve, too. He just, well . . . all ex-athletes have their stories of bad ju-ju. The pro athletes' richness, in our minds, came from the fact they could continue the endless game and *get paid*. They didn't have to go to work. And if Ralph the dog chowed down on some well-tended glove leather, it meant little difference to the pro; the team would fork over a new one, presumably a glove like mine, that was hidden in the darkness under my bed and wrapped in twine and Vaseline and oil with an old ball in the pocket. I had this vision as a child. In my mind there were a million old bunk beds covering oily and greasy gloves, maturing like fine bordeaux, only to appear with the Tribe or the Pirates or the Cubs in the spring.

We loved Colavito and Doby and Minoso and even Mantle, of course. But, from our perception of their status, they were no different than the hangers-on. To us, Hal Naragon or Preston Hardy or even Harry Chiti was as important as Colavito. They got to play too, right? And they didn't have to go work either. Right? And when a second-liner like Gary Geiger or Dick Brown came to the plate, his name floated across the neighborhood as easily as any star, the soft Georgia tones of Jimmy Dudley on transistor radios wafting from the porches of the city and, until the batteries wore out, on the sidelines of our games.

Until the recent past, we believed, or pretended to believe, something else about the college games and, if we were lucky, it might have been something more than pretend. Maybe. We fantasized these to be the games of our childhoods, but with something other than the fans of our imaginations and the realities that one's mind can conjure. There is something in the average sports fan (in me) that wants to hold onto this, that wants to believe that the games just go on and we are a part of it, though we know this part is well-buried in our pasts. Six seconds are left on the clock. Ross dribbles to his left. He is being held and hacked by Berggren. He struggles free. Berggren grabs him again with his clawlike appendages. Chaney yells at his minion. "Put him down! I want you to put Ross down!" But Ross eludes the defender. He jumps. He hangs in the air. He scores!! West never made a move against Berggren like that! And, of course, the Wolverines edge VMI for the NCAA championship. This is the game we have all imagined, a mixed metaphor lurking just beneath the surface of all who continue to play or try to play or once played. But writing about it can be a drag, a cynical exercise, something that takes the naiveté out of what is loved. And burns the romance from the fantasy, Tom Sawyer digging his way out of jail with a spoon while the door is open.

But here is the strange thing. Over the course of the year, while writing this book, I began to care less about the outcomes of the games and the games began to mean more. In September, the winning and losing of contests was important to me, at least as important as the aesthetic of the events. By April, I was more jaded and blasé about the outcomes. These are all people, after all, even those as lowly as Spartan Bob, and the winning and losing are symbiotic, one no more or less meaningful than the other. And I began to become more tuned to the elegance of the contests. The answers to questions like, "Was the game fun?" and "Did we play well, given our abilities?" seemed more important questions than "Did we win?" Yet, in this, I began to envy the Worst Fan or the Iowa Crows, certain that a ball seen from a hundred feet was butchered by a deranged and venal umpire. The sense of injustice can be sweet. This sense of being part of a hard-fought win, though doing nothing other than having it in your heart, is much more than sweet and is an emotion that only the real fan comprehends. No other.

This is what I want. I want my innocence again. I want to track the neighborhood for Ralph the dog and take my glove back from that ratty cur. I miss Ralph. I miss shoveling the snow and shooting the ball until my hands are red, numb, and frozen, and the basket, in a mystical blurring of fugue and vision, becomes as large as Lake Erie. And I even miss Maynard Bloat, an older kid who used to jump my brother and me from the bushes with stones and anti-Semitic invective, despite the fact we had never set foot in a temple or any place of worship. The religious world was as mysterious to me as girls, yet here was Maynard and his flunkies, cursing and swearing and threatening until they made us fearful and ashamed. I worry about Maynard, what became of him. But most of all, I miss right field being out.

I will try again next spring. I can do nothing else. And, after all, the Worst Fan promises (as he does every year) that the Tribe will come out of the gates hot, and the Wolverines will be unstoppable in the fall. It will be 1948 all over again. The year when I was born, and the year Chappuis led Michigan to a national championship. The year when the Indians won their only World Series and the hockey Wolverines won the NCAAs. John promises.

Go to sleep, Bertha, you will be able to look it up.

Bibliography

Albom, Mitch and Bo Schmbechler. *Bo.* New York: Warner Books, 1989.

Albom, Mitch. *The Fab Five.* New York: Warner Books, 1993.

Bacon, John U. *Blue Ice: The Story of Michigan Hockey.* Ann Arbor: The University of Michigan Press, 2001.

Canham, Don B. *From The Inside: A Half Century of Michigan Athletics.* Ann Arbor: Olympia Sports Press, 1996.

Carrol, Bob, Pete Palmer and John Thorn. *The Hidden Game of Football: The Next Edtion.* New York: Total Sports, 1998.

Cromartie, Bill. *Michigan vs. Ohio State: The Big One.* West Point, NY: Gridiron-Leisure Press, 1981.

Falls, Joe. *Man In Motion.* Ann Arbor: School-Tech Press, 1973.

Hemingway, Tom. *Life Among The Wolverines: An Inside View of U of M Sports.* South Bend, Indiana: Diamond Communications, 1985.

James, Bill. *The Baseball Abstract.* New York: Ballantine Books, 1982-88.

Lamb, Kevin. *Quarterbacks, Nickelbacks, & Other Loose Change: A Fan's Guide To The Changing Game Of Pro Football.* Chicago: Contemporary Books, 1984.

Merchant, Larry. *The National Football Lottery.* New York: Dell Publishing, 1974.

Mortimer, Jeff. *Pigeons, Bloody Noses and Little Skinny Kids.* Dexter, Michigan Thompson-Shore Publishers, 1978.

Perry, Will. *A Story of Michigan Football: The Wolverines.* Huntsville, Alabama: The Strode Publishers, 1974.

Peterson, Robert W. *Pigskin. The Early Days of Pro Football.* New York: Oxford University Press, 1997

Strom, Earl. *Calling the Shots: My Five Decades in the NBA.* New York: Simon and Schuster, 1991

Watterson, John Sayle. *College Football.* Baltimore and London: The Johns Hopkins University Press, 2000.

Wolf, Alexander and Armen Keteyian: *Raw Recruits.* New York: Pocket Books, 1990.

Yaeger, Don. *Undue Process: The NCAA's Injustice For All.* Champaign, Illinois: Sagamore Publishing Inc. 1991.

Yaeger, Don and Dan Wetzel. *Sole Influence: Basketball, Corporate Greed, and the Corruption of America's Youth.* New York: Warner Books, 2000.

Yaeger, Don and Douglas S. Loney. *Under The Tarnished Dome.* New York: Simon & Schuster, 1993.

Zimmerman, Paul. *The New Thinking Man's Guide To Pro Football.* New York: Simon & Schuster, 1984.

Craig Ross grew up in Lorain, Ohio, the home of Guido Sarducci, Laslo Toth, and Toni Morrison. He now lives in Ann Arbor, Michigan, with his wife, Sue.